Praise for Vonda Pelto's
Without Remo

"In unflinching language, Vonda Pelto escorts us into the claustrophobic bedlam of a giant jailhouse and lays bare the behavior of notorious serial killers. Pulling no punches, she allows us a voyeuristic look into that will leave you reeling."
—**Don Lasseter,** Author, Journalist

"Dr. Vonda Pelto's brutally honest book, **Without Remorse**, takes the reader on a forbidden tour behind the gates of the men's jail, a haunted house where Serial Killers live. But most powerful is the juxtaposition of Pelto's personal and professional life, with its conflicts between men and women, sex and violence, and intimidation and vulnerability."
—**Carole Lieberman,** M.D., M.P.H., Forensic Psychiatrist/Expert Witness

"Vonda Pelto scares me. This book is way too much fun. I hear she's the favorite pin-up on Death Row. Pour yourself a cup of warm arsenic and settle in for the ride."
—**Brian Alan Lane,** Bestselling Author, *Cat & Mouse: Mind Games with a Serial Killer*

"Without Remorse is an incredible journey that only Vonda could undertake, with her eyes wide open and a determination that even the most horrendous killers of society couldn't break. This is a brilliant book!!!
—**Jeff Hathcock,** Film Producer

"I sentenced nine men to death row from the bench. Dr. Pelto had to deal with sadistic killers who had no remorse for their actions. She does an incredible job of revealing the depths of the soul of these killers. One hell-of-a-book! So well written that you feel as though you actually knew these killers. I felt like I was right there with Vonda. I loved the book. **Without Remorse** shows a side to these killers that the general public never sees. It puts you right there in the jail with them. What this great book reveals are the two sides of these men, the dark side and the human side. How could these killers be so charming and yet, be able to murder and mutilate a follow human being?"

—**Judge Donald McCartin,** Retired Superior Court Judge "The Hanging Judge of Orange County, CA."

"This is a one-of-a-kind book by a one-of-a-kind author. Vonda L. Pelto has written a disturbingly factual account of her years as a unique psychologist in L.A. County's Men's Jail. She met with the area's worst serial killers to prevent them from wreaking havoc on themselves."

—**Tedd Thomey,** Award winning columnist for *The Independent Press Telegram,* author of eighteen books and a successful Broadway play.

www.WithoutRedemption.com

WITHOUT REDEMPTION

Vonda Pelto, Ph.D. is a Clinical Psychologist based in Southern California whose first book, **Without Remorse: The Story of the Woman Who Kept Los Angeles' Serial Killers Alive**, came out in 2008. Her time spent working in Los Angeles Men's Central Jail with notorious serial killers and murderers, from September 1981 till February 1985, provided the basis for **Without Remorse** and **Without Redemption**.

Michael B. Butler's first book, **A World Flight Over Russia**, published in 1998 by Wind Canyon Books, was the result of a last-minute July 1992 assignment to document a flight of 12 small planes flying 17,500 miles around the world while crossing the entire landmass of Russia and Siberia. His work in public relations, marketing and as a photographer resulted in documenting travel junkets to Tahiti and Ireland, the 50th Anniversaries of Pearl Harbor and D-Day and a Pilgrimage to the Holy Land with 750 Christians from all over the world.

WITHOUT REDEMPTION
Creation & Deeds of Freeway Killer Bill Bonin, His Five Accomplices & How One Who Escaped Justice
Vonda L. Pelto, Ph.D. & Michael B. Butler
www.WithoutRedemption.com

Copyright © 2022 Vonda L. Pelto & Michael B. Butler
All rights reserved. First edition published 2022
Flotsam Publishing

Legal Disclaimer

No part of this publication may be reproduced, distributed, or transmitted in any form or by any means, including photocopying, recording, or other electronic or mechanical methods, or by any information storage and retrieval system, without prior written permission from the publisher, except for brief quotations embodied in critical reviews and certain other noncommercial uses permitted by copyright law.

ISBN: 979-8841931249

Dedicated to My Loving Husband Jim Lia
—Vonda Pelto Lia

Dedicated to Angela & George
—Michael B. Butler

Contents

Preface		14
What is *Without Redemption*?		15
Intro: What's a Nice Girl Doing in a Place Like This?		16

PART ONE—1940 TO JULY 1979

1	Los Angeles Men's Central Jail Vonda Pelto, Ph.D., August 31, 1981	21
2	Bonin Family, Boy's Home & Orphanage 1940 to 1955	23
3	New House, Abuse, School & Neighbors 1955 to 1962	33
4	Move to LA, New Schools & New Troubles 1962 to 1965	39
5	High School Dropout & Vietnam War Service January 1966 to October 1968	43
6	Coming Home & First Arrest October 1968 to June 1969	48
7	Atascadero Mental Hospital—First 90-Days June 17 to September 18, 1969	60
8	Atascadero, Vacaville Prison & Parole September 1969 to June 1974	70
9	Freedom & Second Arrest June 1974 to December 1975	80
10	CMC Prison & Unexpected Parole January 1976 to October 1978	90
11	Probation, New Friends & The Death Van October 11, 1978 to July 28, 1979	98

PART TWO—AUGUST 4, 1979 TO JUNE 11, 1980

12	Origins of the Freeway Killings 1973 & May 1979	105
13	Bill Bonin & Vernon Butts Light the Fire Mark Shelton, August 4, 1979	108
14	Bonin Kills Alone #1 Markus Grabs, August 5, 1979 As Told to Vonda Pelto by Bill Bonin	114
15	Third Arrest & Immediate Release August 9 to 13, 1979	122
16	Bonin Creates Alibi for Grabs Murder August 17, 1979	124
17	Bonin & Butts Victim #2 Robert Wirostek, August 20, 1979	127
18	Bonin & Butts Victim #3 Donald Hyden, August 26, 1979	132
19	Sgt. 'Jigsaw' St. John of LAPD & Sgt. David Kushner of LA Sheriff's Dept.	137
20	Bonin & Butts Victim #4 David Murillo, September 9, 1979	139
21	Court Hearing, Jailtime & Early Release September 18 to November 12-13, 1979	144
22	Bonin Kills Alone #2 Wallace Tanner, November 14, 1979	145
23	Bonin & Butts Victim #5 John Doe, November 21, 1979	150
24	Bonin Kills Alone #3 Dennis Fox, November 29 or 30, 1979	155
25	Bonin Kills Alone #4 John Kilpatrick, December 10, 1979	159
26	Bonin Kills Alone #5 Michael McDonald, January 1, 1980	161
27	Reporter J.J. Maloney, Law Enforcement & An Evidence Breakthrough	164
28	Bonin Kills Alone #6 James Moore, February 1, 1980	166

29	Bonin Recruits Greg Miley for Murder Charles Miranda & James Macabe, Feb. 3, 1980 As Told to Vonda Pelto & Gene Brisco by Greg Miley, March 27, 2003	167
30	Bonin Kills Alone #7 Jail & Early Release, Feb. 4 to March 14, 1980 Ronald Gatlin, March 14, 1980	183
31	Bonin Kills Alone #8 and #9 Glen Barker & Russell Rugh, March 21, 1980	188
32	Day of Crossroads & Consequences Monday, March 24, 1980	197
33	J.J. Maloney Breaks the 'Freeway Killer' Story March 24, 1980	198
34	Bonin Recruits Billy Pugh for Murder Harry Todd Turner, March 24, 1980	201
35	Press Coverage & Bonin Misdirection	209
36	Bonin Kills Alone #10 Steven Wood, April 10, 1980	211
37	Bonin & Butts Victim #6 Darin Lee Kendrick, April 29, 1980	215
38	Bonin Meets Jim Munro May 1980	222
39	Bonin Recruits Eric Wijnaendts for Murder Larry Sharp, May 17, 1980	226
40	Bonin & Wijnaendts Victim #2 Sean King, May 19, 1980	232
41	Billy Pugh Provides Vital Tip May 29, 1980	239
42	Bonin Recruits Jim Munro for Murder Steven Jay Wells, June 2, 1980 As Told to Vonda Pelto by Jim Munro	244
43	Surveillance & Bonin's Final Arrest June 3 to 11, 1980	253

PART THREE—JUNE 12, 1980 TO AUGUST 1981

44	Bonin in Custody & Munro Skips Town June 12 to June 29, 1980	270
45	Scott Fraser Interview, Butts & Munro Arrested June 30 to August 21, 1980	275
46	Miley Arrested, Arraignments & Butts Interview August 22 to November 13, 1980	289
47	Hearings, Media, Snitches, Eric Arrested, Sgt. St. John's Letter & Secret Deals November 14 to December 18, 1980	296
48	Holidays at LA Men's Central Jail December 19 to 31, 1980	312
49	Arraignment, Trial Dates, Pugh Arrested, Dave Lopez Interview & Butts Suicide January 1 to 11, 1981	325
50	Butts Suicide Fallout, Pugh Charged, Jailhouse Tales & Eric Released January 12 to February 28, 1981	338
51	Hope for a Deal, Mind Games, Protecting Eric & Major Decisions March 1981	351
52	Why Bonin Helped Eric & March 24, 1980!	367
53	Munro's Deal, Tim Alger's Articles, OC Files Charges & Lawyer Changes April 1981	368
54	Witness Developments, Pugh Strategy, Jailhouse Tales & Bonin Gets Engaged May 1981	382
55	Love Triangle, Reporters, OC Charges & Jurisdictional Fights June thru August 1981	391

PART FOUR—AUGUST 1981 TO PRESENT DAY

56	Vonda Pelto Arrives at LA Men's County Jail August 1981	402
57	Pelto's First Session with Bill Bonin August 31, 1981	405
58	Pelto's Second Session with Bonin September 7, 1981	412
59	Bonin Lawyer Change & Trial Delay September 14, 1981	416
60	Pelto's Third Session with Bonin September 21, 1981	419
61	Session with Greg Miley October 3, 1981	424
62	Trial Starts, Lawyer Change, Jury Selection & Roadblocks October 19 to November 3, 1981	430
63	Opening Remarks & Family Testimony November 1981	434
64	Lopez & Alger Testimony Rulings December 1, 1981	441
65	Bonin Gets Beat Up & Postponement December 8, 1981	442
66	Pelto's Fourth Session with Bonin December 11, 1981	444
67	Dave Lopez Decides to Testify December 14 & 15, 1981	447
68	Final Arguments & Jury Gets Case December 21 to 28, 1981	452
69	Jury Verdicts January 9 to 20, 1982	455
70	Death Penalty & Pelto's Last Session with Bonin Monday, March 15, 1982	457
71	Execution Friday, February 23, 1996	462
72	Epilogues, Why Bonin Covered for Eric & Importance of March 24, 1980!	469

Acknowledgments

In 2003 Gene Brisco contacted Vonda Pelto, Ph.D. when he was in the process of investigating a series of related murder cases for the Riverside County Public Defender's Office.

Following their association, Brisco handed off to Vonda scores of boxes with reams of investigative documents related to Bill Bonin and the Freeway Killer cases. Without those documents, this book would have been impossible.

James Lia, accomplished attorney and husband of Vonda Pelto, Ph.D., provided invaluable insight on court procedures, how the criminal justice system operates and how judges, prosecutors and criminal defense attorneys think and operate. His input was vital in smoothing out the legal aspects of the story.

In addition, his patience and support, over many years, was a shining example of selfless sacrifice, devotion and love for his wife.

Thanks also to British historians Andrew Roberts and Paul Johnson for producing stellar books that involve first-rate historic scholarship which informs, entertains and inspires.

Preface

State of California
Department of Corrections
San Quentin Prison

September 3, 1982, RE: Bonin, William G., C-44600 (Condemned)
Neuropsychiatric Committee Examination Summary

Psychiatric Evaluation: The subject of this evaluation, William Bonin, is a 35-year-old white male 2nd termer received at San Quentin State Prison March 22, 1982 from Los Angeles County for ten counts of Murder 1st under the sentence of death. The commitment offenses include luring of ten young men to a van whereby they were murdered. Subject has served a prior term in 1975 for multiple counts which include sex offenses. This report is based on an examination of the central file, psychiatric file, medical file, and several psychiatric interviews.

DIAGNOSES: Axis I (302.84) Sexual Sadism
Axis II (301.83) Borderline Personality Disorder with antisocial features

SUMMARY: The diagnosed personality disorder is directly related to the commitment offense. Mr. Bonin's long history of aggressive sexuality toward young males can be seen as acting out of his conflicted feelings about dependency, anger, and his own identity and sexuality. At this time he appears to be coping well with the stress of being on Condemned Row and facing trial on further charges in the near future. With his long familiarity with incarceration and considerable intelligence he is expected to continue to maintain a stable adjustment.

What is *Without Redemption*?

This book was written on a number of parallel tracks that constantly intersect: First, it is the most detailed historical biography ever written about Bill Bonin, the notorious Freeway Killer responsible for murdering 22 teenage boys over ten-months in 1979-80.

Second, it is a comprehensive psychological roadmap which charts the evolution of Bonin's personality from abused child to sexual predator to serial killer. This is accomplished using documents from his childhood, war service, multiple California government mental health and penal institutions, witness testimony and the expertise of Clinical Psychologist Vonda Pelto, Ph.D., who had many sessions with Bonin and two of his accomplices while working in Los Angeles Men's Central Jail.

Third, it is a narrative which, using a trove of long hidden documents, reveals the inner workings of Bonin's mind, showing how he thought, felt, planned and viewed the world. The narrative displays Bonin, an abused high school dropout, cleverly manipulating lawyers, judges, psychiatrists, social workers, friends, family, probation officers, government bureaucrats, detectives, journalists and, most tragically, the innocent victims of his rage.

Fourth, ***Without Redemption*** reveals the complex and interconnected stories of what took place after Bonin's final arrest, when so much was in flux and so many moving parts were swirling about. Archived investigative documents, collected from a variety of sources, brings to light a number of surprising, shocking, sad and even funny events from those tumultuous ten-months from June 1980 to March 1981.

Finally, it is a book which solves two murder mysteries and unlocks how one day of crossroads and coincidences, in the midst of the murder spree, profoundly impacted many lives and future events.

Introduction:
What's a Nice Girl Doing in a Place Like This!

The Los Angeles County Men's Central Jail was a strange, surreal world; a mustard-gray, cement encased ecosystem filled with LA County Sheriff's tan uniforms, multi-colored inmate jumpsuits and pale faces.

It was a world where, on my first Halloween, a gang riot broke out and an inmate was dropped from the second level tier, his brains splattered on the cold concrete floor below.

It was a world where convicts, linked by foot-shackles, shuffled down the sides of the halls, against the walls, because the center of the corridors was forbidden territory to them.

It was a world where trustees stood patiently, like waiters in a high-class restaurant, waiting to take our orders in the officer's dining room.

It was a world where I found myself alone, in my office, having coffee and cookies with rapists and murderers.

More than anything else, it was a world filled with rage, terror and pain. It was here that men, arrested for a multitude of crimes, were incarcerated until the completion of their trials, or awaiting reassignment to San Quentin, Chino, Mule Creek and other prisons.

This was a place for them to quietly meet with me, Vonda Pelto, Ph.D., Clinical Psychologist, for the express purpose of evaluating them for suicidal ideation. Many of the serial killers and murderers relished in the practice of reliving their crimes, taking pleasure in making me uncomfortable as they recounted the gruesome details, often trying to explain their rationale for torturing, raping and murdering. I learned these men sought me out to calm fears and anxieties about their future punishment, most every of one lacking any guilt or remorse for their behavior.

Here was a world that invaded my life as I struggled to maintain my own sanity and keep the darkness from my two daughters. Divorced and feeling alone, I was forced to compartmentalize various personas in order to survive emotionally, spiritually and physically.

Although much has been written about these men and their crimes, few have experienced their inner minds and thoughts as I did during my time, as it were, at the LA Men's Jail. Many books are written about killers by authors who had a limited number of formal interviews with them, but those types of conversations differed dramatically from the barriers down, tell me what you really think confabs I had with serial killers who were **Without Remorse** and **Without Redemption**.

From my first day at the jail, I kept a diary and took copious notes of the meetings conducted with the inmates I was assigned to keep alive. My mandate was to support them through their trials and to *not* engage in therapy. Even after they were transferred to prison, many continued to communicate with me through letters and calls. Their letters, like the conversations, revealed a need for human contact and a total lack of guilt or remorse. My office was a converted cell located quite close to those of the Hillside Strangler, Freeway Killers, the Sunset Strip Killer, the Trash Bag Murderer and the Wonderland Murderers.

The primary focus of this book is Bill Bonin, the Freeway Killer who recruited five others to help him murder teenage boys. As you will find out in this book, Bonin killed just as many alone as he did with the accomplices. I had direct contact with Bonin, Greg Miley and James Munro, but never got a chance to speak with Vernon Butts, Billy Pugh or Eric Wijnaendts.

My first book, **Without Remorse: The Story of the Woman Who Kept Los Angeles' Serial Killers Alive**, and this new publication resulted from those meetings and sessions. While **Without Remorse** covered the entire experience and featured all the killers and criminals I encountered, **Without Redemption** focuses on the entire evolution of Bonin's personality from young boy in Connecticut to serial killer in Southern California. The region was in fear while the killings went on and enthralled as the details of their crimes emerged after Bonin and company were arrested.

It may be the stuff of nightmares, but it is all frighteningly true and had, as mentioned, a tremendous impact on my life. As far as unusual jobs go, especially for a woman in 1981, working in the jail chatting up serial killers and unrepentant sexual predators is close to the top. Place an attractive, single woman working in an environment comprised of five thousand male inmates, and that makes it even more unique.

In this book, Bill Bonin, Greg Miley and James Munro tell me personally about some of the murders and it often seemed as if they were talking about a ballgame or a vacation trip. In addition, a number of other conversations I had with Bonin, before and during his trial, populate the final sections. Coming from a sheltered and strict religious background, I struggled to differentiate between the troubled and the evil.

During many years working at the jail, I developed relationships of varying types with a number of different men. John Holmes, famed porn star and suspect in the Wonderland Murders, proposed marriage to me; Hillside Strangler spoke of his son and the sadness he felt knowing he would not watch his only child grow up; The Trash Bag Murderer almost cried when he recounted watching the dismemberment of two people and hearing the cries of the mother for her children.

Many are curious about what makes a serial killer tick. How do they think? What are they like personally? What are their lives like while incarcerated? What did they do while involved in their criminal activities and what are their interactions with jail staff and other inmates? How do those tasked with being around serial killers deal with emotional baggage they take home every night?

It is my desire that more research will give us the ability to spot serial killers in waiting and devise ways to change the outcomes. Learning the history and cataloging the danger signs, many seen in this detailed telling of Bonin's story, may provide a roadmap for such work.

In the aftermath of traversing through Bonin's world, and trying to make sense of it, I can only hope that one might come away with renewed appreciation for family, love and life. Bonin was betrayed by his family, the people he depended on for love, protection and guidance failed him.

Years spent overcoming persistent nightmares resulted from what Bonin and others dished out to me during multiple conversations. Finding my way back to an emotional equilibrium involved pain and many sleepless nights. Through it all, I learned that the pain we inflict has tremendous impact beyond our imagining, directly and indirectly.

Vonda Pelto, Ph.D.

PART ONE
1940 TO JULY 1979

1

Los Angeles Men's Central Jail
Vonda Pelto, Ph.D., August 31, 1981

Monday, August 31, 1981: "I hate Monday mornings," I mumbled to myself. Pushing open the door to my office, I took time to lock the bottom half of the Dutch-door, leaving the top half open. I inhaled the stale cigarette smoke still hanging in the air, giving the impression of a smoky nightclub from the thirties. Ashes flew airborne with the intake of air created from opening the door. The flakes settling down on a brown sealed envelope addressed to me, Dr. Vonda Pelto, Forensic Outpatient Unit, Los Angeles County Men's Jail.

Two half empty Styrofoam coffee cups, one with curdled cream floating on top, sat to the left side of my desk. Stains circled the bottoms of the cups leaving dried rings on the scared surface.

After I dropped down on the hard, wooden, swivel chair, wishing I would remember to bring in a soft cushion to sit on, I pulled open the crammed file drawer and pushed my purse into the tiny crevice created by jamming the files closer together.

"Morning Doc." I looked up to see the smiling face of James Munro, one of the Freeway Killers, leaning on the bottom half of the door.

"Good morning to you too."

"Can I talk with you later? I'm feeling real bad. By the way, it's those FBI jerks who sit around here shooting the bull at night. They make the mess while interrogating guys," Munro informed me.

"I'll have a deputy call you out." Munro was still leaning on the door when the ringing of the phone startled me.

"Hi Doc, this is Deputy Jerger down in 1750. Can you come down this morning to talk with William Bonin? He saw you here the other day and asked who you were. Told him you're the Shrink, I think he needs to see you."

"Sure, ten o'clock work for you?"

"Works for me," he said.

Bonin's crimes and notoriety required the Sheriff's Department to house him in the high-power module (1700-1750), located on the first floor of the jail off the main corridor. Raping boys, a rung below raping girls, was on the lowest end of the prison hierarchy. This marked him as a prime target for someone in general population wanting to score points amongst other inmates if they offed him.

The prospect of talking with Bonin, an accused serial killer, starting my heart racing…

2

Bonin Family, Boy's Home & Orphanage
1940 to 1955

One might guess that on the morning of March 30, 1940 Alice Cote woke up, rolled over on the mattress and smiled, knowing it would be the last night she would be sleeping under her father's roof. Stretching out to her full five feet and no inches, she read the face of the clock sitting on the nightstand, 7:00 a.m. In four hours, at the Catholic Church where she had her first communion, Alice would become Mrs. Robert Leonard Bonin of Willimantic, Connecticut, a mill town situated on the lush banks of the river with the same name.

Alice sat upright, swung her legs around, and sat on the edge of her bed realizing she would never be vulnerable to her father's sexual advances again. She remembered shivering with fear, dreading the sound of the door opening, knowing her father would soon be on top of her. Alice reported the abuse to her mother, but she dismissed the accusations. Even though her father was known in the neighborhood as a pedophile, no one stepped forward to help her.

With no one to turn to, at age 14 Alice summoned up the courage and ran away to the all-girls St. Joseph's Orphanage in Fall River, Massachusetts. The girls were assigned numbers and never called by their names. Stories have emerged in recent years of the abuse children suffered in this facility and many other orphanages throughout Massachusetts. Two years later, missing family and friends and weary of abuse at the orphanage, Alice returned home. Sadly, the sexual abuse by her father resumed. Alice cried and pleaded with her mother to let her leave, finally her mother agreed, and Alice entered a convent in Canada. She lived there until she turned eighteen.

The Bonin's marriage was troubled from the start, with constant fighting over money. In May 1940, Alice found out she was pregnant. Barely able to contain her joy, she believed the baby would love and accept her unconditionally. Now, her life felt complete with a husband and a child on the way. Robert Arthur was born on March 27, 1941. Shortly after the baby's birth, Robert, Sr. joined the National Guard, and being a father, obtained a deferment from active duty. The young couple felt relieved, knowing the extra money would ease their financial difficulties.

The following November, on a snowy morning, Alice walked to the baby's crib and picked her son up. He felt cold to the touch, his skin a bluish tinge. Snow covered the barren trees and sat quietly on the outside windowsills. Alice prayed he just needed more blankets. In a fit of frenzy, she shook him, ran to her husband and screamed out in horror. Her baby was dead. Years later, some in Alice's family said she never recovered from that blow. She continued talking to her lost child, telling him how much she loved and missed him. A doctor speculated that most likely the baby died of Crib Death.

Weeks later, the Japanese bombed Pearl Harbor on December 7, 1941, and all Guardsmen were called to active duty. After Alice's husband left, she refused to get out of bed. For the next year she remained withdrawn from the world, unable to deal with her grief. Alice's grief did begin to lift at discovering she was pregnant again.

Her second son, Robert, Jr., arrived on June 18, 1943. Unable to support herself and care of baby, Alice went to live with her parents. Her worst fears were realized. Her father again came to her bedroom in the middle of the night. She called Doris, her sister, and pled with her to pick them up, Doris agreed. Young Robert, called Bobby, was nearly three years old when her husband returned home from the service. They moved 18-miles away to Willimantic. However, like so many who served, Robert came back a changed man, unpredictable and violent. He had developed a taste for gambling and drinking, neither of these vices having been apparent before he left. Robert's tolerance for frustration was extremely low. Almost anything could throw him into an uncontrollable rage.

Alice bore the brunt of the outbursts when her husband beat her with clenched fists. She blamed the war, believing the stress of the battles and atrocities he witnessed had caused the changes in him. Unwilling to hold him accountable for his actions, Alice made excuses and refused to take any actions against him.

Having been through abuse from her father, Alice rationalized the situation and tried to move forward. Although Robert maintained steady employment as a machinist, his salary wasn't adequate for a growing family. Robert paid little attention to his family, spending most of his nights and weekends in bars drinking and gambling.

Birth & Early Years

William Bonin was born on January 8, 1947 in Willimantic, Connecticut. Alice described him as having a "low birth weight, he was always a tiny child." He was baptized at St. Mary Roman Catholic Church by Reverend Henry L. Cabot, the same church where his parents were married. Alice's pregnancy proved difficult. Never knowing when Robert, Sr. might blow up, she stayed on edge, trying not to upset him; but his moody and unpredictable personality made it nearly impossible. Fearful of a miscarriage, and the loss of another child, Alice prayed to God for a healthy baby.

Born into a family with a myriad of multi-generational problems, Bill described his early home life to Vonda Pelto, Ph.D., co-author of this book, during one of her conversations with him at the Los Angeles Men's Central Jail:

"It was fucked-up, anyway, that's what a social worker told me after I grew up. I didn't know if we was fucked up or not because I was a kid and figured everybody's family was just like ours. My old man was a drunkard and beat the holy shit out of mom and us kids most every night. I never knew when the next punch was coming, anything could set him off! Like if mom cooked somthin' he didn't like or if she forgot to pick up his favorite beer. One time Bobby, my older brother, tried to defend mom and dad threw a cereal bowl at him, cut his face real bad.

"He needed stitches, but they didn't take him to the doctor. Mom begged him to take Bobby to the doctor, he refused. The old man didn't spank us he beat us. I want to believe they wanted me cause I wasn't their first kid or their last. They ended up having four kids, all boys. Who knows maybe they didn't want any us, you know cause of the way they treated us. They was Catholic, so they couldn't go against the church. You know the birth control stuff. In spite of everything, though, I need to believe they loved me, and wanted me."

Alice wondered if, while pregnant with Bill, the beatings and her anxiety possibly damaged him before entering the world. The last child born to the disordered family was Paul, who was born on November 23, 1949. Robert continued gambling, he loved the racetrack, causing the family financial problems and prompting Alice to find work at the American Thread

Company.

In time the Bonin's used the GI Bill to buy a house in Andover, close to where Alice's parents lived. In January 1950, when Bill turned three and his older brother was about seven, Robert Sr.'s addiction to gambling accelerated and in a high stakes poker game he lost their home. They were forced to move again, this time in with Alice's mother, where they remained until August 1956. Trying to cope with her husband's abuse, Alice escaped by drinking heavily and spending prolonged periods of time at The French Club, a locale bingo parlor.

Bill's older brother, Bobby, later lamented, "My father was a gambler and a drinker, and nothing was allowed to interfere with that—or else you got beat. I remember that the beatings were all the time and my father really hurt me; I remember always having busted lips. Most of the time I was trying to figure out how to survive, not knowing if I would make it to the next day."

With the children too young to be left alone, Alice left them with her parents. Unfortunately, this gave her father access to Bill. A custodian at a local drive-in theater, Bill spent long periods of time with his pedophiliac grandfather. Bill generally received money on these visits, supposedly for assisting him at work. The man who sexually abused both sisters, during childhood and into adulthood, was strongly suspected of sexually abusing Bill. She recalled the time he came into her bedroom, after Alice was married, and tried to sodomize her. Alice never let a man come at her from behind again.

Caught up in her own problems, she never investigated the possibility. Rather than stopping the dysfunctional family pattern, Bill's mother paradoxically surrendered her children to the man who sexually abused and damaged her.

Robert, Sr. worked for Jilson Mills, along with the majority of the town's people. The mill produced cotton thread at a complex, built in 1824, where men worked ten to twelve hours a day operating noisy machines kicking up dust. Willimantic was a small and safe town, like many riverbank textile towns throughout New England.

Boy's Home, 1952

Bobby began getting into trouble, stealing and fighting, setting a bad example for Bill. Alice worked the day shift and her husband the night, leaving the boys with little supervision. Requiring Bobby to babysit created resentment and he often took it out on Bill. This often resulted in Bill either getting beat up by Bobby or left with Paul alone for long periods of time. While Bill was afraid of his older brother, like many younger siblings he wanted to be accepted by him. Bill was dependent and hated to ever be left alone.

At age five, Bill began attending kindergarten at St. Mary's Catholic School in Willimantic. The Nuns complained that he continually broke the rules with frequent fights, not paying attention in class and ditching school. His marks were poor and once he purposely rode his bike full speed into a group of girls, an offense considered serious enough to get him a weekend at a State Juvenile Facility as "a serious warning."

In a continuation of his conversation with Vonda Pelto, Bill described what happened, "My parents couldn't handle me and they got the authorities to ship me off to one of those boys' homes. Don't know why they called that place a 'Home,' it was a shithole of a reformatory. Dumping us in ice water was the counselors' favorite punishment. Older kids had knives and threatened me if I didn't do what they wanted. The time I spent there seemed like years. It was only a month.

"The first night they put me in a room with four other kids. I was a scrawny little kid and really scared. I got on my bunk and stayed there trying to kinda hide out from everybody. Then out of the blue one of the other kids reached over and hit me. I don't remember doing anything to bug him. This older kid, I think he was thirteen, told the boy to leave me alone or he would beat the shit out of him. He was a good guy, cause he wanted to protect me from the other kids.

"The next night he took me into the bathroom and asked me if I wanted to do some sex. I told him yeah if I could tie him up and he said okay. So I tied his hands with a towel. Then he ordered me to jack him off. Guess I was pretty dumb cause I didn't know what that meant. After he explained it to me, I started rubbing him. All of the sudden he was massaging the back of my neck; I hadn't tied his hands very well. I perfected that skill later in life.

"He pulled out his dick, it was already hard and he wanted to put it in my mouth. I didn't want to. He told me to pull down my pants and he started sucking on me. It felt pretty good. Then he said, see that's not so bad. So I sucked his dick. He started kissing me and it was okay. I felt comfortable because he was gentle. Then he told me to take off all of my clothes and get down on the floor on my hands and knees. He had already taken his clothes off.

"He came up hard behind me and raped me. I screamed out. 'Shut up you little punk.' He pushed me over and rammed it in my mouth, when he started comin' I gagged and jerked away. But it was too late I threw up all over the bathroom floor. I vowed that day that I would never let anyone do that to me again.

"Looking back now, I realize that this would be the beginning of my homosexual life. After that I started feeling other kids up and let them feel me up. From as early as I can remember back my grandpa would fondle me and make me suck on him. I didn't want to do it, but he'd get mad at me if I didn't. Mom would drop me off at his place a couple times a week for him to baby sit. She liked to play bingo. I'd beg her not to make me stay there but it didn't do any good."

Incarceration at the Boy's Home didn't have the desired effect on Bill, instead he became more rebellious by refusing to conform to his parent's rules. He shared a bedroom with his younger brother, Paul, and he began sexually abusing him. Paul tolerated the abuse for six months before confiding in his mother, leading her to immediately separate the boys into different bedrooms. Unfortunately, the records don't indicate whether this change stopped the abuse.

Franco-American Orphanage, September 1953 to May 1955

Alice and Robert Bonin had a dual problem on their hands. Their two oldest sons, Bobby nine and Bill six, were acting out, they were out of control and becoming seriously delinquent. Pressure to control their children's behavior began coming from all sides: neighbors, local police, probation officers, school authorities and the Church.

The children were lucky because their father spent little time at home. He continued to beat them over the slightest provocation, clearly not understanding the value of or how to offer appropriate guidance, discipline and love. Alice kept drinking, chain smoking and frequenting the local bingo parlor, equally out of her depth when it came to properly caring for her sons. Inept at the demands of giving her sons the protection, love and attention they required and needed.

All of the elements in the Bonin's lives combined to force a decision serving multiple purposes; satisfy local authorities, give the boys a structured environment, relieve pressure on the parents and keeping the boys away from their father's physical abuse.

On September 6, 1953 the Bonin's two older sons were placed in the Franco-American Orphanage at 357 Pawtucket Street in Lowell, Massachusetts, a Catholic boarding school for children, to be cared for by Nuns with a mandate from society and God.

Most of the children placed there were not orphans, rather coming from families unable to care for or control their children. The facility was maintained by the Catholic Archdiocese of Boston and run primarily by Nuns. Located 83-miles north of Willimantic, the school consisted of a three-story red brick building complex situated on the banks of the Merrimack River.

Originally built as a stately mansion in the 1870s by prominent Lowell industrialist, Frederick Ayer, it was designed in the Victorian style of the time to reflect Ayer's wealth and power. Vacant for eighteen years before it was purchased in 1908 by the Missionary Oblates of Mary Immaculate, it was to provide a home for orphaned children of Franco-Americans, thus ensuring a continuity of French-Canadian heritage from families who settled in Lowell from Canada.

During a campaign stop for John F. Kennedy's second senatorial campaign, in October 1958, Jacqueline Kennedy visited the facility, and a picture was taken with her and all the students.

When Bobby and Bill arrived, the facility was surrounded by a 15-foot-high chain link fence covered with metal nubs and topped by loops of barbed wire, looking more like a prison than an orphanage. Newcomers were teased, one student recalling "it took a while to learn not to cry." Passersby viewed the sad faces of the confused children pressed against the fence, looking for help which never materialized.

They spent almost two years at the orphanage. Bill attended grades one thru three in this structured environment and maintained acceptable grades. Cut off from the outside world, the Nuns running this rather scary institution could and did treat the children as they pleased. A daily routine consisted of "morning wake-up, go to church, eat, go to school, go to church, go to lunch, go to school, go to church, go to dinner, go to church, then bedtime. Once you went to bed at night, you were not allowed to get up and would be physically punished if you did."

Their lives were strictly regimented with playgrounds segregated by sex and age. Should boy and girl siblings see each other through the playground fence and attempt communication, severe punishment followed; one incident saw a young girl, who tried to talk to her brother, "jerked away from the fence by her hair and severely beaten." Siblings might see each other in the community dining room but were not allowed "to sit together or talk with each other." Bill became severely depressed. He was scared and lonely, not allowed any interaction with his brother.

Perimeter fencing kept children inside and served as a punishment tool. When Bill misbehaved, the Nuns forced him to hit the fence with his fists until his knuckles bled, the fingers becoming unmovable once scabs formed. When subjected to this severe punishment, children "cried and begged not to have to hit the fence."

Begging, crying or pleading brought neither sympathy nor relief from the Nuns, whose Christian charity came from a sense of their duty to the children. They never held, hugged or offered any emotional support. A number of sisters spoke only French, leaving many of the children unable to understand them; of course, blood curdling anger and punishment is the same in any language.

One teacher, who sat at a "really big, imposing desk in front of the classroom and was the scariest sight in the world," wielded a half-inch thick, one-inch wide, 14-inch fiberglass ruler that was a weapon of fear and humiliation. She banged it on the desk so hard the sound reverberated throughout the room; one student still vividly recalled the terrifying sound decades later. She hit one student over the head repeatedly until it broke in half, sending the other students into crying jags begging her to stop.

Robert Doucette, who attended the orphanage in 1953, told investigators that "life was pretty regimented at the orphanage. It was a large institution and children just couldn't get individual attention or emotional support. It was very structured. I remember some of the boys had a pretty rough time. Discipline meant physical punishment in those days. Beatings were pretty normal."

The dreaded "Clackers" were the scariest and most formidable of all weapons wielded by the Nuns. Made of two small pieces of two-by-four pieces of wood, attached by a hinge, it was used to physically punish errant children and as an instructional noise maker. The sound could mean many things such as wake-up, go to the bathroom or the community breakfast table or even which door to enter.

One former resident stated, "They hurt like hell when I got hit with one of them. The Nuns would hang those clackers from their belts, we could hear them walking down the hall before we even saw them. I would run and hide, even if I hadn't done anything wrong. I was always afraid. They taught us Jesus could see into our minds and know if we were thinking bad thoughts or did anything bad. I figured the Nuns could get the word from Jesus and know we needed to be punished. To this day, I can still hear the sound of those clackers and I feel an electric jolt run up my spine."

One boy got hit so many times on the head it made him dizzy, another said he "believes it made him deaf in one ear." Blows from the dreaded Clackers quite often left lumps, or hematomas, on their heads. Bill may have suffered a head injury at the orphanage. Later examinations found evidence of frontal lobe damage—an area of the brain important for impulse control.

Other punishments involved a Nun holding a child's head in the kitchen steam cleaner, the one used to clean and sterilize dishes with high heat; or spreading rice on the floor and making the children kneel on it for long periods of time, causing extreme pain and exhaustion.

Spending too much time in the bathroom was grounds for punishment, with some Nuns actually "kicking down the door and coming in after you." Nuns might discipline violators by holding their heads under water in the sink or toilet, eliciting crying and pleading for mercy as the children feared drowning.

Every child was forced to sleep on their right side, facing a crucifix on the wall, and if they turned before going to sleep a Clacker hit was issued for correction. At bedtime, Bonin and forty-nine other children were locked in one of the large dormitory rooms with eight rows of beds, six deep, separated by just enough room to walk around. Sounds of sobbing children could be heard nightly throughout the austere rooms.

A bed wetting incident sent one child into the closet for hours before a vicious beating with a strap. One former resident recalled waking up one night when a Nun, for no apparent reason, "yanked my friend out of bed and forced him into a closet, where she made him strip down and beat him with a strap until welts appeared and his body was bloody."

One Nun feared sending a child to the dorm room alone, believing he might jump out of an upper floor window. Another former student said,

"Once you're there, you don't forget it. I won't go past the orphanage because it brings up such bad memories. I try not to think about it."

Bonin was subjected to the severe punishment, and he was also molested, "Father Fortier molested me while I was in the orphanage. Later he came to St. Mary's to celebrate Mass, near my home in Willimantic, and had me taken to the house that houses all the priests. He molested me again. That day I never forgot; it made a lasting impression on me. I think about him often and still wonder what happened to him."

His vivid memories are sad at best, "I always dreamt of running away from the cruelty, but I was little and didn't have any place to go. I'd pray to be rescued by someone who would protect and love me, but no one ever came. I can remember one-time crying cause I thought my parents were dead. It was because they didn't come to see me. When we went back home, the neglect and abuse from our parents started up again. But at least there only my old man would beat us."

3

New House, Abuse, School & Neighbors
1955 to 1962

On May 31, 1955 Bobby and Bill, ages 12 and 9 respectively, left the Franco-American Orphanage to return home to an abusive family and an uncertain future? Both returned to St. Mary's Catholic School and their troublesome behavior continued as before. Nine months later, on March 23, 1956, Father Guilmette of St. Mary's confronted Bobby after he brought nine ball point pens to class.

Based on young Bobby's history, he accused him of stealing the items in question. Bobby claimed he bought the pens for 19 cents each, at Grant's, with money he earned shoveling snow. Whatever the case, the parent's didn't believe their son and, four days later, both of them were taken to Backus Hospital for psychological testing by Dr. Lichtenstein from Norwich State Hospital.

The doctor reported that Bill showed "a desire to please and is adaptable to the situation. Has pride in his appearance and seems orderly and serious to protect his possessions." Dr. Lichtenstein also noted the "implication of his peculiar desire for boys, his aggressive behavior, fears others in the community, suspect he influences other children. Lacks continuity in home supervision."

In a separate portion of the report, the doctor noted that "Bill's chief need centered on the family with an acute need for maternal affection. He appeared to be seeking protection and love, but expected punishment instead. There are no indications of a personality disorder. His active fantasy and organizational activity fall within the normal range and are controlled by adequate reality awareness. It is felt that his occasional acting out could best be controlled by more maternal affection and supervision. This child is not feeble minded to the extent requiring commitment to an institution for the feeble minded."

This sums up Bill's life to that point: like all children he desperately wanted, and needed, love and protection. Instead, he received abuse and punishment with no means of protecting himself physically or emotionally.

Before his fifth birthday, he had been physically abused by his father and physically and emotionally abandoned by his mother, in addition to molestation by a maternal grandfather.

Alice Bonin, victimized throughout life, was incapable of giving her children a safe and loving environment. She possessed little capacity to love or communicate feelings of love, and neglected children develop dysfunctional patterns since their self-esteem emanates from parental treatment. Learning to love and appreciate ourselves is predicated on a parent's ability to love and appreciate each other, and their offspring.

An April 6 meeting in Willimantic followed in order to talk over Court Action and Disposition with the Bonin parents and local officials. Two possibilities were explored: 1) Both would be shipped off to boarding school, 2) Bobby would go away to school and Bill would be left behind, this option relieving Bill from getting beaten up by his brother.

Options were hashed out in extensive discussions with the boys, Judge Gill, Mr. and Mrs. Bonin, Father Guilmette and Probation Officer Carley Hough. They came up with nothing. Costs prohibited sending them to certain schools and, since they were about to move to Mansfield, 15-miles from Willimantic, it was decided the boys would remain at home.

However, before the move a key event took place. Young Bill was befriended by a local florist, a 40-year-old man named Burt. Considered an upstanding citizen of the community, Burt was also a member of the local police auxiliary. Bill expressed an interest in rare pennies and was invited to view Burt's collection, at his house. Burt seduced young Bill was ushered into the world of what may be termed "more sophisticated homosexual activities." Sex with an adult had a profound effect on Bonin, relegating previous encounters, with boys, to the realm of "unimportant."

Encounters with Burt were few and ended when the Bonin's moved into a house owned by Alice's father in Mansfield, on Route 32 now designated as 465 Stafford Road. Bobby enrolled in E.O. Smith Middle School and Bill attended the Annie Vinton Elementary School for grades four thru six from 1956 to 1959.

Multiple changes in just over three years were hard on young Bill; St. Mary's School, Boy's Home, back to St. Mary's, two years at the orphanage, back to St. Mary's and then moving to a new town followed by enrollment at Annie Vinton. Being shy and trying to continually make new friends tested Bill's nearly non-existent socialization skills, a problem which he never sufficiently resolved. Difficulties with class work made an already difficult existence more problematic, thus leading to extensive absenteeism from school.

Wanting to avoid uncomfortable feelings around others, he also struggled with sexual identity. Young Bill was confused and receiving nothing constructive from those around him. Fearful others would discover his hidden secret of being attracted to male teachers and other boys, he was isolated and embarrassed. Unable to come clean about his dysfunctional home life, unequipped to deal with the feelings fighting it out in his brain, he cloistered himself from classmates and family.

Their new house was in a rural setting, characterized by widely separated residences surrounded by thick woods populated with American Elm and Chestnut trees which dominate New England. A short distance to the Willimantic River, and swimming holes, gave the brothers ample room to explore and, with fewer neighbors, less of chance of causing trouble. Bill went to school one mile away with his little brother, Paul, while Bobby attended middle school five miles away in Coventry. Each afternoon, the boys returned to an empty house with no parental supervision and little food to eat.

Robert Sr., a serious gambler and drinker, was never at home; Alice quit her job but was rarely home. A chain smoker nicked named "Buttsey" by the neighbors, she drank heavily and endeavored to find any available bingo game around town. They were latch-key kids in the full sense of that term; left to their own devices, the Bonin boys were often dirty, hungry and free to cause trouble without implications.

When at home, the father was prone to beating his wife, with closed fists, and turning his fury on twelve-year old Bobby when he tried to defend his mother. Frightened by the ruckus, the younger boys would scurry away and hide. Bill was not immune from physical abuse and this, combined with a lack of caring attention, goes a long way in explaining his adult behavior.

During fourth grade his classmate, Phillip Pavone, was left with vivid memories of Bill Bonin, "I clearly and distinctly remember that Bill was very much a 'loner' who did not have many friends. He was very different from all the rest of my classmates, not fitting in to the so-called normal type of kid behavior or mannerism. He appeared to be a little odd and acted strange and different. Bill would get into trouble while in school and be disciplined, on occasions getting into physical fights with other classmates. Often time he would be picked on just because of the way he acted and behaved.

"The way Bill dressed was messy and unkempt. I do not recall his specific hygiene but remember he was not neat. I talked to Bill from time to time, but I did not hang around him like he was a good friend, don't forget, he was different. I talked with him because I felt bad for him—no friends, no attention—just kind of there. As a child I felt that William had some difficulties which resulted in the way he acted and behaved. I felt that something was not right with Bill and his family. He was possibly from a dysfunctional family. Something made Bill different from all the rest of the kids."

Next door neighbor Wilmot Dyer told investigators that "for the six years, 1956 to 1962, that I resided next to the Bonin family, I recall the children were never supervised and cared for by their parents. It seems, based on my observations over the years, that the children did not receive a healthy, happy normal life." Bobby was in charge of keeping the house and looking after his younger siblings, a duty he often abandoned, and thus the young boys were left at home to fend for themselves. When he did stay around, Bobby would pick on Bill constantly, yelling at him "an awful lot and would beat him up on occasion. I do know that Bill was very much afraid of his older brother."

Left alone, Bill made Paul go everywhere with him. He "seemed to dominate him" as they roamed "the neighborhood without having to answer to their parents. I do vividly recall that I observed Bill throwing sharp darts at Paul, who was positioned up against a tree in the yard. It was like playing chicken with the darts or like knife throwing at the circus."

Concerned about the boys, Dyer sometimes invited them over and "spent a reasonable amount of time with Bill, more than Paul, and it seemed that he was not allowed to eat enough food. I would feed Bill and Paul and they both would eat fast as they were always hungry."

Linda Dittrich remembered Bill from Mrs. Ruth Porter's sixth grade class at Annie Vinton, "I can vividly remember classmate Bill Bonin because he was quite different from all my other classmates. It is easy to remember him as a very unhappy child. His body and clothes were always dirty. He was a 'loner' type person. He seemed to be unapproachable and shy, seldom interacting with other classmates, male or female. I remember that he got into trouble a lot. He wanted and needed some positive attention. In fact, Bill needed attention but never received any positive attention by classmates, teachers or school-based adults. He was pretty much left alone. I feel that something bad had to be going on in Bill's life for him to behave the way he did and appear to be so unhappy."

Observations from Bill's classmates paint an accurate picture of his public personality; closed off, difficulty making friends, shame about his personal shortcomings, family life and proclivity for other boys. Bill began to molest younger boys, usually by oral copulation. About the age of ten, Bill and a girl about his age got undressed and looked at each other. He first masturbated at 11 or 12 and, at about 13, got into bed nude with his 17-year-old female cousin in a bit of sexual experimentation.

Bill later talked about becoming a serious juvenile delinquent and the punishment from his father, "Guess it all started when I was about ten or eleven. Me and some other kids started stealing hub caps, license plates; little shit like that, no big deal. Neighbors complained about us, that really bugged my dad cause he didn't like his drinking being interrupted. He wanted me off his back. He'd yell and cuss at me.

"His belt buckle would leave red whelps, even blood sometimes, but I wouldn't give him the satisfaction of crying. That fucking made him crazy. At about 12, I started stealing cars, could hardly see over the steering wheel. One time I picked up a stolen car and rammed it into a police car. The case was dismissed by paying damages of $250 for the stolen vehicle and $50 for the damages to the police car. I got put on probation. That didn't stop me. I just got more determined to do what I wanted."

By this time, 1959 and 1960, Bill attended Coventry High School, a good distance from home, and continued to get failing grades. However, events were about to take a dramatic turn in the lives of the Bonin family. Having suffered from her husband's abuse for twenty years, Alice reached the limit and kicked him out in late 1960. A short time later the court awarded her custody of the children and declared him an unfit father. Even though money would be tight for the family, Alice could no longer tolerate the cruelty and the fear it inspired.

The beatings may have stopped, but the neglect did not. In 1961, Darwin G. Gebbie began delivering the ***Hartford Courant*** newspaper to the Bonin house. A report indicates he got "to know who Bill Bonin was, but never really got to know him very well." They were both 14-years old.

Darwin said, "I guess you could say I was one of his few friends. Really though, I was not really his friend, nor was he my friend. William did not participate in anything that I was aware of at the time. William just did not fit into the normal crowd. He kept to himself."

Darwin noticed the family was "not well off financially. Mrs. Bonin would almost always have an obvious odor of liquor. She consumed an awful lot of liquor, probably beer, and probably often. I always used to go to the side door of the house which had a small porch area. This area was always completely cluttered with beer bottles."

Sometime in 1961 Robert, Sr. lost his job when the American Screw Company was purchased by Noma Lights, causing many job losses. Finding work was difficult because he was trained on a specialized type of machinery, one used by a limited number of companies. After many inquiries, a company in Downey, California offered him a position.

A small city 12-miles southeast of Downtown Los Angeles, it was basically an engineering town dominated by aerospace and defense contractors. Facing the prospect of her husband relocating across the country, with a well-paying job, Alice rethought their separation and the family moved in early or mid-1962.

4

Move to LA, New Schools & New Troubles
1962 to 1965

In early 1962 the Bonin family moved from Connecticut to California and Robert Bonin, Sr. went to work at the Olympic Screw and Rivet Company in Downey. Southern California was a hub of defense industry contractors and Olympic was one of many, large and small, spread throughout the area. During the 1960s about 25,000 employees worked in Downey, a city of 12-square miles, solely on the Apollo Space Program.

They settled in the city of Torrance at 2415 West 187th St., 15-miles from where Robert, Sr. worked and not far from the beach. Everyone, especially the kids, had difficulty adjusting to the large metropolitan area.

With family and friends over 3,000 miles away, they felt untethered from emotional support and help. Bill and his two brothers were left to their own devices to find new adventures, and new troubles. Rural Connecticut made fewer demands, with small-town values and a slow pace giving way to big city chaos and uncertainty.

The whole region was in the midst of an incredible economic expansion, one which started after World War II. Previous to the war, Southern California and Los Angeles were known for agriculture and Hollywood, but following the war millions of former combatants, from all over the country, settled in the area, went to university on the GI Bill and stayed to begin new lives.

A booming suburban sprawl, with new housing tracts and business districts, was all of connected by something new which became part of Bill Bonin's fate and legacy: The Freeway.

In fact, the opening of the famed San Diego Freeway, a north-south main artery that is now the busiest freeway in the world, coincided with Bill Bonin's arrival. Car was king and the area would see many developments centered around motoring: drag racing, drive-in theaters, drive-in restaurants just to name a few. Unlike many Eastern cities, having a car in Southern California was a practical necessity.

Essentially, moving to Southern California from Connecticut, for young Bill, was akin to landing on a new planet. To be uprooted and put in a faster paced world at fifteen years old would be difficult for anyone, let alone an abused and troubled teen like Bonin. For six years they lived in the same house and neighborhood in a quiet rural environment, the longest run of stability in his short life. Torrance, with houses closely situated in grid blocks, had no nearby meandering rivers, lush forests or swimming holes.

Having experienced sexual abuse and a rather chaotic family life, it is no wonder Bill grappled with his social and sexual identities. Continuing to feel ashamed of his emerging feelings, Bonin kept his homosexual tendencies a secret. Possessed with the social ability to make friends, he probably didn't talk much about his parents or the horrifying experiences at the orphanage and other abuses.

The three brothers enrolled in the Torrance Unified School District. Bill was the proverbial new kid from the other side of the country with no friends and the same raft of insecurities. He didn't fit in with the kids from this different world, but he understood why the family had to move. There was no choice with his father's unique job skills and, after a year in Torrance, Bill was still kind of lost. His older brother ignored him, and his younger brother was in grade school.

Exhibiting problems with his sexual identity, Bill was always self-conscious about his appearance and rarely smiled due to poor dental health. Although he had experimented sexually with a few girls, it never felt comfortable. Unable to communicate or feel comfortable with girls, he found it easier to deal with boys. From all outward appearances, no one knew what was going on inside of him, the hurt and rage which overpowered him.

Bill was bright, but he couldn't keep his grades up and had always been a marginal student. However, his natural aptitude for math indicated an analytical mind combined with an obsessive nature, both allowing him to concentrate on the topic at hand. Discouragement led to more absences from school and the situation deteriorated.

He began forging absence excuses with his mother's signature, a violation which eventually caught up with him and led to a three-day suspension. Decades later he told me this at LA Men's Central Jail, "I figured they were doing me a favor, I didn't want to go to school anyway, and now they were making it legal for me to stay home."

Bill wasn't interested in school sports, but he did become very active in bowling and harbored dreams of going pro. At 16, he spent most of his nights at a local bowling alley keeping league scores, often not returning home till well after midnight. The next morning, when it was time to go to school, he was wiped out. On the off chance he did go to school, Bill would invariably fall asleep in class.

In the middle of his junior year, on January 8, 1965, he turned 18: "I always did what I wanted, nobody ever supervised me. My parents were both working, and they liked to go to the horse races on the weekends." During high school, Bill met Linda and they began to date. Although he was not completely comfortable with her, he wanted to be normal. His mother was happy and encouraged him. They later got engaged right before he entered military service.

That summer, on July 4, he was arrested for **Petty Theft** and **Burglary**. Bill and his brother's friend were out joy riding and were running out of gas. They stole a weight scale machine and a newspaper receipt box from a supermarket. An alert citizen called the police and patrol officers easily found the boys, busting them cracking the machines open for a paltry sum in coins. Bill was frightened they would discover his troubled past and send him to prison. In a sign of continuing poor judgement and impulse control, his days of theft and stealing cars remained a problem.

Lacking money for an attorney, the court appointed public defender made a deal for Bonin to plead guilty to a first offense **Petty Theft** charge. He was given a suspended 30-day sentence, one-year probation and a $56 fine. More than happy to pay up, Bonin admitted his first offense in California was stupid. But realizing his good luck did not translate to learning from the experience.

Still officially in school during the 1965 fall term, Bonin's school attendance was practically nil as he still committed petty crimes. Feeling above the law, like he was too smart to get caught stealing from the liquor store where he worked or the vending machines at school. Over ten years of abuse, uncertainty and lack of family stability had put a stamp on young Bill that was showing through.

5

High School Dropout & Vietnam War Service
January 1966 to October 1968

Records indicate Bonin dropped out of high school in early 1965, not long after turning 19-years old. He obtained work with his father at Olympic Screw and Rivet in Downey and signed a contract to purchase a horse on a monthly payment basis. But Bill was still skirting the law. Alice lost sleep from the familiar nightmare of her song getting arrested, possibly for involvement with young boys. He preyed on kids in the neighborhood, with one neighbor recalling Bonin's "offerings of X-rated movies and free beer to the boys on Angell Street."

She pointed out the dangers and prayed for him as a good Catholic mother would. Growing weary of the nagging, Bill told her, "Mom, you worry too damn much!" She tried to protect him, the second of her three sons and the most fragile. Throughout the pregnancy, she lived in fear of a miscarriage from her husband's beatings. Alice always had a nagging suspicion Bill suffered brain or physical damage in utero.

While fairly smart, Bill bored easily and lacked motivation or any concrete goals. Always broke and borrowing money, Alice talked him into volunteering for the Army, rather than waiting to get drafted. The Vietnam War ramped up in 1966 and millions of young men found themselves called to duty. After agreeing, Bill talked a friend into joining up and in mid-December they enlisted together. He disliked doing anything alone and had not overcome his insecurity/dependent personality.

Alice felt relieved for the first time in years, believing military service would take care of him for a while, possibly injecting some discipline into his chaotic life. Bill and his girlfriend, Linda, decided to wait to marry until he returned, offering an incentive to work through his sexual identity.

After Basic Training, Bill served as a cook in Alaska for four months and then signed up for helicopter school to fulfill a dream of becoming a pilot. He failed to get in and his ego took another blow (his first dream was to become a professional bowler). Instead, Bonin trained as a door gunner on a Chinook CH-47, a twin-engine heavy-lift helicopter, and an Aircraft

Mechanic. Alice knew Bill was disappointed but was pleased when he wrote, "Mom, I've been made a door gunner in a helicopter."

On October 25, 1967, while on leave in San Francisco before getting sent to Vietnam, Bonin was arrested on suspicion of **Grand Theft Person**. Bill denied the charges and, since departure to the war was imminent, he would not be able to attend the hearing. Bonin later said, "The beef got cleared up when my commanding officer sent the court a letter. He got me out of having to appear." He netted five dollars in the botched robbery and again Bonin circumvented the law.

Bonin arrived in Vietnam about two-months before the North Vietnamese launched the massive Tet Offensive, on January 30, 1968, which commenced a massive and bloody eight-month struggle. This became the political turning point in the war for the U.S. and Allied nations. Attacks took place all over the country by forces of the Viet Cong and North Vietnamese People's Army, constituting the largest military operation of the war by either side to date.

Numerous websites and biographic publications mistakenly report that Bonin served with the U.S. Air Force on-board helicopters for search and rescue operations, looking for downed pilots. This is a mistake.

A Disability Application Claim, found in the documents of a private investigator, contains the relevant facts regarding his Vietnam service. Bonin's Army Serial Number was 56-700-885. He obtained the rank of Private First Class E-3 and was stationed at the Pho Loi Base Camp, north of Saigon, with the skilled 205th Assault Support Helicopter Company, the "Geronimos," of the 11th Combat Aviation Battalion, nicknamed "Red Dog Firefly."

Airmobile companies dropped soldiers into combat zones and evacuated them as necessary, essentially Air Calvary operations, a new advanced form of highly mobile warfare first tried only years before and still in early stages of development.

Bonin arrived in late 1967 and spent the last six-months of his 12-month tour operating as a door-gunner on the Chinook CH-47, amongst the fastest helicopters in the world. During 1968, Chinooks carried in supplies of all types, often under fire, and ferried out wounded soldiers for urgent medical attention. Countless numbers of soldier's were saved by these operations and the famed MASH units staffed by nurses and doctors—200 of the 750 Chinooks deployed to Vietnam were lost in combat or "wartime operational accidents."

In February 1968, while Bonin was at Pho Loi, ground patrols found a large contingent of North Vietnamese troops dug in for a long siege less than 1,000 meters from the perimeter. After ground assaults by U.S. troops failed, an Air Calvary assault resulted in a seven-hour battle sending enemy troops, minus 277 dead, retreating into the jungle. An 11th CAB May 1968 Operational Report, declassified in 1980, indicates that during February 1968 alone it conducted 207 combat assaults using ten or more lift aircraft.

Bonin flew with the 205th during their 1968 Counteroffensives IV and V, from April to October 1968, and no doubt combat was hot and heavy. Records indicate the 11th CAB operated on a 400-mile front, with their operational footprint heavily increased in 1967 just prior to major battles of Tet Counteroffensives.

A hallmark for U.S. Forces was employing helicopters like the Chinook to resupply and support isolated garrisons. During many hazardous combat operations, Bonin logged in over 700 hours in a CH-47 manning a 7.62-mm M60 machine gun, one of two mounted near the front for self-defense.

Alice knew he was afraid when Bill wrote, "I don't know if I will get back to the states with my ass. Being a machine gunner in a helicopter and being shot at is nerve wracking. Many of the men in my unit are coming home in boxes."

Bonin received a commendation for risking his life to pull a downed airman into the back of the helicopter. North Vietnamese troops were shooting down CH-47s as they dropped off supplies. To Bill's credit he received a Marksmanship Medal, the Vietnam Cross of Gallantry, Good Conduct Medal, Vietnam Campaign Medal, Vietnam Service and Air Medal. He also earned his high school diploma, GED, while in the service.

According to one report, Bonin had five heterosexual encounters, all with prostitutes and the last one in Hong Kong with a 25-year-old. However, shortly after arriving in Vietnam he forcefully sodomized two men, at gun point on separate occasions, and had a number of homosexual encounters. Because the victims were too ashamed to report the crimes, he skirted through legal disaster yet again.

Vonda Pelto, Ph.D., co-author of this book, wrote this about Bonin, "While speaking with Bill in 1981, at LA Men's Jail, he said that he enjoyed his time in the service, being away from home and feeling a powerful independence. He said he felt less lonely in the service; he had a girlfriend and number of pen pals. The regimented structure provided the external structure Bill needed in order to feel safe.

"Children push their parents trying to find out where the limits of their patience exists. Parents who do not provide a proper structure will ultimately raise insecure and dependent adults. Bill's lack of internal impulse control, combined with poor judgement and an inability to learn from punishment, spelled trouble at every turn."

Bonin's life during combat operations was stressful with close calls and dangerous adventures. While not a ground combat soldier, he witnessed destruction while U.S. armed forces were engaged in major operations all over Vietnam. Bonin also saw the brutal treatment South Vietnamese soldiers doled out to their enemies, which included something he later used extensively, handcuffing and restraining.

6

Coming Home & First Arrest
October 1968 to June 1969

In late 1968 Bonin came home to a time of free love, college anti-war protests, race riots and revolts against long-held cultural norms and the "establishment." America and the world were torn apart in a political upheaval which altered all levels of society. Those changes bled heavily into the government institutions Bonin soon had to deal with—dramatically impacting his future and that of many others.

Alice Bonin thanked The Lord for keeping her son out of trouble and bringing him home safely. After reaching the rank of Private First Class, Bonin received an Honorable Discharge on October 25, 1968, and returned home at 187th Street in Torrance.

She felt joyous watching her son unpack his gear and get settled back into his old room. She offered to wash his clothes and put them away for him, but he told her it was time for him to start taking care of himself. She believed that his time in the Army had helped him change and become more mature, she was right and wrong! During his time away his girlfriend married another man, which made him feel betrayed.

Bonin settled in by working nights as a gas station attendant at the U-Sav-On Gas in Torrance. He bought a Norton motorcycle for $900 with a loan from Bank of America in Long Beach, paying $45 a month. He began a new phase of his life, but he had changed and not for the better. Now the objects of his attention were young boys, and this obsession began with 14-year-old Billy Jones.

At 9:00 P.M. on November 17, within weeks of returning home, Bonin was cruising around Arcadia, 35-miles northeast of Torrance, when he spotted Billy Jones walking home. Driving his mom's white Chevrolet station wagon, Bonin pulled up next to Jones and asked him for directions, a tactic he often used as an icebreaker with many victims, then and later.

"What did you say?" the boy asked.

"See, I'm not familiar with this area." Bonin modulated his voice to a soft whisper.

"I'm looking for the Santa Anita racetrack. Do you know where it is?" Mrs. Jones would remember later she had warned her son many times to never talk to a stranger. But to Billy Jones the man seemed harmless.

"Sure, I know where it is. But you're too late to catch the races."

"Thanks, but that's not what I'm interested in. I'm looking for a good place to stable my horse." Bonin knew he had used the perfect ploy when the boy's facial expiration turned into a wide grin.

"You got a horse?" His curiosity was palpable.

"Yeah, hope to have it running in the quarter mile races as soon as the season opens. Once I can get him stabled, you could come over and have a ride," Bonin said, seeing doubt on his prey's face. "That is if it's okay with your folks."

"What's your name man?"

"Billy Jones."

"Hey little buddy, can you believe it? We got the same first name and who knows; soon we may have a whole lot more in common. My name is William Bonin, but my friends all call me Bill. Hey, why don't you just crawl in? It's getting late and you're beginning to shiver. It's nice and warm in here. I'll give you a ride home. I can find the track tomorrow."

"Well, I am kinda tired." Billy said and got in the car.

"You ever been blown?"

"Huh? What's that, some kind of sex stuff?" Billy asked.

"You know suck dick. Head, you know what that means don't you?"

"Well yeah, sure I know what that is. But I'm not into it"

"I'm sure you'd like it. It feels good."

"If it's alright I'll get out here. I can walk on home." He reached for the door handle, but it was locked. He jiggled it harder and looked for a lock to disengage.

"Hey, I can't get this open." His throat was suddenly dry, and he began to feel panic.

Holding the steering wheel with one hand Bill reached over, grabbed Billy's crotch and squeezed.

"Hey that hurt! Why'd you do that?" Billy looked uncertain about his vulnerable position.

"I want to fuck you in the butt!" Bonin growled with anger and anticipation.

"Let me out," he screamed, his body shaking.

"Listen you, stupid kid, I'm not about to lose you now."

"Please let me out." Billy pleaded, banging on the window, hoping to get someone's attention.

Bonin had to get to a safe place fast, aware that someone might see the kid's signals. He wormed his way to the back of a closed shopping center, got out of the car and dragged his victim out onto the ground, sat him on his back and handcuffed his wrists. As the kid struggled to get up, Bonin grabbed him around the neck choking him.

"If I count to three and you don't nod your head, I'll kill you and then fuck you in the butt."

"Please, please don't kill me," Billy said, sobbing uncontrollably.

Bonin ignored the pleading boy while ripping his blue jeans down to his ankles. Billy opened his mouth to scream just as Bonin struck him in the face with a closed fist, his head snapping backward. The child's eyes wild with fear. The predatory Bonin settled on top of him.

After regaining consciousness, he was released and told to sit on a bus bench with the further admonition, "Don't look back until I'm gone, or I'll come back and kill you!"

Mrs. Jones later said she had barely dosed off, vacillating between anger and fear. When she heard the front door open quietly her anger took precedence, "Billy is that you?" She called out.

Billy stood transfixed, not moving from the frame of the front door, his face tinged with purple, his bottom lip broken, bleeding; testimony to the brutal beating he had been subjected to. Blood evidenced on his pants. His mother crossed the room put her arms around him while gently wiping his tears, as her own flowed freely mingling with her child's.

By 10:30 p.m. Mrs. Jones and her son were at the Arcadia Police Station to report the crime. With evidence of the beating still clearly on the young boy's face, the officer asked him, "Son can you tell me what happened?" Young Billy hung his head down, trying to hide tears and shame.

The police had a first name, a description of Bonin, the car and details about his M.O., but he wouldn't be back in Arcadia anytime soon. Bonin started operating closer to home in the South Bay coastal beach cities, far away from Arcadia and not far from his home in Torrance.

Four more attacks, almost exactly like the one just described, took place in roughly weekly intervals over the next six weeks. Since he was driving a motorcycle for basic transportation, the attacks occurred at night or on weekends when he was able to borrow the station wagon.

The following information is taken from court documents on those incidents: "On November 26 at 12:00 a.m. John Treadwell, age 17, reported to the Redondo Beach Police Dept. that he had been hitchhiking on a public street and accepted a ride with Bonin. He began asking me about 'fags,' etc. Then he slowed down and I thought he was going to stop and let me out at my house. But instead he accelerated the vehicle pointing a hand gun at my head. Then he said, 'Okay, shut up and sit still, don't worry, I'm not going to hurt you…you know what I'm going to do don't you, you'll find out soon enough.'

"He drove to some place I didn't know and tied my hands behind my back with handcuffs. Then the man pulled my pants and underpants down to my knees and raped me. Then he released me and said, 'I can go to jail for a year for this, I know where you live and where to start looking for you and I have a lot of friends in this area but don't tell The Man…if you tell The Man I'll get you with more than my fists'

"On December 4, 1968, it was reported to Torrance Police Department by Allen Pruitt, age 17, that he had been hitchhiking when a male driver offered him a ride. While driving with the driver, the victim was asked if he knew about queers? At this time the suspect turned quickly off the highway and forcibly handcuffed the victim, forcing him into a prone position pulling his pants down and placing his erect penis in the victim's rectum. The victim reported the incident to his instructor at Torrance High School who in turn reported it to the Vice-Principal, which caused the delay in reporting…

"On January 2, 1969, it was reported to Hermosa Beach P.D. by Lawrence Brettman, age 12, that on January 1, 1969, at approximately 8:00 p.m. he had been hitchhiking on Pacific Coast Highway and accepted a ride from a male driver. The victim told the driver that he wanted to get out of the car at a desired location, but the suspect refused to let the victim out threatening force. The victim stated the suspect drove to an area north of Hawthorne Boulevard and Palos Verdes North for acts of sodomy and where armed robbery occurred…

"On January 19, 1969, at 1:00 a.m., it was reported to the police department by Jesus Monge that on January 12, 1969, at 9:00 p.m. he had been hitchhiking on the highway and had been picked up by a man who asked him about homosexuality. The driver offered him $20 if he would give him a blow job. The victim attempted to exit the vehicle and the suspect punched the victim in the stomach and chest area with his fist.

"The suspect then unzipped the victim's trousers and grabbed his penis, stating 'I'll rip your nuts off if you don't cool it.' The victim's hands were handcuffed behind his back. The suspect then removed the victim's trousers and underwear and without removing his own clothes lay on top of the victim. The suspect then had the victim orally copulate him..."

The police realized they had a serial rapist on their hands. Alerts were distributed to law enforcement agencies throughout Southern California. All of the attacks were similar in nature, obviously perpetrated by the same person driving the same vehicle. Then, on January 28, 1969 at about 02:30 a.m., El Segundo Police got a break while patrolling the 1800 block of East Walnut Street. Officer Peggy Duval noticed a white station wagon that fit the description given by several of the witnesses.

"Get on the horn and call it in, see if we got a match to the partial plate," she said to her partner. He hit the button, turning on the flashing red light and trailed the car until it pulled over to the curb. Bonin rolled down the window, beads of perspiration shining on his forehead, "Is there a problem sir?" Bonin asked working to appear calm.

"License and registration please!"

The driver fumbled around in the glove compartment, located the paperwork, pulled his license from his wallet and with shaking hand, thrust them out through the window. The uniformed officer stepped back and shined his flashlight on the license, "William Bonin, age twenty-two. Is that you?"

"Yes sir." Bonin answered barely above a whisper.

The male officer shined the light into the car and noted a young man with brown hair and crooked teeth, then compared Bonin's face to the picture on his credentials. It matched. The officer also saw a young male sitting in the passenger seat.

"Would you both step out of the car please?"

"What's your name son?" Officer Duval asked the boy.

"Timothy Wilson." She discovered Wilson was a run-a-way from Kansas, barely 16. Duval would testify later that "the kid was scared shitless."

"Mr. Bonin, raise your arms." Duval ordered.

"What's the problem? I wasn't speeding," Bonin began shifting his weight back and forth, his face turning red and the veins on his neck throbbing.

"Turn around. You got any needles or knives?"

"No." The officer proceeded with the pat down looking for weapons and found metal, tarnished handcuffs.

"What are these for?" she pointedly asked Bonin. "You care to explain?"

"Please, you got to help me. You should incarcerate me, not let me be free because of the way I am."

"Put your hands behind your back. You are under arrest."

"You don't understand, no one does! I can't help myself. None of this is my fault," Bonin exclaimed in a pleading, sobbing yet unrepentant rant.

Walking back from the police car, with Bonin sitting in the back seat, she said, "Poor kid, Bonin picked him up at the airport promising to take him for something to eat. That man scares the holy crap out of me. Something about the look in his eyes, ice cold. Bonin pled for my help," Duval continued. "He kept saying he should be incarcerated and not let free because of the way he was. I'm telling you this guy's capable of committing homicide, and I truly believe this is only the beginning."

That night he was booked on suspicion of **Kidnapping**, Penal Code Section 207, and **Sex Perversion**, Section 288 (a). Quickly the pieces fell into place and Bonin was connected to the five attacks. He knew it was big trouble and that, in prison, men who rape young boys are on the lowest rung of the food chain and get targeted. Treatment dealt out to them can be disgustingly gruesome, brutal and ongoing, sometimes resulting in a tortuous and painful death.

Bonin's arraignment was followed by a preliminary hearing in Municipal Court, where they bound him over for trial in Superior Court. Knowing additional charges were pending, he was moved to LA County Men's Central Jail in Downtown LA.

This is where Bonin's cunning ability to work the system begins to emerge. He was searching for a legal loophole by painting himself as a victim of childhood abuse, essentially a "sexual psychopath" who didn't "know why he did what he did." He faced multiple counts of **Kidnapping** (207), **Crimes Against Nature** (286), **Crimes Against Children** (288) and **Sex Perversion** (288 a).

California law, at the time, stated that a "sexual psychopath is any convicted criminal, not punishable by the death penalty, who suffers from abnormal sexual desire of a kind and degree to constitute him a menace to others."

Atascadero State Hospital had been established to treat sexual psychopaths along with other patients with a myriad of psychiatric disorders. Bonin's personal history of abuse, run-ins with the law and dealing with the stress of war were all presented to the court as justification for his request.

As a result, on March 11, 1969, prior to the actual legal proceedings, Judge Newell Barrett issued a Court Order for Bonin to undergo a psychiatric examination to determine if he was possibly a "sexual psychopath" who required treatment. If accepted, he would be remanded for a 90-Day Observation period to see if he would be labeled a ***Mentally Disorder Sexual Offender*** (MDSO) and confined for "an indeterminate period of time" for treatment.

The proceedings were instituted and Albert Boner, M.D. and Frederick Hacker, M.D. interviewed Bonin. The two psychiatrists were to make evaluations and a recommendation regarding Bonin's ability to benefit from treatment. Boner completed the first report on March 14, 1969. After going through Bonin's history, he stated that Bonin "frankly admits his guilt in all charges. He described his sexually deviant behavior and his narrative approached very closely to the evidence incorporated in the preliminary transcript."

He then went on to describe Bonin in this manner: "Mentally, the defendant is of average intelligence, in good contact with reality and verbalized freely, relevantly and coherently. In narrating his deviant sexual behavior, he revealed no emotion, anxiety or remorse. He admitted that he was fully aware of the seriousness of the crimes alleged at the time that he committed the acts, he was not aware that there would be charges of kidnapping.

"He also admitted that in each instance he did have a climax. In answer to a pointed question he stated that he prefers heterosexual contacts, and doesn't understand why he involves himself in the deviant sexual acts charged. His memory for recent and remote events was quite satisfactory. Insight and judgement is markedly impaired. There was no evidence of psychotic ideation. The defendant gives no history of psychiatric hospitalization. He advises that he saw psychiatrist several years ago, three times, when he was living in Connecticut."

Frederick Hacker, M.D. was a bit more pointed in his detailed four-page report, completed on March 28 and filed with the court on May 9. Dr. Hacker stated that the "Defendant who originally denied any trouble during childhood and early adolescence, recalls that he was interned in some reform school when he was approximately 8-years old. At that time he was forced by an older boyfriend to touch him and feel him up. He believes that during the ages of 9 and 12 he had various homosexual experiences, usually with people much older than himself; he subsequently had many homosexual relationships sporadically (but never accepted any money or gifts for it)."

Key to this story is the following observation: "Defendant claims that these recent episodes are incomprehensible to him; they must have something to do with his war service in Vietnam but he doesn't exactly know how." He admitted to Hacker that he carried handcuffs and "always bound his victims that he picked up as hitchhikers and then proceeded to forcefully have anal intercourse with them, while they had their hands behind their backs."

Additionally, as a psychiatric observation, Hacker noted that "Defendant shows signs of depression, aside from his realistic worry about the present involvement; the disturbances in the area of affective responses making for tenuously retained reality contact and stiff, somewhat inappropriate emotional expression is very definite."

Hacker ends the report with a paragraph that is straight forward, ominous and yet provides hope, thus giving the court enough to consider that Bonin be evaluated for rehabilitative psychiatric treatment.

"The defendant certainly is not mentally ill by legal standards; he has sufficient capacity to know and understand what he was doing, he is at present capable of understanding the nature and the purpose of the proceedings against him to cooperate in his defense. Defendant definitely represents a distinct danger, since the mixture of uncontrolled sexual drive is explosive with great likelihood of recurrence. Therefore, under all circumstances, confinement of this possibly treatable individual for a prolonged period of time is strongly recommended."

Hacker notes that Bonin is not capable of being able to control his sex drive, however, he opens the door with phrases like "possibly treatable" and "prolonged period of time." On May 9, 1969 he was formally charged with five counts of **Kidnapping**; five counts of **Crimes Against Nature**; one count of **Crimes Against Children**; and two counts of **Sex Perversion**. Knowing the victim's testimony would result in a conviction, Bonin pled guilty. He asked his mother to pray for him.

At trial, Bonin admitted to offering money or drugs to induce the boys to get into the car with him, then asking them about "queers and fags. I would ask them if they wanted a blow job; get their consent and then drive to an isolated spot. We would crawl into the back and make love. If they struggled, I would reach down and squeeze their testicles and handcuff their hands behind their backs to restrain them. Then I would sodomize them."

He was found guilty of one count of **Kidnapping**; two counts of **Crimes Against Nature**; one count of **Crimes Against Children**; and two counts of **Sexual Perversion**. At the sentencing hearing, scheduled for June 4, it would be determined if Bonin was headed for psychiatric evaluation or prison.

In mid-May he was interviewed by Kenneth E. Kirkpatrick, a Probation Officer, in relation to his desire to be sent to Atascadero for "rehabilitation," communicated in a letter Bonin wrote to the court.

"I was given this opportunity to write you, and give my explanation to why I did what I did. There's no good or bad reason for committing these crimes. The only thing I can say was that I wasn't thinking straight. I have never used any force on anyone for the purpose of homosexual acts or any other reason before.

"When I got back from Vietnam I was supposed to have gotten married. I found out that she had gotten married when I got back. I felt bad for a while but got over it. I think that I should be sent to Atascadero for rehabilitation. I want to try to be cured of this unnatural sickness. I would say whatever I get as far as time, I have it coming to me. I should have thought before I acted.

"Whenever I do go back on the streets I am planning on getting married and raising a family. I'll also get a good steady job to support a family. I know that I am capable of leading a useful and a good life as a good citizen.

"I know I can be cured of this sickness because it is my desire to stop doing these unnatural, immoral acts against nature. I was thinking of going to school to learn and get a license for flying helicopters. I was a crew member on a helicopter in Vietnam. I like being on a helicopter a great deal. I intend on doing this if the opportunity presents itself when I am released. This will help me in being a good and useful citizen.

"I will say that if you send me to Atascadero to be rehabilitated you can rest assured that when I am released from there I will never again do these things. It's not a good but a bad life in jail. It's a life of non-achievement and it is shameful. Once I go back to civilization, I can guarantee that I will do my utmost and then some to abide by all laws in the county, state and nation."

Bonin pushes all the right buttons, while bending the truth, in a letter he probably wrote with coaching from his attorney. Bonin is a 22-year-old, just back to civilization from the Vietnam warzone, who has descended into an entirely different world emotionally and psychologically. His desire for help might be genuine, but the motivation to avoid hard time in prison was paramount.

When speaking with Kirkpatrick, Bonin recounted some of his childhood experiences, and trauma, while relating that he "is overcome by this problem and did not know to gain help for his problem." He hadn't had a "normal relationship with women since his return from Vietnam" but says "he is not afraid of girls, he has only found it hard to seduce girls. He feels that female relationships in a normal manner are preferable."

Around the same time Kirkpatrick met with Bonin's mother, who told him that she knew of "her son's illness when the defendant began practicing sodomy on his younger brother. She attempted to correct the situation by placing the defendant in another room. At no time did she take her son to a doctor or attempt to communicate with her son about his problem. The mother stated she wanted to help her son."

Mrs. Bonin also wrote a letter to the court trying to help the cause: "Our son, William G. Bonin, knows that what he did was wrong. He promises that he will try to be cured of this problem in any way possible. When he was ten years old, some men did something to him and he began to practice this on our youngest son. When we were told about it, we honestly thought that this was a childish curiosity and separated the boys. We made Bill sleep in a room by himself. We never suspected that he had a mental problem that should have been dealt with by a doctor.

"Maybe it is our fault that he is like this today. If we had taken him to a psychiatric doctor when he was ten, he may never have grown up with this problem. I asked the veteran's hospital in Long Beach if they could help him out. Their answer was that the charges would have to be dropped in order for them to get Bill into the psychiatric ward and help him to be cured. My husband and I want Bill to be cured and we want what is best for Bill.

"We will do anything you ask of us. Is it possible, for him to be paroled to us? We love him very much and hope you give him and us a second chance. We want him to get help in one way or another, because we don't believe he can be cured without this help. I don't want to see any more young boys hurt. We will abide by what you say, one way or another. It took a week before I had the courage to write this letter. Please help us. Alice Cote-Bonin."

In the final evaluation, Kirkpatrick leans heavily toward psychiatric evaluation by concluding that the "defendant is seriously lacking insight and responsibility for the infamous crimes he stands convicted of since his Grammar School years. Openly candid and cooperative, defendant explains involvement in these crimes because of not knowing where to look for help. Defendant now asks for help by requesting that he be referred to the State Mental Hospital at Atascadero.

"This officer questions defendant's statements because of the defendant's background which was totally involved in sophisticated society. Defendant, a Vietnam War Veteran obviously knew more about mental health before his arrest in this matter. This officer feels that defendant realized the consequences for these crimes and with this in mind will cooperate to that extent which will allow him to be returned to society. It is this officer's opinion that the defendant is a threat not only to himself but to others."

This must have been the deciding factor for the court because Kirkpatrick's May 28 report recommended the "Defendant be committed to the Department of Mental Hygiene for placement in Atascadero State Hospital for observation and diagnosis pursuant to Section 5512 Welfare and Institutions Code."

On June 4, 1969 the judge decided that Bonin would go to Atascadero to determine if he "could benefit by treatment" and if he was in fact a ***Mentally Disordered Sexual Offender.***

Two things are important; 1) Atascadero is a maximum-security facility founded, in large part, for treating sexual psychopaths; 2) If the authorities at Atascadero determined Bonin was faking, or gaming the system, he would be remanded back to court for sentencing and prison time.

Bonin arrived for "diagnosis and evaluation" at Atascadero State Mental Hospital on June 17, 1969.

Observations of Clinical Psychologist Vonda Pelto, Ph.D.

A turning point in the life of Bonin, and his victims, had been reached; he entered the Army in December 1966 as a troubled teenage with a prediction for petty crimes and homosexual activity, and returned as something else indeed. He had seen death and destruction doled out in massive doses; viewed and felt how in war human life is cheap and aggression is valued.

People handle the psychological and physical strain of combat in different ways, some are suited to the task and seem unaffected during and after serving in combat, others collapse after the first shot is fired and never recover. Bonin returned with a penchant for violent aggression based on homosexual rape of young men.

Bill suffered sexual and physical abuse as a child. Later doctor's also found evidence of possible brain damage from being battered about the head by his father and at the orphanage. He entered an institution designed to help people overcome trauma and turn their lives around. It was now up to the doctors at Atascadero to help Bill Bonin.

7

Atascadero Mental Hospital—First 90-Days
June 17, 1969 to September 18, 1969

Atascadero State Mental Hospital (ASH), located along the Central Coast of California mid-way between Los Angeles and San Francisco, opened in 1954 under part of California's Program for the Sexual Psychopath.

In 1960 Superintendent and Medical Director at ASH, Reginald S. Rood, M.D., wrote that the basis for the whole program is that the "legal provision which establishes a state hospital as an alternative for prison for certain nonpsychotic, convicted offenders, legally defined as sexual psychopaths."

This maximum-security facility, with an all-male population from 1,200 to 1,500, is nestled in beautiful rolling hills and lush pastoral landscapes, an area where families could spread out blankets on the inviting grass and enjoy picnic lunches under the shade of tall, stately trees. Inside the weathered walls of Atascadero, the cookie cutter construction of the pre- and-post war era cement blockhouses were, by appearance and design, depressing all by themselves.

Within the walls is a lack of color, nauseating smells and the sameness of everything which, taken together, might drive anyone mad. ASH is ringed with chain link fences festooned with loops of razor wire and guard towers, a veritable assault on such beautiful surroundings.

This treatment facility, like many mental institutions, is overcrowded, understaffed and run by officious bureaucrats. In society's effort to deal with those considered mentally unstable, those who endanger others, mental institutions are always a reflection of their own time. Dealing with extreme defects in human behavior is never easy and, unfortunately, such institutions often do more harm than good. Over the decades, the range of patients at Atascadero expanded in concert with laws and institutional guidelines.

During the 1960s, according to Rood's report, 60% of the patients were sexual psychopaths and 40% criminally insane. All the strictures governing what was happening to Bonin—laws, treatments and length of incarceration—were enacted in the 1930s. Tamara Rice Lave in a *Louisiana Law Review Report* described what happened, "Citizens across the United States were terrified that they were being engulfed by a wave of sexual predators, and the politicians responded. Between 1937 and 1967, twenty-six states and the District of Columbia passed legislation calling for the indefinite civil commitment of so-called sexual psychopaths."

Bonin was facing an uncertain future, living on the knife edge between time in state prison or an extended stay in a maximum-security treatment hospital. Bonin's life had changed drastically; only months earlier he was in the Army flying resupply and evacuation missions in and out of battlefields in Vietnam, enjoying military leave in Hong Kong, a soldier operating in a stressful wartime atmosphere with relative amounts of power.

The court diverted him from prison for a 90-day evaluation and diagnosis, but rejection for long term treatment means immediate resumption of criminal proceedings. Undoubtedly nervous during his first encounters with medical staff, he is evasive, hides certain aspects of his life and is forthright about his family history. The first Psychiatric Examination report, by George Baier, M.D. on June 19, 1969, stated that Bonin "realizes that he is a sick person mentally. He does not understand why it has happened in a vague way, attributes it to his experiences in Vietnam where he learned to become aggressive. He admits his guilt. He does not blame others. He makes statements that are reasonably valid, and he is anxious to have treatment."

Bonin reveals to Baier that he got the "idea about handcuffing while seeing prisoners handcuffed in Vietnam." A tactic he later used in more heinous crimes. Baier finished his report by stating he "realizes that his crimes are serious and is very cooperative, and willing to abide by whatever is dictated for his punishment and cure." He was diagnosed with 301.82, *Inadequate Personality* and 302.20, *Sexual Deviation, Pedophilia, Male*.

Every new patient is first given a psychological interview to determine if he posed a danger to himself, others, or is gravely disabled, has psychotic features or is dealing with any type of drug abuse. Bonin's psychiatric interview/mental status examination didn't reveal any psychotic symptoms. He denied hearing voices, seeing things not present, any paranoid ideation such as believing the FBI was following him, or delusional thinking, believing he was a famous historical figure.

After the interview he, along with the other new patients, were showered with quale soap to eradicate body lice or crabs, given a physical, including x-rays, new clothes, photographed, and fingerprinted. If a patient becomes violent, he is treated as a medical emergency and given medication. Since no weapons are allowed inside the hospital, the staff has access to restraints and protective gear available in locked boxes along the long, dreary corridors.

Patients lived in individual rooms measuring six by ten feet, a mere sixty square feet, with heavy wire mesh covering the windows, allowing little sun light to seep in and thus adding to an already gloomy atmosphere. Room doors remained unlocked, allowing patients to roam the halls as long as he is involved in a myriad of therapies. Regulations prevented patients from personalizing their tiny spaces in any fashion.

When someone is transferred between wards, they cart what few possessions allowed in a box, and it is fairly common for patients to bounce from ward to ward depending on circumstances.

A single dormitory has twelve to fifteen rooms, more like cells. Center of all activity is the wardroom, a kind of living room gathering place, therapy center and sleeping area for those without rooms. Budget, design, societal norms and accepted medical practice created an environment where someone who might benefit from treatment can get lost in the shuffle.

In 1969 Atascadero had a completely different atmosphere, it was far less dangerous and bears little resemblance to that which exists in 2023.

Issues in Criminology, distributed internationally to scholars, doctors and mental health professionals, published a well-researched article in the 1966 edition by Michael Nasatri, D. Dezzani and Mimi Silbert, ***Atascadero: Ramifications of a Maximum-Security Treatment Institution***, which sheds light on Atascadero State Hospital when Bonin arrived.

After describing it as a normal looking hospital, with a nicely decorated entrance lobby, they note that once through the "double-doored sallyport one realizes this is a maximum-security prison. Two immense corridors, painted a depressing gray and filled with men, lead at right angles away from the sally-port entrance and give access to the cells and dormitories of the twenty-seven wards. Despite the dungeon-like construction, a second glance reveals immediately that this is no ordinary prison.

"Women walk freely and unescorted among the patients. Technicians, clothed in white, are actively working among the prisoner patients. Though most of the men are uniformly clothed in khaki, many wear civilian clothes. Moreover, seventy-five percent of them are allowed fairly unrestricted movement within the building area. Atascadero, then on second impression is more a hospital than a prison. The tense atmosphere and strict regimentation of a prison is absent and the therapeutic aura of a hospital is somehow present in these two great tunnel-like corridors."

Medical staffs endeavor to help patients bring their symptoms under control. Sexual offenders, such as Bonin, are taught to recognize their impulse to seek out children for sexual gratification and what to do to keep them from acting on these impulses. Molesters who choose female victims generally blame the child, saying "she seduced me." Justification for their behavior lies in the notion that they are giving the children love and positive attention denied by parental figures, thus displaying a shocking lack of any empathy or understanding of the damage the children are suffering.

For the most part, child molesters are unable to feel basic human emotions such as happiness, fulfillment or love, emotions learned in early childhood. Most of the men did not have the advantage of a healthy environment growing up, their parents unable to give them necessary nurturing for proper development.

Bonin is stuck with no power over mundane activities with full knowledge failure would spin his world in a far harder direction. Nearly his every word, expression and movement would be tracked, noted and analyzed. Bonin's restless nature and impulsive sexual drive would have to be bottled up as he shuffled around drab hallways, lived in depressing rooms and was surrounded by a variety of psychiatric patients. He also will be subjected to ongoing therapy and self-examination from psychologists, social workers and psychiatrists.

The medical staff works to understand the dark side of human behavior where dangerous murderers, rapist and child molesters reside. Men, both charged and found guilty, have been committed by the court for treatment under a variety of classifications: ***Mentally Disordered Sex Offender***, ***Mentally Abnormal Sex Offender***, ***Mentally Ill—Incompetent to***

Stand Trial, Not Guilty—By Reason of Insanity or *Mentally Ill— Civilian Commitments.*
Today Atascadero is considered one of the most dangerous facilities in the country, in part because the patient population has been expanded to include the most violent offenders. Bonin was initially labeled a **Sexual Psychopath**; today he would be called a **Sexually Violent Predator** and the laws for crimes he committed are taken more seriously and the penalties reflect such a designation.

In contrast to 1969, ASH is now for all practical purposes a city unto itself, containing a fire department, police department and a large pharmacy which is always well stocked because 90% of all patients are on some form of medication. Since the patients are not shackled or constrained, the medical staff must rely on meds for their own safety. The psychotropic drugs also serve to make the men more amenable to treatment.

To further understand what Bonin went through on the road to becoming a vicious serial killer, a glance at the nature of organization and treatment at Atascadero is necessary. This gives a snapshot of those with the power to decide Bonin's future, the nature of designated professionals who would hold sway over a man who is aggressive beyond his own understanding, a man filled with a longing to inflict his sexual urges and willpower over helpless victims.

When Bonin arrived, Atascadero grouped the wards into five equally sized psychiatric sections: two were run by Assistant Superintendents, one by the Chief of Professional Education and two by Senior Physicians. While all section chiefs are psychiatrists, their administrative duties result in minimal or no contact with patients. With seven psychiatrists on staff, this left only two fully trained psychiatrists treating upwards of 1,500 patients.

After careful organizational analysis, an **Issues of Criminology** report cited a key factor which Bonin experienced at Atascadero, one that may have contributed to what happened later: Those with the least amount of formal training had the "most direct contact with the patients." The structure placed "an administrative psychiatrist in a position of dealing with the courts of a certain geographic area in hopes of establishing greater rapport between the hospital and courts."

Within that plan was also the desire to "develop a small hospital setting to combat the impersonality and anonymity of this huge and depressing maximum-security hospital." Their report concluded that the "objectives seem commendable" but created "lost benefit to patients" by making it virtually impossible for psychiatrists to deal directly with them.

Each geographic ward had a treatment team consisting of a physician, psychologist, social worker and rehab therapist, the latter three working amongst multiple wards. But the primary point lies in the fact that "the workhorses of the team, however, are the psychiatric technicians who, though they possess relatively little formal training, are in the most direct contact with the patients." Each Psych Tech, who is assigned permanently to a ward, acts as a sponsor for "ten to twelve patients who are his particular responsibility."

Group therapy, conducted by a psychologist or social worker, is at the heart of treatment with "informal therapy groups" broken down into Rehab Therapy and Industrial Therapy. Each patient must participate in at least one-hour of group therapy weekly, with about 50% involved in many hours each week. In addition, every sponsor conducts a "sponsor-led group which is a patient-discussion groups, with the presence of a sponsor to allow for the new title." An article by Dr. Fred Cutter notes that these "provide a supplementary psychotherapeutic experience for the patients in the group" but definitely "doesn't replace existing treatment methods nor is it psychotherapy in the strict sense of the word."

Bonin was assigned to Ward 5 and, according to staff chart notes, was judged a poor candidate for therapy. He verbalized trying to change but his actions proved otherwise. Like many sexual predators, he proved to be manipulative, untruthful and sexually dangerous to the other patients. His diagnoses did not require any type of anti-psychotic medication, and he was a reluctant participant in group therapy.

An interesting incident took place during his first interview with Dr. Alfred Owre, a psychiatrist who figures prominently in Bonin's story, then and later. Forced to confront the homosexual pedophilia which landed him at Atascadero, Bonin got highly agitated about his "homosexual problem" and lack of consciously coming to terms with his "own homosexuality." The June heat and a growing conflict anxiety ramps up the discomfort and Bonin's emotions boiled over, causing him to "faint dead away and remain unconscious for ten minutes."

Apparently, all the implications of childhood abuse, stunted socialization skills and aggressive sexual activity overwhelmed Bonin's mind and body all at once, delivering a stark realization of what Bonin had become like a hammer blow.

A July 24, 1969 report noted "his involvement and participation has been minimal which suggests little motivation to help himself. Patient has expressed the desire to remain for treatment. Responds to direct questioning, by the group, in a flat, evasive manner and very defensive." It also related Bonin proved helpful repainting the ward and keeping it clean, but in socializing he irritated other patients with a braggadocious, know it all attitude.

Bonin had full hall privileges and retained them as long as he had an Industrial Therapy Assignment, such as painting the ward, and participated in formal and informal treatments. He played board games with other patients, watched TV and spent time roaming the corridors, often passing the nurse's station, trying to pick up males for sex. "He particularly liked young retarded ones," a nurse reported. "He was restless and irritable and would often come by the desk saying he had lost his appetite and needed something to help him sleep."

Staff perceived Bonin to be immature and someone who "lacks insight into himself and others and relates to others only through aggressive self-assertion," which was indicated in an August 5 Psychological Evaluation Request and Report by Alfred Owre, Jr., M.D. He noted that Bonin had no idea what made him behave aggressively and possessed even less desire to change.

An IQ test revealed him to be bright to superior in intelligence, but he exhibited little insight into his behaviors or the consequences of them. Bonin followed the program when it suited him, which the doctor described this way: "He handles his inner conflicts regarding sexuality by utilizing sociopathic defenses such as acting out, rationalization and denial of emotional problems. He is most comfortable when inspiring guilt, anxiety, and fear in others."

The final sentence of the Report on Psychological Testing concludes with a key observation: "Before Mr. Bonin can be strong enough to face his problems, he needs to be reinforced for relating to others in situations where he can neither withdraw nor be aggressive."

After eight weeks of acclimation, with some setbacks as he settled into the motions of schedule, staff, patients and therapy, his fate hung in the balance. In mid-August, he had a crucial meeting with doctors who would decide if he remained at Atascadero or was sent back court and thence prison.

On August 14 James Hollingsworth, M.D. dictated a Mental Status Examination Report which contained a series of cogent observations and a decision. He observed that Bonin "is alert, cooperative and his speech is quiet, coherent." A dull mood and inappropriate affectation coupled with a good memory of long past and recent; a solid grasp of current events and a superficial notion of his actions with no remorse; a reluctantly voiced belief that his arrest prevented more violent events coupled with cloudy discussions of childhood and family relationships; no hallucinations, delusions, "ideas of reference or apparent thought disorders."

The Staff Findings portion of the report states that his "extensive homosexual acting out" has increased in violence over time with severe "control deterioration." Their psychological testing pointed to him as an "extreme sociopath" with "high potential for psychotic breakdown when threatened" while dehumanizing his victims. The Staff Psychologist expected a "long and difficult treatment" for a person who talks about his crimes "frankly and with no remorse."

Despite the staff believing that Bonin was "extremely dangerous" with little chance of benefiting from treatment, Hollingsworth's diagnosis and decision was that Bonin was a "***Mentally Disordered Sexual Offender*** amenable to hospital treatment." Treatment would progress as established and be reassessed in 90-Days.

While the report was dictated on August 14, it wasn't transcribed till September 3. Filed on September 8 at LA Superior Court, it stated that Bonin was committed for an "indeterminate period as provided by Section 6316 Welfare and Institution Code."

Bonin was given another three-month reprieve. Despite staff misgivings, the doctors decided he would stay and the diagnoses of ***Inadequate Personality and Sexual Deviation***, ***Pedophilia***, ***Male*** remained the same. The retention decision was approved by Edward E. Edlund, M.D. and Hollingsworth. He was made aware of all facets of the decision immediately and with frank honesty, thus bringing home two messages: he had passed the first hurdle but faced big uncertainty.

Bonin took the strong message to heart and six days later, on August 20, he willingly participated in an "all-day marathon group therapy" session and "was attentive and participated more than usual in the discussion." Despite a willingness to participate, the barrier of his horrendous socialization skills was on full display.

Ward 5 Progress Notes from Program Coordinator Charles Hall, Master of Social Work, reported that "it came to light today that Mr. Bonin was quite unpopular among the patients because of his pushiness and his dogmatic, opinionated point of view. The patients feel he is unopen to suggestions and they are at a loss as to how to handle him." As a result, after the sessions he became depressed, downcast and "withdrawn."

But knowing his situation, he shook off the criticism. According to Nursing Notes, on August 26 he fell while running in a courtyard and suffered abrasions on his left leg, hip and shoulder. Bonin received visits from friends, regained full hall privileges by rejoining the Industrial Therapy Assignment of painting the ward and participated in ward cleanup, made friends, was groomed nicely and slept well.

Staff definitely noticed the change in his behavior when, on September 9, it was noted he was "endeavoring to obtain benefits from the program and he is trying to improve his adjustment." Bonin picked up the pace by performing admirably on two ITA assignments, in admissions and the kitchen, while attending therapy on a consistent basis. He also became involved in Atascadero's Emotional Security Program, a form of Patient Governance, which was open to anyone holding full hall privileges.

Patients in ESP elected ward officers, who kept it running smoothly, participated in town meetings and were allowed to collectively air grievances and offer suggestions to staff. Considered controversial by other psychiatric authorities, Atascadero defended the program as necessary to run the facility and noting it gave patients a certain measure of responsibility and authority which assisted psychological health. In fact, administrators responded to critics by reporting it would have been impossible to run the hospital without it.

Even at this early stage, in report after report, it always came back to the heart of the matter: poor impulse control, poor judgement, lack of insight, anger, and lousy socialization skills. A September 9 Ward Report sums up his first 90-days at Atascadero: "From the results of psychological tests, which were reviewed with the patient, and his ward behavior, it is evident that his relationships with others are extremely disturbed. He does not know how to cope with other people at even a most basic level and he cannot tolerate closeness. When individuals get too close and threaten his defenses, he drives them away through various obnoxious behaviors. Mr. Bonin will have to work through these problems before he can accept help from anyone."

On September 18 Bonin was served with the Order of Commitment, giving him ten days to request a court hearing on the decision, something he was unlikely to do considering the alternative, prison. He signed to "acknowledge receipt of the above number Order of Commitment" and was able to breathe a sigh a relief while contemplating what lay ahead.

His next 90-day deadline would be mid-December. Being committed for an unknown period of time put him in a place of relative security. The ever-present sword still hung over his head should progress prove regressive, or his behavior become detrimental or dangerous.

8

Atascadero, Vacaville Prison & Parole
September 1969 to June 1974

Bonin entered the next phase of dealing with the California mental health system following an "indefinite commitment" to Atascadero as a ***Mentally Disordered Sex Offender*** "amenable for treatment." Having skirted state prison, for now, Bonin is in a safe place and can rightly assume he is at Atascadero for the long haul, however, it is important to note he is constantly being reassessed on 90-day time frames for possible return to criminal proceedings in court.

Once a patient is diagnosed and committed, public health medical bureaucracies, and the doctors who run them, are notorious for not wanting to admit professional and institutional failure. They will slog forward with faith in the treatments available and eschew responsibility with double-talk when one of their patients blows a gasket.

A mix bag of good and bad reports allows Bonin to retain full hall privileges. On October 15, 1969 Bonin is transferred from Ward 5 to Ward 25 that is classified as an "administrative transfer." He must now face his problems while also meeting and dealing with a new group of patients, staff and Psychiatric Technician. During October and November, he adjusts to the new ward, writes to friends and family and is elected, by the other patients, to be Assistant Sargent-at-Arms while continuing with his ITA job in Admissions.

Bonin felt anxious in therapy, with that 90-day reassessment always in the back of his mind. On November 25 he voiced a "sincere desire to return an 'A' recommendation from hospital reports, and it is noted he "is a friendly individual who will usually speak first and is cooperative on the ward." He still does not require any medication.

Bonin energetically sailed through his reassessment and into 1970, often with too much energy as he tended to boss patients around as Sargent-at-Arms. He sexually pursued patients his own age, and this tendency went wrong when struck by a patient on December 12. Bonin tried to force his sexual will on someone and got paid back with a punch in the face.

At the end of January, he was cited for "deviating with a patient from Ward 3 in the hallway of the medical area." Bonin seduced a young, mentally retarded patient and aggressively sodomized him. This violation, plus being too bossy with patients as Sargent-at-Arms, caused him to be reassigned to kitchen duty and told "he can work his way back to a higher status assignment when he shows regard for himself and others by functioning in a realistic and practical way."

In February Bonin withdrew, only socializing with younger patients as his hall privileges were revoked due to the sexual assault. On March 5 he was again caught having sodomy, probably with a different patient, and three-days later got punched out again. Bonin is aggressively forcing his sexual desire on unwitting victims. Alfred Owre, Jr. M.D. reported, "This man has not been reached in therapy." He has been at Atascadero for nine-months and has been tagged as unresponsive to treatment; Bonin must get back in line or face the music in court.

Throughout March and April, he writes to friends and family consistently, four letters a month, and displays an avid interest in sports of all kinds. On April 25 his Psychiatric Technician reports Bonin is "working hard in hopes that he will not return to court with a 'B.' He keeps busy with his work assignment, plays hand ball in the gym. He writes to his girlfriend and receives letters from her. His brother has returned from the Army and has been visiting him. He has stabilized more in that he has made some more permanent relationships with people. Before that he was very much alone."

During May, and the first two weeks of June, he keeps to himself and buckles down in therapy, leading Owre to issue a positive June 11 report: "Patient Bonin is making good progress in therapy. He is more frank and open than he was upon admission. Homosexual preoccupations are less pervasive. He is doing well in his industrial therapy assignment. Insight is developing. Decision: Retain and treat."

Bonin skirted thru yet another 90-day assessment period with his first anniversary at Atascadero one week away. The next day Ward 25 Psych Tech detects a hint of positive developments and uplifted spirit after Bonin's parents and girlfriend visited, leading him to note Bonin might have a "change in interest from boys to girls."

While active in therapy, "the trouble is he sometimes talks to dominate the group" with lots of aggressive chatter. The Psych Tech made Bonin "more aware of his extra talk" and reported he is active with work assignments. However, all is not as it appears because he developed a relationship with a patient that results in repeated urinary infections throughout July.

The true cause of the condition came to light on August 4, when it is learned he repeatedly sodomized and performed "acts of perversion" with the "new friend," the latest one in the auditorium on July 30. Bonin admitted to acts with the current friend, and others, and had his hall privileges revoked. After illegally using hospital phones, for the first time a Ward Report puts forward two important observations, "He appears to be putting on false front to hide his real selfish intentions. He is a real manipulator and is a past master at it."

Here is Bonin the serial killer to come; smart and clever intriguer, able to mold people to take part in nefarious activities, then masking guilt and responsibility in a blizzard of explanations and false remorse.

One fellow patient/inmate, Phillip Gonzales, who was convicted of a felony, remembers two chilling comments from Bonin. One part of therapy involved an important question: What would you do if you were in similar situations again? Twice Gonzales heard him say, "I will make sure they don't take me alive, and if they did, I will leave no more witnesses whatsoever." Discounted as bluff among inmates, who are also mental health patients, the statements reveal a deep Bonin character flaw.

On September 18, 1970 he was approved for transfer to Ward 3 for a "special training program" and, facing little choice, was "amenable to the transfer." Bonin had learned a key trait for survival in correctional institutions: parroting back what therapists, doctors and social workers "want to hear" to keep up the notion, or falsehood, of progress.

He would remain on Ward 3 till mid-November, but events moved rapidly towards a reckoning for Bonin. During those eight weeks in Ward 3, for special training, he wrote many self-analytical, autobiographical materials trumpeting progress and seeking continued treatment. Patients in group therapy confronted Bonin, calling him out for not dealing with his own problems. They strongly voiced dislike for him.

In early December, the wheels were in motion to send Bonin back to court. Dr. Owre and the Staff, on December 10, 1970, filed a report determining that "although he says he has changed, his actions prove him to be manipulative, untruthful and sexually dangerous to other males.

Typically, he victimizes mentally ill or retarded victim who are eager sexual converts. Since he is untreatable at this time and all treatment programs available to the sex offenders have not produced personality change in him, the staff recommends disposition under Section 6325(b) WI. In my opinion, he is sexually dangerous to males, both children and adults."

Twelve days later an order was issued for Bonin to return to court, filed with the LA Superior Court. On January 14, 1971, he was transported to LA Men's Central Jail. This is another key event in the future of Bonin and his victims: Judge Allen Miller must decide whether to accept Atascadero's findings and reinstitute criminal proceedings.

While awaiting the hearing, Bonin penned a 9-page letter to Judge Miller pleading for more treatment at Atascadero, resulting in a January 26 phone call from Miller, to doctors, for more info. Miller was informed similar communications were created by Bonin during a "special program" and he "still proved dangerous by performing sodomy on other patients. Additional treatment would not be considered beneficial at this time." The phone call is in the Ward Progress Notes and signed by S.W. Morgan, M.D., with copies going to Dr. Eklund and Dr. Owre.

The next day Bonin was in court, represented by a Public Defender, R. Briggs, to face a judge who knew first-hand he was deemed "beyond treatment and a danger to others." DA Joseph P. Busch, Jr. pushed for him to be formally sentenced and sent to prison. Bonin expected a prison sentence but was blessed with a reprieve when Judge Miller ignored the doctors, reprimanded Bonin for his behavior with a stern ultimatum and sent him back.

Doctors and staff were furious; Judge Miller not only ignored their recommendations but sent Bonin, a man they believed to be a dangerous and disruptive force, back to their hospital. Even after being told over the phone of their firm decision, the opinions of trained professionals were tossed aside. Bonin's work around, with a letter sent directly to Miller, was a clever move and may have been the difference. Judge Miller's inexperience with Bonin's refined ability to manipulate overruled the opinions of those most familiar with his machinations.

Immediately the wheels were set in motion to rid themselves of Bonin by different means. Readmitted on February 8, 1971, he was given an updated diagnosis and disposition on March 17. 301.78, **Anti-social Personality, Severe**; 302.80, **Sexual Deviation, Aggressive Sexuality**

(Forcible Sodomy); 302.60, ***Sexual Deviation, Sadism***.

More importantly, the updated disposition was ***Transfer to Department of Corrections***.

On April 1 Dr. Eklund wrote to E.F. Galioni, Deputy Director, Division of Mental Health Programs in Sacramento, requesting Bonin's transfer to the Department of Corrections with no specific facility recommended. One week later, the transfer to the Department of Corrections was approved by T. Aller, Assistant Chief Classification Services.

Doctors employed a horizontal bureaucratic move to bypass the court, but Bonin still has tricks to play on his own behalf. He writes his own plea, to Galioni, seeking a reprieve from transfer. During April, Bonin received a sympathetic reply from Galioni, which was countered on April 29 when doctors resent the March 17 diagnosis and decision report reaffirming their recommendation. Doctors refused to be outwitted by a man who continued to pursue patients for homosexual encounters, asking targets "how long is your penis" and other alarming questions.

Bonin tried to convince therapists he would only seek out consenting adult males, but he got reported for targeting younger known homosexuals on the ward. One patient reported Bonin for wanting to use his room to have sex with a patient from another Ward, causing restriction to his home Ward. Team members stopped believing Bonin and, on June 10, forwarded a suggested letter of reply for Galioni to send to Bonin, undoubtedly denying any hope of remaining for further treatment.

July 1971 to June 1974, California Medical Facility, Vacaville & Parole

Bonin was officially discharged from Atascadero to the Department of Corrections on July 7, 1971. The California Medical Facility at Vacaville, halfway between San Francisco and Sacramento, is a male-only, medium to maximum security, state prison medical facility with a capacity of over 2,000. Procedures at Vacaville's mental health facilities are similar to Atascadero, and Bonin knows how to play the game.

His initial Custodial Evaluation reveals him as a pleasant natured, willing worker who has "made a satisfactory adjustment to the institution."

An interesting aspect of the August 3, 1971 intake report is what Bonin told them of his personal history; by eliminating enough words and info to appease authorities, bits of truth come through. "I felt there was no who cared about my well-being; I didn't get any love from anyone after returning from Vietnam, my girlfriend married someone else and my parents gave me the impression they only wanted my help. I craved love and if I could not get it I would force it out of people. I continued doing it like a mad man until I got caught which was a relief to me."

Here are grains of truth slipping through what Vacaville Correctional Counselor Marion L. Strickler calls Bonin's "superficial insight."

Bonin's primary supervising Therapist during group sessions at Vacaville was C.H. Ostby. In a March 1972 report Ostby noted that "there is a strong possibility that his homosexuality is of a compulsive nature. He frankly admits to a homosexual orientation, but states that when released from custody he will limit activities to consenting adults in private." Ostby states he "hadn't reached the point of maximum insight or self-understanding of which it is felt he is capable."

Bonin's diagnosis was ***Explosive Personality and Homosexuality with Aggressive and Sadistic Features***, and he is deemed by the Psychiatric Council on April 5 as "unable to be returned to Atascadero at this time." By August he had been granted minimum security privileges.

Group session reports, from the Psychiatric Resident, note Bonin was forced by other patients to confront the discrepancy between his expressed beliefs and actions, thus enabling him to make Bonin look closely at his own progress.

Initially reluctant to deal with the observations, the Psychiatric Resident soon becomes more upbeat as Bonin realized "there had been significant change in his patterns. This encouraged him and positive change in attitude followed with what seems to a valuable improvement in hope and outlook for the future."

After almost two years at Vacaville, it appears Bonin made good progress, increasing steadily in the second year according to Ostby. A May 1973 report sees him coming to terms with the crimes and deviations which landed him in trouble. Dealing with hostility towards his father and older brother, Bonin accepted his homosexuality and curbed his sexual activity at CMF, leading Ostby to note he is "comfortable in his present sexual role, but strongly avers that he no longer has a need to act out sexually in an aggressive manner."

Bonin's diagnosis of ***Explosive Personality and Homosexuality with Aggressive and Sadistic Features*** was upgraded as "improved" with a proviso that "it is felt that there is still a strong underlying psychosexual pathology which requires working through. Emphasis should be towards inter-familial relationships."

The Psychiatric Council agrees Bonin "could not safely be returned to Atascadero and the Department of Mental Hygiene." CMF doctors noticed, during group therapy sessions when confronted by patients about violently raping young boys, he became defensively aggressive. Such confrontations prompted him to flash out in anger and retreat into a shell.

A September 20, 1973 report shows this aspect of Bonin's personality giving C.H. Ostby, his primary group therapist, reason to worry. Citing his preoccupation with sex and violence, he believes there is strong possibly for "withdrawal and deterioration into psychosis under pressure, it is felt that treatment in this case is most difficult."

The report indicated that Bonin appears to have avoided homosexual contact in the first two years at CMF, a conclusion which seems implausible. Ostby, dealing with Bonin for around two-years in group psychotherapy sessions, decided he still had "not reached the point of maximum insight of which he might be capable." Focusing on the words "might be capable," Ostby also notes that "progress has been slow but generally seems to be positively directly."

Bonin has been under psychiatric care for almost five years, two at Atascadero and three at Vacaville, and the team of therapists at CMF found themselves at a crossroads. Ostby, in a defeatist tone, wrote that he is "almost at a loss in how to proceed in helping this individual. He clings to his homosexual orientation but states positively that he will no longer engage in aggressive and sadistic activity if he is released."

His updated diagnosis was **Antisocial Personality** "severe, somewhat improved" and **Sexual Deviations** "sadism and aggressive sexuality."

Bonin is yet again deemed completely unsuitable for return to Atascadero and a report is filed with William C. Keating, Jr., M.D., a Deputy Director at the Department of Mental Hygiene in Sacramento, stating Bonin "has not yet recovered from his mental disorder" and is "still a danger to the health and safety of others."

Five months later CMF doctors reversed course and given up the ship. Seemingly overnight they washed their hands and totally dismissed all the previous concerns about Bonin's danger to others and rationalized his "superficiality of insight" with their superficial beliefs that "criminal offenses will not recur."

A March 24, 1974 report, by Staff Psychologist J.W. Fleming, Ph.D., states Bonin's "identity as a homosexual and his identification with the gay community should provide what outlets he needs." Bonin's diagnosis was reduced to a single condition of ***Homosexuality with Some Aggressive Features***, and on April 3 the Council decided he be sent to court with a recommendation for probation.

On April 22, 1974, T.L. Clanon, M.D., Superintendent of the California Medical Facility Vacaville, issued a final report to LA Superior Court with the March 15, Staff Clinical Analysis, Report and Recommendations Report attached.

The cover page issued the ***Psychiatric Diagnosis of Homosexuality, with Some Aggression, in Remission***, leading to a conclusion that Bonin "has been treated to such an extent that it is my opinion he will not benefit from further care and treatment in the hospital, and he is not a danger to the health and safety of others at this time. He should be returned to Court under the provisions of Section 6325 (a) of the Welfare and Institutions Code with probation. It is requested the Court notify the Sheriff to call for the above named without delay."

LA County Superior Court Judge Allen Miller was alerted by Sacramento on May 1, and Bonin was discharged from Vacaville on June 6, 1974. Bonin was transported back to court and released on June 11. He was on probation for five years with conditions that will be reviewed later.

Observations of a Clinical Psychologist who knew William Bonin, Vonda Pelto, Ph.D.

For five years Bonin was confined to mental hospital treatment wards at two facilities. Put through hundreds of hours of group therapy, he talked about his crimes, family, war experiences, sex, childhood abuse, disappointments, anger, abuse, women, marriage, guilt, aggression and more. He learned much about himself and the underlying reasons for his behavior, but the question remained if he could control the base sexual desires fueling aggression and rage, or if he would act out violently in a psychopathic manner?

Other questions of vital importance are institutional failures, within the criminal justice and mental health systems, which are supposedly designed to curb and rehabilitate people like Bonin. Once sent to Atascadero, for diagnosis and evaluation as an *MDSO*, three outcomes were possible: 1) Cure him and send back to court for prison; 2) Decide he was beyond help and send him back to court for prison; 3) Decide he was sufficiently cured for release back into society.

My experience as a Clinical Psychologist, with doctors and government institutional mental health treatment, can shed some light on what happened. While hindsight allows for the citing of systemic failure, it should be acknowledged it was nearly impossible to predict how far Bonin would break from himself and commit such horrendous crimes. In the same vein, the documents and careful deconstruction of events allows for identifying crucial events and turning points, along with reasons why certain people made certain decisions.

In light of Bonin's ability to manipulate people and the system, the first error was the court believing he desired help, felt guilty about his crimes and needed treatment to overcome his problems. The Probation Officer interviewed him, and his mother, then gave a recommendation to the judge, who then made the call derailing his journey to prison and sent him to Atascadero for re-evaluation.

Doctors then diagnosed him as an MDSO amenable to treatment. He was given two years of treatment, continued to engage in egregious homosexual behavior and was sent back for criminal proceedings. Leading to the second error; the judge ignored doctor's recommendations and shipped him back to Atascadero. Aside from the nine-page letter to the judge, it is unknown what Bonin said to sway the judge's decision.

Not wanting him back, Atascadero arranged for him to be transferred to Vacaville for treatment, a prison-like setting. For three more years Bonin received good and poor reports, making slow progress with doctors wary of his lack of remorse tied to a fragile and volatile personality. During that time, they viewed Bonin as dangerous and never agreed he was fit for return to Atascadero.

But rather than sending him to court for prison sentencing, Vacaville reversed course, sent him to court reporting he wasn't dangerous and recommended release on probation. What happened?

Thus, we come to the third error, one that is systemic and bureaucratic. I well know that psychiatrists, psychologists and the institutions they serve don't like to admit failure. Five years of taxpayer funded treatment and incarceration gone to waste. Even if they had given up on helping Bonin, the doctors were not going to give their hospitals and professional calling a black mark in the eyes of the court and government bureaucrats.

9

Freedom & Second Arrest
June 1974 to Dec. 1975

During five years of commitment, 1969 to 1974, William Bonin, his family and the world changed dramatically. President Nixon was re-elected in 1972 on a promise to end the Vietnam War and was about to resign after the Watergate scandal; the war is winding down in a humiliation for the West; riots and student protests of the late 1960s gave way to high-stakes Cold War tensions; the 1973 OPEC Oil Embargo altered energy markets while creating panic and launching years of crippling inflation. The long gas lines, from the embargo, ended months before the 26-year-old walked out of court a free man in June 1974.

Years earlier, Bonin's parents moved from Torrance to a house in nearby Downey, at 10282 Angell Street. His parents are in their mid-fifties; his father is not working anymore, classified as a Disabled Machinist, and his mother is a Licensed Vocational Nurse at the Long Beach Veterans Administration Hospital (VA).

Robert, Jr., now 29, moved to Tennessee and his 23-year-old younger brother, Paul, has been out of the Marines for a couple of years and lives in Southern California.

Bonin's August 6, 1974 court hearing is a resumption of previous criminal proceedings. A probation recommendation by Vacaville doctors, of the Department of Corrections, is not the final word. Even if the Probation Officer's report is positive, the judge can rule otherwise. As it turns out, Bonin's Probation Officer is the same guy, Kenneth E. Kirkpatrick, who recommended "diagnosis and evaluation" at Atascadero five years earlier.

In the Supplemental Report for the hearing, Kirkpatrick notes Bonin's activities as related to him by the "defendant." He moved into his parent's house in Downey, applied for work "through the Department of Vocational Rehabilitation and Veteran's Hospital" and inquired about attending "a truck driving school with aspirations of becoming a diesel truck driver." Following advice from his attorney, and invoking what he told doctors at Vacaville, in July Bonin got an apartment in Hollywood at 4956 Romaine St. with the intention of circulating within the adult gay community.

In the Remarks section of the report, Kirkpatrick writes that "as a result of the defendant's apparent adjustment into the community plus the referrals to community agencies which he seems to be taking advantage of, this officer feels that probation should be granted and can provide the community with the observation plus providing the defendant with counseling both, both of which seem to be needed at this time. It is felt that in compliance with Section 6300 of the Welfare and Institutions Code a substantial period of time on probation with additional treatment, if it appears to be needed, aid in an educational or work program and an understanding mature adult may help this defendant refrain from further law enforcement contacts."

The report was submitted by Kirkpatrick to Judge Barrett as signed by Andrew W. Wallace, Deputy Harbor Area Office. Barrett went along with the recommendation and Bonin was granted five-years of probation on Terms and Conditions listed below. For the second time in five years Kirkpatrick has intervened on Bonin's behalf and spared him prison, this time with a different judge.

Here are the conditions of his parole:

1. Not use or possess any narcotics, dangerous or restricted drugs or associated paraphernalia, except with valid prescription, and stay away from where users congregate.

2. Not associate with persons known by you to be narcotic or drug sellers or users.

3. Not associate with persons disapproved of by the Probation Officer.

4. Cooperate in a plan for psychiatric or psychological treatment to be terminated only with the consent of the therapist and the Probation Officer.

5. Seek and maintain training, schooling or employment as approved by the Probation Officer.

6. Maintain residence as approved by the Probation Officer.

7. Obey all laws, orders, rules and regulations of the Probation Department and of the court.

According to California sex registration laws, passed in 1947, Bonin had to register with local law enforcement wherever he lived. Enacted nationally in 1994, California was the first state to pass such laws.

While in Hollywood, Bonin frequented gay bars but finds the experience difficult. His social skills, never refined, are even less in tune after five years of commitment and intense psychotherapy. It remains unclear how long he stayed in Hollywood, but later statements show it was maybe a couple of months.

Back at his parent's house by August, he began working as a bartender at Pizza Burger on Brookhurst in Fountain Valley, 20-miles south of Downey. He was receiving $200 in monthly social security benefits and had become eligible for VA educational benefits under the GI Bill.

Bonin attends weekly group counseling sessions supervised by Carol Rogers of the Southeast Mental Health Dept., although he finds them less productive than those experienced at Vacaville. This is only natural as Bonin interacts with a new group and a new counselor in a far less-structured environment.

He commented later that Vacaville "was the only place he had ever been able to receive help from an experienced therapist with the result he managed to convince himself and the staff that he benefitted from treatment to the maximum degree and that it would be safe for him to return to the community."

Never a drinker or drug user, this aspect of parole was easy for Bonin to comply with. An accomplished bowler, who once harbored aspirations of turning professional, he joined a local league and frequents billiard parlors for socializing and relaxation. Trying to find a new way forward, he frequents gay bars in Long Beach but finds the experience difficult and unsatisfying, resulting in no meaningful relationships or associations.

When 1974 closes out, Bonin quits the bartending job and starts work at Dependable Drive-Away, in Montebello at 546 Greenwood Ave, six-miles northeast of Downey. Delivering trucks as needed on a per job basis, work at Dependable involves sitting around the yard for hours on end waiting for an assignment, and it ends in February when Bonin wrecks one of the trucks. Bonin claims the accident wasn't his fault.

Around March, driving a dark blue Opal, Bonin starts to get anxious and reverts to constantly trolling the streets for hitchhikers to find homosexual partners. Encounters are "of a transient and promiscuous nature" because it seemed Bonin never really "felt like maintaining a continuing relationship of a homosexual nature."

Bill Bonin, the emotionally conflicted, socially inept person who has never experienced a strong emotional bond with anyone, drives around finding hit and run affection to release sexual tension.

Deep down he wants and craves love, even that of a woman, but doesn't know how to express, receive or socially engage properly to form such bonding relationships. Akin to a damaged soul trapped in series of conflicted boxes within his brain, Bonin was molded by abuse, reformatted by war and is now driven by physical desire mixed with an inability to find a place in the world.

He signed up for the summer session at nearby Cerritos Junior College, taking a variety of classes with the intention of continuing into the fall. In another departure from the norm, and trying to make progress, Bonin meets 30-year-old Sharon Nitz at the Beverly Social Club in Los Angeles. She has a five-year old mentally challenged son. Bonin and Sharon, who lives 23-miles north in West LA, see each other often and even decide to get engaged. This constitutes Bonin's first heterosexual encounter since Vietnam, and it appears positive developments are in the works. The summer of 1975 concludes uneventfully, with Bonin passing his classes and reupping for the following semester.

Knowing Bonin began picking up hitchhikers for sexual contact in March, it is reasonable to assume the activity continued during the summer, after which the wheels came off the wagon.

His old friend from Atascadero, Phillip Gonzales, kept in touch with Bonin and around this time they met up in Hollywood. During the evening Bonin suggested "that they pick up some boys." Gonzales asked how he "would handle the situation if he got in the same trouble he had been in before?" Bonin told him, "There would be no more witnesses." He asked Bonin how he planned to eliminate them and was told matter-of-factly, "I would kill them if I had to." Startled at the notion, Gonzales pressed for confirmation of his plan and Bonin replied flatly, "Yes."

For three years he was under strict control at Vacaville; then after getting released he kept himself in check for 13 months before the teapot blew up again. September 8, 1975 at 7:00 p.m. is another watershed moment in the life of William Bonin; sadly, it is also one for 14-year-old

David McVicker, who was walking east on Westminster Avenue when a dark blue car pulled up and the driver asked if he wanted a ride.

He relates what happened, "Well, I was walking home that late afternoon when a guy in a blue Opal pulled alongside of me, he was friendly, you know, all smiling and cheerful, he seemed ok. Bonin asks me where Euclid Street was and offered me a ride home, I stupidly got in the car and we started talking about stuff and then he asked me if I had ever had sex with a man, and what did I think about gays and stuff like that? I said I'd never done something like that and didn't care as long as they stayed away from me.

"Then I got kinda nervous, you know, things felt bad, and I told him to just drop me off, my street was coming up anyway, I wanted to get outta there fast. But that son-of-a-bitch didn't pull over, instead he kept driving and when I realized Bonin wasn't stopping I freaked out, what was going on? I was scared to jump out of the car, but if I had to I was going too, fuck it, I sneaked the door open and got ready, but Bonin saw me and pulled out a fucking gun and pointed it at me, I couldn't believe it, 14-years old with a gun pointed at my head, fuck I couldn't believe what was happening, I didn't know what to do, so I just froze and didn't say anything.

"He kept on driving, I don't know how long, it wasn't real long, but Bonin kept that damn gun pointed at me with his left hand, driving with his right, you know like you see in the movies. Well, we ended up in some place with dirt hills all around, seemed no point in screaming cause there wasn't anyone around, it was almost dark, if I tried to run away, who knows what he would do, I didn't know where the hell I was or how to escape?

"Bonin stopped the car, acting paranoid to make sure no one was around, then he starts taking took off all his clothes and orders me to strip down, he grabbed my penis and made me touch his, it was so fucking gross. Bonin started giving me a blow job and ordered me suck him back, I said 'no way' and he got real mad, pissed off enough to put the gun right next to my neck, it was real close, like so close I couldn't see it and he told to me to do it.

"Oh my God, that moment is burned in my memory forever, like time just froze as I just stared at Bonin in blank horror wondering what the fuck to do? I try to imagine what my face looked like staring at him at that exact moment, a 14-year-old boy staring into unknown evil with total fear, it scares me years later thinking about it. The moment ended when he punched me in the chest, God he was big and strong and I was just a kid, I thought he would break my chest, but I did what he said. It was disgusting and I gagged and tried to open up the car door to spit on the ground, and this got Bonin real pissed off, fuck he was so mad he punched me right in the face and screamed to 'roll down the window instead.'

"After he calmed down, Bonin began to play with my penis and told me to do the same with his, it was awful, when Bonin got hard, he told me to turn around and bend over and he tried to rape me, oh God what a horrible feeling, fuck I hate him for doing that to me. Well, it hurt so much I began to cry really hard; I mean like begging for my life kind of crying, guess me crying must've made him stop, maybe it wasn't exciting enough, I don't know, fuck, I don't care? Anyway, the creep actually apologized for hurting me.

"He then put Vaseline on his fingers and on mine and, well, he touched me, and I touched him, but nothing happened, and Bonin gave up, I thought he might punch me again because he wasn't able to do anything, or maybe he would shoot me and dump out of the car and leave me to die in the dirt? All these horrible things racing through my mind, I was so fucking scared, I wanted to get home so badly, really, I never wanted anything so bad in my whole life.

"After giving up on everything, Bonin just masturbated himself into a rag and told me to get dressed. He asked me where I lived and dropped me nearby, but as I walked home, he drove up and down the street looking for where I lived. I couldn't get inside our house fast enough. It took me hours to calm down, telling my mother what happened, crying and still scared to death. I knew he saw our house; was he going to come back and get me again? I wish the memory could just be wiped from my brain, but I can't forget it, I probably never will."

David McVicker and his mother went to the Fountain Valley Police Department at 1:04 a.m. to report the incident, informing officers he was kidnapped and forced to engage in acts of sodomy and sexual perversion. Police had a description of Bonin and the car, but no license number or even a partial. Unfortunately, this incident had a devastating impact on David's life.

Bonin continued the rampage when, in the City Stanton adjacent to

Long Beach, he made a run at another young boy at 3:00 p.m. on September 10. Bonin pulled up beside a 15-year-old boy on Beach Blvd. and solicited sex from the car window, asking if he "knew what it meant to be gay?" and if would "sell his body for $35.00?" Picking the wrong boy, he yelled at Bonin to "get out of here" and kept walking, upon which time Bonin drove up the curb and nearly ran him over. The observant boy provided police with a "possible license plate number" and thus Bonin was on their radar screen.

Bonin did not know, but probably assumed, that the incidents were reported to police. Either way, he has reverted to the aggressive sexual predator hunting for young boys. Arrest will mean new criminal charges on top of serious parole violations. It is unknown if, after the two attacks, Bonin began attending classes or continued contact with his girlfriend. But five years of therapy failed to instill any sense of control in Bonin over his base instincts, while the failing socialization skills continued to frustrate and isolate him.

On October 10, 1975 Bonin was pulled over by a Stanton police cruiser and arrested for probation violations based on the attacks. Now he knows for sure at least one of incidents was reported to police and prison is a real possibility. During the arrest he utters a prophetic phrase to one of the arresting officers, further signaling Bonin's gradual, decades in the making psychological collapse. Officer Patricia Johnson later testified that, after getting him into the police car, Bonin chillingly told her, "The next time there won't be any more witnesses!"

David McVicker and the other victim positively identified Bonin and he was booked by Stanton PD for *Assault and Battery* and *Soliciting Sex in Public*. Four-days later he was sent to Fountain Valley PD for booking on *Kidnapping*, *Sodomy and Sex Perversion by Force* charges in the brutal September 9 David McVicker attack. All charges were incorporated together for proceedings in Orange County Superior Court. LA Superior Court was alerted about Bonin's arrest and parole violations, thus requiring a hearing with Judge Barrett, who granted him parole a year earlier.

Knowing Bonin must appear in Los Angeles for parole violations, on November 5 Orange County Superior Court accepted a guilty plea for one count, 288 (a) *Perversion by Force*, serving to lock in the LA County parole violations.

Sentencing and the balance of Orange County charges are continued to December 23, labeled ***Mentally Disordered Sex Offender Proceedings*** that will take place after Bonin sees Judge Barrett in LA on December 18. Both decisions can later be consolidated for final sentencing. Treating Bonin as an **MDSO**, given that label by Atascadero, offers him certain advantages in the ultimate disposition.

Prior to the Los Angeles hearing, Judge Barrett receives a damning report from Acting Probation Officer Clarence E. Cabell, one approved by Roger Carlson, Deputy Bellflower Area Office.

Previous August 6, 1974 parole proceedings are deemed "suspended" and the report lists Bonin's previous violations, parole obligations, notes he is in custody at Orange County Jail, current violations, whether adjudicated or not, and other relevant facts.

Cabell wrote that the "defendant appears to be in violation of probation as evidenced by his plea of guilty to violation of Section 288 (a) Penal Code. It is apparent that defendant is not willing or capable of functioning in an open setting and it is also apparent that he is a real and present menace to the community. Consequently, a commitment to state prison would seem to be the only logical alternative. Therefore, the following recommendation is submitted: It is recommended that defendant be found in violation of probation; that probation be revoked and sentence imposed."

A key moment in Bonin's story is at hand. Unforeseen circumstances regarding court decisions, terms of release 13-months earlier, designation as an MDSO from Atascadero and poor oversight will all impact on terrible events to come. Making harsh judgements looking back in time is easy, thus rendering statements about this or that broken system ineffective and worthless.

Government agencies are staffed by human beings doing their best within bureaucratic, political and highly inefficient public institutions. Mistakes and oversights take place, and judgements about people like William Bonin, with keen manipulative abilities, are often flawed with terrible consequences.

At the LA hearing Bonin's probation is revoked and he is scheduled for the most important appearance in early February. Bonin was sent back to OC for the December 23 sentencing hearing.

Believing LA County District Attorney John Van De Kamp will pursue, and obtain, a stiff sentence on multiple charges from Bonin's 1969 arrest, Judge Williams passes a watered-down sentence on the one charge he pled guilty to, as a result the 288 (a) went from *Sex Perversion by Force* to *Oral Copulation*.

Despite Bonin's desire for assignment as an *MDSO* to Patton State Mental Hospital, located in San Bernardino County, Williams gives him 15-years with a 6-month minimum at the California Men's Colony (CMC), a state prison. Events will reveal this as yet another lucky break for Bonin.

OC is saved from pursuing further charges, which involve mental health implications, and the onus to put Bonin away for a long time falls on those who unsuccessfully dealt with him previously, LA Superior Court. Orange County's official proceedings in this case are closed.

Bonin arrives at CMC on December 31, 1975 and it must be noted that Bonin's designation as a *Mentally Disordered Sexual Offender* (MDSO) is the reason he lands at CMC East. Without the *MDSO* tag he would have been dealt with in a different manner, meaning hard time inside a dangerous state prison. Bonin lands in a relatively safe prison, considered "easy time" when compared to other violent, high-security facilities. Child molesters are considered the lowest of the low in most jails and prisons.

Split into two sections, East and West, CMC is a men's only prison with a capacity of about 4,000 inmates on 356 acres run by a staff of 1,800. CMC East is medium security with individual cells, armed perimeter fencing and licensed hospital and mental health delivery systems. CMC West is minimum security. Bonin is in a neighborhood he lived in for two years; CMC is 200-miles north of LA but only 20-miles south of Atascadero. Just as Bonin's reappearances in LA court brings him back into contact with Kirkpatrick and Barrett, life at CMC ushers in familiar faces in the form of doctors from Atascadero.

Bonin appears back at Los Angeles Superior Court in early February and DA Van De Kamp convinces Judge Barrett to convict on four counts, from the 1969 arrest due to parole violations, and he receives 25-years with a 1-year minimum. Documents are a bit confusing, but it appears that, on April 21, 1976, the California Attorney General adjusts the sentence on the OC 288 (a) charge to 15-years maximum. The full sentence will be adjusted again in 1977 while Bonin is at CMC. Documents indicate a final sentence is 25-years with a one-year minimum, but on another part of the LA case summary a term of three-years minimum is indicated.

The final sentence is vague and a legacy from California's indeterminate sentencing policy, which is about to change with the passing of a new 1976 California Determinate Sentencing Statute. Amendments in 1977 meant the statute was in full effect and thus will alter Bonin's final sentence.

Without the new law, Bonin's stay at California Men's Colony might have been much longer.

10

CMC Prison & Unexpected Parole
January 1976 to October 1978

On Bill Bonin's 29th birthday, January 8, 1976, he had been at the California Men's Colony for a week as he filled out a detailed Personal Information questionnaire during the intake process.

Broken down into four parts, it starts with basic info—a drawing exercise, sentence completion and essay questions. Checking the box for regular psychological help during his stay in prison, the sentence completion portion of the questionnaire sheds light on Bonin's current state of mind.

Here are a few examples with pre-written portions differentiated from Bonin's completion words.

I thought of myself as *really mixed up and very confused.*
I gave in because *I was weak mentally.*
When nobody cares, I *withdraw and rebel out.*
Sometimes sex *thoughts get in the way of things I am doing.*
When upset, I *get out and drive for hours.*
I wanted my mother to *show me more love and understanding.*
When I lost my temper, I *hold it in and act out my hostility.*
If I fail *it is my own fault.*

One essay question is rather interesting: *How, or in what ways do you wish to change while in prison?*

His written answer was, "I wish to change my previous orientation and become a more stable person. I will do it as I have one thing I didn't have before, the desire to change and the determination to do it."

Another section of the intake form, titled *Your Story of the Offense*, asked Bonin to write a "a brief account of the offense for which you are here. Tell how you feel about the whole situation now. Tell how you got involved in the offense and why you think you did it."

Here is Bonin's answer: "Most of the facts are true in my case. I do have a problem and intend to get straightened out this time. I'm not going to go back into society this time until I know I am a fully changed person. I don't mean until you think I am changed. I mean until I know I am changed. In the Christian Fellowship Vacaville and when I was released left religion at Vacaville. That was my first mistake. I intend to go back to my Christian religion because it is where I should be.

"It is the power I need to make the change in my life. Let's face it. The change I am talking about cannot be done alone. It is a 24-hour struggle and I intend on coming out the person I desire to be. It can only be done with the power of God with me. If you think I'm running a game then I'm sure my attitude and conduct will show you different.

"There's no turning back as once I do it is very hard to gain back what you lost. It's like a bank account. The more time you go straight the more you have. Once you start withdrawing it doesn't take long to lose everything. If drug addicts and alcoholics can do it, I can also."

Senior Psychologist E. Rivlin is the first to evaluate Bonin and readily grasps the vital issues. From the first report, dictated on January 12, Rivlin believes he will benefit from therapy and be deemed suitable for clinical treatment after release on parole, which will not happen for at least three years according to his sentence.

Here are the two key paragraphs from the two-page report:

"Personality Evaluation:

"The outstanding finding in the test material and on interview is this inmate's passive-dependent orientation. He is a person who seems to be searching for much dependency gratification. Apparently, such desires were frustrated during his early childhood formative years. He seems to be searching for an all giving, warm mother figure who will give him affectional care, emotional support, and guidance.

"He relates to such an individual submissively in the manner of a small boy. Feeling dependent and weak, this individual equates himself with adolescent boys. He engages in sexual relations with them, hoping to receive affection, love and warmth. Evidently, because he forces such offenses, he does not receive what he so avidly desires, namely affection and love, and he goes from one person to another, engages in sexual relations, only to feel frustrated and guilty.

"Recommendation:

"This individual is young enough, flexible enough, and anxious enough so that he can derive benefit from intensive psychotherapy. Psychiatric evaluation is indicated in this case at the outset of therapy, periodically thereafter, and upon parole consideration. If given parole consideration, he would likely candidate for the parole outpatient clinic."

He was diagnosed as 307.89 **Personality Disorder, Passive**, 302.2, **Sexual Deviation, Male Pedophilia**.

Bonin adjusts easily and was courteous with staff while the rhythm of prison life took hold, but the instruction is for "close supervision." Doctors, therapists and social workers know all about Bonin's psychiatric and social history—family and institutional abuse, acting out with his younger brother and other boys as a teenager, aggressive homosexual attacks in Vietnam, incidents with five boys in 1968-69 leading to the first arrest and the 1974 attacks leading to the second.

What doctors don't know is that Bonin may have suffered a severe frontal lobe head injury as child, either at the Boy's Home, the Orphanage or from his father's brutal beatings. This type of injury can affect moods, behavior and impulse control.

Bonin, unaware it may have been an issue, never mentions the incidents and medical technology wasn't capable of detecting those types of brain injuries. All the same, his "sincerity and ability to benefit from treatment" is viewed as a false front with realists tagging him as "recidivistic individual" incapable of avoiding "deviant behavior."

In the five years since Bonin was at Atascadero his old doctor, Alfred Owre, Jr., was promoted to Chief Psychiatrist at the CMC. Yet another person from Bonin's life within courts, mental hospitals and prisons reenters the picture. Owre and Bonin got reacquainted in July for his first Psychiatric Evaluation for Adult Authority, internally classified by CMC as the August Board report.

Irony abounds in this twist: The man who gave up on Bonin at Atascadero, sent him back to court and hopefully prison, forced to deal with him again when Judge Miller sent him back; the man who then engineered Bonin's transfer to Vacaville prison-mental hospital finds himself engaged in the same discussions five years later after Bonin was re-arrested. But now Owre possesses less power over Bonin's disposition while other events will also impact his term of incarceration.

A professional who takes his job seriously, Owre states he will do his best to assist Bonin slay the demons which plague his mind. He reports most of their conversation as "amiable" and focused on "tactics which he might use to improve his adjustment when and if he is released to society." One hard hitting observation is that Owre sees "truly pathological and sociopathic areas" when Bonin downplays the aggressive acts and blames the victims, stating he "would not pay the victim who was a hustler."

Chillingly, Owre compares his justifications to those of the San Simeon Slayer, whom he interviewed for San Luis Obispo Superior Court five years earlier. Owre concludes this about Bonin, "Here again this is a thoroughly pathological and thoroughly sociopathic area of thinking."

Owre believes all previous psychotherapy has been ineffective and only made him a "better adjusted homosexual pedophiliac." Right out of the gate, Bonin was informed by Owre that he has run out of ideas but truly wants to help solve his problems. Bonin is given credit for desiring help and signing up to receive individual therapy. But Owre must think Bonin was capable of murder; basically, he had more "Bonin experience" than anyone else in this realm.

Numerous visits from his parents and fiancé Sharon Nitz must have lifted Bonin's flagging spirits because he, in the first four months at CMC, mounts a vigorous letter writing campaign. Besides letters to family, friends, Sharon and her parents, the recipients include California Governor Jerry Brown, the Prison Mission Association, Universal Life Church, various State Senators, Public Defenders, The Way Ministries in Illinois, the Nicky Cruz Outreach in North Carolina, Scripture Investigation Course, Reverend Chuck Smith and famed preacher Billy Graham. Raised a Catholic, Bonin must have been looking for guidance in his time of need.

In May of 1977 the CMC prison bureaucrats contacted the County Clerk of Orange County for information regarding the specific subsection of 288 (a) Bonin was convicted of "in order to accurately compute his term under the new Determinate Sentence Law." The 1976 law, mentioned earlier, is about alter future events, and not for the better.

A detailed 1978 analysis by Berkley Law's Phillip E. Johnson and Sheldon Messenger, **California's Determinate Sentencing Statute: History and Issues**, sheds light on the reasons for Bonin's sentence review.

"Before 1976, California was famous or notorious as the state whose laws seemed most thoroughly committed to the idea that sentences should be indeterminate.

"The laws implied or said that the length of imprisonment should depend more on the individual characteristics of the criminal than on the nature of the crime; maximum discretion over length of sentences should be given to an administrative agency shielded from public accountability; the purpose of imprisonment is to rehabilitate the offender and to protect society from his further misdeeds; and the released prisoner should be subjected to a lengthy period of parole supervision to protect the public and to insure his rehabilitation.

"The Uniform Determinate Sentencing Act of 1976, commonly known in the state as S.B. (Senate Bill) 42, seems to be based on the opposite assumptions in every respect. As originally passed, it provided a relatively narrow range of fixed penalties for each crime; replaced Adult Authority discretion over release with a complex system of 'good time' credits; greatly lessened the period of parole and the importance of parole supervision; and, perhaps most significantly, stated flat out that the purpose of imprisonment is punishment.

"The California sentencing reform is an event of national significance. If other jurisdictions did not go as far as California in endorsing indeterminacy, they nonetheless went very far indeed.

"Unchecked discretion is a feature of criminal sentencing law everywhere, whether the discretion is lodged primarily with the courts or the parole boards. Reforms based on the considerations which inspired the California innovations are in the air in many states."

Events move towards changing everything that would keep Bonin behind bars for a long time. In August 1977 Bonin retains a new attorney, Mark Woolpert from San Luis Obispo, and a sentence review hearing is set for January 12, 1978. While his parents continue to visit, the fiancé is no longer in contact and stopped visiting. Over the previous year, Bonin refused to participate in group therapy, and he is still on the waiting list for individual sessions.

Prison doctors are powerless to force him into group therapy, and Bonin does finally start private psychiatric treatment in October 1977. Enrolled in Vocational Machine Shop, Bonin gets an "A" grade in Algebra I and utilizes the math in machine shop. His intelligence is considered "Superior" and his monthly disability checks have piled up to $5,000 in a Bank of America savings account in San Luis Obispo.

In the meantime, Bonin's annual 1977 August Board report is coming up, which have been renamed the Psychiatric Evaluation for Community Release Board due to the new Determinate Sentence Law. On July 11 the Psychiatric Council, six psychiatrists including Dr. Owre and another old friend from Atascadero, Dr. Hollingsworth, interview Bonin for over an hour. Preceded by a case review and followed by a discussion, it is noted that Dr. Owre prepared the 1976 August Board report.

Bonin is described as "inarticulate in recognizing, labeling or recognizing his emotions" and he uses only one word in relation to his own personality, "aggressive." Thriving in the controlled environment and kept busy, Bonin believes he overcame a "negative self-image through vocational training, school, friends, self-control and a positive outlook."

Bonin was absolutely considered as "demonstrating little psychological change during the present period of incarceration," but he nonetheless had gained an "intellectual understanding of some of the dynamic features."

Doctors view him as still "likely to seek sexual acts with minor boys under stressful circumstances in the community. If released, he should be in a closely supervised program and should be encouraged to attempt therapy or at least to maintain a counseling relationship in which he can explore appropriate behavior alternatives for stressful circumstances as they arise."

Doctors have no way of knowing that, within about six-months, the long "indeterminate" length of stay for Bill Bonin will become much shorter and more determinate. Their ability, and that of prison authorities, to "decide" to keep Bonin behind bars by classifying him "a high risk to strike again" have ended. While each of the individual sentences is supposedly increased, the total "determinate" sentence is far less than the "indeterminate" and possible 25-year sentence.

On January 12, 1978 a three-member panel of the California Community Release Board meets and sets about assigning a set amount of time for each convicted offense and the total adds up to nine years and eight months. The final Order in the Application of Law section reads, "Special Condition of parole to be imposed in this case is Parole Outpatient Clinic."

Seeing an opportunity to reduce the final sentence total, Bonin obtains hearing transcripts, requests documents from LA and OC Superior Courts and submits a written appeal that is highly lucid and well-organized.

Citing various mathematical errors and time credits due, the total sentence is knocked down to eight years and four months. On February 21, 1978 another appeal is denied, and further appeals disallowed.

Bonin's father suffered a minor stroke, in December 1977, which landed him in the Long Beach VA Hospital for two-months, where his mother worked as a vocational nurse and could assist in his care.

Bonin's path forward was really clear at this point—the most he would serve had been substantially reduced and his record at CMC was flawless. He continues to work at the Vocational Machine Shop while planning how to get released quickly. A possible pretext arises when, in March 1978, his father suffers a second, and major, stroke which lands him back in the VA hospital, at least for a year and probably for good.

By May, he has been in individual therapy for about seven months and, according to reports, is making good progress "acquiring a positive self-image and insights into his previous 'hang-ups.' Along with this he acquired enough self-knowledge about himself to realize that he really wanted to become a practicing adult homosexual rather than attempt to fulfill the heterosexual identity that his mother had always given him."

Apparently, after discussions with his parents, they came to accept that their son needed his own identity. This is Bill Bonin at his manipulative best, playing a game honed over eight years of incarceration, many of them being psychoanalyzed and picked apart by teams of psychologists, psychiatrists and social workers.

On May 10, calculating that recent events and good behavior make him eligible for early release, he writes a letter pleading his case to a variety of prison officials. In the letter Bonin cites four primary reasons for early release: 1) Helping his mother because his father is hospitalized, 2) Having completed 2,400 hours of vocational training with good work reviews, 3) Solid progress in individual therapy, 4) Job prospects and financial viability.

He meets with Dr. Owre on July 27, 1978 for what turns out to be the final August Board report. It is the shortest one since Bonin arrived at CMC and Owre breezes through his progress and recommends parole. Diagnoses of **Anti-Social Personality** and **Sexual Deviation, Male Pedophilia** are upgraded as improved with the Psychiatric Conclusion that "his prognosis for non-recidivism is noticeably improved and better than average, in the opinion of the examiner."

The Community Release Board agrees with the recommendation, noting

Bonin will return to reside with his mother in Downey, seek employment as a machinist, receives $240 a monthly in social security disability benefits and must participate in Patient Outpatient Clinic therapy as part of his parole obligations.

The decision has been made, the die is cast, and Bonin is about to be set free.

An August 22 request was issued for a medical examination so he can "maintain his Class I California Driver's License in good standing" and states "that Bonin will be released in December 1978." Parole will be for one year and he must participate in outpatient "psychiatric treatment" and will be reporting to Parole Officer Walter R. Daly of the Southeast Division, near his mother's home in Downey. Bonin has secured employment at Freight Movers, also in Downey, and he uses this to appeal for even earlier release, it works.

For the last time, William George Bonin was released from state prison on October 11, 1978.

11

Probation, New Friends & The Death Van
October 11, 1978 to July 28, 1979

Bonin left the California Men's Colony, in early October 1978, a changed person yet again. In contrast to previous incarcerations, he was not required to engage in psychotherapy, although he did to a certain degree.

This time he took classes and was intensely involved in productive vocational work in the machine shop, along with deftly and systematically working the criminal justice system to gain release.

Eight of the last nine years were spent in some form of incarceration, with a variety of assumptions regarding his personality postulated and debated by psychologists, psychiatrists, social workers, probation officials and judges. While hints of the dangerous sociopathic killer in waiting peeked through in a few reports, predicting the storm to come was practically impossible.

Bonin returned to his parent's home in Downey, on Angell Street, and started work at Freight Movers, not far away, driving a delivery truck while attending his parole required weekly therapy sessions. Within a month he changed jobs and began working at Products Development Company in LA, a company, according to reports, unaware of his parole status.

On November 1, 1978 he moved into apartment #307 at the Kingswood Village, located less than a mile from his mother at 10000 Imperial Highway.

Comprised of a dozen or more three-story buildings, separated by gardens and pathway, it is a large complex separated from the busy thoroughfare by a looped street fronting the property.

Through his new neighbor, Scott Fraser, Bonin would find party friends, sexual partners and murder accomplices.

Around mid-November Bonin and his friend, Neil Mendez, contacted Fraser through the building intercom system to ask about an incident at the building. Scott's place, apartment #F220, was party central for a wide variety of young people, many homosexual men, who gravitated to the seemingly endless festivities.

Fresh out of prison, with homosexual desires, Bonin gravitated to Scott's and fit in with the ever-changing scenery. Fraser's drug dealing business also increased the numbers and types of people hanging around and coming thru.

Bonin spent three to four nights a week at Fraser's and the two became, according to Fraser, "social friends." They would go out to eat occasionally, but the majority of their contact was at Scott's apartment. Fraser never tired of entertaining and setting his friends up for sexual encounters. Bonin liked bowling and, in early 1979, he joined the same league team as Neil Mendez at Keystone Lanes. Through others, Bonin found out Mendez was gay, and they became friends after Bonin inquired about his preferences.

Fraser, who met Vernon Butts after watching his magic act at Warren High School, in Downey, introduced him to Bonin and they became fast friends. Born and raised in nearby Norwalk, Butts was extremely close to his father, who passed away at a young age and left the devastated nine-year-old rudderless. His father taught him magic card tricks and he continued to be intrigued with magic and fantasy stories.

Vernon Butts left his mother's house a year earlier, then lived in Anaheim before moving to the Quo Vadis apartments back in Norwalk. Located at 11026 E. Imperial Highway, near Studebaker Road, he was blocks away from Bonin and Fraser. Downey and Norwalk are small unincorporated cities, within LA County, adjacent to each other and close to north Orange County. In late 1979, after being evicted from his apartment and leaving it a wreck, Butts moved into a converted garage at back of a properly at 7310 Dinwiddie Avenue, in Downey.

Vernon Butts was tall, about 6 ft. 3 in., and skinny with long stringy hair framing a skeletal visage. He worked at the Knott's Berry Farm amusement park, in their magic store, and performed an amateur magic act for small parties. He believed in witchcraft and black magic and belonged to a Satanic Cult with his fiancée, Cati Poore Razook. Actively bisexual while abusing drugs and alcohol in equal measure, he met Cati at one of the Mystery Parties he organized and ran.

They actively participated in Pagan religious rituals and sometimes visited graveyards to "communicate with the dead." Her real name was Pam, but she went by Cati and boasted a 180 IQ. She was active in witchcraft and accepted into the inner circle of witches in her own coven.

According to James Meurer's girlfriend, Tracy, they enjoyed an active sex life as Razook spent days on end at his place.

Part of Butts occult/witchcraft pursuits, with mentors James Meurer and Razook, was an intense interest and participation in the game Dungeons & Dragons. Classified as a Fantasy Role Playing game with "overt violence and death themes" involving a Magical World View.

The game involved a series of supposedly "authentic magical rituals" and this imagined MWV was "far outside the cultural norms of most societies" and applies "the understanding of how to manipulate the universe to get what you want."

Black Magic rituals in the game are designed to call up demons and the game was directly responsible for a number of suicides, mainly young men, and murders during the 1970s and '80s. Suicide notes from several teenagers, who killed themselves by gunshot, hanging or carbon monoxide poisoning, revealed the serious effects D & D had on their minds. A 14-year-old whose interest in hard core Satanism began with D & D killed his parents and a convenience store clerk and became the youngest inmate on Death Row in Oklahoma. Another 14-year-old, from Texas, took his D & D training and created a ritual murder circle in the living room, stabbed his mother to death, slit his wrists with a Boy Scout knife and died in the snow in the neighbor's yard. Another boy's suicide note indicated he killed himself believing he would come back in the game.

Vernon Butts was "obsessed with death" and into various cults which met for rituals in sewers and cemeteries. He threatened a friend, by putting an ax blade to his throat, and bragged to inmates, after his arrest for murder, to have carved Satanic symbols into murder victims with Bonin and others. Butts was inflating his dangerous nature, to scare others, for no one he killed with Bonin had symbols carved on their bodies and no "Satanic related" killings took place in the area. Razook later told police that Butts was learning paganism and "would not kill anything."

Another of his favorite activities was organizing Mystery Parties. James Meurer related that Butts "would set a game similar to a game of Clue except he would hide the clues for the game throughout the city, giving various clues to their whereabouts." Fraser, Mendez and Bonin all participated in these Mystery Parties, usually involving about 16-people in the pursuit of finding common objects which might be used to kill someone, like an icepick or a hairpin. An icepick was used in the killing of

Darin Kendrick, committed by Butts and Bonin.

They were often seen together at Fraser's apartment and became friends and lovers, with Butts describing Bonin as a "dominant, drill sergeant type, a very passionate lover." Butts was a troubled person subject to the whims of more dominant individuals, possessed by his own set of demons which brought him to a place he never expected.

His residential garage on Dinwiddie Street in Downey, where he moved to sometime in late 1979, was decorated with a coffin standing in the corner and another one for sleeping, with flashing black lights, occult posters, figurines and multiple spider webs creating a bizarre atmosphere. Loud music, drinking, drugs, Star Wars costumes, promiscuous sex, and movies with violence and death were ever present.

In April 1979 another Frazier came on the scene. Blane Frazier become friends with Scott Fraser, and they dealt drugs out of Scott's apartment on Imperial Highway. Blane had already served time in jail, and his business with Scott suffered a setback when they were arrested on narcotics charges. Out on bail, Blane was hanging out with Bonin and learned how much he liked young boys and about him driving around Hollywood looking sexual prospects.

While driving around Bonin saw a young boy and asked if Frazier was interested in picking him up, Frazier said, "As long as you drop me off before doing anything." While Bonin's attempt at picking up the boy was unsuccessful, the incident offers a first-hand account of Bonin's unceasing search for young boys and a desire, even need, to recruit accomplices. As noted earlier, he hated doing things alone.

But Bonin was on probation, and the rules of parole, let alone the actual laws, precluded having sex with underage boys. On that note, Bonin's progress with weekly outpatient therapy was going smoothly. His April 1979 parole report showed that the "subject's adjustment continues satisfactory." Bonin was required to check in by phone regularly with his parole agent, who was also supposed to visit his home monthly.

Around this time, Bonin's still loving mother obtained a second trust deed on the house and loaned $30,000 to Bill and Paul, the younger brother, to possibly purchase the Alpine Inn Restaurant & Bar in Silverado. Located about 40-miles southeast of Downey, in Eastern Orange County, Silverado was a small town up in the hills of Silverado Canyon.

They moved to 28901 Cactus Way and Paul applied for a license to run the establishment. As Bill's parole case was transferred to an OC office, Paul was granted a conditional, or temporary, license to operate an establishment already under scrutiny by the Department of Alcoholic Beverage Control's District Administrator (ABC), Norman Pearson.

Noise violation penalties, music so loud neighbors couldn't hear their TVs, had been issued previously and local residents filed immediately to oppose the license transfer. Sometime in June, Vernon Butts and Cati Razook visited Bill for a couple of days to hang out and party.

A police officer assigned to Silverado, named Wit, met Bonin in June 1979 at the Shady Brook Market. Aware the Bonin brothers were attempting to buy the Alpine Inn, he described it as already being "a chronic trouble spot where he made numerous investigations and arrests." When Wit first met him at the market, Bonin admitted he was a registered sex offender and was "nervous and perspiring heavily."

While Bonin lived in Silverado, Wit talked to him about twenty times; each time noting his agitated and sweaty manner and driving either a light green mustang, with a whip antenna, or a white utility van with Beach Cities Plumbing on the side. After the Alpine Inn deal collapsed, Paul bought a Costa Mesa plumbing business. Wit later told OC Sheriff's investigators that "he heard rumors in Silverado pertaining to Bonin being involved with a 16-year-old boy, stating Bonin accosted the boy at the Alpine Inn and locked him in a room. However, the boy escaped through a window and got away."

In July ABC investigators monitored the Inn each weekend for noise violations. A July 18 report, citing the ongoing violations and Bill's arrest record, concluded that the "continued operation of the temporary license issued would be contrary to the public welfare." They remained in Silverado and Bill worked for Paul's plumbing business.

Near the end of July, Bill purchased a vehicle destined to become famous in serial killer history, the dreaded "Death Van," a term coined by Bonin. Downey Ford was one of the busiest car dealers in the area.

On July 19, 1979 he walked in and purchased a 1972 Ford E-100 Shorty Van from Albert Chatel. Green with new green carpeting, installed by Sunset Van Conversions six-months earlier, it had faux wood paneling and curtains which prevented viewing past the front seats through the windshield. Bonin's new van had a roof vent, standard double-doors with a sliding window, on the right side, and double-doors in the rear.

Freeway Killings Begin & Dispelling Myths by Vonda Pelto, Ph. D.
Purchase of the van helped unleash Bonin the world-famous serial killer we know today. Some detectives believed Bonin killed earlier and claimed over forty victims, others that he never killed before August 1979. Just like the detectives directly involved, and figuring on time, opportunity and mindset, I believe he didn't start till after purchasing the van, which became a mobile death wagon and set the stage for all that followed.

Bonin had become more aggressive and, after spending many hours with him and having read his diaries, I believe his relationship with Vernon Butts was the spark which lit the fire. Their strange chemistry served to create a high-octane cocktail, one which let loose the murderous beast lying beneath Bonin's already shaky surface.

Previously, he had assaulted young boys because his sexual thoughts and tensions caused him to act out in frustration and anger. He may have been picking up young males for casual sex, but there no violent sexual attacks reported in the months between his release from prison, October 11, 1978, and the first killing, August 4, 1979, that could be tied to Bonin.

Butts was a timid individual absent an intimidating physical presence. He was a passive-dependent "follower" easily manipulated by dominant people like Bonin. His fascination with the occult, death and violence never came to actual violence. The cults he was part of were never implicated in anything close to murder. They surely talked about death, and that included methods of killing since Butts' Mystery Parties were all about solving murders.

Did Bonin acquire the van because they talked about and wanted to kill people, or was it for homosexual activity? I am quite sure it was for the latter and became the former. Then living up in the sparsely populated Silverado Canyon, the van gave him a mobile platform for sexual activity. After having the van ready for action, it was place, opportunity and combined mindsets which coalesced and went from talking and speculating to acting and doing.

The storm was about to begin.

PART TWO
AUGUST 4, 1979 TO JUNE 11, 1980

12

Origins of the Freeway Killings
1973 & May 1979

The "Freeway Killer" cases, as they came to be known in March 1980, began in February 1973 when a 17-year-old boy was found strangled on the shoulder of the Terminal Island Freeway in San Pedro, 23-miles south of Downtown LA.

Over time, as more victims were found over the years, they were classified as a "homosexually oriented" series of murders involving young males, mostly over 18, being tortured, raped and dumped along freeways or in public places around Southern California.

Two accomplished homicide detectives, Sgt. John "Jigsaw John" St. John of the respected and powerful Robbery-Homicide Division at LAPD and Sgt. David Kushner, LA County Sheriff's Department, were involved from the beginning. By the time Bonin started operating, six-years later in August 1979, about 20 young men and boys were attributed to the same killer or killers. Whether it was one-person, multiple persons working together and separately, or multiple copycats, was a mystery.

The first murder thought to be committed by William Bonin was 13-year-old Thomas Lundgren, a slight boy with light brown hair and a broken arm in a plaster cast. He lived in Reseda, a middle-class suburb northwest of LA in the San Fernando Valley, with his parents, brother and sister. A neighbor reported that he had last seen Lundgren riding his skateboard in front of his home on May 28, 1979.

Around mid-day, Mr. Childs was sightseeing on Mulholland Drive, north of Malibu, when he noticed something wrong, "I pulled off when the road curved and that's when I saw the body. It was about thirty feet down the side of the hill caught in some bushes. I barely noticed the boy's torn t-shirt. All I could see was the blood. It was bright red. It was fresh! Then, oh my God, I saw the boy's crotch. I thought I would be sick, couldn't believe what I was seeing. It felt unreal like something in a movie. I ran to my car and called the cops."

LA County Sheriff's homicide detectives, Sgt. David Kushner and his partner Deputy Jack Fueglein, were dispatched. Kushner later described the scene in court, "When I first arrived, the first thing I observed was that the body had been emasculated. The penis and scrotum appeared to have been removed from the body and there was a large pool of blood under the victim's head. I walked on up to the boy and saw a complete slashing through the throat. There was a ligature mark, too. I looked around and saw the penis, scrotum and testicles about two feet away lying in the dirt and bagged them. I saw a lot of blood emanating from the skull."

Lundgren's tennis shoes were found up in a tree approximately 10-feet from the body along with a pair of short cut-off pants and undershorts.

Dr. Joseph L. Cogan, an autopsy surgeon, stated, "Lundgren died of severe slash wounds to the throat that severed his carotid arteries and larynx which extended nearly to the back of the neck." Cogan also noted that "bruises on the organs could have been bite marks. The boy's chest and skull had been fractured by a blow from an object like a tire jack handle."

The pain had to be unbearable when the court asked Russell Lundgren to identify the pictures of his murdered son, with the amputations of the boy's sexual organs on display.

Author's Notes

The following murder sequences were constructed using transcriptions from Bonin's 11-hours of "confession interviews" with detectives in December 1980, official investigative documents, Bonin's written stories and jailhouse diaries, newspaper articles and conversations that Vonda Pelto, Ph.D. had with Bill Bonin, Greg Miley and Jim Munro.

13

Bill Bonin & Vernon Butts Light the Fire
Mark Shelton, August 4, 1979

August days, and nights, in Southern California can be hot in the flat, desert basin, but that wasn't the case on Saturday, August 4, 1979. A comfortable 75 degrees during the day, the temperature would drop to about 65 during the evening hours. Bonin had been living up in Silverado Canyon for two months and had limited contact with Vernon Butts.

He told Butts several times he would stop by to see him but never did, making him feel guilty. Hoping to make up for past slights, and wanting to show off his new Ford van, Bonin called him up for an evening out. Bonin later wrote, "I told him for sure I'd pick him up and we'd go to a Drive-in movie, at the time I had no idea how the night would end."

Bonin picked up Vernon Butts and they headed for the famous Highway 39 Drive-in movie theater. Located in Westminster, on Trask Ave adjacent to Beach Blvd., which is Highway 39, it opened in 1955 and was one of the largest Drive-ins in the area with 1,600 parking spots, a snack bar a quarter of block long and a screen nearly ten-stories tall. During the first movie of the double-feature, they relaxed in Bill's new van and caught up on the latest events in their lives.

Bonin continues the story, "During the break between movies we got around to talking about murder and picking up a guy and having sex with him and then killing him. I was sort of joking at the time. Vern thought the idea was real neat. He told me, 'I always wanted to see what it was like to kill someone. One of my fantasies is to kill someone using an icepick and putting it into his ear.'

"We continued to talk and then I thought I noticed he was very serious. I was surprised, so I asked him, 'Are you serious?' He said, 'Yes.' Still not believing it, I asked Vern again, 'Are you sure you could handle it, killing someone?' He said, 'Yeh.' I then said, 'If you can handle it, so can I, okay then why don't we leave right now.' Vern said 'Ok, let's go' and we left. You know, I was kind of testing him, really I didn't think he would go for it, but he did. I don't like doing stuff by myself. I never did, even when I was a kid I always made my younger brother come along with me. The only way I went into the service was a friend of mine went in, and that's what prompted me to go in, even though I wanted to, guess I just feel kinda insecure."

No longer interested in the second movie, they had seemingly goaded each other to go over a line neither had ever crossed. What must have been their feelings at that moment, was it anticipatory, or were they just daring each other, not wanting to appear weak, to see what might happen?

Bonin removed the speaker from the side of the car door and placed it back on its stand, then slowly guided the van out of the theater and on to Trask Avenue and south on Beach Boulevard, towards a place where Bonin had seen hitchhikers before.

At the corner of Beach and Edinger, where the San Diego freeway on-and-off-ramps are located, he spotted what he thought were two hitchhikers near the freeway entrance and turned left towards them.

"There's a hitchhiker, are you sure you want to go thru with this?" Bonin asked ominously, making sure Vernon Butts was serious.

"Sure, let's do it," he replied with an anxious and excited look.

Bonin and Butts inched closer to that point of no return, but even at this juncture the first of the Freeways Killings was not a sure thing, as Bonin later told police investigators: "During the whole time driving out there, I had no intention of killing the guy. I was gonna have the sex and then I figured I'll just leave him off there, you know."

Bonin later said the kid was hot hitchhiking, just walking home. Bonin pulled up and asked 17-year-old Mark Shelton for directions to some nearby street, then he asked if he needed a ride? Shelton said yes and hopped in the van. Bonin asked him straight out if he had ever gotten head from a guy before? Shelton said no and appeared hesitant, that is until Bonin asked him if wanted to make an easy $400 and proceeded to whip out five crisp $100 bills to wave in his face.

After hearing Bonin only wanted four or five hours of his time, and would be returned in the morning, Shelton readily agreed and Bonin headed south on the 405 to catch two freeways before getting on Interstate 15, the road to Las Vegas and about sixty-to-seventy miles from their starting point. Bonin's destination was the desolate mountains of the Cajon Pass.

"How late can you stay out? I have a cabin and we can go to it, but it's going to take a while to get there" Bonin said, anticipating at least having sex with the young boy.

"All night, it doesn't matter really."

"Ok, hey, uh, what's your name?"

"Mark Shelton."

"Hey, come on up here," Bonin said, patting the console between the seats, "I want to see what you got." Mark squeezed between the seats and got into a kneeling position with his back to the console. Bonin reached over unzipped Mark's pants, reached into his shorts and began rubbing his penis.

"Nice package, Vern check it out. I can't wait to get to the cabin."

Vern reached over and squeezed Shelton's crotch real hard. The kid screamed out in pain.

"Real nice," Vern said cracking up.

"Shit man, that hurt!" Shelton zipped up and moved to the back of the van.

Vern got in the back and kept the kid occupied with card and magic tricks during the hour-long drive up into the Cajon Pass, lying between the San Gabriel and San Bernardino Mountains. Bonin could hear Shelton laughing and enjoying himself in the back of the van, commenting later, "He was happy, he was gonna earn four-hundred dollars."

Shelton, at the very least, was in for an aggressively abusive homosexual experience, maybe a beating and being dumped out on the street with no money. Bonin detested hustlers and had expressed that to doctors in prison. He found a boarded-up gas station and parked in back, then he went to join the others to get the sex party going. Vern was sent up front as a look out.

"I told the kid it would be an hour before the cabin was free and we began make out French style, I took off all his clothes and really got him going and got him hard, I could tell that the kid was real relaxed and sexually excited, making little groans of contentment.

"Vern's thing was that he liked to give head to guys, not my thing. I used that as a coax to get people into a situation because my thing was sodomy. After Vern finished, I pulled down my pants and told Mark to give me some head. He did, at least for about a minute, he was nervous and shivering. I told him to lie down on his stomach to let me fuck him, he did and I was talking to him in a very nice and gentle voice. He nodded yes and looks like he is kinda in a trance.

"He's eyes are closed, barely aware of his surroundings, moving slowly with his eyes still closed. Vern's moved over to the side of the van just watching. I spit on my fingers and wet Shelton before moving into him. I do it slowly, gently. But Shelton screams out in pain and rears up, I panicked and came around and off him. He was on his right side, facing towards the back of the van. 'Man you scared the shit out of me,' I screamed out, 'you little bastard!' I was now pissed off."

Sent into a blinding rage, Bonin delivered a punishing one-two punch to Shelton's stomach and chest, grabbed his testicles and squeezed hard before, with coiled and compact power, violently driving his right knee square into Shelton's face again and again and again till he was limp and unconscious.

Now the moment of truth was at hand, whether to continue over the boundary and into unpredictable circumstances and consequences, or stop and move away? As if walking through a shimmering veil between worlds, Butts and Bonin strolled right through the dark passage.

"We can't let him go. We'd better just go ahead and finish him off right now," Bonin told Vern in a panic, who readily agreed.

"We flipped the kid back over to his stomach, he had a long sleeve shirt, so I tied the sleeves and wrapped it around his neck, then slipped the tire iron through the loop started twisting. Vern was on top of him, holding his hands behind his back. I twisted and twisted the shirt around his neck real tight. Then the kid woke up and started wiggling around and Vern couldn't hold him, so I used my right hand to keep his hands from getting free and kept a strong grip on the tire iron with my left. Vern got a better grip and after three or four minutes the kid stopped moving and we let go, we thought he was dead and relaxed.

"I untied the shirt and within about 10-seconds we hear this loud inhaling of air from Mark, Vern panicked and screamed, 'He's not dead.' That put me into a panic also, I jumped up and put the shirt around his neck again and began twisting, I screamed at Vern to get back on top of him and hold it tight while I drove."

Bonin got the van going south on Interstate 15, and within ten minutes Vern relaxed his grip, young Mark Shelton's life was definitely over. After a time, they found a gravel road and parked. Bonin and Butts then carried

Shelton's nude body further down the road and put him in some bushes.

"Then Vern starts talking about the ice pick thing. I looked around for something to use, I knew there wasn't anything like that in the van. I found a rusty wire in the bushes and pushed the wire into his ear as hard as he could. I didn't get any reactions, but I was actually still not sure he was dead. As we walked back to the van I saw a short dried out tree branch and picked it up and walked back to Mark's dead body and shoved it up his ass. He didn't move, now I could relax. He was definitely dead."

One night that changed all to follow, an accidental yet purposeful deed which altered William Bonin's mind and soul for good, thus setting him on a course of destruction and pain. Vernon Butts was also changed for the worse. Indeed, both of their lives can be divided up as before and after the night of August 4, 1979.

In his written confessions, Bonin offers these chilling thoughts on the murder and aftermath: "We left there and headed home. We were laughing as we felt we had gotten away with it. Actually we did if we would have stopped right there. No one knew Mark got into the van and the guy who saw him get in didn't know who it was. No one saw him while he was with us and no one saw us drop him off or us near the site where he was dropped off. That ended the first night of a nightmare for both Vern and me. It was the beginning of 10-months of hell for Southern California and many victims and their families and friends.

"There wasn't anyone safe. If a youngster was out there at night or at times during the day and got into my van then it was all over for them. There were some exceptions that were the lucky ones. I can think of five young boys off hand and three girls who could have been put to death also. Those were the very, very lucky ones."

Shelton's nude body was found on August 11 in the Cajon Pass north of San Bernardino. According to Tim Alger, of the ***Orange County Register***, Shelton's nude body was so ravaged by animals and the elements that it was unrecognizable.

A hiker walking along a gravel road noticed something partially hidden in thick brush and, thinking it might be a body, called the police. Mark's parents, Donald and Ramona Shelton of Westminster, did not learn of their son's whereabouts until April 1980, an eternity later.

During these months Mark's unidentified body lie on a cold metal tray in a San Bernardino County morgue. His frantic family continued to search for their lost child, always hoping for any news, positive or negative. They needed closure, as any parent would. Finally, at the end of March 1980, the identity was revealed; this occurred after Mr. Shelton drove to their dentist office and picked up his son's dental records. Then he took the records to the Westminster Police and requested they forward them to the Department of Justice for identification.

A month later the grieving Shelton family was informed of their child's whereabouts. Over a year later, in August 1980 the Shelton family filed a complaint in Superior Court alleging that police "recklessly and wantonly failed to conform" with the state regulations requiring them to file a request for dental records for any unidentified body.

They filed a lawsuit contending the murdered youth would have been identified quickly if detectives had followed state law. Nothing resulted from the litigation.

14

Bonin Kills Alone #1
Markus Grabs, August 5, 1979
As Told to Vonda Pelto, Ph.D. by Bill Bonin

LA Men's Central Jail, November 1981
I had barely arrived at my office, a converted jail cell adjacent to serial killers, when I received a call from the Senior Deputy in 1700 asking me to meet with Bonin, who was on the ragged edge from his ongoing murder trial and a sleepless night. Bonin arrived at my door 30-minutes later, with dark circles under his eyes showing his weariness. Having barely gotten myself organized, I didn't know what to expect from him; did he want to engage in light chit chat or get really serious?

It was a mystery to me as the world-famous serial killer slumped down on the hard-wooden chair across from me. Bonin asked for a cup of coffee, and even before it arrived the discussion turned to murder, in fact the bloody murder of Markus Grabs, his second victim.

"I felt really strange that morning, after all Vern and I had killed that first kid the night before, that would make anyone feel jumpy. But, man, I really felt a new kind of power from killin' that first one, I'd never done that before, and it was a real high, still kinda' can't believe we actually killed him. I needed to get out, I was so jumpy, and driving always made me feel peaceful, guess that's why I liked driving trucks. Hell, I would just go out and start driving anywhere, just to gear down. Thinking back to that day, I didn't go out to kill anyone, really, I can truthfully say killin' wasn't on my mind when I left that morning."

Markus Alexander Grabs was the second boy Bonin killed and the first one he confessed to killing alone. Grabs had left Germany in February 1979 with $,1,200 in American Express Travelers Cheques, equivalent to about $5,000 in 2023, with the intention of going to Paris, London, New York, Vancouver, Canada and then down the Pacific Coast to Los Angeles and on to Mexico and beyond. Equipped with an orange backpack and a sense of adventure, he ended up in Los Angeles in early August.

On Thursday, August 2 Grabs was hitchhiking south on Pacific Coast Highway in the Seal Beach-Huntington Beach area. Miss Byrnes, and her friend Bruce Simpson, were stopped at a red light and noticed Grabs walking along the highway wearing a backpack with a British flag on the back. They started talking and learned he was from West Germany.

Grabs told them he planned to sleep on the beach that evening before continuing south. Byrnes advised him that it was illegal, and he risked being arrested, so they invited Grabs to stay with them. After three days, on Sunday, August 5, he went to lunch with Miss Byrnes, in Costa Mesa, before she dropped him off, around 4 or 5:00 p.m., on Pacific Coast Highway in Newport Beach.

After final goodbyes, she used Grab's Polaroid camera to take a picture of him, a final snapshot where young Markus started hitchhiking that fateful day.

Bonin continued to tell me the story, "I headed south on PCH, wanting to get down to the ocean, I eventually ended up in Newport Beach. It's a nice area, the ocean breeze felt good. Well, I spotted a kid hitchhiking and, you know, I started getting horny. Figured I'd just pull up and feel him out about gays.

"He came over to the van as soon as I pulled onto the gravel, I found out he was a student from Germany and was backpacking around during summer vacation. I think he was goin' to Mexico, I can't remember, but I'll tell you his looks turned me on, tall and lean, nice tight body with light-colored eyes and hair.

"I started talking about sex and asked him if he was gay, he smiled and crawled up in the front seat with me. I made a U-turn and headed back up on PCH, wanting to park along the ocean. I started feeling a little better thinking about fucking him. There were a lot of cars parked along the highway, so I pulled in between a couple of campers. Most of the people were out walking along the water, but I still closed the windows, I didn't want anyone to disturb us.

"We got in the back of the van and took our clothes off, then we started giving each other head. It was good. We did that for a little while, then I had it in my mind somewhere about trying out bondage. I'd never dun it before, so I got out some electrician type wire out of my tool kit and hooked him up."

"Didn't he object?" I asked.

"Nah, and that surprised me, I wouldn't ever let some stranger tie me up! But guess he thought it wouldn't hold him if he wanted to get free."

"Maybe he trusted you because you were about his same age?" I asked.

"Well, yeah, and I didn't tie him up real tight. When I finished hooking him up, I looked down at him lying there on his stomach, with his hands tied behind his back. I felt good, I felt like I was really something, I felt strong, you know, growing up I always felt helpless. I started caressing his body by running my Buck knife blade up and down his skin. His body was almost hairless, nice and smooth. All the while I kept telling him how easy it would be to kill him, guess I kinda' wanted him to be afraid."

Bonin's demeanor changed as he sat up straighter, readjusted himself, and put on a wry smile.

"I still didn't plan to kill him. I wanted to play with him, show him who was boss. I held the knife up to his throat, told him I should cut him," animated, and smiling, Bonin's face broadcast the pleasure he was feeling as he relived the experience.

"He looked at me, like he was starting to feel scared, all the sudden realizing he was helpless. The kid couldn't tell if I was serious or not, I didn't know if I was or not either. I backed off cause I wanna enjoy him some more. We were getting excited, so I reached between his legs and checked out his dick. It was hard, like mine was too," he coyly smiled and looked to see if I was uncomfortable with the topic, I wasn't.

"I got him up on his knees and pushed inside of him stroking back and forth until I exploded. Then I grabbed hold of his nuts and squeezed them real hard. He screamed, broke loose and I fell back, then the kid twisted around and faced me with his fist raised in the air, ready to punch me. I had to defend myself, I didn't have any choice. He was strong and he might overpower me, maybe kill me!"

"Did you plan to kill him?" I wondered if he had changed his mind.

"Oh, shit no! I just wanted him to be afraid of me. To look up at me, know I could kill him at any second, I wanted him to show me respect," he said with venom, then softened his gaze and kept going. "Anyway, I'm afraid of knives and didn't have no intention of using it as a weapon, I didn't want blood all over my new van, but I had to defend myself, I had no choice. He was strong, maybe stronger than me. What could I do? What if he got the knife away from me, he might have killed me?" Bonin said with false fear, fixing his gaze on the ceiling as thought about this pathetic excuse for his actions.

After regaining his composure, and taking a few sips of coffee, he continued to describe what happened, "Well, the kid landed a hard one on my jaw, and I fell back and hit my head against the van, I was shocked, he nailed me good. The knife was in my hand, I didn't know what to do, so I raised it up and dug it hard into his upper arm," he said with a demonstration of bringing his arm down. "The kid screamed in horror, really loud, his eyes were wide open, he couldn't believe it, fuck, I couldn't believe I'd dun it. Never imagined stabbing anyone," he said with a blank stare, lost in the moment before continuing.

"Then something inside me clicked and I was on automatic pilot," Bonin said, all of the sudden animated in expression. "I had to survive, so I got a better grip on the knife and started stabbing him wildly, over and over, but he was twisting and turning. I hit him in the back and in the butt, I don't know where else, I was just stabbed blindly. His blood squirted all over the place, on the walls, the curtains, on me. He was trying to stop me, putting his hand out where he thought I might hit next. He tried to grab the knife, but I couldn't let him get it.

"Doc, I couldn't let him live" he said, pleading with me to understand. "He would tell the police and I'd be in prison again. I'd been in too many times, raped and beaten by other inmates and no one helped me out. My heart was pounding in my throat, I just kept stabbing him frantically until he stopped fightin.' Then I had to get out of there fast, I didn't know what to do, but the kid was asking me to take him to the hospital. I told him sure, no problem, what else could I say? But he was getting on my nerves with all the whining.

"For a minute, I thought I would be sick from the smell of all the blood. After getting a window open and some fresh air in the van, I felt a little better. I had to get my mind clear, but when I looked down and saw the blood all over myself I froze. I tried wiping the sticky stuff off, but it was impossible. The kid's backpack was lying over to the side, it was soaked with blood too. I had to find some place to get rid of him, so I hit the freeway heading to somewhere by Malibu Canyon. Figured I could finda' place where no one would see me. It was a long drive and dark by the time I got there."

"Why didn't you drop him off at a hospital and split?" I asked.

"Someone might have seen me or got my license plate number. I couldn't take the chance. Also, I drove for about an hour just to get to Malibu Canyon, my gas was running low, what if I ran out of gas with the kid in the back? I couldn't stop, he was still alive. That little shit would've cried out for help. My mouth was dry and my heart racing," Bonin related, trying to communicate his state of mind. Hiding my own state of shock, I listened without showing any emotion.

I didn't realize it could get worse, but it did as Bonin continued the story.

"Finally, I told him to shut him up, I said I was going to take him to a place, drop him off and then call a doctor to come and help him. He quieted down. After I got off the freeway, I drove down Malibu Canyon and found a lonely side road and took the turn.

"I started draggin' him out, he was screamin' all over again. I got him out and down onto the ground. He was weak and I had to hide him real good, so I wrapped him up in a blanket, but then I was all covered in blood again.

"So, I got him on his stomach and started strangling him. That wasn't working cause I couldn't get enough leverage, but I had to kill him. I wrapped an orange cord around his neck and tried to strangle him, but I couldn't manage it. I didn't like using the knife, I didn't like that blood going everywhere, but there was no other way.

"I got the Buck knife out of the van and put my mind in a sort of Zen state order to bring myself to the point of being able to stab him again. I stabbed him, I don't know how many times, but I just kept stabbing him like I was in frenzy. Now he was quiet, he didn't fight me no more. I had to make sure he was finished off, so I rammed my fist up his ass and he didn't flinch.

"His blood had splattered all over me, even got on my face. I started thinking about how it was when I got beatin' as a kid. I used to beg my ole man to stop. Shit, he wouldn't."

I could not believe what I just heard. Bonin exhibited a wanton depravity and a complete and total indifference to the boy he heinously murdered, no slaughtered. Throughout his description of the Markus Grabs murder, he maintained an excited quality. Was he ignorant of the horror he wrought on this boy or the pain he caused his family? I scrutinized his face throughout the conversation, searching for any sign of guilt or remorse. I never detected anything close. Was I was reading his expression correctly?

"By this time it was late, probably after just after 10. After it was done, I dragged him into some bushes, oh shit, was I so tired from everything. I headed back to the freeway, then I stopped at a gas station, but the guy said they were closed, so I got back on the freeway and ran out of gas. While I was standing there a police car came by, I waved and they kept driving, that scared the shit out of me. I was a nervous wreck, but I got lucky. A guy finally stopped and drove me to a gas station that had a little store. I went in and bought some water, God I was so thirsty. People were giving me funny looks cause I had blood all over my pants. I told them that I was painting a house.

"The guy drove me back to my van, I tried to give him some money, but he wouldn't take it. He told me that if I ever saw someone in distress to stop and help them, I said okay and he left, jeez Doc, if that guy only knew what I just dun?" Bonin asked me with an ironic smile on his face.

"Anyway, I drove back real careful cuz I couldn't get pulled over, there was blood all over the van and my clothes. I called Vern and told him to get some cleaning stuff and some Pepsis. I didn't want to take a chance on stopping again cause of the blood, but I had to clean the van, oh man, the smell of blood was really makin' me sick," he said, seemingly drained from tell the story.

"At Vern's, I used paper towels to soak up the blood, it was everywhere, on the seat belts, the carpets, shit, even on the curtains. After working up a sweat, I quit cleaning and told Vern to stop. I decided to rent one those shampoo machines after I got home. We sat down to relax, and I told Vern the whole story while drinking a Pepsi before heading back to Silverado Canyon. He asked me all kinds of questions, wanting to know everything that happened."

On Monday morning, around 6:30 a.m., Harold Posada was picking up a friend on Las Virgenes Canyon Road. About four miles from the Ventura Freeway off Malibu Canyon, across the road from a Youth Camp, Posada spotted what he thought was a body and pulled over. Upon closer examination, he realized it was a male who was unclothed and covered with blood. It was partially hidden in a bed of Ice Plant.

After dealing with his shock, he contacted the Los Angeles County Sheriff's Department. Malibu Canyon lies within Los Angeles County and thus the crime scene became an L.A. County Sheriff's Dept. investigation. Sgt. David Kushner, a Sheriff's homicide detective, and his partner Deputy Jack Fueglien were dispatched. Like famed LAPD homicide detective Sgt. John "Jigsaw" St. John, Kushner had been investigating a string of "murder cases involving homosexuals and sexual deviates either as victims or suspects" for six years. Most recent of those cases was Thomas Lundgren and Mark Procter, neither which Bonin had committed.

Kushner observed Markus Grabs, with bruises around his face, a victim of multiple stab wounds with an orange cord still wrapped around his neck, and blue wires tied around his ankles. The body was still warm with ligature burn marks, from the strangulation with the cord, clearly visible around the neck but especially up front. Bonin had strangled him behind while he was on the ground.

Grab's tennis shoes were laying across the road. No money, traveler's checks, passport or any other official papers were found, but his backpack, blood splattered sunglasses and Polaroid camera in a pouch were scattered about. The coroner reported severe injuries to the anal region, consistent with Bonin's claim of using his fist inside to ensure he was dead.

During the trial, Sgt. Kushner's testimony offers a vivid description of seeing Grab's body, stabbed over 70 times, and the nature of his killer:

Q: You made the statement in answer to the District Attorney's question that the stab wounds on the back, in your opinion, were done in a frenzy. Is that true?

A: Yes

Q: What do you mean by that?

A: I can only liken it in my mind to a rabid dog that has gone insane and does not know when to stop biting. It occurs quite often and it is mostly seen in homosexual type murders where the person who is doing the stabbing stabs so many times in a rain of pattern that really have no great injury value each of themselves other than to inflict a lot of pain and to drain themselves of a lot of heat. That's my experience.

Q: Well, similar to like you said the rabid dog, it just bites and bites?

A: It's just the stabbing begins and it doesn't end until the person's energy level is worn down to cause him to stop.

Markus Grabs was an unfortunate victim at the front end of a ten-month horror show inspired by Bonin with help from Butts, the latter helping set off a murderous time bomb that consumed innocent lives and destroyed families. Bonin was transformed from homosexual pedophile predator to homosexual pedophile predator/murderer.

From a psychological standpoint, Bonin does not yet fully grasp the changes taking place within his mind and soul. Unfortunately, for people who were part of or stumbled into his world, Bonin came to realize he liked having the power of life and death and embraced those feelings.

15

Third Arrest & Immediate Release
August 9 to 13, 1979

Five days after killing his first two victims, dumped about 80-miles apart in different law enforcement jurisdictions, Bonin was right back at it in Orange County. On Thursday, August 9 he went cruising in the van and found someone willing to enter his evolving world of horror, but luckily a police officer happened upon the scene. The Charge Sheet from Deputy Duncan, Badge #334, reveals what happened.

"Orange County Sheriff's crime report #562-395 indicates that on 8-9-79 at about midnight, Mr. Bonin was arrested for ***Sex Perversion***. Officer Duncan, while on patrol, observed a van parked in a school parking lot. The van was moving slightly due to movement inside. Investigation revealed that inside the van were two occupants, William Bonin and a 17-year-old male. The 17-year-old related that Mr. Bonin had picked him up as he was hitch-hiking a ride.

"Bonin agreed to take the boy to a friend's house. Shortly after the ride started Bonin reached over and fondled his genital area stating, 'Does this feel good?' He replied, 'I don't get into this' and pushed his hand away. Bonin then said he was bi-sexual and he should try it. Bonin again touched his genital area while driving. As they passed the school parking lot, Bonin pulled into the lot and stopped in the center, facing the street, stating 'What is this park?' Bonin once again fondled his genital area stating, 'Can't you get it hard for me?' He became confused and wanted to leave but wasn't sure what to do.

"Bonin then climbed into the rear of the van and said, 'Come back here with me.' He hesitated and Bonin took his hand, pulling him into the back, saying, 'Don't you want a good blowjob.' Bonin then unzipped his own pants, pulling them down to about his ankles. Bonin then turned to him and tried to kiss him. He turned away, telling Bonin, 'Hey, I'm not into this.'

"Bonin turned to him and said, 'Just lay down and relax.' Bonin unzipped his pants and pulled them to his knees. Bonin then put his mouth on his penis and began orally copulating him. Bonin told him, 'Just jack me off.' At that point, the patrol unit arrived. On 8-13-79, Mr. Bonin was released from custody and efforts to contact him to get his side of the story have been to no avail. Note prior commitment to similar behavior."

How lucky was this boy? Bonin never indicated that he intended to murder him, but it was a few days after he murdered Shelton and Grabs. Guessing that Officer Duncan saved a life that day seems like a safe bet.

Bonin's attorney filed a Writ of Habeas Corpus, compelling his release, and called for the charges to be filed against him by September 7. He was released by the court and set to appear for a disposition hearing on Friday, August 24. While the wheels were set in motion to decide this matter, with possible parole violations, Bonin continued killing. A parole report, dated August 23, recommended that further jail time would not serve any purpose.

Bonin's progress was reported as such:

"In December 1978 he moved into an apartment of his own and established a heterosexual relationship. During the period from December 1978 to June 1979, there was reported regular POC attendance and no criminal behavior. In June, Mr. Bonin moved to Orange County and resided with his brother. He was hopeful of going into a business with his brother, but the deal turned sour in late July."

A verbal report to his parole officer, from Dr. Illing, stated, "Mr. Bonin has been very cooperative during his period of parole. Dr. Illing feels there is always a chance for this type of behavior from this type of case. He does not feel custody will serve any positive purpose in Mr. Bonin's case."

A Parole Revocation Hearing Decision was set for September 18, 1979 to decide whether to vacate his parole, sending him into custody with the possibility of new charges and additional punishment. Not mentioned in the arrest report was that a controlled substance, marijuana, was found in the van, something which played a role in later events.

While all these hearings and decisions took place, Bonin participated in the murders of Robert Wirostek (August 20), Donald Hyden (August 27), and David Murrillo (September 9). Bonin, who obviously shouldn't have been released, called Scott Fraser for a ride and uttered a phrase reminiscent of one he used five years earlier, "No one's going to testify again, this is never going to happen again." Fraser dismissed the comment as Bonin venting his anger.

16

Bonin Creates Alibi for Grabs Murder
August 17, 1979

Ten days had elapsed since Bonin committed his first two murders and his mindset was a mixture of uncertainty, turmoil, excitement and confusion. Already with a history of preying on young boys for sex, now Bonin had added killing to the equation. What should he do now, stop and hope the killings drifted into the world of unsolved murders?

Bonin needed to talk to someone and perhaps convince them he had killed Markus Grabs in self-defense. Only days before he had blurted out to Fraser there would be "no more witnesses," and now he attempted to create an alibi about the Grabs murder.

Bonin became good friends with Scott Fraser during the months he lived at Kingswood Village apartments. While living there, he frequented the ongoing party scene at Fraser's apartment three or four nights a week. Still a consistent visitor to Fraser's place after moving out, many of the characters involved in the murders came from meetings at Fraser's where partying and homosexual activity were ongoing.

Around 1:00 p.m. on Friday, August 17 Bonin picked up Fraser and took him to the Magic Cork restaurant, near Lakewood and Rosecrans in nearby Paramount. Regulars at the Magic Cork, after ordering drinks Bonin came right out and said, "Scott, I think I've killed a man." Proceeding to lay out the circumstances of what happened to Grabs, Bonin left out a number of relevant details.

He painted it as "acting in self-defense" and included Vernon Butts in the story, which he was not. Bonin said Grabs got scared, lashed out at him and he was forced to defend himself. Weaving a tale of half-truths, lies and reality, Bonin needed Fraser to truly believe him and possibly vouch for him, should the need arise.

Bonin said he was "using the knife as a form of sexual teasing, had no intention of killing him, was just trying to scare him, and had no choice but kill him to save himself." There were some grains of truth in Bonin's testimony to his friend; from this point forward, no other victims were stabbed by Bonin. He hated knives and never used one again as a primary instrument for killing, although one was used to ensure Sean King was dead after Eric Wijnaendts delivered the initial wounds.

Fraser did not seem to be shocked, asked logical questions, and was sympathetic and supportive as a "friend" might be. He said, "You had to defend yourself, Bill, he was going to kill you." Bonin made it sound like he "left the kid alive and hoped someone might find and take him to the hospital" and that "the whole thing taught me a good lesson." All lies designed to gain Fraser's sympathy. Bonin had stabbed him repeatedly to make sure he was dead during the drop-off in Malibu.

Bonin told Fraser about steam cleaning the van to get all the blood stains out and then, knowing that Fraser subscribed to the ***Los Angeles Times***, wondered if he still had issues from the last couple of weeks. Fraser did and they went back to Scott's apartment to start digging through the stacks of back issues. Fraser later testified about thinking to himself that "it couldn't be made up because he wouldn't involve someone else." Failing to find anything in the first run through the stack of newspapers, Fraser was about to ask Bonin if he was just "playing a practical joke" when Bonin shouted out, "I've got it, I found it."

Bonin showed him the article, read the text aloud, and then handed it over for Fraser to peruse. He then "figured it was probably true" and believed Bonin's version of events.

Bonin was playing "master manipulator" and it worked. Could Bonin have believed that a post-murder, self-justifying conversation might help if he was arrested for the murder? Fraser could hardly be called a credible witness, but the facts of the murder may nullify anything Fraser had to say. All of it became moot as the bodies piled up over the coming months.

A logical question would be why didn't Fraser contact authorities immediately? Such action would have saved many lives, not only the victims but the others Bonin sucked into his swirling vortex of despair. Fraser's inability to connect Bonin with the unfolding murder spree has many valid reasons, as will be seen.

In December 1980 Bonin wrote this about the "alibi" meeting with Scott Fraser, "After the Grabs affair I was really shook up. I had never stabbed anyone before. It took a lot from me to get myself to finish him off after I got to the dump site in Malibu. It shook me up so much I told Scott about it. I told him Vern was with me yet he wasn't.

"I told him Vern wouldn't help me and made it sound like a self-defense thing. I told Scott that after we dumped off the body that Vern looked at me and said, 'You know what, I'm hungry.' Scott and I were at the Magic Cork Restaurant at the time and Scott was just about to eat a chunk of steak when I told him. It became a private joke with us.

"Vern never did say that the night of Grabs killing as he wasn't there. He did say it after the killing when we dumped the body off in Kern County. It always stuck in my mind as a sick statement. You just don't go out and eat after killing and dumping off a body. But we did as Vern was hungry."

Guess the final comment was about etiquette for murderers—don't eat right after killing.

17

Bonin & Butts Victim #2
Robert Wirostek, August 20, 1979

During hours of confession interviews with detectives and prosecutors, in December 1980, Bonin was asked about the about the murder of Robert Wirostek. Two versions of the murder are chronicled below: first the interview and then his written confession, penned before the interview.

Two interesting points come out of comparing the two: 1) At the end of the interview Bonin talks about one boy he had sex with and intended to kill, then decided against it and let him go, 2) The written confession contains more details about the gruesome, brutal treatment Robert Wirostek experienced at the hands of Bonin and Vernon Butts.

ESPOSITO: Okay, we'll get to Robert Wirostek, and you mentioned last night that he was hitch-hiking on Pacific Coast Highway near Newport Beach.

BONIN: Correct, That would be north as your coming down, there's a street to where, you make a left turn, it goes up the hill and around that. So it was north cause…

ESPOSITO: Okay

BONIN: That's the street we took to get over to wherever Ralph's Market was, uh, to the best of my knowledge that is the street we took. I can't remember what the, I thought it was Newport…

ESPOSITO: Newport Boulevard Interchange.

BONIN: Okay and then that's it.

ESPOSITO: About what time of day was that?

BONIN: Daytime, that's all I can say. I…

ESPOSITO: In the afternoon?

BONIN: I don't know.

ESPOSITO: Okay. Did he say where he was going?

BONIN: Yes, to work, Ralph's Market.

ESPOSITO: Okay you mentioned he was all for getting some head…

BONIN: Yes. I went, I went all the way to Ralph's Market and I went into a parking lot about two parking lots down from Ralph's Market into another big parking lot.

ESPOSITO: Say how much time he had to get to work or anything like that?

BONIN: Uh I believe he did, but I don't remember how much time. I believe he still had a half-hour by the time we got there.

ESPOSITO: Okay, you said, you said last night you tied him up. What did you tie him with?

BONIN: The string. I'm almost certain of that.

ESPOSITO: How'd you get him tied up?

BONIN: I tied it around one hand and wrapped it around his throat and then went around and tied it around the other and back up to the throat.

ESPOSITO: Kind of like hog tying?

BONIN: I guess, yeah.

ESPOSITO: Why did you get him subdued, you know, to, to tie him up, did you produce a knife?

BONIN: I pulled a knife.

ESPOSITO: How long had you been with him when you pulled a knife?

BONIN: I got back there and started sucking on him and then I says, uh, well I don't take the come, let me get some, uh, toilet paper and I went up, this would have been about fifteen, thirty seconds after we started, and I went up and when I came back I had the knife?

ESPOSITO: Okay. So you held a knife on him and...

BONIN: Yes, to his throat, and he turned over and I tied him up.

ESPOSITO: Okay, did you sodomize him?

BONIN: Yes, I believe I did.

ESPOSITO: Did you pick him for the purpose of killing him, or just for sex, and it turned into killing, or what?

BONIN: Believe, uh, when I first picked him it was strictly sex. But, uh, we talked on the way up there, and the only thing he would do for twenty dollars was let me give him head, and what I wanted to do is I wanted to fuck him, and I knew I wasn't gonna be able to, so that it turned around to where I was gonna have to tie him up and to do that.

ESPOSITO: You have a situation where if somebody wasn't agreeable and you wound up where you had to tie them up and all that, you know stuff in order to fuck 'em, that would prompt you to kill them?

BONIN: Yes, I would say that, uh, a lot of time, as I said, I was more into the killing as I went on, uh, if I would come then it would be very, very difficult for me afterwards to kill him, uh, I couldn't do it. Like for instance I picked up a kid, uh, that lives off Lakewood Boulevard and Candlestick, somewhere down in Los Angeles, or Lakewood, and uh he was sixteen, he looked more like twelve or thirteen, and I got it on with him. I made him give me head, I didn't tie him up, and I butt fucked him, and I came, and then I gave him head. But I couldn't bring myself to kill him. I had already come. I was by myself and end up giving him thirty dollars, and I never did hear from him again. Nothing was ever turned in, he was happy to get thirty dollars, uh in fact I'm positive he didn't say nothing because, uh, I played a role. I told him how sorry I was all that, and I says, 'Wow, I really think I ought to turn myself in, we're gonna find a cop.' And no way did he want to find a cop, cause he had warrants out for him, juvenile warrants. So I says, 'Okay, you got your thirty dollars, you go, I'll go,' and that was it.

Now read the written confession and notice the differences. When Bonin talked with detectives, he was playing a variety of angles in terms of his ultimate conviction and disposition.

"It was a sunny day and I felt like taking a drive. I headed for the Pacific Coast Highway where it enters the Long Beach Traffic Circle, I wanted to do some driving and look at sailboats. I took the coast highway south and was at peace with myself, there were no hitch-hikers and the traffic was light. I found that in a short time I was in Newport Beach, just north of Newport Beach, that is when I saw a guy hitch-hiking.

"I picked him up and had no intention of doing anything, until he got into the van and seems that he is around 16 to 18 and quite good looking. I decided to see what I could do. He said he was going to work and I offered to drive him there. I asked him if he was into the gay scene and he said no, and then I offered him fifty bucks to just give him head.

"We got in the back of the van, I started sucking on him and rubbing his chest. 'Oh yeah that feels great,' he said. I had him hooked, he was laying back and really enjoying it. I went in the back to get some tissue and came back with an eight-inch steak knife, I held it to his throat and said, 'If you move, I'll stick you with this knife.' He was petrified, 'I'll do anything you say.' I tied him up and told him, 'One false move and I'll stick you.'

"I could see his sweat on his tan skin and it really turned me on. I pulled down my pants and butt fucked him. He started complaining and I told him, 'If you make any noise, you're a dead mother fucker.' I drove my dick into him and fucked him real hard. I then found a phone booth and called Vern. All the way up to Vern's place, he asked me to loosen his hands because they were hurting, I told him to 'shut up.' After I got Vern in the van, I headed out towards the I-10 freeway going east to the inland desert area.

"During the time I was driving, Vern learned his name was Bob Wirostek, Vern gave him head and slapped him around a bit. Then Vern drove and I got back there, I rolled him on to his stomach and hit some on the side, then I asked Vern if he'd like to hear him scream, and Vern said, 'Sure, why don't you do that finger trick.' That was thing we discussed the night before, where we break the guy's fingers. I said okay and grabbed Bob's little fingers and bent it back till it breaks, he screamed in pain. After I finished, I went for the little fingers on the other hand and he begged me not too. I pushed it back for a while but didn't break it.

"I then grabbed his nuts and squeezed, then I took the tire iron and rolled him over on his back and hit him as hard as I could on both knees and ankles. I hit him on his shoulders and elbows, then told him, 'We are going to let you out, but you will be unconscious.' I gave him the choice of either choking him or hitting him over the head?

"He didn't say at first what he wanted, then he said, 'I don't know.' I hit him with the tire iron and I thought he was out, I hit him again and he raised up saying, 'You fucking bastard.' He had momentarily scared me. I said, 'I'll choke you instead, just let yourself go and it won't be as bad, don't struggle as it will only make it worse. And don't try to pretend you're out, I can tell.'

"I started choking him with his t-shirt and twisting with the tire iron, after I got it tight I saw he was fully conscious, he was trying to stay that way. I said to him, 'If you try to fight it would use up the oxygen faster. It won't help to try and stay conscious, it's all over, you're one dead dude.' He started to struggle when I said that, I said, 'struggle baby, it will only make your death come faster.' In fifteen seconds he was out, I relaxed and held the shirt and tire iron tight for five minutes. We dumped him in the desert around Palm Springs and went home."

The badly decomposed body of young Robert Wirostek was found on Wednesday, September 12, almost three weeks after the murder. This was left within the jurisdiction of the Riverside County Sheriff's Department, which runs all the way to the California-Arizona border.

18

Bonin & Butts Victim #3
Donald Hyden, August 26, 1979

Bonin woke up that morning feeling anxious and restless. Four murders in three weeks and an arrest cast a dark cloud over his future. During a break at work on this hot August day, Bonin phoned Vern to see if wanted to "go out hunting?" Vern was up for it, having already helped Bonin murder two young boys in the past three weeks.

Vern sounded excited and that charged up Bonin, he felt like "they were a couple of big game hunters on the prowl." Of course, as has been noted throughout Bonin's life, he preferred to not be alone when going out and it had been that way since early childhood.

Knowing what lay ahead, Bonin was keyed up for the rest of the afternoon, thinking about, fantasizing and anticipating what might happen.

"Hey, Billy you have to catch a train or something?" Bonin's boss yelled at him after noticing he kept checking his watch.

"Yeah, I got a hot date later," he screamed back, wanting to laugh because his boss would never have guessed what was really on his mind. Bonin had to gas up and clean out his truck before leaving for the day. By the time he picked up Vern, it was mid-evening.

They drove around Long Beach, no luck; next various areas of Orange County that Bonin knew may have ripe pickings, no luck as well. Frustrated, Bonin elected to troll the streets of Hollywood, a place with plenty of late-night activity that, Bonin wrote, "had always been lucky for me; lot of hitch-hikers or kids trying to get discovered for the movies."

Just after 2:00 a.m. Bonin drove west on Santa Monica Blvd. and then decided to take La Cienega Blvd. up to Sunset, in the heart of Hollywood. He spotted a good-looking boy and possible target crossing La Cienega, it was 15-year-old Donald Hyden. He was not far from his home, where he lived with his parents. In the left turn lane, Bonin suddenly jerked across two lanes to the right while also noticing a police car observing his crazy move. Bonin was sure he would get pulled over for the maneuver, but nothing happened.

"Billy, you got some kind of charmed life," Vern said in the midst of a good laugh. He was lying down in the back of the van, out of sight from the boy.

"Do you know where George Street is?" Bonin asked, using his usual ploy and employing the name George Street when unfamiliar with the area.

"No, I don't know that place."

"You wanna make fifty bucks?"

"Sure, for what?" Hyden asked.

"Give me some head," Bonin said, trying to be casual and non-threatening.

"I don't know, is that all?"

"C'mon, it won't take long, maybe I'll give you more, if you're worth it."

"Sure, OK," Hyden said, innocently entering the van.

Bonin headed north on La Cienega towards Sunset, found a place to park and got into the back of the van. Vernon was lying there, pretending to be asleep. Bonin made it like he had to wake Vernon up, then he told the boy to get in the back of the van. He hesitated after seeing Butts.

"I don't like him being here, you said it was just for you," Hyden said, getting more nervous as the seconds ticked away.

Already anticipating what he could do with him, fantasizing about the sex and killing, Bonin wasn't about to let him escape after driving for hours and finally luring someone into his grasp. Sensing he wanted to leave, Bonin decided to call his bluff.

"Go ahead, forget the fifty bucks and get out of the car, and stop wasting my time," he said to the boy, betting he preferred not losing the money.

After noticing he calmed down, Bonin said, "Look, I'll have Vern drive up and down on Sunset, so you'll know where we are."

This did the trick, and the final piece of the puzzle was in place. Hyden got in the back of the van while Vern started driving around. Now firmly in his clutches in the Death Van, Hyden and Bonin began having sex, both responding to each other as the heat rose between their bodies. Vern made a turn off Sunset by mistake and Hyden panicked, jumping up while tugging on his pants.

"Just relax," Bonin said. "Vern just made a wrong turn."

"I don't care, let me out, I wanna get outta here, let me out," the boy screamed.

That was it, Bonin was through playing and reacted with rage, grabbing rope and twisting Hyden's left arm behind his back and high up between the shoulder blades, inflicting pain and immobilizing the victim. After wrapping his left arm around Hyden's neck, Bonin tried to pin him down, but Hyden struggled to free himself. He went for the side door latch to pop it open. Bonin responded out of instinct to reverse the latch, then remembered the side door didn't open from the inside.

Bonin pushed the boy to the back of the van and pinned him against the door. Hyden raised his right arm, made a fist, looked Bonin straight in the eye with the intention of hitting him in the face.

"I wouldn't do that if I was you!" Bonin said, twisting the boy's arm higher up the back. Instead of trying to hit Bonin, the boy angrily hit the side of the van five or six times and screamed, "When I get out of all this, I'm going to tell the cops and you're going to jail."

"You broke my arm," Hyden screamed, continuing to fight.

"No I didn't, shut up," Bonin said as Hyden tried to free his legs from his pants to kick Bonin. They continued to struggle while Butts drove around, leaving the Sunset Blvd. area and heading south to Santa Monica Blvd.

"Tell you what, I'll give you another fifty bucks if you let me tie you up," Bonin whispered in Hyden's ear. He wasn't going for it. Bonin got a rope around Hyden's left arm and wrapped the rest around his neck for leverage.

"Put your right hand behind your back right fucking now," he whispered menacingly.

Hyden stopped fighting and Bonin tied his hands, his pants around his ankles preventing him from moving about. With triumphant pleasure Bonin said to Vern, "See how nice he's being now."

With complete control of the situation, Bonin's temper, frustration and pent-up anxiety burst forth in a shower of rage. He slapped the helpless 15-year-old boy hard across the face a couple of times, just like his father had done with him.

"So, you're gonna tell the cops on me, well, I may as well get my nuts off," Hyden was told in a threatening manner before Bonin delivered multiple punches to his chest and slaps to the face, causing the boy to double over with pain.

"Hey Vern, you want some of this"

"No," Vern said from the driver's seat. Bonin drove his knee hard into the boy's side, reached between his legs, grabbed his nuts and squeezed hard. Hyden screamed out in pain. Bonin pulled down his own pants and sodomized the boy, releasing his pent-up tension in an aggressive act of sexual violence. After he was done, he continued to beat him as contempt and rage spilled out.

"You entered the Death Van, and when someone enters, they don't go out alive," Vernon Butts said with the intention of scaring Hyden out of his wits. Bonin later commented that Vern really liked instilling "psychological fear" in their victims, he like to get them "scared shitless because he really got a nut off of it."

Hyden didn't seem to take Vern seriously, believing Butts was just trying to scare him. By this time, Vern had the van headed north, on the Hollywood Freeway, towards the San Fernando Valley. Bonin took the bandana tied around Hyden's head and put it around his neck, telling him he didn't want to lose it. Hyden still didn't know the final intentions of Bonin and Butts.

"Okay, here's what's going to happen, I'm just gonna choke you until you're unconscious then we're gonna drop you off, it's that or I can squeeze your nuts and beat the fuck out of you until you pass out."

"Okay," a frightened Hyden said.

"Don't you try to pretend you're out, cause I'll know, and don't struggle cause that will make it worse for you," Bonin said firmly.

Bonin got out the tire iron, slipped it into the bandana and started twisting it, squeezing bit by bit around Hyden's neck. Then he started twitching and struggling a bit when Bonin whispered his in ear, "Sorry kid but I can't let you live to tell about this." Hyden reacted to the news and began to struggle, but he was unconscious in a few seconds.

Bonin untied him, took off his shoes, socks and pants, and then took over driving, going north on the Ventura Freeway towards Malibu Canyon.

"Billy, you know what one of my fantasies has been for a long time?"

"Yeh, I know, an ice pick to the ear to kill someone," he replied.

"Yeah, that's one of them, but I have another one, to suck on a guy after he's dead."

"You fucking with me? Shit, the guy wouldn't even be able to get it up," Bonin said, shocked and repulsed.

"Well, that's my fantasy," Vern said, pleased at shocking Bonin.

"Well, there's your corpse,' Bonin motioning to the back of the van.

Much to his surprise, Vern got in the back and started doing his thing. Even for a deviant like Bonin, Vern's behavior struck him as strange. How much of this is true is up for speculation?

Bonin got off at the Lost Hills exit, the first one after Malibu Canyon, where he had dumped Markus Grabs. He found a construction site not far from the freeway. They stripped the boy of his clothes and Bonin got out knife to make sure he was dead. He stabbed him twice in the right side of the neck, once in the middle of the back and in the scrotum, leading investigators to speculate he tried to cut off his testicles.

On Monday, August 27, 1979 Robert Cassano, a construction worker, found Donald Hyden dumped on his head, nude, in a Dempsey Dumpster. LA County Sheriff Homicide detectives Sgt. David Kushner, and his partner Deputy Jack Fueglein, were back three weeks later at another Bonin crime scene, this one about five miles from where Markus Grabs was dumped.

They had to view another teenage boy who had been beaten, raped and murdered by a homosexual killer. No money or ID was found, and Kushner observed blood running from his anus. Donald Hyden's mother was the first parent to testify at Bonin's first murder trial, in November 1981.

From my point of view, as Clinical Psychologist Vonda Pelto who knew Bonin, his need to satisfy his base instincts had reached a point of no return. Four victims in 21 days, and now all he fantasized about was the next hunt, the next victim, the next kill.

19

Sgt. 'Jigsaw' St. John of LAPD & Sgt. David Kushner of LA Sheriff's Dept.

Bonin had committed four murders in three weeks and legendary LAPD Robbery-Homicide detective, Sgt. John P. St. John, was alarmed. A 38-year veteran of the LAPD, St. John became famous after solving a murder in the Griffith Park area, near Downtown Los Angeles. A difficult case because the victim was completely dismembered, St. John was affixed with the moniker "Jigsaw John" and it stuck. Involved in hundreds of murder cases, St. John had been investigating a series of murders, classified as 'homosexually oriented,' since February 1973.

Officially started when a 17-year-old boy was strangled and dumped on the Terminal Island Freeway in San Pedro, Bonin's murder spree seemed connected. St. John was partnered with Sgt. Kirk Mellecker in the Robbery-Homicide Division, a department with a sterling reputation amongst law enforcement agencies internationally.

During the six-years from the first victim to when Bonin started killing, over 20 homicides were deemed part of that series. That entire time Sgt. St. John was tasked with "the responsibility of coordinating and monitoring similar murder cases throughout Southern California."

Randy Kraft was operating at the same time killing, raping and mutilating men 18-25 years of age, but the victims were older and killed differently. Unlike Kraft, Bonin didn't mutilate his victims nor use a belt to strangle them to death, but who could know since Grabs was stabbed so many times and Hyden was pierced with a blade postmortem.

Questions would have been raised: Was this the same killer or killers changing tactics or was a new player in the game? Were there multiple killers playing copycat or was it one person? Was it a group operating together or one person? From experience, they knew serial killers rarely change their methods, however, St. John and Kushner never discounted anything.

20

Bonin & Butts Victim #4
David Murillo, September 9, 1979

In the previous five weeks Bonin had committed four murders, three with Vernon Butts, and was interrupted during a possible murder scenario by an OC Sheriff. Arrested on **Sexual Perversion** charges, he was released and scheduled for a September 18 hearing on the charges, which also included a drug violation component, and to determine if he violated parole. Parole violations would bring up old charges and could send him to prison for many years. With his immediate future looking murky, Bonin went on the hunt for another victim.

In the city of La Mirada, which borders North Long Beach, Bonin was cruising on Valley View Blvd. when he saw his next victim, 17-year-old David Murillo. David was just getting off his bike and walking it slowly to a bus stop, just short of the corner. His mother warned him to be careful, but David thought he could handle himself in any situation.

Like the previous Robert Wirostek murder sequence, this murder story is also split into two versions. First is from the December 1980 interview with LA Deputy District Sterling Norris and detectives, the second from Bonin's written confessions.

Bonin left out many gruesome details during the interview as he was still hoping to avoid the death penalty. Here is interview version:

"So he put his bike in there, and he got into the seat. We continued on down the way, and I started talking to him about having sex and everything. Uh, I believe this youngster's name was David Murillo, yes. We, uh, he was kind of for it, kind of against it. I got on Valley View, or a street before that, I'm, I'm not sure of the street, there was a gas station on the southeast corner, I went around pulled around on the east side of the gas station where there was a wall, and an apartment building on the other side of the wall, and at this time the youngster got out of the van, and, uh, he wanted to get his bike and everything, and he says, well, you know, they got all these things happening, uh you might have a gun or knife around there."

"I opened up my side of the van and told him well go and ahead and look, and he looked around and seen that there was nothing. So I says well we won't do nothing then, I said go ahead and get in and I'll drive you on down to Valley View, so okay we were still west of Valley View. He got in, and then I shut the door, rolled up the window, and locked the door, and I said oh come in the back, I said just let me give you some head, he goes no and so I pulled him back there.

"At that time I tied him up and gagged him, and uh did nothing more, drove over to Vern's and, uh, Vern, had some company at the time, it was a guy named Neil Mendez that was there, along with I don't know who else, and Vern said he couldn't get away.

"I said well at least come with me so I can gas up, cause I cannot go gas up with this person in the van at the same time, so he did, and on the way to the gas station, he started fondling with the boy, and uh, started sucking on him some. And when he came back, he says look, he says I'm gonna go in and tell Neil, and there was a girl there, in fact I, here there was girl, uh, that he told me of. He went in and told them he had to go out on a magic trick thing, he brought some magic stuff with him, and he decided to come with me, and uh I went on the freeway and drove.

"He started uh, sucking the kid off. At that point he got done, he took over driving, and, uh, and I did my thing with the youngster, and, uh, at this point in time were somewhere way out on Highway 101, heading out towards Malibu again, uh, Vern kept driving, and I strangled the youngster, and then we, uh, I un, I untied him, and turned and headed back southbound on the freeway, stopped along the side, and Vern helped me get him out of the van, and at this point the youngster was dead, and uh I had a crowbar behind there, and hit him in the back of the head two or three times. And, uh, we threw him off the embankment. We drove further south on the freeway, and Vern was driving, and I wiped off the bike fingerprints, and we pulled around and dropped off the bike on an on-ramp that was coming onto the freeway, and got rid of the rest of the stuff somewhere along the freeway down below, including the crowbar."

In contrast to the above statement, the following text is Bonin's written confession of what happened to David Murillo. Bonin's written confessions are more forthcoming with details and how he tormented his victims till the very end. His desire to control the situation, making him helpless, is palpable in the written confession.

"I was traveling east, I saw a kid walking his bike, called him over and asked him where Valley View is? I used this tactic a lot as then I could offer them a ride. The first thing is to get them in the van and then into the back, then they were all mine. Before I could say anything else, he said, 'could you give me a ride in the back.'

"I went around and he put his bike in the back and crawled in. I asked him if he would like to 'earn twenty dollars for giving him head?' He said, 'No, could you let me out here.' I parked behind a gas station and asked him, 'Why are you so scared?' He said, 'Because kids got killed in this type of situation.' I told him I was only interested in giving him head, then he told me, 'You may have a gun in there.'

"I told him to come on over and look around, he checked it out and was still against it. I said, 'I'll give you fifty dollars, you can get in the front seat with the door open.' He got back in, I started fondling him and said, 'Someone may see us, let's go in the back.' He refused and I told him, 'This is too dangerous, I'll just take you where you're going.' I reached over, shut the door and locked it. That done, all I had to do was get him in the back. I took his wrist and said, 'Come on in the back.' He resisted so I put my around him and pulled him back, I told him to lay there on his stomach, he was very frightened. I tied his hands behind his back to his neck, took his shoes and socks off and tied his feet, then gagged him. Then I told him he was being kidnapped.

"I called Vern and told him I had a package, that is how I would refer to a guy tied up. Vern told me had company, I told him I only needed him for about ten minutes so I could get some gas. Vern came out and I said, 'Hey Vern, take a look at this beauty.' I showed him his smooth chest and that turned Vern on. Vern was fondling the kid and even gave him some head, by the time we got back from getting gas Vern said, 'I'm going with you, he is too good to pass up.'

"He told his friends he had to do a magic show and go for an audition. I headed off to the Freeway 605 north, I told Vern to take over driving. I got in the back with the kid and took the gag off, I slapped him once, pulled out my dick and told him to suck on it. I got his pants off and squeezed his nuts real hard, he screamed. I pulled down his pants and fucked him, I told him 'he was the best fuck I ever had.' I traded places with Vern and he started sucking on him. After a while he said he couldn't get him hard, I told Vern to hit the kid a little for encouragement.

"Vern squeezed the kid's nuts and he screamed, about five minutes later Vern said he was half hard. I pulled over to the side of the freeway and parked and told the kid, 'You get hard or I'll fuck you up so bad you'll wish you were dead, and I squeezed his nuts.' The kid was terrified. Watch this I told Vern, I started masturbating him and told him to get hard, within a minute he was hard. I looked at Vern and said, 'All it takes is a little something to convince him.' Vern went back to sucking and I continued to drive.

"Vern got bored and told me was through. He took over driving and I got in the back. I told the kid, 'Sorry kid, you're going to die.' I told him how we had killed the other guys, then took the iron bar and hit him across the chest, and squeezed his nuts, I hit him many times on the chest and throat. He didn't cry on any of these, I don't think he could. I told him I was going to torture him like this until he was ready to die. I told him that I'd strangle him at that time.

"He asked him to stab him instead, and I said no. I hit him some more and asked him if he was ready to die, he said yes. I put the iron bar across his neck and pushed down until I felt he was dead. I untied and took his clothes all off. I headed south and stopped along the freeway, put my flashers on, I waited till there was no traffic coming and through him out."

On Wednesday, September 12, 1979 the nude body of 17-year-old David Murillo was found near the 101 freeway. For the third time in less than five weeks Kushner and Fueglein, of the LA Sherriff's Department, were called to a Bonin murder scene.

After viewing Murillo's bruised and battered corpse, the experienced detectives must have strongly suspected that Grabs, Hyden and Murillo were all perpetrated by the same person or persons. He collected evidence at the crime scene and attended the autopsy, which was conducted by Dr. Ronald Kornblum, an employee of Ventura County. When he testified at Bonin's trial, Kornblum was Chief of Forensic Medicine for LA County.

At the autopsy, Dr. Kornblum reported ligature marks on the neck, wrists and ankles. There was injury to the skull and the victims' rectum was distended. During court testimony, he indicated the windpipe was fractured from the pressure of the iron bar being pressed on the front of his neck.

Essentially, Bonin used the tire iron to bash Murillo's head. Sgt. Haas testified that Murillo and his bike were found just off two freeway onramps eight miles apart. The three victims Kushner was investigating were all dumped a short distance from each other and just off or near the Ventura Freeway, Highway 101, at the border of LA and Ventura County, north of Malibu.

In 1979 the communications amongst law enforcement agencies were handled by bulky and large Teletype machines, phone calls and exchange of paper files. Originally conceived as an automatic telegram printing device, the 1970s Teletype machine was a typewriter mounted on a metal platform and hooked to the phone lines. A message could be typed in and sent to single or multiple locations where the message would be printed out automatically.

When pictures or wanted posters needed to be sent, law enforcement agencies used a forerunner of the fax machine where a piece of paper was strapped to a rolling metal disk that sent info to the receiver to be printed out in single sheets of paper.

At this time, an interesting incident took place with Vernon Butts. Three years earlier, Ron Close was introduced to Butts, by Neil Mendez, at a pizza joint next to the Keystone Lanes bowling alley in Norwalk (Mendez also introduced Bonin to Scott Fraser). They hung out together, partied together and had a number of mutual friends.

He participated in the Mystery Parties, which Butts organized, and knew of his occult practices. Close later told investigators that, in September of 1979, Butts started acting really strange; considering how bizarre he was this must have been disturbing behavior.

One night, at Butts' house, he took out an ax blade, put it up to Close's neck and said, "I'd like to see your blood gush out and hear your screams." When Vern removed the blade, Ron Close picked up his things and never saw him again.

21

Court Hearing, Jailtime & Early Release
September 18 to November 12-13, 1979

On Tuesday, September 18, 1979 Bonin appeared for his hearing regarding the August 9 arrest and parole revocation. His parole was revoked, and he was remanded into custody for a six-month sentence.

Then on Monday, October 15, 1979 the Parole Revocation Hearing Decision was surprisingly reversed, claiming an "error in judgment led to a decision which is unreasonable in view of the facts." It requested that "the decision of September 18, 1979, revoking the parole of Mr. William Bonin be reversed and that the Parole status of Mr. Bonin prior to the hearing be reinstated."

The application was based on two stipulations: "1) Alleged unlawful possession (11357c Health & Safety Code) it is undisputed by the evidence that the controlled substance was the property of the passenger of the vehicle who had hid the substance in the vehicle unbeknown to Mr. Bonin.

"Therefore Mr. Bonin did not exercise requisite dominion or control over said substance to fall within the meaning of the said code section. 2) 288a (b) (1) all evidence that was available clearly reflected that (a) Mr. Bonin was informed by 'victim' that he was eighteen years of age (b) that said victim's physical appearance supported a reasonable belief of minor's declaration that he was in fact 18 years of age. Therefore, Mr. Bonin, with no contrary evidence present, entertained a reasonable 'Good Faith' belief that said 'victim' was of the age of majority. Said 'good faith' belief being a defense to the alleged code violation."

Bonin lucked out again. Due to a technical error, he gained release after serving two out of the six-month sentence, had his parole status reinstated and escaped having to serve out the remainder of the original prison sentence. As mentioned previously, the new California sentencing laws caused considerable confusion when calculating how much time he had to serve, thus leading to an early release.

As a result, based on the killing timeline and other evidence, Bonin was released November 12 or 13 and wasted no time getting back to business!

22

Bonin Kills Alone #2
Wallace Tanner, November 14, 1979

Two months of confinement, along with realizing he was extremely lucky to have been released, increased Bonin's appetite for the hunt and the kill. His sixth victim was Wallace Tanner, the only one dumped in San Diego County. Bonin was familiar with the area, having made a number of work deliveries there. He decided it was a good place to keep the police on the back foot, unable to pinpoint a specific area from where he was operating from or lived.

At 11:00 pm, Bonin started cruising around Long Beach, deftly prowling the fog shrouded streets of the coastal city. Late on a Wednesday night, in mid-November, the streets were largely empty, devoid of anyone walking, seeking a ride, or possibly hustling on the streets. For hours Bonin visited spots where potential victims might be lurking. His anxiety growing as the hunger propelled him forward, devoid of any feelings of compassion, only aware of the base needs gnawing at his brain.

Around 2:00 a.m., after three hours of cruising around, Bonin decided to give up and go home. He headed south on Pacific Coast Highway to the Long Beach roundabout, which connected to Lakewood Blvd. going north. Still living up in Silverado Canyon, he would go north to Chapman, a road which took him on a straight line into the canyon.

Tragically for Wallace Tanner, Bonin spotted him hitchhiking home at the very moment of him giving up the search. Having just attended a Jethro Tull rock concert in Long Beach, Tanner was seeking a ride home to the City of Orange, east of Long Beach.

Bonin pulled over, "Where you goin?"

"I was at the concert and am going home, near the Orange Circle, I have to get to Carson Blvd.," Tanner innocently replied.

"I can give you a ride there, it's on my way home, get in," Bonin said.

"Thanks," he said, crawling up into the van.

"You're in luck, I live up in Silverado Canyon. You're on the way, but you know it's dangerous being out so late and hitchhiking" Bonin said with false concern, creating small talk.

"Yeh, I know, but I dun it lots of times."

"Really," Bonin said, setting up the next move, "you ever get picked up by guys."

"Sure, all the time."

"Did they ever approach you, you know, for sex?" Bonin excitedly asked.

"Yeh," the innocent boy replied, sinking deeper into the net.

"They ever offer you money."

"No."

Bonin, using his most common approach, altered it slightly to lure in the unsuspecting victim.

"Well, what if a guy told you he'd like to give you a head job, and would pay you $50?"

"Wow, that's a lot of money, I don't know," Tanner said thinking about it for a few second, "Yeh, I'd probably take him up on it."

"Well, I'll do just that, if you're interested?" he said alluringly. Bonin looked at him and reached over to softly run his hand up Tanner's high towards his crotch.

Bonin was pleased when Tanner looked at him with the "smile of someone who couldn't believe he was being offered 50 bucks for this." Keeping his hand up against his crotch, he noticed that young Tanner was responding to his touch.

"You have a lot of dick for a youngster, what about it?" Bonin said with an inviting smile.

"Okay, where?" Tanner quickly responded.

"We'll park someplace," Bonin said, happily anticipating the emotional release from killing again. He turned right on Carson Blvd. and found a safe place to park.

They proceeded into the back of the van and Bonin got to work. He pulled the boys pants down, got him fully excited and then began sucking vigorously. Tanner responded to Bonin with moans of pleasure, appearing to be enjoying himself. After a couple of minutes, Bonin stopped and played the next card.

"I'll get some tissue, I don't like taking the cum, you just keep jacking yourself off."

Tanner was on the right side of van, unable to see Bonin pull out string and an eight-inch knife and leave them on the front seat. He nestled back up to Tanner, then got ready for the final move.

"You want to make another $25?"

"Sure."

"Let me tie your hands behind your back."

"No way, that ain't too cool, you might decide to butt fuck me." Tanner protested in horror.

"No, I just get a nut when I suck someone off while they're tied up," Bonin flashed back, trying to get him to cooperate voluntarily.

"No, I don't wanna do it," he told Bonin emphatically.

Knowing it wasn't going to work the easy way, Bonin reached over the seat and grabbed the knife and a slightly broken pair of handcuffs. He put the cuffs in his pocket and the knife in his right hand, then whirled around at full speed and pounced on the boy. Straddling the helpless boy, he pointed the knifepoint against his throat, "Yes I am, now fucking turn over or so help me I'll stick you right now."

Scared and shocked by the knife, Tanner refused to surrender without a fight.

"There's no way I'll let you tie me up. You'll butt fuck me for sure, so go ahead and stick me," Tanner bravely told Bonin.

"Look, I'm not interested in fucking you. All I want to do is suck you off while you're tied up. Hey, the handcuffs don't work good," Bonin told him with false sincerity.

"Handcuffs, forget it," he screamed back.

"All right fucker, turn over." Bonin exploded at him, "the game playing is over." Tanner refused to comply. "I'm going to start pushing this blade into your throat until you turn over. If it penetrates before you turn over, I'll shove it in."

Tanner had attempted to call Bonin's bluff, but the moment of truth was at hand. Bonin started pushing in the knifepoint as he twisted his left arm, causing him to relent and turn over. His fate was sealed!

Bonin pushed Tanner's left arm up high up, behind his back, and then put his full weight on him while getting the handcuffs out. He secured the left wrist in the working side of the cuff and told him to put his right hand behind his back. Tanner refused, still exhibiting fight mixed with hope. Bonin put the knife between his teeth and punched him with all his power in the stomach, causing pain and bringing compliance.

"You waste any more of my time and I'll fucking kill you," Bonin whispered with full menace. He fumbled around, getting the other wrist in the handcuffs before securing both hands with three-inch wide surgical tape. While Bonin breathed a sigh of relief, Tanner drowned in fear, his heart blasting out of his chest because he was at the mercy of an unhinged sexual predator and sadistic murderer.

"So you want to cause trouble and you don't like getting fucked," Bonin said while stripping off the child's pants. "We'll see how you like this."

After delivering a series of devastating punches to Tanner's side and back, Bonin reached around to cover his mouth with his hand. Having absolute control of the situation, Bonin brutally and forcefully sodomized the boy, taking out months of frustration, anger and tension on Tanner. The musty van filled with muffled screams of pain and the disgusting sounds of Bonin's furious sexual assault.

After a few minutes Bonin was done, the sexual tension was gone but the total release only half complete. A thick chain was retrieved, and then Bonin tied a loop in it before lying it down with a tire iron next to Tanner's face.

"You ain't going to say one fuckin' word to anyone, are you?" Bonin asked with command.

"No, No, No, I won't, I swear, please let me go," Tanner pleaded.

Bonin grabbed his nuts and started fondling them and put his other hand on Tanner's handcuffed wrists, making sure he was tied securely and couldn't wiggle out of confinement.

"If you want a little taste of what you'll get," Bonin said before yanking his arms up between his shoulder blades, eliciting a soft cry from him. Bonin squeezed his nuts hard, and the boy screamed aloud in pain. Startled from the realization he was not gagged, and the noise might attract attention, Bonin again straddled Tanner.

"Here is what I'm going to do. I'm going to render you unconscious. Then, I'll dress you and put you out somewhere."

"You don't have to do that, I won't say anything," Tanner said, pleading for mercy.

"You have no choice kid. That's the way it's going to be, if you don't shut up, I won't stop strangling you when you pass out,"

With the chain around his neck and the tire iron inserted in the loop, Bonin starting twisting until Tanner started struggling for air.

"If you want to struggle, well, you'll die for it," a resigned and satisfied Bonin said as Tanner began to lose consciousness. Right at the moment when it seemed he stopped struggling, Tanner's right hand broke free. Bonin quickly grabbed it and tightened the loop around his neck to make sure he was dead.

"I felt powerful as the kid's life drained out. I felt tired but fulfilled, I don't need anyone else with me, I am strong enough to go it alone," Bonin later wrote.

Wallace Tanner was gone; another destroyed life, another family damaged; another community shocked; another future ruined. All his tomorrows were gone so William Bonin could sleep easier and put his mind at rest, till the next time!

Bonin headed south on the I-5 for the Ortega Highway and then decided to continue south, checking roads along the way till he found a deserted place near San Diego. As in Long Beach, the area was socked in with coastal fog that concealed his movements. Tanner was the only victim dumped in the San Diego area. From Malibu to San Diego and on to Palm Springs and up to the Cajon Pass, hundreds of miles separated the areas where police were finding bodies deposited by Bonin.

23

Bonin & Butts Victim #5
John Doe, November 21, 1979

One week after getting out of jail and immediately killing Wallace Tanner, it was time for Bonin and Butts to get back together for another "outing." After a short conversation, they decided to go out the next day and "find somebody, have sex with them, and kill him."

Crawling into bed, Bonin already knew sleep would allude him, being much too excited thinking about what tomorrow would bring. Anxiously, Bonin twisted and turned, willing the sun to come so he could get going. Vern told him he wanted to kill someone using an ice pick, Bonin was willing to try it to keep Vern hunting with him. On his way to the van, he grabbed the newspaper off the front lawn, drove to McDonalds and picked up a cup of coffee, black, having learned to drink it that way in prison.

Sitting in the booth, he plowed through the paper hoping to find an article about himself. But there were none to find since he had been incarcerated for two months, and his latest victim, Tanner, was dumped in San Diego a week earlier. His exploits were so sporadic, and geographically so wide, that no set pattern had emerged, and law enforcement was still in the dark while sharing little with the press.

In 1981 Bonin told Vonda Pelto at LA Men's Central Jail: "It got to the point that I couldn't live without it, I had to go out and kill. It was a driving force within me, as if there was something inside that took control and made me kill. I have no power over these decisions."

He said at times it felt like The Devil was leading him to the boys who were "chosen to die." There were other times when he would pray, "Lord, lead me to where you want me to go so that I will find the boys you know must die."

Bonin knew that Vern liked to party late and wake up late, but since it was a weekday, he probably would be up by now. Bonin parked beside Vern's garage house, walked up, and started banging on the front door. After a couple of minutes, he answered.

"You want to go out and get someone?" he asked, already knowing the answer.

"Yeh, let's go, I'm ready to roll."

After getting dressed, Vern grabbed some rope, two different types, and an icepick. They set out and cruised around locally for a couple of hours. Having no luck, they headed to Hollywood, a good hunting ground and where they had found Donald Hyden three months earlier.

Shortly after turning onto Santa Monica Blvd, a notorious hangout for young male hustlers, he pulled up beside a young boy hitchhiking at a bus bench. He fit the bill perfectly; five-foot six-inches tall, shoulder length light brown hair and about 130 pounds. He claimed he was 18-years old but looked younger; he was just another lost soul on the streets of Hollywood hustling to stay alive. Bonin's contempt for this type of person knew no bounds.

Bonin signaled the teenage kid over to the van, "Hey, how ya doin?"

"Ok, what do you want?"

"You out hustling? Bonin asked.

"Are you a cop?"

"No, I'm out for a little action, you up for it?"

"How much?" the boy pointedly asked, not wanting to waste time.

"Twenty bucks, sound good?"

"Ok, I'll do it."

"Get in and we'll find a place."

Unaware of the danger, he got into the back. He sat behind them with Bonin driving and Vern in the passenger seat. Around 12:00 noon on a cool November day, Bonin headed east on Santa Monica Blvd. and entered the Hollywood Freeway, heading north towards the San Fernando Valley. The further the Death Van progressed away from Hollywood, the more agitated and nervous the boy became.

"I didn't agree to an all day, unless you want to pay extra," he told them.

Vern started asking questions, trying to distract and calm him down. He said he lived in Huntington Beach, close to the ocean, and his family owned a bakery. Bonin got off the freeway in Studio City, about a 15-minute drive, and found a place behind a closed gas station to park. He threw the van into park, crawled between the seats, sat down and looked down at the boy's trusting face.

"Hey Vern, do you want to do him first?"

"Nah, I'm trying to think up some new magic tricks for my act," he replied, preferring to stay up front.

Bonin leaned down, took the boy's face into his hands, and French kissed him. To Bonin's surprise, he felt nothing, no sexual arousal whatsoever. Bonin unbuttoned the kid's shirt, removed it, and ran his hands over the almost hairless chest. He was shocked at feeling nothing, especially in that situation.

"Listen kid, if you let me tie you up, I'll pay you some extra."

"Sure, but can we just hurry up? I want to get back to town. I got plans for later."

"No problem, you'll be finished here before you know it."

As directed, he laid down on his stomach and allowed his hands and feet to bound. Bonin rolled him over onto his back, then sat back on his hunches.

"Well let's get going, do your thing so I can get out of here," the boy said anxiously.

Bonin was devoid of sexual excitement. What was going on? Bonin looked down at the boy lying before him and thought back to the time when he was gang raped. Suddenly he realized it wasn't about sex anymore, it was about killing and the power over life and death. Being in total control for the first time in his life; having another's life in his hands became the primary motivation for William Bonin.

Bonin straddled the boy's back.

"This is something new, I don't even have my clothes off. Don't see how you can butt fuck me now," the boy said with sarcasm.

"I don't want to fuck you," Bonin while leaning closer to the boy's ear. "I'm going to kidnap you and hold you for ransom." Then he punched him multiple times in the chest and stomach to make sure he was scared and cooperative.

Facing Vern and Bonin, the boy knew the odds were against him and he had to play along. Bonin got back in the driver's seat, headed for the Hollywood Freeway and thence to Interstate 5. One hour later, they were in the desolate hills of the Tejon Pass, better known as The Grapevine. This road travels high into the hills and drops down to connect Southern California with the Central Valley. The sixty-mile drive must have been agonizing for the boy, stuck in the back of the van, not knowing where they were going, or his ultimate fate?

High in the hills, Bonin exited the highway and found a deserted spot. Vern and Bonin immediately started beating him up all over again, roughing him up in between pointless questions. Then Bonin put his hands around his neck and began squeezing the life out of the innocent boy. Fighting his captors with every fiber of his being, Bonin's grip loosened, and the boy bucked him off. Bonin fell against the side of van as boy was attempting to gain leverage by sitting up.

"You little shit!"

"Here, use this iron bar," Vern said. "It will make it easier." Bonin grabbed the bar, shoved the kid back down, pressing the rod down on his neck.

"Are you going to kill me, why are you doing this to me?" the boy screamed and sobbed in horror. Bonin gave him no answer and pressed down harder, then Bonin let up on the pressure and said, "Do you really want to know why you have to die?"

"Yes! Why? Why? I don't ..."

"Your folks paid me to find you and kill you." The boy's eyes widened, staring straight up. Bonin pressed the bar down again till the life drained out of his body.

"Why did I lie to him?" Bonin asked. Vern's face went blank, having no answer. Bonin realized he wanted this boy to die believing that nobody loved him.

"I wanted him to feel like I have felt all of my life. No one has ever loved me."

After believing he was dead, Bonin untied him and shoved the icepick into both nostrils and his ear, just to make sure the job was done. About 85-miles from home, in the mountains, Bonin needed to figure how to dispose of him. Rather than drive back to the city, with the risk of getting pulled over with a body in the van, Bonin drove 35-miles in the opposite direction. After dropping down from the mountains, into the flat Central Valley heading towards Bakersfield, they diverted off Highway 5 and headed west on 166 into an agricultural area near the town of Taft.

Victim number seven, forever known as John Doe, was dumped in a shallow irrigation ditch off a lonely road between crop fields. He was discovered nine-days later, on November 30, in Kern County. In an effort to confuse authorities, Bonin had dumped bodies in five county jurisdictions throughout Southern California: the others being Mark

Shelton in San Bernardino County, Robert Wirostek in Riverside County, multiple victims in the northwest LA County and Wallace Tanner in San Diego County.

Orange County, south of LA, had yet to experience Bonin's handiwork; but that was about to change. Bonin and Vern quickly headed back to The Grapevine and towards home, over 120-miles away. While traveling through the hills, Vern told Bonin he was hungry and they stopped to eat at a local restaurant, near the middle of the mountain pass. Nothing like a kidnapping and a murder to give one an appetite!

24

Bonin Kills Alone #3
Dennis Fox, November 29 or 30, 1979

One week after killing with Vernon Butts, Bonin was consumed with hunger for another victim. Four months into his murder spree, Bonin had claimed seven victims, five with Butts and two alone. One lucky boy got away when Bonin was arrested.

Mrs. Fox stated that Dennis lived in Long Beach and didn't have a car, saying, "He usually took the bus, or I drove him to classes at Long Beach City College at Pacific Coast Highway campus. He was 17 and independent, living in his own apartment in Long Beach. We had occasional contact, he was a responsible young person who always carried his California ID, money and pictures in his wallet. Unfortunately, he also hitchhiked around Long Beach. November 17th was the last day I saw him."

More than likely Bonin encountered Fox on November 29 or 30, when he was cruising around Long Beach looking for his next victim. His written confession offers a grim, depressing description of the murder and shows Bonin's callous attitude towards life.

"I was down in Long Beach again and I picked up a guy who was obviously a hustler. I said, 'How's it going.' He told me, 'Not so good.' I asked him where he was headed and he said home. 'You into the gay scene?' He said yes and I asked him, 'You interested in getting it on.' He said, 'Yes, for a price, I have rent to pay.' I offered him twenty bucks, and told him, 'I'd like to fuck you.' He said, '30 bucks and you got a deal.' I said 'Ok.'

"We parked and got into the back of the van, I fucked him and had a good nut. Then I brought out the knife and told him to put his hands behind his back. He said, 'What's this?' I told him, 'I don't have no 30 bucks, I don't even have five, so I'm going to tie you up and put you out.' He told me, 'Hey you don't have to do that, just let me out and there will no hassle.'

"I told him, 'Look, put your hands behind your back and there won't be no hassle, either do it or I will stop wasting my time and just stick you. He put his hands behind his back, I tied him up with string, then I took his shoes and socks off and tied his legs. 'You didn't want to do what I said the first time, I'm going to drop you off a long way away from here.' Fox said, 'Come on man, I did what you wanted me to do.' I hit him several times and then squeezed his nuts, I said, 'You don't say one word unless I ask you a question, you do and I'll stop and give you double what you just got, do you understand?' He said, 'Yes.'

"I drove out the 91 East, found a frontage road and got off, I parked right on the road and got in the back with him. I hit him a couple of times and then I told him I was going to strangle him until he was out and there wasn't any way he was going to talk me out of it, and if he tried I'd just kill him instead. I told him it was easier if he just let himself go, if he fought against it, it would be hard to tell when he was out and I might accidentally kill him. I killed and untied him. I took the rest of his clothes off, and looked to see if it was clear.

"I saw a car coming from behind me, so I couldn't drop him there where I planned to. I had found the place first, then killed him. I started up the van and drove off. I got to where I could turn and headed in the opposite direction. There was a center island right after I made my turn and headed back toward the freeway, I saw the car that had been coming up behind me, it was a California Highway Patrol cruiser, he slowed and I just kept on driving. I watched my rear-view mirror, he didn't turn, it was a close call.

"I got back on the 91 west and then I got the 55 south, then took I-5 south and got off at Ortega Highway, I went down Ortega till I found the wilderness park far away from San Juan Capistrano and found a place, I kept the van on the road and my parking lights on as if I had something wrong. I opened the side doors, then I looked and listened, there were no cars coming. I dumped the body of Fox out."

Dennis Fox's nude body was found in the late afternoon of Sunday, December 2, 1979. Devoid of any personal data, his identity would not be determined for several days. Fox was discovered in Casper's Regional Park in Southeast Orange County by a Mr. Alvarez, who later reported that he pulled off the road on Ortega Highway, about 2 to 3 miles from the park.

He noticed what he thought was a body and notified Park Ranger Joseph Perry.

The body was laid out up towards the mountains and away from the highway, about half a mile from a rock quarry where people go swimming. Perry notified the OC Sheriff's, and they arrived in about an hour. Tony Rojo, an OC investigator, told the court that he met Perry at the site.

After he was led to the area where the body was found, Rojo saw a male subject lying down in some bushes. Rojo also stated that he found some tire marks, and he did not know if they were related to the crime scene or not, so he protected the crime scene.

Criminalist Sandy Wiersema collected penal swabs and a ball of fibers from the victim's penis. She reported that his body was at the bottom of an embankment of a hill. Fox was laying on his right side and had apparently been rolled down the hill, coming to rest against a metal post that was part of the barbed wire fence. The body had ligature marks on its wrists, ankles, neck and had been there for several days prior to discovery.

William Clarence King, OC Sheriff's Deputy Coroner, reported that Dennis Fox had been dead for nearly three days based on postmortem and the coagulation of blood. No clothes, property or ID were found around or near the body. A component of saliva, amylase, was found on his left nipple as well as on his penis, with abrasions to the scrotal area. The cause of death, according to Dr. Robert Richards, was ligature strangulation.

Marks found on the victim's neck were consistent with the ligature being twisted during strangulation. Fox's ankles and wrists were wrapped with a very thin material prior to death, while facial injuries, caused by a closed fist to nose and mouth, all occurred prior to extremis.

The dumping of Dennis Fox in OC marked the sixth different Southern California county jurisdiction to investigate a Bonin murder. Eight murders committed in four months, all of a similar nature, dumped all over Southern California with little or no hard evidence. Just connecting them all together would have been a Herculean chore for even the best of detectives.

Dennis Fox was the first Bonin victim to land on the desks of OC Sheriff homicide detectives Sgt. Bernie Esposito and Sgt. James Sidebotham. Both were involved in the Bonin cases till the end. Sidebotham became famous as the chief investigator in the Randy Kraft case, a man who drugged, raped, mutilated and strangled young males, from 18 to 25, with a belt. His murder spree overlapped when Bonin was operating and their methods were eerily similar, although Bonin went after younger victims and never drugged them.

Kraft's methods of mutilation were gruesome, something which Bonin generally never did. In retrospect, it is easy to see why detectives suspected Kraft's murders belonged to Bonin. Kraft was not arrested till 1983, when he was pulled over for suspected drunk driving with a dead victim in the passenger seat.

25

Bonin Kills Alone #4
John Kilpatrick, December 10, 1979

Bonin was totally in the "killing zone." Little else mattered as the obsessive power of killing, combined with a loathing of feeling powerless, meant four victims in less than a month were murdered.

Bonin's written confession puts that on full display, "I went out looking for someone to get it on with. This was actually an excuse for going out and killing someone. I'd say to myself I was going out for sex, yet I knew it was actually going out to kill. I wanted to see the life leaving their bodies. I went to Long Beach again and cruised down Long Beach Blvd. I got down to the Bus Depot and spotted an extremely good-looking blond I figured to be about 17 years old. He was on the phone so I drove around the bus terminal and came out next to the phone. He had just gotten off it."

Bonin watched as John Kilpatrick, 15-years old, crossed the street and began walking north on Long Beach Blvd. After shadowing him for a few minutes, realizing he was attracted to him, Bonin slowly rolled up to chat. Kilpatrick lied to Bonin about his age, saying he was 18, before being offered "20 bucks for showing me some of Los Angeles." Knowing Bonin wanted sex, he jumped in with little hesitation. After coming to terms, they got in the back and Bonin harbored second thoughts about killing the boy. Blond, young and slim, he hit the right buttons and Bonin fantasized about a relationship with him.

Then everything went sideways when Bonin tried to finger Kilpatrick's anus while receiving a blowjob. Kilpatrick jumped up and protested, saying, "I don't get fucked." That was all the motivation Bonin needed.

Bonin acquiesced, then asked him about doing a 69, which Kilpatrick agreed to and calmed down. Bonin did his classic "I need to get tissues" move and retrieved a knife and string from the front, then put the knife to Kilpatrick's throat and told him to rollover. Shocked and frightened, he readily acceded to Bonin's wishes before getting his hands behind his back.

"You don't get fucked, huh, well fuck you," Bonin said menacingly and then proceeded to violently sodomize the boy, although he did not climax.

Bonin stopped after a few minutes and then drove to his mother's house. He took Kilpatrick inside, using his van to cover their movements. Once inside, the frightened boy revealed his true age of 15 in hopes of obtaining mercy, none was forthcoming.

"Well kid," Bonin said, while squeezing his testicles to make him scream, "you'll never make it to 16 if you don't do exactly what you're told." A glimmer of hope and overwhelming fear filled every corner of the boy's mind, something Bonin enjoyed instilling in his victims. Bonin went to the kitchen, to get some string, and then whipped him with it until he cried. Then he wrapped it around his neck and strangled John Kilpatrick to death. Bonin put him in the van and drove 55-miles northeast to Rialto, a city adjacent to Interstate 15 in San Bernardino County. Bonin found a spot near Rialto Airport and dumped him in the brush.

Killing was now part and parcel of a twisted personality which evolved over decades. Claiming power over a powerless existence brought him to a place where nothing was sacred, for Bonin life was cheap and his for the taking. John Kilpatrick was Bonin's ninth victim and the second one left in San Bernardino County. His first victim, Mark Shelton with help from Vernon Butts, was dumped in the mountains of Cajon Pass four months earlier.

26

Bonin Kills Alone #5
Michael McDonald, January 1, 1980

On New Year's Day 1980, while Bonin's mother was on vacation in Hawaii, he celebrated The New Year contrary to most everyone in the world. Putting aside resolutions for positive change, Bill Bonin hit the road in the Death Van looking for action.

Three weeks after killing John Kilpatrick, he decided to pick up someone in another county, later admitting, "Where I was going was getting kind of dangerous, I felt the police were watching everyone hitchhiking and I should get out to places where no one might be watching. I needed a place where no one had been picked up."

He drove 50-miles inland, east of LA on the 10 Freeway, to the area around the Chino Airport near Ontario. Bonin quickly found a young boy walking along the road and pulled up next to him, it was 15-year-old Michael McDonald.

"Do you know where the freeway is?" Bonin asked, using his tried-and-true opening line. McDonald pointed down the road in the direction Bonin had just come from.

"Thanks, where you headed?"

"Home," the innocent boy replied.

"Is it far?"

"No, just down the road."

"Well, hop in and I'll give you a ride," Bonin said. Hoping to secure success he pulled back into traffic and baited McDonald with a $50.00 bill.

"How would you like to earn this?" he enticingly said to the boy.

"How?"

"Sell pot for me."

"Sure," he replied, brightened by the prospect of easy money. Bonin reeled in the fish one step at a time, carefully pulling on the line to keep the catch comfortable now that it was within grasp.

"Tell you what, I'll give you 5-ounces, you sell and keep $10 from each ounce. Sell them at $50 apiece. Then call me when you need some more, Okay?"

"Okay!" Michael agreed.

Bonin turned off the street and into the parking lot of an apartment building, now time to pull the fish out of the water and kill it.

"Why are you turning in?" McDonald asked with alarm.

"So I can give you the ounces without anyone seeing me."

"Okay."

While looking for a place to park, Bonin said, "Get in the back, if no one saw us I'll get in the back and give you the ounces."

While the kid crawled over the seat, Bonin drove slowly, looking for a parking place, carefully watching for prying eyes. Confident no one was around, Bonin moved to the back, eyeing the prey. When McDonald looked away, Bonin grabbed his knife and violently yanked the boy onto his stomach and straddled his back.

"I don't want to hurt you, all I want is your money," Bonin said, offering misdirection and false assurances.

"I don't have any," he screamed. Bonin searched and found no money, giving him the pretext for his next demands.

"Put your fucking hands behind your back!"

Bonin tied his hands, making sure they were secure. Then he turned the frightened boy over, unzipped his own pants. "No, money, so you are going to give me head," Bonin demanded with fury.

McDonald's brain was on fire, adrenalin rushing through every corner of his young body, his heart pumping blood at such a pace it was beyond feeling. Everything happened so fast, his conception of events rapidly pushing past his naïve understanding. He stared blankly at Bonin, looking into the cold eyes as Bonin's fist crashed down on his chest with full force.

"Give me head," Bonin menacingly told him, trying not to be too loud.

Michael complied, but after a few minutes Bonin told him to stop and rolled him over on his stomach, then yanked the boy's pants down. Bonin punished him by squeezing his testicles, eliciting screams of pain. Having no idea what lay ahead, he could only pray for deliverance. Bonin vigorously raped him, but only for a short time. Enjoying the power of sexual domination, with cries for mercy ever present, quickly bored Bonin because he was there for the killing.

Bonin strangled 15-year-old Michael McDonald, watching life leave his young body, robbing another child of his future. Within the cloak of night, Bonin searched for a place to dump the body. After going past two freeways in search of a lonely spot, he ended up on a desolate road in Chino. Unlike other victims, McDonald was dumped fully clothed.

While mass murderers kill many at once and expect nothing more, serial killers want to keep killing, always looking for the next one. Paradoxically, while diligent about disposing of clothing, weapons and ID papers, he never bothered to hide the bodies. Bonin's method of evasion was spreading them out geographically. Everything else, nature of victims, method of death, manner of disposal, remained largely the same.

When I asked him, during one of our meetings, if he wanted to get caught, he looked me in the eye with disbelief and said, "What, you kiddin?"

27

Reporter J.J. Maloney, Law Enforcement & An Evidence Breakthrough

Bonin had claimed ten victims in five months. Previous to his first kill, on August 4, 1979, detectives had cataloged 20 victims in six-years in "a series of homosexually oriented" murders. By January 1980 they are looking at half as many murders in an infinitely shorter time span. Leaving little evidence behind for detectives, it is nonetheless clear a serious pattern of rapid killing, with nearly identical methods, is underway and accelerating.

Should a single serial killer be responsible for the latest victims, detectives must walk a number of delicate lines:

1) Keep the public informed, 2) Maintain enough secrecy to not tip their hand and scare the killer into hiding or switching locations, 3) Try not to feed the killer's ego with media publicity. Viewing their handiwork on TV news, or in print, often fires up serial killers for more activity.

Another phenomenon is also possible: When law enforcement ignores obvious signs of a serial killer pattern or fails to devote sufficient resources to confirm, deny or explain what is happening.

Large bureaucracies move slowly and in this case four major ones were involved: LAPD and the Sheriff Departments of Los Angeles, Orange and San Bernardino Counties. Adding various small city police departments piled on more bureaucratic muddle. Up until January 1980 local reporting treated the murders as routine and unrelated police stories, but all that was about to change!

J.J. Maloney, famous for hard-hitting exposes and "straight-forward, piston driven prose," had recently started working for the **Orange County Register**, the major newspaper in the county. A native of St. Louis, he spent years in reform school before being sentenced to four life terms, at 19, for murder and armed robbery. Self-education in prison transformed him into an artist, poet and then a book reviewer for the **Kansas City Star**.

After release on parole, in 1972, Maloney went to work immediately for the **Star** and made a name for himself by co-authoring an award-winning series on prisons and his own investigative stories on the mob's control of Kansas City's River Quay. During the 1970s Maloney was nominated for five Pulitzer Prizes, won the American Bar Association's highest award, The Silver Gavel, and Best Investigative Story from the American Society of Newspaper Publishers.

Maloney would soon alter the public and political landscape regarding all the killings. Sensing a big story, he began digging around till he found enough to convince his editors. Detectives were struggling on whether the recent victims, dumped all over Southern California, were murdered by the same person? Collectively leaning towards the multiple perpetrator theory, their thinking changed when a major break came through from an Orange County criminalist.

Using a "tape-lift" technique, several "microscopic twists of avocado-green carpeting" were procured. Testing on victims from LA yielded the same fibers and, according to Sgt. Sidebotham, this led "detectives to suspect a customized van was being used. It was the first common link among the victims later traced to Bonin."

28

Bonin Kills Alone #6
James Moore, February 1, 1980

One name not on any Bonin official victim list is James Moore. As far as we know, his body was never discovered, or if it was, he was never linked to Bonin. But Moore's name does appear on Bonin's master list of victims and was described in the hand-written confessions.

Bonin describes his encounter, "I picked James Moore up on a freeway on-ramp hitchhiking, drove towards Palm Springs, killed him and dumped him in some kind of garbage dump site or official landfill location."

Maybe Moore was one of many lost kids who ran away from home and was never reported as missing? Maybe he came from out of state and is listed as a John Doe on a missing person list? Apparently, no one noticed or reported he had gone missing. The only way we know about James Moore is from Bonin himself.

29

Bonin Recruits Greg Miley for Murder
Charles Miranda & James Macabe, Feb. 3, 1980
As Told to Vonda Pelto, Ph.D. & Gene Brisco
by Gregory Miley on March 27, 2003

Key to the murders of Charles Miranda and James Macabe, with Gregory Miley, is that Bonin was slated to report to county jail the day after, February 4, 1980, to serve a six-months as part of a parole revocation sentence from his August 1979 **Sexual Perversion** arrest.

Greg met Bonin at Scott Fraser's apartment and they quickly hit it off as friends and lovers, with Bonin also viewing him as someone easy to manipulate. Two days earlier, on February 1, Bonin killed James Moore, alone, and was driven to "get in a few" before going to jail. He went to Miley's house on the night of February 2, where a family party was in full swing, to recruit him for some nasty business. Preferring to have someone along, it was easy to convince Greg to go out. He looked up to Bonin, indeed viewed him as something of a father figure. Against the wishes of his mother, who hated Bonin, Greg made the fateful decision to go with Bonin.

February 2003, Vonda Pelto's Office:
I still remember the phone call which pulled me back to a time I had struggled to leave behind. Many decades after leaving my job at Los Angeles Men's Central Jail, the nightmares had stopped while my fear and paranoia were a dark shadow from another life.

Then, with one call, my thin tissue of protection was pierced. In private practice, as a Clinical Psychologist, I had just finished up a difficult week and was leaving when the phone rang. I wanted to let it go, the door home to wine and pleasant conversation steps away. At the last second, I raced back across the office and grabbed it after the sixth ring. Beginning to regret my decision, the man hurled words at me in a staccato fusillade.

"Are you Pelto...sorry...I mean Dr. Pelto...the psychologist who worked in the LA County Jail in the eighties? The woman who saw the Freeway

Killers?" A bitter taste of bile backed up into my mouth.

"Hey, wait, just hold on for a moment please," I said before stretching the phone cord around to the back of the desk and plopping back down in the leather chair. Oh God, I'm tired and now am I going to have to deal with some nut case.

"Yes, I am," I admitted with trepidation.

"I'm Gene Brisco, I work for the Public Defender's office for Riverside County as an investigator, and I need your help. The police have a suspect in custody they believe is guilty of a murder, but I'm not satisfied that they have the right guy."

"Go on."

"The thing is this man is accused of killing a kid, I don't think he did it. It has all the earmarks of being a William Bonin kill, you know, one of the Freeway Killers you talked to."

"I don't understand what…?"

"This guy is being railroaded, and you might be a last hope in saving his life," Brisco pleaded.

My memories of the night terrors came hurdling back; dread of falling to sleep, fear of people, anxiety, anger, feeling like an outsider with friends. Decades of healing and Gene Brisco wanted to plunge me back into that world. Why should I? Did I have a responsibility to help this man? The silence on the phone hung heavy.

"Can we just please meet and talk? Sorry, guess I'm not being clear," he continued. "James Crummel, he's been arrested and is the police's prime suspect. He came under suspicion back in '97, after happening upon the remains of a kid's decomposed body. He found it dropped off Ortega Highway where we know Bonin dropped at least three bodies. But the Sheriffs figure he is good for the murder, figure he wanted to go back to the scene of his own crime."

Bonin did indeed dump multiple bodies along Ortega Highway, and I remembered him telling me about some of those murders.

"I think one of those Freeways Killers might be able to give me some information about who did kill the kid."

My stomach began to get queasy.

"I don't have any contact with them, I wrote to Munro and Bonin for a short time after I quit the jail, but I stopped answering their letters. I wanted to move forward with my life and leave the jail behind. I didn't want any part of Munro or Miley," I emphatically told Brisco.

"I've written to them at Mule Creek State Prison but haven't gotten any response," he said, "I could force them to meet with me, but they aren't going to open up. Would you mind writing to them to set up a meeting for me?"

The coroner reported the body was a young, white, male in his early teens. Due to advanced decomposition, little more could be learned. However, a few body characteristics fit the Bonin victim profile. This raised questions about Bonin possibility being responsible. I sat rocking in my chair, trying to block out Brisco's voice, as he lobbied for my assistance. Me, a possible only hope?

Bonin's co-murderers still at Mule Creek were James Munro, convicted of second-degree murder and sentenced to 15-years to life, and Gregory Miley, 25-years to life for first-degree murder (Basically Miley got two life sentences). Up for parole every few years, it was likely they would spend rest of their lives in prison. Munro's next parole hearing was in the fall of 2004. He had written to me asking for help, with a favorable letter, for the hearing. On the other hand, being unpopular with inmates and bereft of visitors, Munro asked the governor for immediate execution, stating that he was unable to cope, "I would rather die than spend the rest of his life without freedom." He was turned down.

I decided to help Detective Brisco and go to Mule Creek.

The town of Ione is nestled among oak tree covered rolling hills in California's Gold Country. A small town of seven thousand sixty-one miles southeast of Sacramento, the beautiful rolling hills are in sharp contrast to the drab prison, which is located within Ione's city limits. A high to medium custody institution, operated by the California Department of Corrections, the all-male population is largely composed serial killers, murderers, rapists, and child molesters.

Opened in June 1987, with a capacity of 1,700, it now houses about 3,600 in dormitories festooned with long rows of metal bunk beds. Bulging at the seams, with a ratio of six inmates to every staff member, tension runs high in this miniature city.

Gene Brisco and I arrived on Thursday, March 27 and were classified as a legal visit, since I was a Clinical Psychologist and he was a public official. Deputies checked our credentials and gave us the necessary paperwork, then guided us to the front of a long visitor's line. Our special treatment ended there.

When I walked through the metal detector, it alerted deputies about metal somewhere on my body. I was ordered back and told to remove shoes, rings, earrings, glasses, and watch before a second attempt. Again, the alarm squealed. The female deputy ran the wand up and down my body, nothing! I attempted another walk through the gate and the alarm sounded again.

"It's the underwire in your bra," the female deputy said. With that announcement she handed me a seam ripper and pointed to the restroom. I thought, because Brisco and I were there on official business, we would be allowed some leeway, that was wrong. Sheriff deputies treated us like we were trying to smuggle in weapons to inmates.

I looked directly at her and said, "This is a very expensive bra and I'll destroy it if I take the supports out."

"After you have removed the metal supports bring them back to me, they can be used as weapons."

"I'll just leave my bra with you and pick it up when I come back through," I suggested with confidence, since I was wearing a heavy blouse.

"You must wear a bra to enter the visitors' area," she said with deadpan finality.

Brisco went ahead as I reluctantly headed for the restroom, where two other women were cussing loudly while ruining their own bras. Since lives depend upon tight prison security, I stifled my annoyance. Once through security, I was directed across the inmate's exercise yard, surrounded by a high chain link fence with loops of razor wire on top. The visitors' building lay about 50-yards away, but it seemed further as I trudged across the cement path.

During visiting hours, Thursday and Friday from 1:30 to 2:45 and 4:00 to 7:30, no inmates were allowed in the yard. Two guard towers, with deputies holding rifles, watched vigilantly over the yard while paying close attention to my movement. After a second security check, I was shown to the attorney's interview room.

"Mileys on his way," Brisco said wearily.

Raised in the Lakewood area of Los Angeles, not far from Bonin's home in Downey, Gregory Miley's early life was characterized by illness, bad luck and tumult. The third of four children, Miley quite likely sustained a bit of brain damage due to a difficult birth.

At two, he suffered an allergic reaction to penicillin which caused a dangerous fever. Both incidents probably contributed to learning disabilities, maybe even mental retardation. Miley's mother went thru a series of abusive husbands, leaving him largely unsupervised. He repeated kindergarten, was enrolled in Special Ed classes and dropped out in the 11th grade. His life consisted of intermittent small jobs, petty crime and drug use.

Accompanied by a deputy, he arrived thirty minutes later. I watched, through the door window, as he crossed the crowded common area where inmates and visitors conversed at long metal tables. Greg pushed the door open, causing the knob to hit hard against the wall beside my chair. Startled from the noise, I bit my tongue to avoid commenting. Glancing around, Miley grinned at me and strutted to the empty chair at the round metal table.

Miley exuded an air of confidence I never saw before, which was over 20-years before at LA County Jail. Back in 1981, he was a timid child trying to avoid the death penalty. Pale with long hair back then, he now sported a tan, short white hair and a Cheshire cat grin. Greg wore a prison blue chambray shirt, tucked into jeans, and heavy brown lace-up shoes. Miley was short, about 5 foot 5, and thinner than I remembered. His recalcitrant prison record and penchant for violence worked against his chances for parole.

I introduced myself, although I felt he was not particularly interested. He checked the room out, then turned back with a sudden look of recognition and exclaimed, "Dr. Pelto, I remember you from the jail, you used to come and talk to me."

I nodded in agreement, showing him that I too remembered. "Long time ago," I commented.

"What ya doin' here?" Greg said as he scratched his head.

Brisco jumped in before I could answer, not wanting to give Miley any clue about the nature of our visit.

"Gregory, can I ask you some questions?"

"Yeah."

"Are you aware I have a tape recorder?"

"Yeah, I got eyes." Brisco ignored the sarcasm and activated the prison issued recorder.

"Mr. Miley, do you mind if we tape you?"

"No, why should I? Nobody can do nothin' to me no more."

"Greg, would you state your full name for me."

"Gregory Matthew Miley," he recited for the record.

Brisco continued, "Today is March 27, 2003, the time is 5:35 p.m., my name is Gilbert G. Brisco investigator for the Riverside Public Defender's office, and we are at Mule Creek State Prison. With me is Vonda Pelto, a psychologist, we're in an attorney room and we're here to talk to Gregory about William Bonin. We'd like to ask if you know about any murders Bonin's committed but was never charged with."

"Okay," Greg said, glancing at the ceiling.

Brisco intentionally left out details, hoping Greg knew something about the victim, who was involved or how the boy was killed? Bonin, who bragged about his exploits to potential or actual co-murderers, may have revealed clues which may assist Brisco's investigation.

"How did you first meet Bill Bonin?" I asked.

"This guy, can't remember his name, took me to Scott Fraser's apartment over in Downey, he lived close to my house. Fraser said Bonin would want to meet me, said I was his type. Well, anyway, I was there when Bonin came by, he walked right over we started talking, hit it off right away. He asks me if I'd like to go to eat and go to a movie, I said all right and we left. From then on, we hung out together, Bill took me places and even bought me clothes, he was nice to me."

"How old were you?" Brisco nodded to me to conduct the interview.

"About seventeen."

"Was your family concerned about you hanging around with a man almost fifteen years older than you?"

"Yeah, Mom never liked him."

"Did she ask you to stop seeing him?"

"Yeah, but I didn't care what they said," Miley said with a bit of sad shame. "Mom thought he was strange, scared he was a cop setting me up or something, like he might arrest me for drugs. I told her Bill was a friend who had his own business. I was real messed up, into drugs. They thought if they moved me to Bellflower, they could get me away from the drug guys I hung with."

"Did that work?"

"Hell no! Cause that's 'bout the time I met Bonin. I got into worse trouble. He was gettin' me drugs and stuff, and we were having sex at his house, I did what I wanted to do."

"How'd you get involved in the murders, I believe there were two?" I asked, searching for key info. Then something happened I never expected; Mylie started telling us all about the two killings he participated in with Bonin.

"Yeah, two kids. Macabe and Miranda," Miley said.

"What year was that?"

"1980, in February, before we moved to Texas. Bonin came over when my parents were having a party to celebrate sellin' their house, so we could move. At midnight he knocks on the door and my little sister answers and Bonin asks for me. My brother followed me to check out Bonin, then he gave me money for cigarettes. Bill drove to Fraser's parking lot, and we fooled around a bit, you know, having sex in the van, but it wasn't good, so we went to the liquor store and back home. I stayed for a few minutes, then went to talk to Bill.

"We're just talking, and he asks me if I ever killed anybody? I almost fell over, I sez 'what?' He sez, 'you ever killed anybody?' Then I sez 'no, never have.' 'Do you want to kill somebody?' he asked, I didn't know if he was serious. 'Well, I don't know, I guess, maybe' I told him, I didn't know what to say. Then my brother comes out to ask about Bonin, wantin' to know all kinds of stuff, I could see my mom in the window, waving for me to stay home, I told Bonin to drive.

"Then Bonin asks me, 'What if we went out crusin' one night and saw a hot chick hitchin' and we wanted to pick her up and make her. Then after she got in the car and wouldn't go along with us, so we made her anyway. What do you think about that?'

"Well, I sez, 'I guess that would be rape. But shit, the bitch shouldn't have got in the car with us horny dudes if she didn't want any.' 'Problem would be' Bonin sez, 'now if we would let her go, she'll go and tell the man on us and we'll get arrested, so what should we do?' 'We'd have to kill her, so she couldn't tell,' I tell him. 'You can handle that?' He asks. 'Yeah' I sez, 'I guess I could?' I was feeling high, feeling good that night," he said with false bravado.

"So, we take off to Long Beach lookin for someone to pick up. After 'bout thirty minutes with nothing, so we stopped to get chips and a drink at the store."

"What time was this?"

"Probably 'bout two in the morning. Anyways, Bonin sez, 'since you never killed anyone, I can take you home, you can forget all about this.' I sez 'fuck no!' Now I was into this, I felt good. Bonin asked if I'd ever been to Hollywood, I said no, so we headed up and started cruising the streets. It was three in the mornin' and there were all kinds of people walkin' around."

Meanwhile, in Hollywood 15-year-old Charles Miranda was partying with friends at the Starwood Disco, on the corner of Santa Monica and North Crescent Heights, near La Cienega Blvd. He lived in Bell Gardens, 15-miles southeast of Hollywood, and worked at a donut shop. Charles had just been paid the day before and was last seen by his family when he went dancing.

One friend, Kathi Vernazza, saw him at the club before going home to 924 Gardner Avenue, two miles east of La Cienega, around 2:00 a.m. Charles showed up at her apartment, after 2:30 a.m., and woke Kathi and her friends up to ask for a ride home. But they had no car and she told him to call his father, he left without calling. Charles walked to Santa Monica Blvd., two blocks north, to somehow find a ride home.

Miley continued, "Bonin spotted someone and says, 'that kid walking over there, how about him?' I sez 'why not' and Bonin agreed."

"Who was that?"

"That one was the first one, Miranda. Anyways, Bonin makes a quick U-ee and drives real slow behind him. We cruised along waitin' till the kid was alone, then Bonin calls out, 'Hey man, where ya going?' Kid stops and walks over to the driver's window. 'Home,' he tells us. Bonin sez, 'want a ride?' The kid sez 'no' and Bonin starts talking real nice to him, he could be good at gettin' people to listen.

"Then he sez, 'you want to smoke a joint?' The kid looks around, kinda uninterested, till Bonin offers him a hundred bucks for some head. He couldn't believe it, 'you just want me to blow you for a hundred bucks?' 'Yeah,' Bonin sez and turns and gives me a wink. I didn't know what's gonna happen. The punk finally crawls in the back and Bonin drives, lookin' for a place to park.

"The kid comes up and sits between the seats and starts rubbin' Bonin's dick, I can tell he is excited. The first chance Bonin gets he pulls off the street and cuts the engine. Then he crawls into the back of the van with the kid, I'm watchin' em from the front seat. Bonin wanted me to stay up there to be a look out.

"He starts feeling the punk off and the kid is feeling him off. Bonin asks the punk if he he's gay, he tells him he can give head for a hundred bucks. Then Bonin asks him if he likes to get fucked? The kid sez no and Bonin pats him on his head real nice like. I'd never done this with him, so I didn't know what the hell was gonna happen.

"Bonin has the kid take off his clothes tells him to lay down, then he starts rubbing him up and down, getting' him real hard, but the kid wants to get the money and leave, so Bonin unzips his pants and whips out his dick and tells the punk, 'Get busy, and if you know what's good for you, you won't scrape your teeth on me.' Then he grabbed his head and shoved it down hard, he's gaggin' but Bonin don't let up, keeps pushing his head down.

"Bonin stops and tells the kid to get on his hands and knees, after he asked about the money again Bonin looked at him, and oh fuck he's mad. He punched him really hard and screams, 'Turn over and get on yur knees.' Punks scared, shit, I'm scared, but he does it. Bonin starts fucking him hard, he's screaming cause it hurts. The kid tried to turn over, so Bonin hit him again and grabbed some rope and tied his hands behind his back, he was pretty strong. The kid was whining, so Bonin tells him, 'If you shut up and lay still, we'll let you go.'

"Now Bonin looks up at me and sez 'Hey man, back in Bellflower you said you wanted to do it.' I said, 'Hell yes, I want some.' So I come back in the van and get on top of the kid and try to fuck him, but I couldn't keep it hard. Bonin leans over and sez, 'You know why, the kid's gonna die.' It kinda shook me up," he said blankly.

"Do you think Miranda heard Bonin say that?" I asked, dreading the answer.

"Nah, he whispered it in my ear."

"How did you feel when you realized you were actually going to kill the boy?"

"Well," Greg shrugged, "We had to do it, the kid would've squealed and we'd be in trouble."

"Did you ever think about letting the boy go?"

"Nah."

"Did he try to escape?"

"He couldn't, he was trapped and hurt. Bonin then sucked me off and I'm hard and ready, so I get up and ride the kid. We're having a good old time, really partying. The punks trying to turn over, to get up, I roll off. Then Bonin throws him and starts punching him, so I got the rope and tied his feet up, he was moving around, tryin' to kick us."

"Did you hit him too?"

"Yeah."

"Where?"

"One the side, in the stomach, you know, body punches, but Bonin kneed him in the balls and he passed out. He wanted my shirt, I didn't know why, but shit, he took my shirt and started strangling the kid, kinda shocked me for few seconds. From behind he's twisting the shirt real hard, fuck, with all his strength, kids turning blue, then he jerks him up and twists harder. Bonin tells me to hold it, then sez to give him the tire iron. He whips the shirt off, rolls him over and starts pushing the tire iron down."

"Bonin has the tire iron across the boy's neck?" I asked with horror.

"Yeah. That's when I throw Bonin off and say, hey man let me get a hand at that. I jump on him and push the tire iron down on his throat real hard, I could hear the bones cracking, then his neck goes flat."

"Was the boy dead?"

Miley looked directly at me and smiled, "Oh yeah, he was dead alright."

"How could you tell?"

"Well, because after I got thru with him, it felt like he was dead. I didn't think he was dead when Bonin was thru cause he was shaking all over. That punk shit and puked all over the place, man it stunk! When I heard those bones cracking, I thought, yeah, okay, he's dead," Greg repeated the phrase, then looked for my reaction.

He got it, my face blanched with revulsion, my stomach nauseated from what I just heard. My previous ability to stay detached was cracked, and I feared the nightmares would resume.

"Bonin looks at the kid, tells me to push the body up close to the back of the seats and get his clothes together. Then he starts driving. After a while he went by some railroad tracks and there's this big dumpster trash can, with a forklift on the side. Bonin grabbed his legs, and I grabbed the head and we dumped him off naked. We dropped a few clothes in each place, tossed the ID and split the money."

"Did you do any drugs with Miranda?"

"Nah, there weren't no money or pot, Bonin said it's just a gig to get a kid into the van."

John Hostetter was looking for boxes in an alley, near Downtown LA in an industrial area two blocks away from the famous Olvera Street, when he discovered Miranda's body, face down, next to a dumpster. Cause of death was Bonin's trademark "twisted knot" method, characterized by a bruise on the back of the neck, and a crushed larynx. Numerous abrasions and bruises were visible on his face and body.

Charles Miranda was declared dead at 9:28 a.m. on February 3, 1980. Sgt. St. John and his partner, Sgt. Kirk Mellecker, of LAPD Robbery-Homicide, whose office was blocks away, were notified.

Miley stood up, looked through the door window and commented on the many visitors. For a moment I thought he was going to leave, then he turned and said, "I got all these here guys writing me wanting to know about Bonin, yeah, they want to know all about the murders." He looked pleased, obviously enjoying the attention.

After a break for refreshments, Miley was ready to continue. I welcomed the break as the memories came flooding back, memories of being at LA Men's Jail and listening to so many gruesome stories told by too many unrepentant murderers. Memories best forgotten.

"By the time we were done it was light out."

"What happened next?" I asked, trying prompt for stories.

"Well, Bonin sez, 'I'm horny again. I need another one,' I couldn't believe it."

"How long after you dumped Miranda did Bonin say that?"

"Almost right after, I said no way, I was tired and wanted to go home."

"You did kill another boy though, didn't you?"

"Yeah, Bonin went lookin' for another one. He wanted to know if I was hungry, shit, I didn't feel like eatin' anything. But he was striking out, one guy and a couple kids wouldn't get it, another kid took off fast on his skateboard like a scalded dog. So, I went to sleep in the back.

"When I woke up, we were in Huntington Beach, I was out for a while. Bonin spotted a kid and yelled at me to wake up. Up front I see this little kid's galloping along like, you know, he's all excited. Bonin following' real slow, I looked and sez, 'No, he's too young.' Bonin sez 'Fuck it. I want him.' I didn't want to do it again, shit, Bonin knew but didn't care."

"This was James Macabe?"

"Yeah."

"How old do you think Macabe was?"

"Oh, 'bout 11 or 12, youngest one Bonin ever got. So, we pull over and Bonin sez, 'Hey man, where you goin.' 'To Disneyland,' the kid sez. 'Want a ride? Bonin asked him. 'No, I'm gonna take the bus,' the kid sez. Bonin wasn't givin' up, he tells him we can take him all the way to Disneyland, but the kid's brother gave him money and said to take the bus. Then he sez, 'You want to smoke some marijuana?' That got him, I jumped out quick to open the back door for him.

"Bonin tells me to drive, he wants to get in back with the kid. Bonin crawls back and tellin' him, 'I'm gonna take you to Disneyland, don't worry.' I could hear all kinda like sex noises, Bonin had closed the curtain so I couldn't see. I heard him saying 'no, no' and crying, I just kept driving but I knew."

"You knew?"

"I knew we wasn't gonna take him to Disneyland. We had to stop for gas. He gets out and the kid asks me what's gonna happen? I sez, 'Well, Bill says we're gonna take you to Disneyland, okay?' Bonin starts drivin' and tells the kid we're gonna go down here a little way and then…out," Miley said as his voice faded.

"You're going to do what? Sorry I couldn't hear you," I asked, shifting uncomfortably on the steel chair.

"Gonna let him out."

"Let him go?"

"Okay, Bonin didn't mean it. I felt sorry for the kid, but I wasn't gonna say anything, Bonin might've killed me too. Finally, we pull into a grocery store, he parks, and we got in the back and tell him to lose the clothes. 'Wait, you didn't say anything about taking off my clothes, you said we're gonna smoke some pot and drop me off at Disneyland,' he screamed. 'We will in a little while' Bonin smiles at him, 'I just want to hold you for a little while.'

"Then he starts kissin' and huggin' him. I'm out of it, I watch but I'm bored, so I reach over and grab the kid on his private parts and squeeze hard. The kid yells and tries to wiggle away. Bonin laughs out loud, me too, so we hooked him up."

"Hook him up?"

"Yeah, you know, tie him up, Bonin grabs him around the neck and bends him backward real hard. Then he asks him, 'What could you get for ransom? Could you get a couple of thousand?' He says nothing, he's crying, wanting to go home.

"Bonin pushes the kid down on the floor, jumps on his stomach and sez, 'This is a kidnap.' The kid starts fighting, jumping around, so Bonin starts beatin' him up good, hittin' real hard in the body, we took turns. Then Bonin gets up and I finish hookin' up the legs. Bonin rolled him onto his stomach, and I got the arms hooked up.

"Bonin wants to fuck him, he starts doin' it but he's crying and screaming, real loud. I kinda pulled Bonin off, saying, 'He's too small, this punk is a virgin.' Bonin sez, 'You want some of this? You got a little dick, see what you can do.' I hesitated, but he screamed, 'Well, you're in this with me and if you don't, I'll kill one of your brothers.' I didn't know what to do."

"Did you believe him?"

"Shit yeah, Bonin could get real mean if you didn't go along, I was scared of him."

"What happened next?"

"We have sex with him for a while, you know, taking turns fuckin' him and having him suck us off, you know, gettin' what we want. It was still lights out, so we had to wait to get rid of him, he's cryin' and cryin, so Bonin sez, 'Relax, it'll be over soon.' Kid thought he was going home, but I knew he wasn't. Bonin said to get dressed, the kid swears he'll never tell anyone, Bonin sez, 'Yeah, I know you won't.' Finally, it got dark.

"Bonin started driving and we ended up on the Pomona Freeway, he pulled off at a construction site, near a trash bin. 'Lay on your stomach,' Bonin sez. I got on his back and Bonin told me to hold down the arms. He got on his knees, you know, on either side of his head, and put the shirt around the neck, the kid starts yellin' 'no, no, please no.' Bonin twists it as he's screaming, saying 'he won't tell anyone.' He was jumpin' all around, but we held him down till Bonin got him to pass out.

"Next thing you know Bonin turns the kid over on his back. He gets the crowbar from the side of the van and starts pushing down on the front of his neck with both hands, the bones started cracking."

"The same thing you did to Miranda?"

"Yeah, same thing, but this time the neck was split, it kinda had a mark, like an open cut. We untied him and took him out of the van, Bonin dropped the kid on his head once, man it made a weird sound when it hit the ground. Then we tossed him into the trash bin," Miley said, then paused.

"You know what Bonin then told me, he sez, 'You know, I didn't really want to kill that little kid.' I told him, 'Yeah, I know, but it had to be done, he could've identified us, and we'd get caught.' We took the money and lost the papers on the freeway. Bonin dropped me and said to keep my mouth shut, he was going to jail the next day, I didn't know for how long."

Bonin was lying, of course he wanted the kill James Macabe, that was why he picked him up in the first place. Feigning such an attitude to Miley shows the hall of mirrors within his damaged psyche. However, the deviously clever Bill Bonin liked to keep everyone off balance, playing all sides through the middle was him through and through.

James Macabe, 12-years old and waylaid on his way to Disneyland, was found on February 6, 1980 in an industrial area of Walnut, 30-miles east of Downtown Los Angeles. Body broken and future gone, Macabe was Bonin's youngest victim. The coroner found ligature marks on the neck, arms and legs. There was bruising to the penis, enlargement of the rectum and a crushing of the skull, as if it had been hit with a ball-pen hammer. He was wearing a pair of blue corduroy trousers, a brown sleeveless coat, no t-shirt or undershorts tennis shoes and a pair of white socks with red stripes.

His final possessions were Disneyland tickets, a watch, a ball, Chapstick, and a comb. Death was from asphyxiation through "bar strangulation" by compressing the neck and crushing the esophagus. His face had multiple abrasions.

"How many did Bonin kill?" I asked curiously.

"Forty-four in all, that's what he told me, Bonin had a plumbing business back in 1971 and he would meet these here guys and go have sex with em. Then he'd take em out in the desert and kill em."

"He started in '71?" I asked, making sure I heard correctly.

"Yeah! See he killed twenty or so then. But he didn't get caught, he took 'em out to the desert and buried 'em good. He stopped cause he was tired of doin' it."

"How do you know about what he did?"

"He told me, he got excited talking about it."

"Did he ever dump any of the bodies in the Ortega Highway area?" Brisco asked. "Or did he kill anyone whose body has not been found in the last few years?"

"Well, he dumped three there I know of, but he got caught for those. Ask Munro, he did three murders, but he only confessed to one. He may have done some that got dumped out there."

After more questioning, it was obvious Greg couldn't shed any new information about the murder Brisco was investigating.

Bonin stretched the truth with Miley, as he did so often with others. In 1971 he didn't have a plumbing business but was committed to Atascadero State Hospital. From 1969 to 1978 Bonin was either in mental institutions or prison, with his time out brief and without evidence of murderous behavior.

"Miley seemed to be honest, but he didn't give me anything new to go on." Brisco said. Bonin affirmed Brisco's conclusion by writing, "When I was sitting in the court room, I can tell you Gregory Miley's testimony was honest. He was dumb as shit, but he was honest."

"The things Miley said jives with all of the records I've read, and what I heard from them in jail," I related to Gene.

"All of the reports I've read state Miley has an IQ of 56, way below average. That may explain why he was easily manipulated by Bonin, but he still should have known what they were doing was wrong."

The other co-conspirator available at Mule Creek Prison, Jim Munro, had written me a letter about his up-coming parole hearing, scheduled for the following year. He asked if I could help him by writing a favorable letter to the board. I contacted Munro and filled him in on my association with Gene Brisco, informing him and Brisco might help with obtaining a release. Understandably, Jim was more than eager to meet with us, however, he was of no help to Brisco either.

This exchange with Brisco sums up our day:

"No matter how many times I listen to these guys confessions, I never get used to hearing how cold blooded they are," Brisco commented.

"I thought I was going to be sick at times," I replied to Gene. "I've sure lost the calluses I developed working in the jail. Couldn't have survived listening to these killers without learning to detach from them."

30

Bonin Kills Alone #7
Jail & Early Release, Feb. 3 to March 14, 1980
Ronald Gatlin, March 14, 1980

On February 6, 1980 James Macabe, naked and battered, was found behind a trash bin on a construction site near the Pomona Freeway in Walnut. Bonin, serving time in Orange County Central Men's Jail, must have read about the discovery of his latest victims in the newspaper. Reading stories about the kills allowed him to relive the excitement, a common pathology among serial killers.

The day after the Miranda and Macabe murders, February 4, 1980, Bonin surrendered to serve a six-month sentence for parole revocation and **Sexual Perversion**. As it happened, he was "re-released" from custody a little over a month later, on March 14, 1980, and then released by the court from all further parole obligations on April 11, 1980. Legal wrangling regarding what Bonin should and should not be charged with led to confusion with his sentencing and disposition. Making sense of available records is difficult.

When Bonin was released from state prison, on October 11, 1978, he was placed under a one-year parole obligation that was slated to end on October 11, 1979. However, in the midst of clerical confusion it was extended and then ended on April 11, 1980.

This tedious, months-long process involved charges filed, finalized and reversed; incarcerations started and stopped; desire for him to serve six-months in county jail instituted and abandoned, twice.

Bonin's attorney took advantage of all the bureaucratic confusion and muddle by submitting a **Writ of Prohibition/Mandate** to the OC Superior Court—essentially compelling the court to vacate the proceedings, which they did, and release Bonin, which they also did. The criminal justice system broke down on this one: Bonin should have been thrown back in prison on the parole revocation aspect alone.

Bonin had to laugh; six months in jail, he could do that standing on his head, and they let him out in six weeks and vacated his parole obligations.

Bonin felt sad that Greg Miley had moved to Texas, and he didn't even get a chance to say goodbye. Bonin easily manipulated Miley and he proved a willing murder accomplice, something difficult to find. Planning to call him, to make sure he kept quiet, Miley happened to ring Bonin's mother and left his new contact info. When Bonin called, he assured Miley he was there for him and promised to help bring him back to LA. That happened, but it wasn't in the manner Bonin intended.

Bonin's release time would be up the next day, Saturday, March 15 at the 6:00 a.m. kick out. On Friday morning Bonin sent a message to the sergeant saying his folks were leaving the next morning and he wanted to see them off to the airport. The ploy worked and he was released by mid-afternoon. Tired of his numerous trips to jail, no one in Bonin's family wanted to pick him up.

After transferring from bus to bus, he finally made it to Pioneer and Imperial Highway, about three miles from his mother's house. He walked home only to find the left front tire on his van was flat. Bonin lost it! He stomped into the house and called Vernon Butts, wanting to see if his old murder buddy wanted to "go out hunting." Vern was set to play Dungeons and Dragons with friends and declined.

While in jail, all Bonin could think about was picking up another kid. Disappointed about Butts, he decided to go out alone. Butts' last murder with Bonin was three-months earlier, in late November 1979, when they found a kid in Hollywood and dumped him near Bakersfield.

After Bonin got some air into the leaky tire, re-attached the whip antenna, connected the 23-channel citizen band radio, he headed to the San Fernando Valley, 30-miles north of Downey. Anxious to the point of distraction, he was ready for some serious hunting; he wanted a young one with soft skin. He later revealed this frightful aspect of his mindset in the written confessions: "I had thought about killing someone during the whole time I was in jail. I couldn't wait. I had it all planned out, drive to the San Fernando Valley, I knew lots of kids hitchhiked up there."

Bonin's needs were changing; he wanted to try different methods and new versions of cruelty, even killing multiple victims at one time, believing he had no control over his obsession.

Early in the evening Bonin started cruising Van Nuys Blvd., heading north on the busy boulevard from the Ventura Freeway. Near Victory Blvd., he spotted 18-year-old Ronald Gatlin hitchhiking and was immediately attracted by his slim build and innocent looks. Bonin offered him a ride and Gatlin accepted, taking the step from life to oblivion. Like many Bonin victims, he was at the wrong place at the wrong time and made the wrong decision.

"Where you headed," Bonin asked.

"Home," he replied. Gatlin lived two miles away at 14733 Saticoy St. with his parents and two siblings. He worked at his father's photography studio, on Santa Monica Blvd. in West Los Angeles, and was the youngest of three children. That night he was wearing tan corduroy pants, a brown and white shirt and a bright yellow ski jacket with orange patches on the shoulders.

"You're going home at 10:00 o'clock on a Friday night?" Bonin asked, testing Gatlin.

"Yeah, nothin' to do."

"You want to cruise around with me? I'll take you home later," Bonin innocently asked, wanting to hold on to his prey.

"Okay."

Completely in his clutches, Bonin began to imagine what lay ahead for the night. The six-weeks spent in jail had been spent plotting and planning, caged up and unable to hit the road scoping for prospects. He was fully transformed into a cold-blooded killer, hunting not for sex but for the kill. No empathy or sympathy was involved in his calculations, only a desire for the next victim.

After cruising around for a while Bonin got down to business. "Boy, I sure am horny, how about you?" Bonin asked, playing the next gambit in the game.

"No, not really."

"You into the gay scene?"

"Nah, that's not my thing."

"Let me screw you and I'll give you $50.00."

"No, I don't like getting screwed. I'll give you head."

"Okay, get in the back and take your clothes off while I find a place to park."

Gatlin got into the back and disrobed while Bonin parked. He wasn't going to be satisfied with the boy's terms, whatever they might be, and took a knife into the back with him. He quickly whipped out his knife and pushed the sharp edge against Gatlin's throat, telling him to lie on his stomach. Holding the knife between his teeth, Bonin tied his hands and his feet. Then he raped the young boy, releasing his anger at the world.

Furthering the psychological torture of the boy, Bonin told him he was kidnapped, and he planned to sell him to a homosexual farm. Unable to move, Gatlin was placed with his head resting on the engine cover, in between the front seats, facing towards him so he could keep an eye on him.

Bonin told Gatlin he would give him a chance to escape if found someone he liked better, instructing him explicitly, "If anyone gets in the van you pretend to be asleep."

Bonin had long fantasized about doing a double-murder, and in his agitated state it seemed the perfect time. He cruised around the valley and then, around 1:00 a.m., he came upon two kids that looked to be about 14-years old. Bonin pulled over and stopped along beside them.

"Hey, you two, you want to earn $50.00 bucks?"

"What do we have to do?"

"I just want to give you some head," Bonin replied, worried that Gatlin would say something from the back of the van, but he was so terrified of Bonin he kept quiet. One boy agreed but the other one said no. Now that they had seen Bonin, he couldn't afford to take just one of them. "Well sorry, there's a lot of others who will like the money," Bonin said, then noticed a California Highway Patrol cruiser pass by and slow down, then the car kept going.

Bonin exhaled a sigh of relief as his heart raced. It was getting late, Bonin needed do something with his captive. He drove to an isolated area, parked the van and got into the back without saying a word. He strangled Ronald Gatlin immediately, coldly ignoring the boy's crying pleas for mercy.

He drove 30-miles straight east from Van Nuys to Duarte and dumped Gatlin's body in the bushes next to the Foothill Freeway. Bonin drove the 20-miles south, back home to Downey, where he expected to get a day of uninterrupted sleep. All that pent up energy anticipating the hunt and kill was washed away, leaving only a mind and soul lost in an abyss of darkness, a place where no light was allowed to penetrate.

On the morning of March 15, 1980, about 7:00 a.m., Roger Perkins was on his morning run along the fence line inside the retirement community where he lived on Central Avenue, which runs parallel to the Foothill

Freeway. On one side of the street are houses and businesses, across the street a fence separated the sidewalk from a short slope, populated by trees and bushes, leading up the freeway. Someone flagged Perkins down and told him to call the police, he had found something. He went home, called the police and returned to the scene.

LA County Sheriff's Sergeant David Kushner, with his partner Deputy Jack Fueglein, arrived on the scene to view yet another nude boy's body. Criminalist Ronald Linhart noticed what he had seen on so many recent young victims; the twisting "windless strangulation" with a large bruise on the back of the neck, where the knot in the t-shirt pressed against the skin.

Testimony from the coroner later referred to this as "the knot imprint." He also observed "a blank space which is perfectly compatible with the loose skin on the right side of the neck being folded up and protected from the windless strangulation."

Miranda, Macabe and Gatlin represent the fourth, fifth and sixth victims Bonin dumped in LA County—14 victims left in six different counties, many in desolate places, within multiple city jurisdictions spread hundreds of miles apart. Such a clever stratagem, combined with Bonin dumping clothes and ID, kept law enforcement on the back heel and dealing with little evidence.

31

Bonin Kills Alone #8 and #9
Glen Barker & Russell Rugh, March 21, 1980

A week after release from jail and killing Ronald Gatlin, Bonin wanted to implement something he had mulled over for a long time: murdering two boys in one-day. Later on, in one of my sessions with Bonin at LA County Jail in late 1981, he said one of his regrets was not being able to kill three in one day.

Bonin mentioned the two-kill scheme to Vernon Butts on multiple occasions, just as Vern always talked to Bonin about killing with an icepick. To date Bonin had claimed 14 victims: seven alone, five with Vernon Butts and two with Greg Miley. Back in custody twice, he was let out early for various reasons and was about to be released from all parole obligations.

Divining Bonin's mindset is easy as the pace and desire for more targets accelerated. He enjoyed seeing his exploits in newspapers and on TV news, while basic insecurities derived satisfaction from power over the helpless victims. Unable or incapable of feeling love, Bonin's rage caused him to lash out to fill the unfillable hole in his soul. Like a drug addict, his brain needed the next fix again and again.

Shortly after release, Bonin began working at Dependable Drive-Away at 546 S. Greenwood Ave. in Montebello, not far from his parent's house in Downey. The job required long hours on the road, long hours alone for possible side trips and long hours for fantasizing. He had worked there for a few weeks in 1975, right before his arrest for the rape of David McVicker, and other attacks, resulted in a three-year prison sentence.

When he showed up years later Ed Demler, who owned the company, only ran his driving record and thus had no clue about the real reason for his extended absence. Since work was doled out piecemeal, when clients needed trucks delivered, lots of time was spent waiting at the yard. No set hours, and no guarantees of work, made for sporadic income and a flexible work life.

But Bonin needed money and he was always in the ready room waiting for a job, no matter how far or where. According to Mrs. Marion Perkins, who ran the office, "He was a nice guy, and he was a very good worker. You could always count on him. He wanted to get into bowling, but he didn't because he felt it might interfere with his work." Perkins was told by Bonin about his girlfriend, Mary, who was married to a serviceman but didn't mind Bonin seeing her. Bonin took her bowling and to Church on Sundays. No one had a clue about his bi-sexual nature, and he never made improper advances to anyone at work.

During long trips, usually with multiple drivers to places like New York or San Francisco, Bonin returned by a different route from the others. On one trip, from New York, Demler saw him pick up a hitchhiker, which was against company policy and caused a number of arguments between them on the way back.

Returning from San Francisco, Bonin usually took the longer, more arduous coastal route rather than the main highway down the center of the state. Demler disliked the practice, but obviously had no clue about what Bonin was doing to hitchhikers in Los Angeles. Detectives later took a keen interest in the dates and routes of these various trips.

Bonin, in pursuit of his two-murders-in-one-day-plan, picked up Russell Rugh and Glen Barker on the afternoon of Friday, March 21, 1980. Glen Barker was 14 years old and lived at 2688 England St., Apt. D, in Huntington Beach. OC Sheriff's Detectives Bernie Esposito and James Sidebotham were assigned to investigate the murders and looked into the last known movements of Glen Barker.

Sharon Diane Barker, Glen's mother, contacted the coroner's office after reading a description of one of the victims in the newspaper. On March 25, arrangements were made to meet her and a friend at Peek's Family Mortuary. Positive identification of Glen Barker was made by Susan Maits, a close friend of Barker's mother.

Sharon Barker last saw her son alive when she kissed him goodbye at 7:30 a.m., on his way to Westmont Elementary School. Last seen at school when he left class at 2:35 p.m.; the last time anyone spoke with him was when he called home, ten minutes later, for permission to spend the night at a friend's house. She expected him to come home for a change of clothes, but he never arrived. Later it was reported by a passerby that Glen was seen hitchhiking south on Beach Blvd.

During his December 1980 confession interview Bonin talked about the Rugh-Barker murders with OC Sheriff's Homicide Detectives Bernie

Esposito and James Sidebotham, LAPD's Sgt. Jigsaw John and Mellecker, LA Sheriff's Sgt. David Kushner along with Kristis and Malmberg from the San Bernardino Sheriff's Dept. All these detectives investigated multiple murders in their jurisdictions related to the Bonin Freeway Killer cases.

While questioning Bonin about the Thomas Lundgren killing, which he denied having anything to do with, he brought up the names of Barker and Rugh:

BONIN: I, I can tell you two right off the bat…

ESPOSITO: Okay.

BONIN: that I know, and was Russell, uh, Rouge…

ESPOSITO: Rugh, R-U-G-H.

BONIN: and Glen Barker…

ESPOSITO: Barker

BONIN: Barker.

NORRIS (Deputy DA): Why don't you tell us about those two.

BONIN: I picked up, yeah, I picked up Glen, I propositioned him, he went for it.

DET. KUSHNER: Who's this Glen?

ESPOSITO: That's Glen Barker.

Bonin then proceeded to finish the story for the detectives, "I picked him, he went for it, I got him in the back of the van, I tied him up, I didn't have any sex with him, no I did, I sodomized him. Yeah I sodomized him, I was alone. I drove around looking for another person to pick up while Glen was in the van, while he was alive. Uh a couple of people said they didn't need rides. I gave another guy a ride. I told that was my cousin, and he was asleep.

"I told Glen that when somebody got in the van, to be quiet, don't say nothing, cause what I was gonna do is look for somebody else to take his place, and I would, I would let him go, and if I couldn't find anybody when he was the one that had to go, and he goes where, and I says 'I'd take you out of state to a homosexual slave ring, where I sell people,' this was a cover story. He went for it and kept quiet.

"This guy, when I finally pulled up and stopped, he wasn't going for nothing, he didn't want to get in the back of the van, in fact he got out, so I drove off, and I finally came around to Russell, and he wasn't gonna go for it either, but uh I says okay I'll drop you off. And I pulled up, stopped the van, I reach over and grabbed him, and pulled him towards me, and he got scared. He says okay I'll do, do whatever you want, you know, in other words I told him I wanted to give him head. I took the knife and held it to his throat. I drove across the street from where I was, he got in the back of the van with me, and I tied him up. I had both of them then.

"I had no more sex with either of them, I never had sex with Russell. I drove out to Ortega Highway, went south of 205, to about the 405, got on Ortega Highway and went out. I found a place, it was late at night, down in that, that lower campground, and uh at that point in time, I killed Glen, then untied him, and I told Russell I would let him go instead of Glen…"

Bonin was lying, basically tamping down the cruel nature of the murders with hopes of getting a better deal, but he also had other reasons for talking to detectives, as will be seen later. This disparity is graphically illustrated in Bonin's written confession about the Barker-Rugh murders.

"I offered Glen Barker $50 to get him in the van and he said okay. I started off by asking him if he hitch-hiked much and if he got good rides? I asked him if got picked up by many gays and Glen said, 'Yes, especially on Beach Boulevard.' Then I asked him 'what do you think of gays' and he replied, 'There ok as long as they leave me alone, a couple of guys offered 10 or 15 dollars.' 'My offer is $50 for a head job, what you say to that.' I asked him. 'Dick for $50, I'd let him, it's his mouth.' I reached and fondled him, and he was already hard as a rock, 'it looks like you'll go for it, right.' 'Sure, it's your money and your mouth,' he told me.

"I found a place to park and we got into the back of the van, I told him to take his pants off. He took 'em down to his knees and I told him to take 'em completely off. He said, 'No, you can suck me just like this.' I told him okay, I went to get some tissue and came back with the knife, told him to roll over. I tied his hands, telling him if he didn't do exactly as I told him he wouldn't see another birthday.' Then I got his shirt off and tied up his feet, then I pulled out my dick and said, 'Now it's your mouth, suck on this punk.' He started sucking, then acted like he was gagging and said, 'I think I may throw up.'

"I told him, 'if you do it, it will cost you your life, well since you can't keep my dick in your mouth, it goes up your ass.' Then I fucked him. Afterwards I told him I was taking him out of state and selling him to a homosexual farm, that he was 'only worth $10,000, which was a cheap price as he couldn't handle giving head.' Then I got on the road to find someone else. Finally, after a few people turned me down, I spotted a kid who was worth at least $25,000. I told Glen, 'I don't need you anymore, so keep your mouth shut when he gets in cause he may get away, and if does I'll kill you.'

"I continued up Beach Boulevard and that is where I found Russell Rugh, I asked him, 'where you headed, he said Westminster Boulevard and I told him hop in, I'll give you a ride over there. I propositioned him but he politely refused, I spotted a market and said 'I'll let you out here, cause I have to get some stuff anyways.' I pulled close to a wall so he couldn't get the door open, I pulled him toward me and said, 'You motherfucker, I'm going to give you some head.' I parked across the street, I threw Rugh into the back, got him on his stomach, tied his hands and feet with a long extension cord. Then I told him to give me a little head and he did.

"I told him to get his clothes off, I pulled his shirt up, put my hands on his bare chest and said, 'You have a smooth body,' as I rubbed his chest. I tried to kiss him but he turned away, I said, 'Kiss me you punk.' I reached down and pulled his pants down, his dick was hard. Then I said to Glen, 'Hey this kids got a little hard on.' I turned him over and stuck my dick up his ass, he started screaming and everything fell out. I hit him as hard as I could and knocked him out. I pulled him awake and said, 'That is what happens when you don't do what I tell you to do.' I pulled him over to Glen and told them to kiss, they did and then Glen went down on Rugh. I then told Rugh about how he was taking the place of Glen at the homosexual farm, I headed up to Ortega Highway where I planned to drop him off.

"I was stopped at a light and I reached down to squeeze Rugh's nuts, my foot came off the brake and I hit the car in front of me. Panic set in, I backed up a little and went around her, said 'I'll pull into the station up ahead.' She was trying to get her car started and I took off. I told them not talk to each other at all. I caught Glen mouthing words about something, I pulled over, went back and slammed my knee into his jaw, and said, 'If you ever attempt to talk to this guy, I'll fucking kill you instead of letting you go.' I started driving and said, 'Fuck it, one of you is going to die and the other will go free.' Glen said, 'You said I was going to go free.' I said, 'You didn't do what I said, now why should I let you go.' He said, 'Because you promised.'

"My response was, 'Okay, each of you is going to have to convince me you should live.' Rugh said, 'You should kill him.' Glen looked at him with tears in his eyes and I told Rugh, 'You get a big 10 points for that one.' I asked each if they would help me kill the other, and both said yes. Finally I got to the lower camp grounds below Ortega Highway, I parked and was talking to both of them, letting them cuss each other out. Then a car came down, I turned up the radio with the back speakers so they couldn't hear the car. 'All right shut up, the first one to say a word is the one who dies.' I waited till the car left, I said, 'Glen you get to go free, I am going to strangle you till your unconscious and then dress you put you out.'

"I told Glen to 'relax and just let yourself go, if you struggle I'll just put a stranglehold on you and kill you.' I used an old t-shirt and I just strangled him to death. I looked at Rugh and said, 'You know what's happening don't you.' He said, 'You're killing him.' 'Yes, you get to go free.' I stopped choking Glen and pointed my pen light at him and asked Rugh if saw any blood? I told Rugh that 'Glen was now free of this world' and put the t-shirt around Rugh's neck and he said, 'you're going to kill me aren't you.' 'Just till you're unconscious, what's your name,' He replied 'Russ.'

"I said to him 'Russ, yes, I am going to kill you, at least I didn't fuck you.' I sat while he prayed and I asked him if he was ready, he continued praying and I twisted the shirt until he was dead. I took off their clothes and dumped them, then I went home."

It was a 50-mile drive from the mountains to the house on Angell Street in Downey.

Glen Barker's nude body was found next to Russell Rugh in the lower San Juan Creek Campgrounds, 16-miles east of I-5 in the Cleveland National Forest. Diana Gill, a lab technician at Santa Monica City College, and her friend Mathew Weintraub drove up Ortega Highway and into the hills back of the campground.

Around 12:30 p.m. Gill and Weintraub were walking along a trail when they came across two bodies lying upside down on a slight incline. Both were naked with marks on their neck and on their arms. Due to their positioning, the blood had drained to their heads and to one arm of one boy. Both bodies were not far from the road above.

Kevin Bushmiaer, a grocery clerk for Hughes market in Laguna Hills, said that two people approached his truck and asked him to call the police. He contacted the Sheriff's Department and later testified about glancing over the embankment and seeing two naked bodies in a little ravine. Rather than go down the hill, Bushmaier waited on top by the highway for authorities to arrive.

On March 22 a Deputy Sheriff from Riverside County, Larry Jernegan, received a dispatch call about the bodies. He drove to lower SJC near the border of Riverside and Orange Counties. He observed two nude white male bodies with ligature marks around the neck area. Careful to protect the crime scene, Jernegan described how the lower San Juan is located off the main highway with is a paved roadway that leads into the campground from Ortega Hwy.

Two bodies were found approximately midway between the Ortega Highway and the Campground, down the paved roadway, and approximately six to eight feet off an embankment. In short order, Sergeants Esposito and Sidebotham, of OC Sheriff's Dept., would have been informed of the murder victims along with every agency in Southern California.

Everything appeared to match the death of Dennis Fox, found three months earlier in the same area. Richard M. Slaughter, Deputy Coroner for Orange County, reported he saw two Caucasian young males 16 to 18 years of age. Killed between midnight and 3:00 a.m. on March 22, his conclusions were based on the state of rigor mortis and post-mortem lividity. Bottom line, neither of them was alive after 3:00 a.m. Rigor mortis commences approximately two hours after death, and normally completes after six to eight hours afterwards. Both had ligature marks on their ankles and necks.

No tire tracks or other evidence was found near the bodies. However, a key discovery was made when, during the Barker autopsy, six yellow-green fibers were found on his scrotum and pubic hair combings. Amylase (saliva) was present on one breast area while the rectal area and mouth tested negative for semen. Penis area was positive for saliva.

As with a majority of Bonin's 22 murder victims, death was by ligature strangulation. There was a pronounced deformity to the mouth that could only have been caused by some sort of binding to hold the victim's mouth closed. Dr. Richards noted that the victim's wrists and ankles were wrapped multiple times with a very thin material, leading him to believe the same material was used to strangle the boy. Skin about the forehead and eyes had particular hemorrhages in the skin, and the whites of the eyes also had hemorrhages.

When a person is being strangled, first the blood goes to a thinner part of the skin, the eyes, and then to the facial skin. As the victim loses oxygen, the pressure increases in the smaller vessels that would produce hemorrhaging. Lack of oxygen produces breakdown of the smaller blood vessels. When the blood circulation is restricted, after the blood gets up to the face, then the face becomes darker blue. These are the classic hallmarks of strangled victims. Glen Barker was trying to get loose, and the moving caused skin abrasions and hemorrhaging underneath the skin on his ankles and wrists.

Bonin took the body well past the area where he disposed of Dennis Fox, months earlier in December 1979. They were found 16-miles away from where Fox's body was discovered, with all three victims displaying the same injuries. No clothes, wallets or ID were found. Rugh and Barker represented the third and fourth Bonin victims dumped in Orange County.

32

Day of Crossroads & Consequences
Monday, March 24, 1980

Certain days in the history of nations, organizations and people are later on discovered to be of supreme importance. March 24, 1980 is that watershed day in the Bill Bonin story. No one else, due to a lack of relevant documents, has been able to divine the web of coincidences and consequences within a day which stands out only because Bonin killed another boy.

Four people within Bonin's personal world crossed paths, and performed acts, which later impacted nearly every aspect of the Bill Bonin story, but it would take months for those consequences to play out and over four decades for them to be fully understood.

In addition, on this same day the public, largely uninformed due to scant media attention, began to receive a full dose of the nightmare Bonin was perpetrating throughout Southern California. While not the only serial killer operating in the area at the particular time, this media blitzkrieg was focused on Bonin's handiwork and will thus ramp up pressure on law enforcement and drive events forward on many fronts.

What was so surprising is how the events of March 24, 1980 will cause many different decisions to reverberate outwards like a bomb blast, touching everyone directly or indirectly connected to Bonin and his deeds.

33

J.J. Maloney Breaks the 'Freeway Killer' Story
March 24, 1980

Three days after the killings of Glen Barker and Russell Rugh, a key event in the Bonin story was about to take place. During three months at the **Orange County Register**, firebrand reporter J.J. Maloney started putting together his first major news story for the paper. Maloney had no fear of confronting criminals, police or his editors. In December 1979 Tim Alger, a young **OC Register** reporter on the police beat, wrote an article noting how bodies of boys were being dumped around the Southland, all strangled.

Police offered few details and answered fewer questions, with opinions on the killings being connected divided among detectives from county to city agencies. Quietly the story went away, while other media outlets failed to join Alger in the hunt for more info. At the time, Southern California media consisted of a few local TV news stations, five or six major newspapers and many small city publications.

While at work one-day, Maloney found an envelope laying on his desk with the ominous words "Dead Gay Boys" written on the front. Inside he found a collection of short, largely back page articles about 13 missing boys found dead, from strangulation, scattered throughout many different counties.

Maloney, unaware who left the envelope, speculated about the victims, wondering why there was "no outcry or task force to catch the killer." His Metro Editor, Marv Olsen, "agreed that it would be an injustice to the victims to even unintentionally imply they were homosexuals, since that might tend to trivialize the crimes—a lot of people would turn up their noses and say so 'so what.'"

Maloney sat down with Olsen and argued that other city papers would be "relentless" in pursuing the truth, not allowing police to "double-talk" them into dropping a line of inquiry. Public knowledge of a "serial killer" on the loose would place additional pressures on law enforcement.

Perhaps LAPD was protecting a recently tarnished image from the blown Hillside Strangler case. After spending millions investigating the Hillside Stranglers, Kenneth Bianchi was arrested after killing two more women by a small city police department in Bellingham, Washington.

From his perspective, Maloney told Olsen, a "psychopathic killer is on the loose and that kind of killer, once he starts, repeats and repeats and repeats." Law enforcement agencies were stonewalling the public, putting other lives at risk, and someone had to take the first step. Besides the public needing to know, would-be hitchhikers had to be warned their lives were in danger when they stuck out their thumbs. With Olsen on board, Maloney was assigned to the story full time while Tim Alger covered the police departments and assisted in developing feature articles.

Maloney quickly figured out these "homosexual strangulation" murders dated back to 1973 and involved numbers far higher than reported, with a total in the mid-thirties by March 1980. Trying to keep a lid on things, Maloney was told by law enforcement that "the strangulation of young men was a normal byproduct of the large homosexual community in the Orange County/Los Angeles area."

Not buying their official explanation, Maloney's research of national and California death statistics revealed startling facts: 1) Death by strangulation of males between 12 and 25 was rare; 2) The rate in Southern California between 1972 and 1980 was 15 times the national average; 3) Murder rates were lower for homosexuals than heterosexuals.

Searching for verification on a "one killer" theory, Maloney and Olsen consulted a forensic psychologist, Dr. Alert Rosenstein. Confirming what Maloney had postulated earlier, Rosenstein "insisted that it was one killer."

On March 24, 1980 the story broke in the ***Register*** that a "serial killer was at work in Southern California." Maloney dubbed him the "Freeway Killer" and it stuck big time. No matter what the police said in response, they ran front-page stories daily "sticking by the position that a serial killer was preying on young boys in Southern California."

Quickly all media outlets joined the chorus as phone tips flooded law enforcement and news offices. Damage control saw Captain Walt Ownbey, of the LA Sheriff's Dept., call the Freeway Killer "a total figment in the minds of journalists" and blaming the ***Register*** for unnecessarily, without evidence, igniting public hysteria. More victims in the weeks ahead forced law enforcement to admit the truth and increase inter-agency cooperation. Schools and community organizations distributed alerts for families to be extremely careful and report any suspicious activity.

34

Bonin Recruits Billy Pugh for Murder
Harry Todd Turner, March 24, 1980

At around 11: 00 a.m. on March 24, 1980, while the public, law enforcement and media outlets digested the "Freeway Killer" bombshell dropped by J.J. Maloney and the *OC Register*, Bonin received a phone call from Eric Wijnaendts. During his recent stay at OC Men's Jail, he met and developed a sexual relationship/friendship with Eric, who was going to turn 20-years-old in two-months.

Released from jail that morning but unable to enter his residence, Eric called Bonin, who picked him up and they went to his mother's house. A few hours later, after some intimate contact, Bonin took him over to Scott Fraser's to party. Eric, who later impacts events for many different reasons, made a scene by getting extremely drunk before Bonin dropped him off late in the afternoon.

That night Bonin was invited back over by Fraser for the express purpose of meeting 17-year-old William "Billy" Ray Pugh. Knowing the type of boys Bonin liked, Fraser believed Pugh's engaging smile and youthful appearance would appeal to him. Living in nearby Norwalk, Pugh had a colorful criminal history which included convictions for robbery, car theft, grand theft and battery on a teacher.

The never-ending party at Fraser's, replete with drugs and underage kids, was in full swing when Bonin arrived. Billy Pugh was playing a card game he learned while in juvenile detention. After finding out where Pugh learned the game, Bonin told him he learned it at Vacaville, and they exchanged various prison life stories. Topics included two of Bonin's favorites: sex and violence.

Bonin began laying the groundwork to start something with Pugh, knowing that killing him was out of the question since people saw them talking. Exchanging stories gave him an idea of what Pugh liked, and what Bonin could possibly offer or get from him. Two guys who spent years in custody were laughing and bragging about how they manipulated and trapped inmates to obtain sex, with force, and inflict bodily harm. Bonin began to have ideas about Pugh, as he wrote later, "I started getting the idea that he just might be a good guy to get into a good murder."

At 11:00 p.m. Pugh announced, "I have to leave, time for me to get home,"

"I can give you a ride," Bonin replied, beginning phase one.

"I have a bike."

"That's ok, I have a van, plenty of room in the back."

"Okay," Billy replied.

After pushing away two bean bag chairs, Pugh squeezed his bike into the back of the van. Pugh crawled between the seats and settled down in the front seat, then Bonin hit the road and began phase two.

"Has Scott ever given you head?"

"No, not yet."

"Are you interested in getting some from him?"

"Sure."

"How come you didn't get any tonight?" Bonin asked, pushing him further along.

"Well, you were there. I didn't want to say anything."

"Would you like some from me?" Bonin said, reaching across to touch Pugh's crotch.

"Sure, why not."

Bonin pulled over and parked in a dark alley behind a closed store. The two of them moved to the back of the van. Bonin began servicing Pugh and things began to heat up. After getting Pugh hard, Bonin stopped.

"I'm really horny, how about if he we do something else?" Bonin asked, feeling anxious and on edge, in fact he needed another kill.

"Bill, I'm one way, I do the fucking and I get sucked."

"Ok, why don't we quit," Bonin said, unbeknownst to Pugh phase three was in motion.

"You like boys?"

"Yeh, but I like girls better."

"Why don't we go out and look for a chick?" Bonin suggested, luring Pugh deeper.

"All right."

"If we can't find a chick, maybe we can pick up some guy. You have to get rid of the bike," Bonin told him, needing to clear out the back of the van for the main event.

After dropping off the bike, they headed to one of Bonin's favorite hunting grounds, the streets of Hollywood where young gay hustlers were plentiful. Pugh was under the impression they were looking for a girl to have sex with, that was never Bonin's intention.

"What if the chick doesn't want to do it?" Pugh asked.

"Fuck her and what she wants! We'd just take it from her, same way with the guys," Bonin said, giving Pugh the first indication of what lay ahead. "The only problem is they may tell afterwards. What should we do about that?" Bonin asked, taking the measure of Pugh.

"Beat the fuck out of her and tell her we'll come back and kill her," Pugh said, trying to impress Bonin but unaware of what lay ahead.

"Maybe it would be better not to take a chance and just kill her?" Bonin asked. Here was the whole reason Bonin had recruited Pugh. Through a series of deliberate manipulations, Bonin pushed him down the road to contemplating murder.

"Do you really think so?" Pugh asked with caution.

"Sure, hell, if no one sees us pick her up, no one will know she was with us. As long as no one sees us drop her off we're clean," he assured him, baiting the hook. "You don't want to get caught and sent back to juvie hall, do you?" Bonin asked, getting the hook into his mouth.

"Well yeah, that's for damn sure."

"Okay, we'll each get our nut and then kill her, Okay?" Bonin said, yanking him into the boat while searching for any doubts.

"Right on," Pugh exclaimed.

Point of no return, entering undiscovered terrain or crossing the Rubicon; any way one chooses to express the sentiment, in less than five-hours, on an ordinary night, many lives were altered dramatically. If Pugh had not met Bonin and joined his murderous escapade, they would not have found 15-year-old Harry Todd Turner on the streets of Hollywood.

They arrived after midnight and went straight to an area populated by male hustlers. Within minutes he spotted Turner with his thumb out. "Hey, there's a likely prospect, you could get a piece and get home in hardly any time at all," Bonin said as he pointed out the boy.

"Okay."

"Let me do the talking."

Harry readily accepted a ride from Bonin, being used to hustling on the streets. Settling on the jump seat between driver and passenger, he had stepped into the Death Van.

"Where you headed?" Bonin asked.

"AJ's" he answered, referring to Arthur J's coffee shop, a popular hangout in Hollywood at Santa Monica and Highland.

After putting the van in motion, everyone introduced themselves and Bonin asked, "How's business tonight?"

"You a cop?" Turner asked with suspicion.

"No."

"All right, we'll its lousy."

"You want to earn a quick 30 bucks?"

"How?"

"Let me give you some head."

"Okay."

Bonin drove past the coffee shop and parked on a side street. He got in the back of the van with Harry, while Pugh remained up front as a lookout. Harry pulled down his pants and Bonin got busy.

"Billy, is anyone around?" Bonin asked.

"No, looks ok around here," he answered.

Confident that no one was walking by or within earshot, Bonin pulled down his pants and ordered Harry to "suck my dick."

"Hey, that's not what you wanted, I don't give head," Harry told Bonin defiantly.

Bonin landed a jarring blow to Harry's jaw. Hearing the commotion, Pugh quickly rolled up the window, locked the doors, went in the back and closed the curtains.

"Roll over now," Bonin screamed at Turner, who complied immediately, stunned and scared at the rapid turn of events.

"Go ahead Billy, get a piece of ass," Bonin said.

"No, I want him to give me some head before," he replied as he pulled down his overalls.

"Yeah cool, I want you to give Billy some good head, or else!" Bonin said threateningly.

Pugh stretched out against a bean bag chair and Turner moved between his legs. Taking in the scene, Bonin's sadistic brain hit on a malevolent idea.

"Fuck, I might as well get a piece at the same time," Bonin said as he moved into a position to sodomize Turner.

He watched Pugh pushing down on Turner's head, saying, "Harder, more pressure, go down further." Pugh was clearly pleased with his power over Turner, who started choking. "Don't fucking throw up on my pants," Pugh screamed as Turner stopped to get a breath of air.

"Wait until I get into him before he continues with your head job," Bonin ordered with pleasure.

"Okay."

Bonin started sodomizing the boy and then told Pugh, "Okay, Okay, go ahead."

"Get on the rod, punk," Pugh said with a wicked smile.

Getting it from both sides, 15-year-old Harry Turner was just trying to survive the shocking encounter. Unable to discern his ultimate fate, he rolled with circumstances and prayed it would end soon. After a couple of minutes, Bonin finished and moved away from behind Turner. But Pugh wasn't done, he shoved Turner's head down hard and yelled, "More pressure, take more of it punk."

Turner couldn't do it and choked. Pugh stopped him, raised up on his knees and cracked Turner in the face with a closed fist, "You fuckin' punk, you're lucky you didn't throw up on me."

"Why don't you get your piece Billy," Bonin suggested, meaning Pugh should also sodomize him. Pugh liked the suggestion and moved behind Turner to take his own pound of flesh. Bonin watched with satisfaction until Pugh finished, anticipating the final part of an established pattern of sex, torture and killing. After Pugh finished, Bonin got in the driver's seat and told him to keep an "eye on the kid."

Battered, bruised and violated, Turner feebly asked if he could pull his pants up and was shouted down by Bonin.

"Billy, why don't you work him over," Bonin suggested while driving east towards Downtown LA. Pugh landed a series of devastating blows to his face, opening up cuts on his lips and cheeks which spewed blood on to the carpet. Fearing Bonin's wrath for getting the van dirty, Pugh stopped and rubbed his fists, checking for damage.

Unhappy with the reason Pugh stopped the beating, Bonin stopped and went back to show Pugh a technique of body torture which elicits no blood flow. Bonin positioned Turner to precisely deliver body blows throughout the abdomen, chest and lower back. Turner doubled over from lack of oxygen and mind-numbing pain. Then Bonin reached between his legs and grabbed his testicles and squeezed hard, bringing forth a high-pitched scream which delighted Bonin. Bonin got back in the driver's seat and continued east.

"Okay, no one will hear you now," he alerted Pugh, meaning it was time to keep punishing Turner with body blows, which he did with zeal. Turner rolled into a protective cocoon, trying to protect his vital organs. Pugh screamed at him, "Open up punk." After a minute of pointless hitting, with no appreciable damage, he gave up and told Turner he was stopping.

Mistakenly believing his captor, Turner relaxed his tortured body. Like a snake in waiting, Pugh reacted fast and clamped down on the boy's testicles before viciously striking him in the face. Bonin told him to stop and drag the boy up front, between the seats. Time was getting short, it would be light soon and Bonin needed to finish the job.

Bonin pulled around the corner from a gas station.

"Take all your clothes off," Bonin told Turner.

While this was going on, Bonin whispered into Pugh's ear, "We'll fuck him up first, no squeezing of the nuts, after he's weak, you hold his hands and I'll choke him."

"Okay," Pugh replied, offering no protest. Pugh didn't know if Bonin would turn on him if he refused to help. Either way, Pugh's moment of truth stood at hand: rape and assault were one thing, murder quite another! He could have run away, but later he claimed to have seen news clippings in Bonin's glovebox about various killings.

They pounced and reigned blows on the helpless boy, already bleeding and badly injured. Satisfied Turner was helpless, Bonin instructed Pugh to hold his hands, tied the shirt around his neck and inserted the tire iron in the loop. Slowly twisting in a circular motion, the noose tightened around his neck and cut the oxygen supply. Bit by bit the life drained out of Harry Todd Turner. When it was over his bowels let loose, spilling forth from his naked body on the carpeting.

Panic set in as morning approached. He had to find a deserted place to dump the body. They cruised around Downtown LA and went down an alley populated by dumpsters in the back of commercial properties. Bonin stopped, opened the side doors, pushed the boy out and quickly drove away. To assure no one had seen them, they drove around for a while before heading past the site again. No one was around and Bonin headed home.

When he dropped off his new partner in crime, Bonin told him, "Don't talk to anyone about this, if you need to talk then you talk to me, understand?" Pugh agreed but was nervous enough to call Bonin two days later. They met and Bonin calmed him down. While the two never saw each other again, their short association proved fateful.

Early morning on March 25, 1980, the nude body of Harry Todd Turner was found in an alley off South Bonnie Brae St. near Downtown LA. There were ligature marks on the neck and no identification at the scene. The penis and shoulder of the victim showed signs of being bitten. The headquarters of the LAPD's Robbery-Homicide Division, about three miles away, was notified immediately.

Turner was Bonin's 17th victim and the seventh dumped in LA County, but the only the second found within the actual LA City limits. Sgt. St. John, RHD's lead detective on this six-year long string of "homosexually oriented" murders, and his partner, Sgt. Mellecker, must have been called to the scene.

Over 40 unsolved murders, nearly half teenage boys in the previous eight months, mocked St. John's professional life. With media coverage gaining steam, Bonin's run was about to cause a panic that was going to rush full force at politicians and law enforcement. Harry Todd Turner was a troubled youth who ran away from the Optimist Boys Home five days before being swept up by evil coincidence.

35

Press Coverage & Bonin Misdirection

J.J. Maloney, Tim Alger and the editors at the **OC Register** had blown the lid off the Freeway Killer story. While the rest of the media played catch-up and joined the chorus, it was the Maloney-Alger team leading the way with daily front-page stories characterized by big headlines.

As March turned to April, their stories chronicled killings going back six years, lack of progress catching the perpetrators and identities of the most recent victims: meaning well over a dozen teenage boys murdered in eight months by Bill Bonin and others.

This development played into Bonin's ego, causing him to go out of his way to buy the **OC Register** in order to relive his exploits. He especially liked issues displaying pictures of the latest victims with their names and details about where they were found.

Such a barrage of news coverage never caused Scott Fraser to suspect his friend. Bonin liked young boys, and Fraser knew about him killing Markus Grabs, but the connection between the two was not made. Three had killed with Bonin; but one was out of state and two were still keeping their secrets. A major factor, concerning Fraser, was that the murders were not heavily reported till late March 1980, but an answer may also be found in a clever tactic Bonin deployed to feed his own ego and test what Fraser suspected.

Once the **Register** began running daily stories, especially about a new victim, Bonin would pick up a copy and take it over to Scott's apartment. He would show him the story and say, "Look, this guy got another one." Fraser's replies usually centered on wishing the guy would get caught "because this gives other good gay guys a bad name." Seems Bonin was testing Fraser to make sure he was in the clear.

He did the same thing at Dependable Drive-Away. Showing up with newspapers and exclaiming, "Look, you know that guy, look he got another one." Bonin relished their reactions to the stories while smiling on the inside, replaying the murders in his mind and thinking about the next one. Seeing his exploits splashed across the headlines was pleasing and he enjoyed hearing about the homicide detectives chasing the wind looking for him.

36

Bonin Kills Alone #10
Steven Wood, April 10, 1980

Two weeks after recruiting Billy Pugh to help murder Harry Todd Turner, Bonin was on the hunt again. Southern California was in a panicked frenzy. LAPD and various Sheriff's Departments, under county control, were in damage control and feeling heat from politicians, press and the public. Detective's legacies were being tarnished by Bill Bonin, who created a rapid string of victims with little evidence, except bodies, left behind. But the victims were not criminals or organized crime figures, they were innocent teenagers or runaways lost on the streets.

A tragic irony is that, during the murder spree, Bonin had been arrested, incarcerated, let out on his own recognizance, incarcerated again from a parole violation, let out again, incarcerated again on the parole case, then released for the last time on March 14, 1980, after serving six-weeks of a six-month sentence. His parole obligations were extended and then officially cancelled on April 11, 1980, one-day after killing Steven Wood.

Smart and dumb describes Bonin's methods: In the first instance he has spread victims in a 150-mile-wide radius and left no clues, in the second he has three co-murderers who are, at best, unreliable and unstable. One outsider, Fraser, knows about one murder but suspects nothing else. Bonin has two-modes; in the zone to find "someone" or cruising around looking to "relieve his frustrations." Sometimes he had sex with a kid and let him go; they were the lucky ones. Steven Wood was an unlucky one.

His mother saw him off for school at 9:30 a.m., gave him $10 for the day and later went to work. On the afternoon of Thursday, April 10 he was going from the dentist, located on Rosecrans, to his driver education class at Columbus High School in Downey. He exited the bus at Rosecrans and Woodruff, then set out on foot going north on Woodruff. A clerk at Manny's Liquor Store, located at Woodruff and Imperial, one mile from Rosecrans, spotted Wood outside the store around midday. He recognized him because Woods previously worked at the store.

Bonin, who lived nearby, was on the way home when he saw Wood hitchhiking. Probably walking up Woodruff, while hitchhiking at the same time, Bonin pulled up and offered him a ride. Unfortunately, he accepted. Steven Wood was just a regular 16-year-old running errands around his hometown.

This short description from Bonin's written confessions is disturbing and depressing.

"I saw this guy hitchhiking and picked him up. He was on his way to a driving class at some school. I told him I'd give him a ride all the way. I propositioned him and he declined, I offered him one hundred dollars if he let me suck him off. He was leery and didn't give an answer. I pulled into a lot at Woodruff and Rosecrans, about a hundred or so yards from a self-service car wash. I said, 'Let's talk a second' and shut off the engine.

"I said, 'Look I live right over there, I'm from this area and I won't hurt you and do anything you don't want to, I'll give you a hundred dollars to let me suck you off, and then I'll drop you off at school. It will probably only take fifteen minutes at most to cum. It would have taken you an hour to get to school, or longer.' He said, 'just a head job, nothing else?' I said, 'Right.' I knew I had him now.

"He said, 'Oh boy.' We got into the back and I got his dick hard and said, 'See, I got it hard. I'm gotta get some tissue, I don't like taking the cum.' He started jacking himself off to keep it hard, I went to the front to get some string and a knife, I came back and put the knife at his throat and told him to roll over, he did. He was really scared. I told him to put his hands behind his back and he did. I tied him up, then I took his pants, shoes, socks and drawers off and tied his legs. I had him take off his shirt before I tied his hands, I then fucked him and didn't bother coming.

"I took the chain and made a loop and put it around his neck, I said, 'where do you live?' He told me it was within a quarter mile. I said, 'That's too bad, you'll never see your house and family again.' He said, 'what do mean?' He was trembling now. I put the tire iron into the chain loop and twisted it until it was snug, then I said, 'Have you heard or read of the Freeway Killer guy?' He looked up at me and said, 'Yes.' I said, 'Well kid, that's me, and you're next.' He was so scared and trembling so much he was beyond crying, I twisted the iron and he died within minutes.

"I then untied him and laid him across the van against the back door and covered him up, I then drove home and parked. I went in the house and made calls looking for a job, Wood was in the van dead. At around 2:45 I finally had a possibility, it was a machine shop in Gardena on Western. I told the lady my qualifications and she sounded excited. She said, 'If you can before here 3:30 you can get an interview.' I told her I would be there at 3:30.

"I left the house and was there at 3:29, I filled out the application and talked to the man, I found out a couple of days later they hired me. After the interview I went home and went to a pizza place where my brother manages. As I pulled up, he was standing outside the door. There was a house at the end of the back parking area that had a back part on fire. The Fire Department was there with other units coming. I stuck around for a while and left. I went to a phone and called Scott and told him all the things I done up to that point of the day, except Wood's murder.

"I was creating an alibi for myself. I figured that if I took Pacific Coast Highway to Long Beach I'd arrive close to dark. When I got there it was still light, I drove around for about 45 minutes and then it was dark. I found an alley and dropped off the body."

Steven Wood's mother, Barbara Biehn, got home from work at 11:45 p.m. and expected to find her son at home in bed, he was not, and his jacket was on the bed. If Steven was out at night, he would surely have had the jacket with him. She began phoning friends and neighbors to no avail. Panic began to set in, the worry of a distraught mother overwhelming her every thought and movement.

The morning he left for the dentist young Steven said to her, "See you later alligator." His mother lovingly replied, as she always did, "After a while crocodile." She told detectives, "He took the bus there and was walking back to school when they got him, they killed him. He was just a little guy, just 5-feet 2, 88 pounds. He wanted to be a jockey."

At 7:40 a.m. the next morning his nude body was found 15-miles from Downey in an industrial section of Long Beach, at the crossroads of Pacific Coast Highway and the Long Beach Freeway. There were ligature marks on the neck, ankles and wrists.

Autopsy results showed a distinct similarity to Hyden and Turner, with a dark abrasion mark on the back of the neck; a knot like bruise the coroner said was caused by something "pushed against the skin." Dr. Carpenter referred to this as a form of "windless strangulation" created by the "twisting motion in the method of strangulation." The classic Bonin "t-shirt with an inserted iron bar for leverage" method of killing.

Even though many of the victims were picked up in various parts of Long Beach, this was first one Bonin left within the Long Beach city limits proper and the eighth in Los Angeles County. Long Beach homicide detectives were dispatched and assigned to the case. Of course, all the other relevant law enforcement agencies would be informed that the Freeway Killer had struck again.

37

Bonin & Butts Victim #6
Darin Lee Kendrick, April 29, 1980

Three weeks after Steven Wood's murder and Bonin was overdue and ready to claim another victim. The notoriously cruel murder of 19-year-old Darin Lee Kendrick was the sixth victim in as many weeks and his sixth and final one with Vernon Butts.

Bonin had racked up 18 murders, from August 4, 1979 to April 10, 1980, in eight-months and six-days while incarcerated for about three-months within that time frame. With victim 19, on April 29, Bonin reached this number during approximately 23 weeks of freedom; a chilling average of one per-week. Unable to control his compulsion, Bonin was now slave to the base instincts invading his every waking moment.

On the evening of April 29, about 9:00 p.m., Bonin was driving around Long Beach. He was agitated and needed another kill. Wanting a kid that turned him on, he ended up driving down Katella Avenue at the same time Darin Kendrick was rounding up shopping carts at Lucky's Super Market.

Having just cashed his $200 paycheck, the nineteen-year-old was probably in good spirits. When Bonin spotted Darin, he knew he had found the next one. He drove slowly as Darin walked back towards the store, pulling up beside the unsuspecting teenager.

"You want to buy some pot?" Bonin asked.

"How much?" the boy inquired.

"$45 an ounce."

"Sounds good, what kind is it?"

"Well, hop in and we'll drive around back, and I'll let you smoke a joint," Bonin said, needing him to get in the van. Kendrick looked around warily, checking to see if anyone from the store was watching. He made the last decision of his life by sliding into the passenger seat of Bill Bonin's Death Van. He pulled behind the store and turned off the engine and headlights. Having snagged his prey, Bonin didn't hesitate, there would be no cajoling or asking for anything. He pulled out a knife and placed the sharp edge against Kendrick's throat.

"You aren't that Freeway Killer, are you?" Kendrick asked with fear and shock. Bonin, taken by surprise at the question, played dumb while keeping the knife on Kendrick's throat.

"I don't know what you're talking about, I'm from out of state, I stole this van. I'm interested in whatever money you have on you, then you get out, but try anything and you're a dead motherfucker."

Kendrick calmed down a bit.

"What's this Freeway Killer shit?" Bonin asked, playing along, wanting to hear the answer.

"It's a guy who is going around picking up guys, raping them and then killing them."

"Look, I ain't no fag and I don't kill people, I rob them, but don't get me wrong. Do what I tell you or I will kill you if I feel threatened," Bonin barked at him, seizing control of the situation.

"Okay."

Bonin took him into the back of the van and told Kendrick he was going to tie him up, take his money and drop him off somewhere. He bound the boy's hands and feet with electrical tape, then tied them both together, leaving him helpless.

"How much money do you have?" Bonin asked.

"About 200 bucks."

A quick search of his pockets yielded about $180 and change. Bonin couldn't believe his luck. This was the largest amount of cash he ever found on someone.

Bonin realized he hadn't seen Vernon Butts for nearly five months, so he decided to go see him. Butts had moved from his apartment on Imperial Highway to a converted garage at 7310 Dinwiddie Street in Downey. Set well back from the street, a driveway bisected two small structures, one a house and the other the converted garage. He decorated it with black light posters, spider webs around the ceiling and two coffins, one for sleeping in and the other leaning against a wall as a phone booth. Loud music, drugs, promiscuous sex and shady companions were the themes of his existence.

Bonin had yet to visit the new dwelling. He pulled down the driveway and right up to Vern's front door and turned back to Kendrick.

"You better shut up and not say a word, if you do, you'll die," Bonin said before exiting the van.

When Butts opened the front door, he was shocked to see not only Bonin, but his van practically parked on his doorstep. Visitors were supposed to park on the street, but Bonin couldn't know that and didn't risk leaving the kid out there alone.

"Meet me at the van" he said, giving Vern a serious look of mischief.

"I can't, I have company."

"Just two-minutes of your time," he said with understated emphasis.

"Okay," he replied and went inside to excuse himself.

Bonin backed the van back onto the street. Butts walked out and found Bonin standing next to the van with the radio playing loudly inside, thus preventing Kendrick from hearing their conversation.

"This better be good," he said to Bonin.

"I have a live one in the van, I thought we could use your house," Bonin stated. Vern knew all too well what the words "use your house" meant. Already in deep by committing five murders with Bonin, was Butts ready to move even deeper by bringing the mayhem into his home?

"I have friends over, just can't do it."

"Fuck, get rid of them," Bonin barked at him.

"No way, forget it."

"Look, the kid has money on him, 40 bucks is yours," Bonin told him, Butts' face lit up.

"Okay, give me five-minutes."

"Vern, I am going to tell the kid not to say anything after I put him in the house. If he says anything, I'll fuck him up, you try and get him to say something but don't touch him," Bonin told Vern, setting a trap for Kendrick.

After Vern's friends left, Bonin backed the van back up the driveway and the two men hustled Kendrick inside and dumped him on the living room floor. While he moved the van back to the street, Butts employed various tactics to get Kendrick to talk.

"Did he say anything?" Bonin asked when he returned.

"This kid is scared to fuckin' death of you, I tried to get him to talk, even threatened to put my foot in his mouth, nothing," Butts reported.

"Very good, you listened well. Now tell Vern here why you didn't say anything," Bonin ordered the frightened Kendrick.

Tied up, on the floor, frightened beyond words, Darin Kendrick began addressing Vernon Butts directly. The 23-year-old Butts possessed a scarecrow-like visage that was rather frightening. At six-foot-three inches tall and 130 pounds, with stringy brown hair and green eyes, Butts probably fit the "serial killer" physical profile look more than Bonin.

"If I said one word and you told I did, he was going to just out and kill me, no questions. I believe he would have done it. I'd rather get a foot in the mouth than be dead," Kendrick said to Vern, who cracked a menacing smile. Their little game played out perfectly.

Had Kendrick figured out that Bonin was indeed the insidious Freeway Killer? Trapped inside Butts' creepy living room, with a coffin against the wall and weird freaky posters on the walls, he had fallen into the twilight zone. Masses of adrenalin were pumping through every fiber of his being as that lost, empty feeling in the pit of his stomach shot through his body.

Bonin cut the ties from Kendrick's feet, helped him up and led him to the bedroom. Bonin laid him down on the bed, on his stomach, and removed the shoes and socks. Methodically setting up the scene, Bonin proceeded to tie up his legs and then cut off the work apron, pants, shirt and underwear.

"He's a good-looking kid, huh?" Bonin commented, hungrily viewing the catch.

"Yeh, he is a sweet one," Vern responded, anticipating the fun.

Bonin got undressed and told Kendrick to give him head while his co-conspirator got undressed. Then they switched places and Bonin brutally sodomized Kendrick while Vern got serviced orally. Sadistic, punishing and just the way Bonin liked to treat his victims; all the energies of Bonin's life focused on nothing but the sexual degradation of children and their deaths.

"Man, this kid gives good fucking head," Vern exclaimed with delight.

"You should try this end," Bonin answered back with disgusting pleasure.

"I will," he said, signaling it would continue.

After Bonin finished sodomizing Kendrick, Vern came around and took his pound of flesh from behind. Thoroughly enjoying themselves, the Bonin and Butts team were about to descend further into the dark abyss of human cruelty.

Once Vern was done, they positioned Kendrick on his knees and sitting on his heels. Butts whispered to Bonin he had some Chloral Hydrate solution they might use. Butts obtained it from his occult mentor James

Meurer, who had gotten it from a friend and was known to them as "knock out drug." From testimony, it appears neither Meurer nor Butts used the Chloral Hydrate much, if at all. A prescription drug used as a short sedative, to ease stomach pain, Bonin was aware of its properties. They slowly began feeding the liquid substance to Kendrick. After a few minutes he was drowsy and stoned, saying, "Is my mouth still there?" Butts then retrieved another solution to feed Kendrick.

"Just drink this one," Bonin told him, eager to see what would happen next.

His answer came quickly when Kendrick began throwing up in a thick stream which left red burns on his lips, chin, chest and face. Some form of poison, like a "lye" solution, must have been the second drink. Chloral Hydrate does not cause burn marks. The coroner reported the liquid didn't move past the teeth and none was found in the boy's mouth or throat. Kendrick was now on his back and looked up at them and said, "Wow, I'm tripping." He was in a stupor when Vern asked Bonin to come in the other room for a chat.

Standing in the kitchen, Vern looked seriously at Bonin and said, "I want to try the icepick thing."

"Okay, go get one."

He opened the drawer next to him and pulled out an icepick. Vern got a hand-held sledgehammer, and they went back in the bedroom. With Kendrick totally out of it, Bonin tied an electrical cord around his neck, tied a loop in the back and began twisting. After Kendrick lost consciousness, Bonin manhandled him into position for Butts to do his "icepick thing." Wanting as little noise as possible, Bonin gagged him with one of his socks and tied it with string around his head. Reaching the final act in a disgustingly macabre scene, Bonin held down Kendrick's head while Butts placed the icepick in his ear and readied the hammer.

Seeing it all lined up, Bonin had a thought it was going to be too messy and went to stop Vernon. But it was too late as the hammer blow fell on the icepick and penetrated the cervical section of the spinal cord. Kendrick let out a high-pitched scream and then nothing. Blood started pouring out of his ear even with the icepick inserted, causing both of them to scramble for towels and the boy's clothes to mop it up.

Bonin tried to pull the icepick out, but the handle broke off in his hand. Most of it was still submerged in his brain, and would remain there, as they put a plastic bag over his head and moved him to the shower. After considerable effort to stop the bleeding and cleaning up, they double bagged all of Kendrick's clothes and put the body in the van. The plastic bag was affixed to his head with a rubber band around the neck to prevent bleeding on the van carpets.

Only Kendrick's wallet was left out, which Vern grabbed and kept with all the possessions contained therein; a small black address book, various cards, a Security Service check cashing card and spring 1980 parking pass for Cypress College. Bonin would have thrown it out, but it slipped through the cracks and Vern kept the wallet and hid it away.

During the previous murder they committed, five months earlier, Bonin had driven 100 miles to the outskirts of Bakersfield to get rid of the body. Since it was already late at night, nearly midnight, Butts didn't want to accompany Bonin on another long excursion. Bonin assured him it would be a short ride. They drove 15-miles to the City of Carson and dumped him near a construction site. Bonin dropped Butts off just before one o'clock in the morning and headed home.

Another innocent young life had been taken at the hands of Bill Bonin and Vernon Butts. Four hours earlier he was a young man chasing shopping carts in a parking lot at work, now he was a notch on Bonin's belt and a chilling statistic; all his future possibilities replaced by pain, loss and the sorrow of family and friends. Darin Lee Kendrick would forever remain that young 19-year-old in their hearts and minds.

On the morning of April 30, 1980 Darin Kendrick's nude body was found in the industrial section of Carson. There were ligature marks on his neck, ankles and wrists. It was determined the icepick and strangulation were the causes of death. Dr. Stovitz could only guess at what "caustic" solution caused the burns, putting it down to an acidic "lye" type of solution.

The City of Carson was policed by the LA County Sheriff's Dept., so it immediately landed with Sgt. Kushner and his team. Darin Kendrick was the ninth victim dumped in LA County; the other totals being three in Orange County, four in San Bernardino County, one in Riverside County, one in San Diego County and one in Kern County.

Bonin later told David Lopez, a journalist covering his trial, that Kendrick was "killed ritualistically at the home of Vernon Butts." What a load of self-promoting bovine scatology—killing Kendrick was quite simply a series of opportunistic coincidences advanced by Butts' accidental participation. This was their last killing together, but not the last Vern knew about.

38

Bonin Meets Jim Munro
May 1980

Jim Munro, 19-years old, is a key person to this story for a variety of reasons. His involvement with the last murder committed by Bonin, his testimony regarding that incident and what Bonin told him about other occurrences proved vital as investigators unraveled the whole story. During their short association, which began in early May 1980, Bonin engaged with Munro in a variety of activities; sex, work, partying, picking up hitchhikers just to chat them up, watching TV and murder.

A tangled web of events and coincidences starts with Jim Munro and Bonin meeting at a Gay Community Center near Hollywood and Highland, the heart of Hollywood.

Munro, born in Germany and adopted by a U.S. Serviceman and his wife, was raised in St. Clair, Michigan, north of Detroit. He was a lean, nice looking 19-year-old man with bleached blonde hair and an engaging personality. Munro was comfortable talking to all kinds of people, easily made new friends and was bisexual. He dropped out of high school and, for a couple of years, repeatedly hitchhiked between Michigan and Southern California.

He was given an Honorable Discharge from the Michigan Army National Guard in December 1978. Hitchhiking trips across the country gave Munro a knowledge of the best truck stops to pick up rides and he made friends with a number of long-haul drivers. His length of stay in either place varied depending on circumstances.

Before meeting Bonin, he had been in LA for a few months living with his girlfriend sometime fiancée, Tammie Capps, in North Long Beach with Stan Hurd, a local businessman. He met Tammie in Redondo Beach and, according to Jim, she was a part time prostitute and "real party gal." Tammie introduced him to Stan, who had taken the couple under his wing as he was fond of Tammie. Munro stayed with Tammie, either at Hurd's house or business.

In early 1980 they went back to Jim's home territory in Michigan, where

Tammie had a miscarriage. She called Stan for bus fare to get back to Long Beach, he agreed but wanted her to return alone. Tammie refused and Stan sent enough to get them both back. Tammie was going to join the Army and Munro considered Stan almost like family because of the all the kindness he had shown them, feelings not reciprocated by Stan.

Sometime in March 1980, because Jim had acquired and lost a series of jobs, he was asked to leave the Hurd residence. Munro still owed Stan money, for the return trip, and this would become an issue in the months ahead. Jim started living on the streets of Hollywood and earned money hustling sex in the gay areas of town. One of his favorite hangouts was Arthur J's coffee shop at Santa Monica and Highland. A well-known gathering place for hustlers like Munro, in fact it was so notorious that management had to douse the restroom floors with ammonia to discourage loitering or illegal activities.

Around May 5 Bonin was up near Hollywood to visit someone he met through a gay magazine, **The Advocate**, who supposedly was a look alike for the famous actor, George Peppard. Bonin went to his house, but he wasn't home, so he went by the Gay Community Service Center nearly Hollywood and Highland. While there he saw Jim Munro and talked to him briefly. He asked Munro if he wanted to come over to his house for the weekend, but Munro couldn't without his friend.

Bonin finally got ahold of the George Peppard look alike and went to his house. They talked for about an hour and Bonin was told that Westwood, six miles west towards the beach, was a good place for meeting gays. On the way to Westwood, he stopped by the Gay Community Center again and saw Munro talking with a possible client as he talked with someone else. Jim saw him at the same moment Bonin's conversation finished, and abruptly ended his own conversation and walked over and said, "Is that offer still open?

Bonin said sure and they headed for Downey, 20-miles south. Bonin's mother was gone for a month, visiting family in Connecticut, so they had the run of the place. On the way back Bonin bought Munro dinner. Bonin said he would see about getting him a job where he worked, at Dependable Drive-Away. Bonin believed Munro had just arrived in town, unaware he had been hanging around Hollywood off and on for months. Munro fit the bill as someone he might recruit for killing; young, impressionable and easily manipulated.

The next day Bonin and two other drivers were scheduled to drop off three trucks in Oakland. Bonin convinced his boss to hire Jim to follow them up in his car. The three men would drive back together and thus relieve his boss of paying for return flights. Munro was hired by Dependable, and Bonin helped him obtain a learner's permit driving license. Munro went to work with Bonin and sometimes went on truck runs, but most often he sat waiting for an assignment while Bonin was driving.

Bonin, one of their most active drivers, could always be counted to arrive on time and was willing to go anywhere at any time. But he also got in trouble taking unsanctioned routes home after separating from other drivers, which nearly got him fired multiple times. What was Bonin doing during those unsupervised routes is a mystery? During off hours they partied at Scott Fraser's or were out cruising Long Beach, looking for guys to pick up for sex. They visited a bookshop where Jim Munro had some friends, as well as picking up and dropping off various individuals during their travels.

Around mid-May Bonin brought up the subject of killing as he explains, "One day Jim and I got into a conversation about killing people He told me that he could do it. We decided to go out and find someone and do it, then the phone rang and I had to go to work. The next day I had to take a truck down to San Diego. Jim was to drive the van down and drive me back. My car was in the shop. We decided to park the van near the freeway near the house and take the truck down and hitchhike back. This way we saved some money. On our way back we decided to kill whoever picked us up and take their car. It took us almost all night by the time we got a ride.

"Then early in the morning a guy about 24-years old picked us up. He was good looking. I made a pass at him and he declined. I put my hand on his leg and he pulled over and let us out. Both Jim and I could have taken him and I was thinking about it. Jim was looking at me saying let's take him with his eyes. I decided it was too risky and we got out. Shortly after that a guy picked us up. He gave us a ride all the way to where we were going. It was getting light so we didn't do anything. I did get it on with the guy though. I jacked him off and gave him some head as we were going down the road."

Bonin has planted the seed and Munro went to Dependable every day but was not earning enough, he was new and not considered reliable. He left Bonin's and went back to Stan Hurd's place. Stan arranged a job for him at a Mobil gas station, at Artesia and Atlantic, hoping to recoup the funds he laid out for the bus fare back from Michigan.

Munro lasted a few days at the gas station before getting fired. Hurd again furiously asked him to leave. Munro went back to Hollywood and appeared back at Bonin's around May 22, having no idea that during his absence Bonin had committed two murders.

39

Bonin Recruits Eric Wijnaendts for Murder
Larry Sharp, May 17, 1980

Days after Munro moved back in with Tammie, at Stan Hurd's, Bonin was back at it and quickly claimed two more victims, Larry Sharp and Sean King, within three days of each other. These murders ushered in a new player, Eric Wijnaendts, someone whose participation in two murders, and his meaning to Bonin emotionally, will have a dramatic impact on subsequent events.

In the meantime, Darin Kendrick's employer, **Lucky Markets**, put up a $30,000 reward for information leading to his killer and a local gay activist organization, **Great Outdoors**, would soon add another $50,000 for the capture of the "Freeway Killer who could be responsible for up to 40 sex-related murders of young men." Greg Carmack of **Great Outdoors** said, "If you make the reward big enough, the guy's mother will turn him in."

Pressure was building on law enforcement, but the ever-elusive Bonin was an unknown entity to them. Bonin's next victim was Larry Sharp; number 20 since beginning his murder spree almost ten months earlier. During this 38-week period, Bonin had been in custody for 12-weeks, thus he claimed those 20 victims during 26-weeks of freedom.

None of his co-murderers, three so far, were talking while harboring their own fears of Bonin's wrath. Of the three, only Butts knew Bonin was the real "Freeway Killer" written about since the **OC Register** broke the story in late March. Bonin would come over to Butts' house with copies of the stories, some with victim picture galleries, and wave them in his face and scream angrily, "See this one, that is one I did, see this one, that is also mine."

Greg Miley, far away in Texas, was no less afraid of Bonin because he had witnessed the brutal killer in action. He also believed, probably because Bonin told him so, that he had friends everywhere ready and willing to kill for him. Billy Pugh had been arrested for car theft and was housed at a juvenile detention center in Downey, less than four miles from where Bonin lived. Scott Fraser, one-time neighbor and continuing party buddy, was thrown off the scent when Bonin showed up with newspaper articles and said, "Look that guy got another one."

Lawrence Sharp, age 17, was last seen by his mother on May 11, 1980 at the family home in Long Beach. Larry was given two dollars by his mother, which he carried in a cloth wallet with a Velcro closing. Not possessing a car, Sharp took a bus or hitchhiked and often left home for weeks at a time. During long absences on the road, sometimes with truck drivers, he often checked in from various locations. Larry's sister, Candy Nikola, later said in court that she and Larry had an argument on May 12. During the argument, Nikola yelled for her sister, who came in and started hitting Larry. He said he was packing his clothes and they would never see him again, which is exactly what happened.

Bonin's written confessions reveal when he first met Larry Sharp and the accidental re-meeting when he was with Eric Wijnaendts, who turned 20 six days earlier. Wijnaendts was born in Holland but grew up and lived in nearby Garden Grove.

"A friend of Larry's and mine had been getting it on for a while and one night when I dropped this guy off down in Long Beach, he introduced me to Larry. This was before any of these other things started to happen. He had the kind of looks I like, so I went down there a few days later and picked him up. He ended up coming home with me and spent the night. The only thing Larry let me do that night was hug and kiss him a couple of times and give him head for a while. We then went to Knott's Berry Farm the following day, getting home around 11:00 p.m. that evening. After Knott's I took him down to Long Beach and dropped him off. I didn't see Larry again until the night Eric and I killed him.

"I met Eric in March of 1980 while in jail in Orange County. He was talking with someone in the vestibule and I struck up a conversation with him. He turned me on. I got his address and phone number and gave him mine. He was out of cigarettes, so I gave him a pack here and there. We got to know each other pretty good in jail, having sex and talking.

"I got out around March 15 and on March 24 he called when he got out, it was around 11:00 a.m. or so. We met for a couple of hours, had sex and then went over the Fraser's to party a bit. I felt quite attracted to him for many reasons. The only guy I ever met who didn't ask for things, such as money, in return for getting down and sharing life together. He asked me for advice on stuff going on in his life.

"Once he called me at 3:00 a.m. to talk, he was upset and needed someone to lean on. After 30 minutes I had to end the call, I had work early in the morning. We had an interesting relationship, and I felt a kind of love for him, even from knowing him only a little while. But we kind of drifted apart after those first weeks after he got out. Eric said he wanted to live with me, but not at my mother's house. He would live with me if I got an apartment and even pay half the way.

"One Saturday in May I called Eric and asked him what he was doing? He said, 'Not much.' I said, 'Why don't' we get together?' He said yes and I picked him at the corner of Valley View and Leffingwell. This was right near the house he was staying at. It was my idea that I pick him up away from the house as I didn't want the guy he was staying with to get jealous. I picked him up and we started cruising around Long Beach and I mentioned the 'hit squad' I had talked to him about a couple times in chow line at Orange County jail. He was still quite interested and here is how the conversation went:

"There's this guy who is thinking about turning over some contracts to me. I'll know in a couple of weeks. We're talking about a bit to start off with but it's not definite yet, are you interested in being in on it?"

"Fuck yeah, it's better money than I could get working."

"Yeah, but it is work."

"Sure, I understand."

"Listen, I'm lining up the people who want to be in on it now and am only choosing only one person. It has to be someone I can count on and know he won't back down at the last moment.'

"Hey, I can handle it, you don't have to go any farther."

"Prove it."

"How?"

"We'll pick someone up, someone we don't know, and then kill him. If you can and do handle it, then you're in."

"Okay, when?"

"Tonight."

"Okay."

"I have to say that at that at this point Eric was drinking. So he had some beer with him. He had been drinking before I picked him up and continued after I picked him up. Anyways, we started cruising down Long Beach Blvd. and I said, 'I tell you what, we'll pick up some guy, maybe even a hustler. I'd like to get a good piece of ass at the same time. We can make it look like this Freeway Killer guy.' Eric said, 'Fine with me.' Then we spotted Larry hitchhiking up Long Beach Blvd. and we picked him up. After he got into the van I saw who it was and recognized him, I had forgotten his name though.

"I asked him his name again and introduced Eric to him. Then I asked Eric to drive. I asked Larry if he'd like to get it on and he said, 'No, not tonight.' I said, 'It's worth 50 bucks' and he agreed. When Eric was driving I got in the back and Larry got undressed. Then I said, 'Get it hard' and he started manipulating himself. I got the knife from up front and came back and put it to his throat and said, 'Turn over.' Larry did and said, 'Hey, Bill, what's happening?' I shoved him and said, 'Shut the fuck up and do as you're told and you will be okay.'

"After Eric pulled over at a safe place, he came in back and I told him to put the knife away up front, then I began again, 'Larry, so last time we met I took you to Knott's and didn't get shit for my troubles. Well, now you'll pay your dues. You owe me you little prick.' I got on top of him and got my piece by fucking him as hard as I could. Then I told Eric, 'Go ahead and get a piece. The semen of both of us will mix together and they won't be able to tell whose it is.' So Eric went ahead and got a piece, he fucked him real hard too. Larry took his medicine and didn't squeal too much.

"Then I told Eric to give me Larry's T-type shirt. He did. I put it around Larry's neck, I really wanted to fuck with him. I told him in my best scary voice, 'How would you like to end right here punk?' Larry was scared shitless and didn't say anything. 'Why are you a hustler Larry?' He answered like it was a plea for mercy, 'I, I don't know, easy money I guess.' Larry was freaking out, but I really hate hustlers and don't mind getting rid of them. I got the tire iron and put it in the T-Type shirt and turned it until the shirt was snug against his neck and told Eric, 'I almost feel like killing him, but we will probably get in a lot of trouble. I'm going to leave you just like that for five minutes. You're not going to move a fucking muscle. If you do, I'll fucking kill you, understand punk.'

"Then I motioned to Eric to come up front. I turned up the back speakers on a little louder than usual, so Larry wouldn't be able to hear what I was saying to Eric. I asked him, 'Are you sure you can handle this.' He said yes and I gave the next step, 'Okay, here's what we're going to do.

We'll go back there and I'll twist the shirt, at the same time you grab his nuts and squeeze as hard as you can.' Eric was concerned, he said, 'But he'll scream.' I had to get him calm, 'Listen, I'll be choking him, no sound will come out and it will help to cause him to lose conscious quicker.' Eric said 'okay' and we got ready.

"We went back and without a word I started choking him and Eric reached down and started squeezing his nuts real hard, Larry writhed around in pain, fighting as I turned the tire iron tighter and tighter. Larry gasped for air but it was no use. Eric then switched his squeezing hands, from right to left and began hitting Larry in the body and face. After a short time Eric pulled his hand up fast and said, 'The fucker pissed on me.' I laughed and said that happens when the person loses consciousness.

"We untied him and then drove around look for a place to dump him off. We eventually dropped him behind a Mobil gas station in Westminster and then I dropped Eric off at the place on Leffingwell. I told him I'd give him a call later in the week. Then Eric said something I still laugh about, 'This guy wasn't too good looking. I didn't get turned on that much from him.' I said, 'Well next time I'll try to get a sweet youngster for you.' He said, 'Yeah, do that.' I went home to sleep, I was really tired after that one."

On Sunday morning May 18, 1980 Jon Hagey went to throw away some trash. The bin was located at the back of a Mobil gas station on Westminster Blvd. He saw a pair of legs sticking out from near the front of a car situated between a Mercury station wagon and an Oldsmobile. Hagey walked closer to see what was happening, not believing his eyes at first.

He followed drag marks and discovered Larry Sharp. There were three to four feet of drag marks that probably were made by the body being taken out of a vehicle. Hagey swallowed hard to keep from vomiting as he walked back and called police, but the station mechanic was already on the phone reporting the discovery. Lawrence Sharp's motionless body leaned heavily against the left front tire of a Chevy truck.

None of the station employees knew who the dead boy was, and no clothing or other evidence was found. The LA Coroner reported finding semen and spermatozoa on the head of the victim's penis, a rectal swab revealed the presence of semen. Sharp had been orally copulated and raped. Fibers were found on the victim's scrotum and head hair.

Those located in the head hair were similar to the fibers found on three other victims, Russell Rugh, Glen Barker and Dennis Fox. Time of death for Sharp, established by OC Deputy Coroner Lendith Lee, was set at about 2:00 a.m. on May 18. Lee told the court that post-mortem is "the settling of the body fluids to the lower most portion of the body. When one applies pressure with a finger to the lower part of the body and it blanches then we know post-mortem had set."

Lee noted Sharp's body was enveloped in rigor mortis, reporting "it started in the jaw all the way down through the lower extremities" as the body becomes stiff. His scrotum had two abrasions along with bruising on both upper and lower lips, caused by a fist. A hematoma on his head was caused by a flat, padded instrument. Four victims, Fox, Barker, Rugh and Sharp, were strangled with the same size ligature. Barker, Rugh and Sharp had engorged skin hemorrhages in the whites of the eye.

Larry Sharp was the fourth victim dumped in OC and the 20th murdered by Bonin and company. Esposito, OC County Sheriff's Dept., and other homicide detectives strongly believed this murder involved more than one individual.

40

Bonin & Wijnaendts Victim #2
Sean King, May 19, 1980

"Laying in my cell I started remembering the gnawing hunger I felt that night, only two days after killing Larry Sharp." Bonin later wrote about the night of May 19, 1980.

Driving his Blue Chevette, Bonin went over to Vernon Butts' place on Dinwiddie Avenue in an attempt to get him to "go out hunting." Vern said no, but he did convince Bonin to give his friend, James Meurer, a ride home before going out. Bonin talked Vern into driving along, believing he might persuade him on the way back. While nearing Vern's house, at about 9:30 p.m., Bonin spotted a boy waiting at the bus stop where Firestone and Old River Road crossed—it was 14-year-old Sean King.

Five-foot six inches tall, slender with dark hair, a fair complexion and green eyes, King was a high achieving student at West Middle School in Downey. Into swimming and surfing, during the previous summer he often hitchhiked to the beach, with friends, but was warned off the practice by his mother, Laveda Gifford. She had seen reports about the Freeway Killings and told Sean, while wagging a finger in his face, "When you and your friends go to the beach this summer, just make sure you don't hitchhike." Sean told her, "I promise, I wouldn't be that stupid."

After getting home from school, Sean left in the early evening to take the bus to his girlfriend's house. He was wearing blue OP shorts, a white t-shirt, white slip-on tennis shoes and a blue sweatshirt jacket.

"Hey, there's a good-lookin' kid, let's pick him up." Bonin said.

"No, I don't wanna do it," Vern flashed back.

"Well, I'll just stop anyway and talk to him," Bonin said with a glimmer in his eye. He stopped the car and casually asked, "Hey, where is Atlantic Boulevard?"

"It's right down the road, about a mile or so," King replied innocently.

"Are you waiting for the bus?"

"Yeah."

"Don't you know the last bus has already run, where you headed?" Bonin asked, baiting the hook.

"Atlantic Blvd."

"Hop in, that's where I'm heading."

"Okay," Sean said, walking over to the car.

"I don't believe this," Vern exclaimed, looking at Bonin with disbelief.

Bonin had smoothly lured Sean King into his web of horror, ensnared by a comforting voice and a false assurance of assistance. King got in the backseat, and they headed south on Firestone Blvd.

"Take me home first," Vern ordered Bonin, knowing the kid's fate was sealed, seemingly having no desire to participate. For five months, until the April 29 Kendrick murder, Vern was absent from Bonin's killings. In that grisly murder, three weeks earlier, Butts fulfilled his fantasy of using an icepick to issue the final blow.

After arriving at Vern's, Bonin told King to wait in the car while he got something inside. He got a blanket, twine and a steak knife from Vern and again urged him to come along, Butts refused. This was yet another steak knife Butts complained about losing during his killing association with Bonin.

Heading out in the Blue Chevette, the first time this car had been used in a murder, Bonin set about luring the boy in deeper.

"You do a lot of hitch-hiking?" Bonin asked Sean.

"No, not usually,"

"Ever run into gay people?"

"No."

"How would you like to earn $20.00 for letting me suck you off?"

"I'm not into that kinda stuff," Sean replied warily.

Bonin sensed Sean was getting nervous and pulled off at a side street and found a vacant lot to park.

"You can let me off here, I don't mind walking home," Sean said while reaching for the door handle and found it locked. "Hey, this is locked," he exclaimed.

Bonin pulled the steak knife, grabbed Sean by the neck and held it to his throat.

"Please don't hurt me, please mister, I don't want to die," Sean said, beginning to cry.

"All I want you to do is suck me off, you do what I tell you and you'll be okay."

"Okay, look I'm putting the knife away. But if you fuck up, I'll take it out and use it," Bonin told him with menace in his voice. Sean's breath was shallow, his body shaking, his eyes filled with fear.

"Put your hands behind your back and you'll be okay."

"Okay, but you aren't going to hurt me?"

Bonin tied his hands behind his back, took off his shoes and socks, tied his legs, then reached down and began to fondle him.

"It isn't very big," Sean said.

"Doesn't matter to me," Bonin said, then pulled out his dick and told him to suck.

After a minute or so Bonin was fed up and gave him a French kiss. He redressed, started up the car and, before leaving, he reclined the passenger seat and put a blanket over Sean and said, "You just pretend you're sleeping, if you try and get anyone's attention, I'll kill you."

He got back on Firestone Boulevard, heading towards the 605 Freeway, but then decided to give Eric Wijnaendts a call. Larry Sharp had not turned Eric on, but Bonin thought Sean King just might. Bonin called Eric from a phone booth, one often used to call Vernon Butts when Vern lived on Imperial Highway.

"Can you talk?" Bonin asked Eric.

"No, not really."

"I have to talk to you, meet me at Valley View, meet me in 20-minutes," Bonin told him rather than asking.

"Okay," Eric replied and hung up.

Wanting to arrive before Eric, he drove along Imperial Highway to Valley View, then went just north of Imperial to Leffingwell. He found a quiet place on a residential street to park.

"I'm going to be talking to someone outside the car, but I'll be watching you. You make out you're sleeping, or you'll be one dead motherfucker, or I'll sell your ass to a farm out of state where you'll be a homosexual slave, do you fucking understand me?" Bonin said in his scariest voice.

"Yes," the terrified 14-year-old replied.

"You'd better, cause I won't hesitate if I think you're doing anything other than sleeping," Bonin barked back at his hostage.

Sean King's young mind was scalded with fear, feeling the hatred in Bonin's words. An innocent boy at the wrong place at the wrong time who gave the wrong answer to a simple yet devastating question. Bonin pushed the door open, walked to the front of the car and looked back through the front windshield. Satisfied he could not be seen by pedestrians or motorists, he relaxed. Eric arrived fifteen minutes later.

"I got a call from that guy I was telling you about. He said I have to prove to him that I can do someone in and hide the body, ya know, so nobody finds it for at least six months," Bonin said, lying to Eric. "I got this kid in the car right now, incidentally he is a sweetheart. So, if you really want in, you'll have to help me get rid of him, so he won't be found."

"Let's go," Eric anxiously replied.

Eric crawled in the back of the car. Bonin started driving and Eric got his first look at Sean.

"You are right, this one is a sweetheart. I'm going to really enjoy him."

"I'll tell you what," Bonin said in a suggestive tone, "why don't I put him in the back with you and you get some head while we're heading out."

Bonin pulled into the Zody's parking lot and Sean was transferred to the back seat. Bonin hit the 605 Freeway and headed to the 10 Freeway, moving northeast to the Inland Empire of San Bernardino. While Sean was being forced to give Eric head, Bonin threatened to kill him if he didn't swallow the cum and he complied, not only with Eric but with Bonin when they switched places.

Bonin later took over driving again and they ended up over 75-miles east of Downtown LA, exiting in Yucaipa then proceeding north into the San Bernardino Mountains. He found a lonely country road running parallel to railroad tracks, stopping at a spot adjacent to a large field and surrounded by thick brush.

He parked the car and Bonin excitedly exclaimed, "Let's get a piece of ass."

First Bonin, and then Eric, raped their innocent young captive in the back of the car, oblivious and uncaring as he begged for mercy, hoping beyond hope all they wanted was sex. After they had enough, Bonin motioned for Eric to get out so they could talk. They walked over and stood by a large tree.

"What do you want to do with the kid now?" Bonin asked, looking for the right answer.

"Let's stick him this time," Eric said.

Bonin handed him the steak knife and said, "Okay, you do it."

"All right."

They went back to the car, untied Sean and told him to take off the rest of his clothes. Bonin told the boy not to worry, "I am only going to choke you until you are unconscious and then leave your clothes behind with you."

They walked Sean across a field. Bonin told him to lie down face first on the ground, grabbed his hands, joined them together behind his back and held them securely with all his weight. Eric began stabbing him, first on each side of the abdomen, then in the back and neck, blood rushing out from all the wounds which the serrated knife created.

"Stick him again in the neck," Bonin ordered Eric, who readily complied.

From what they could tell Sean King was dead, however, after walking a short distance away from the body they heard noises and stirring. They whirled around, shocked to see Sean's legs raised up in the air, quivering in spasmodic fits. Angrily, Bonin snatched the knife from Eric and hurried back to finish the job.

"Shut up motherfucker," he said as he started to choke Sean with his hands, but that didn't seem to work so Bonin began stabbing him repeatedly in the sides, the back, legs, buttocks, neck and then through the side of his mouth. Sean King was silent, for the second time it appeared he was dead.

An innocent young boy violated and cheated out of life to fulfill Bonin's dark fantasies of power and pleasure. Another family bereft, broken forever.

Bonin and Eric got back in the Chevette and drove down the hill to a Circle K store for gas and food. For Bonin, such an activity was normal, his bodily functions and mindset hardly altered from the bloody proceedings.

"Let's go back and make sure he's really gone and can't tell on us," Bonin told Eric and they went back up the hill. Not wanting to get to close to where the body was dumped, in case someone was around, Bonin pulled into a road parallel, cut the engine and rolled down the windows to listen. Only crickets and bugs could be heard, Sean King lay silent.

Suddenly a car approached, driving off the main road and near to where Bonin was parked. A police car was trolling the area, causing Bonin to panic a bit. He turned on his lights, started the car and began to leave the area slowly, waving to the officer so show everything was alright. Soon Eric and Bonin were down the hill and headed west on the I-10, during which time Bonin tore up Sean King's various ID cards and threw them on to the four-lane highway.

After Eric was dropped off, Bonin went back to Vern's house to return his blanket and pick up a trash bag to dump the clothes and the knife. He knocked on his door at 3:00 a.m. and was greeted by a curious Vernon Butts.

"Was it good?" he asked in an excited manner.

"Yeah, you should've come along, it was a lot of fun," Bonin told him.

"I want to know everything," Vern exclaimed, "Yah know, just as you was leaving I yelled at you. I had changed my mind and wanted to go. I guess you didn't hear me, I'm sorry I missed this one. Actually, we would have done everything right here and then put his body into a truck and gotten rid of him." Bonin stayed for 90-minutes and shared the grim details. He left at 4:30 a.m., dumped the clothes in a trash bin at the Kingswood Apartments and went home.

The last statement by Vernon Butts brings up numerous questions and possibilities that could have changed future events:

1) Only hours earlier he was adamant about not wanting to pick up Sean King and getting dropped at home after Bonin got him. Was Butts appeasing Bonin by telling him he wished he went along to stay on his good side, or was he sincere about wanting to go along?

2) More importantly, if Bonin had heard him, he would never have called Eric and King would have been killed at Butts' house and probably dumped nearby. King's body would have been discovered the next morning instead of disappearing into the mountain wilderness. As will be seen, this particular set of decisions will have interesting ramifications on future events.

41

Billy Pugh Provides Vital Tip
May 29, 1980

Famed LAPD Homicide Detective, Sgt. John P. "Jigsaw John" St. John, was frustrated and mad. For nearly a year the bodies of teenage boys were piling up all over Southern California, and now the press coverage had people in a fearful panic. Screaming for action, parents were scared to let their children walk the street. Schools and communities were sounding the alarm with posters and warnings; no hitchhiking and don't talk to strangers!

The threatening calls flooded into St. John's department, LAPD Robbery-Homicide, and the political pressure was getting intense; it is one thing when criminals kill each other, quite another when innocent teenage boys get picked off weekly.

The broken bodies of nine boys had been found since the year began, with over 20 since the previous August. St. John, a homicide detective with over 30-years of experience, and many other fine investigators, were stymied with few leads or hard evidence. "Jigsaw John" got his nickname from solving a body dismemberment case and went on to close scores of difficult cases. All St. John possessed was an ever-thickening binder of victims, an ever-widening breach of public trust and an ever-louder media barrage.

The first solid break in the Bonin Freeway Killing spree came on May 29, 1980, ten days after Sean King was murdered. His body hadn't been found but he was reported missing. William Ray Pugh, age 17 and the one who helped Bonin kill Harry Todd Turner, had been arrested for car theft and was incarcerated at the Los Padrinos Juvenile Hall in Downey, a few miles from where Bonin lived.

A little over two months after helping Bonin commit murder, Pugh was meandering across the rec room at Los Padrinos when he grabbed a recent issue of the ***LA Times***. The front-page headline grabbed his attention. In bold letters it cried out that another boy's nude body had been found; discarded behind a Mobil gas station in Westminster, about 20-miles from

Downey.

Scanning the article, Pugh quickly looked for more details: "Larry Sharp, eighteen years of age, had been the victim of ligature strangulation. Ligature marks were also found on Sharp's wrists and ankles, similar to the wounds found on at least a dozen young male victims. Undoubtedly, the signature of the notorious Freeway Killer."

Billy remembered seeing newspaper clippings about killings in Bonin's van glovebox, plus he helped him kill Turner. But could Bonin really be a serial killer? Pugh put the pieces together and concluded Bonin just might be the Freeway Killer.

Pugh must have been shocked at the idea of Bonin killing so many, but if it was true then he must be stopped. Plus, if Pugh helped catch a notorious serial killer, then he would receive a reduced sentence for his part in killing Turner, along with his other crimes. Pugh must have also thought about the fact that he was a juvenile when Turner took place. But if he was wrong, and Bonin wasn't the Freeway Killer, then Pugh might still get arrested for murder and end up worse off.

At this point law enforcement was in the dark, having no clue who Bill Bonin was before Billy Pugh pointed in his direction. In order of importance, logic dictates shock, self-interest and guilt created Pugh's call to action. This key event ties back to the day, March 24, 1980, when the paths of Bonin, Fraser, Pugh and Wijnaendts crossed, a day that was only beginning to reverberate through the Bill Bonin story.

In addition, Pugh might never have seen a Freeway Killer article without the tireless work of award-winning journalist J.J. Maloney. For months he pursued the story, badgered his editors, coined the moniker Freeway Killer and then broke the story on the **OC Register's** front page on that key date in this narrative, March 24, 1980. What followed was a relentless media firestorm and part of the reason Billy Pugh stumbled on the front-page article two months later.

Clutching the newspaper, Pugh searched for his counselor, Columbus Batiste, showed him the front page and exclaimed, "This here guy, I know him."

"What? What are you saying?" Bastiste picked up the paper and searched the page.

Pugh leaned forward and pointed to the headline, "Bill Bonin killed Larry Sharp! He's the Freeway Killer!"

"How do you know that? You're not kidding me, are you?"

"No, no Mr. Bastiste, it's I've met him, I know him. I'm telling you this is the Freeway Killer. I just know, you gotta believe me," he repeated. Pugh related his involvement with Bonin, careful to omit incriminating facts.

They went straight to Director Weigle's office. When Bastiste entered he crossed the room, laid the newspaper down and pointed at the article, "Here, this headline." Bastiste said forcefully, "Larry Sharp, another victim of the Freeway Killer, Billy thinks he knows who this guy is, tell him what you told me."

Pugh again recited the litany of crimes Bonin claimed to have perpetrated. Weigle listened intently, and then he said, "I believe you. I've have been following these cases."

Weigle contacted St. John and he came down to Los Padrinos, 15-miles south of Downtown LA, to interview Billy Pugh. Having received so many false leads, he was praying for a solid break but was experienced enough to keep his emotions in check.

St. John arrived and was seated in the Director's office, looking at the long hoped for break in the Freeway Killer case.

"Where did you meet Bonin?" St. John pointedly asked him.

"At a party at Scott Fraser's place."

"You are talking about Bill Bonin?"

"Yes sir."

"Where does Fraser live?"

"In Downey, he's always got a bunch of people partying at his place," Pugh gushed forth.

"Tell me about this guy you think might be the Freeway Killer," the detective inquired.

"One night, during a party at Scott's place, he sees me playing this card game, and asks me if 'I learned it in jail?' I say, 'Yeah, why?' He tells me he's been in Vacaville, that's why he recognizes the game. Scott told him about me, thinking I had the kind of looks he liked.

"Since then, he had been wanting to meet me, we talked about stuff from jail, the party started breaking up about midnight and he asks me if I needed a ride home, we went out to his van and..."

"Can you describe the van?" St. John asked.

"Sure, it's a green Ford, it has double doors on the side and in the back, the side doors can't be opened from the inside. Van is nice, with wood paneling and carpeting, a curtain so you can't see in back. Anyway, he reaches over and starts rubbing my leg. He tells me I turn him on, and he wants to have sex with me, I told him I don't go for that," he related with the hope of gaining trust.

"Did you have sex with him?" St John asked.

"No sir," Pugh blurted out. "Then he says, 'I'd like you to help me kill somebody,' I got scared. I grabbed the door handle trying to get out, but he stopped at a red light, I figured this was my chance, but he grabbed me by the neck and yanked me back," Pugh said, fabricating certain events for the detective.

"Did he have a weapon?"

"I didn't see any, then he tells me, 'I can't do that to you.' I asked what he meant, and he says, 'People saw us leaving together, I couldn't get away with anything.' I was pretty scared, so I just stayed in the van."

"What happened next?" St. John asked.

"Then he starts talking about killing people, saying he'd killed people, young boys, you know, using their T-shirts to strangle them, I told him I wanted to go home. He's making me nervous cause I don't know this guy, maybe he was lying," he said, muddling fact and fiction.

"Did he take you straight home?"

"No, he drove around Long Beach and all over the place. It's getting about 2:00 in the morning, when he reached over to get something out of the glove compartment and a wad of papers falls out, I leaned over to help and they're newspaper articles about kids getting killed, and he kept talking about it, saying you gotta have a plan and know a place to dump the body before you pick up a kid, he also sez he likes to kill on Friday and Saturday nights and then goes to see his girlfriend on Sundays."

"You said Scott knew him?" the detective asked.

"Yeah, they used to live in the same apartment building."

"Listen Pugh, if you want me to help you, you got to be straight with me," St. John commanded.

"I am being straight with you. I'm telling you that he told me he likes to kill boys," Pugh said convincingly, even though he left out his active and willing participation in the torture and murder of Turner. Despite all this, one can say that Billy Pugh did do something noteworthy: he broke the case of the Bonin Freeway Killer scourge that was plaguing Southern California.

Analyzing events offers some conclusions: Following the murder of Turner, Pugh only saw Bonin one more time, two days after the murder when he was nervous and needed calming. He never went back to Fraser's apartment and, despite Bonin talking about killing kids and helping kill Turner, there is no way Pugh could have known about the "Freeway Killer" cases.

The reason is simple: they didn't exist in the public mind till the day he met Bonin, the day they killed together, the day J.J. Maloney's famous Freeway Killer story broke in the **OC Register**, March 24, 1980. Up till then, the public was mostly in the dark because law enforcement had kept a tight lid on info, thus making it largely a back page story. Maloney lit the media firestorm with a big front-page story and coined the term "Freeway Killer."

So relentless was the ***Register's*** daily front-page coverage, despite LAPD and other agencies still stonewalling, that even the national media began to print and broadcast more Freeway Killer stories. Billy Pugh then got arrested and, many weeks later, sees the story on Larry Sharp and realizes that Bonin, the guy he helped kill Turner with two months earlier, might be a notoriously brutal serial killer responsible for murdering over 20 teenage boys.

To the benefit of many, Billy Pugh then alerted authorities.

All Sgt. St. John knew was that maybe, just maybe, they had caught a break in the biggest mass murder case in Southern California history. The drive back to Parker Center must have been better than the drive to work that morning. Pugh's help breaking the case was taken into consideration when Bonin and all his accomplices went on trial two years later.

42

Bonin Recruits Jim Munro for Murder
Steven Wells, June 2, 1980
As Told to Vonda Pelto, Ph.D. by Jim Munro

LA Men's Central Jail, November 1981
Unaware he was now on LAPD's radar screen, as May became June Bonin's appetite for killing continued unabated. Bonin was placed under surveillance starting on Monday, June 2, as this official LAPD report indicates:

"On 6-2-80, 1900 hours, the detectives of the Detective Support Division, SIS, were requested to conduct a surveillance of William Bonin at 10282 Angell, Downey. Detectives were informed that Bonin had a green Ford van, Calif. license 948255, and had made statements about the 'Freeway Killer' not admitting he was the killer, but that he had killed people, boys in particular, by using their T-shirts to strangle them, using a tire tool for leverage to twist the T-shirts.

"Detectives were informed that Bonin was a registered sex offender and had previous felony convictions for crimes similar to those attributed to the so-called Freeway Strangler. Detectives obtained this information from CII and observed Bonin's rap sheet."

Jim Munro moved back in with Bonin in late May. They picked up Steven Wells on the afternoon of June 2, the day when the police surveillance began but, tragically, a few hours too late to save him.

In the fall of 1981, having worked at Los Angeles County Men's Jail for several months, I was familiar with Munro. He came by my cell/office almost daily, usually wanting hot coffee and diversion from being in his cell. Today his demeanor was different, worried and serious. He wanted to talk about what happened on the day his life changed forever.

"Doctor Pelto, can I come in?" I looked up to see Jim Munro standing at my open office door. "I gotta talk to you. I wanta get this off my chest." I nodded for him to come in and have a seat next to my desk, then ordered hot coffee from a passing trustee.

"You gotta believe me, I didn't know Bonin was the Freeway Killer. He was good to me. One night coming home from work 'bout 5:00, Billy sez, 'Do you wanna go out and pick up a hitchhiker and have sex with him and kill him?' I was shocked, I really thought he was kidding, so I sez, sure. I didn't want him to think I was a pussy."

Munro looked at the celling, tapping his foot nervously, in a way oblivious to my presence.

"We were drivn' around Downey, in his van, and he has a western music station and begins to sing along, I can tell he's excited. Bonin says to me, 'Jim, be on the lookout for some kid hitchhiking, or some little asshole hoping to turn a trick and make some bread. They're usually looking for a sucker to take advantage of and we're just the guys to give it to them.' I spotted a punk leaning on a tree with his thumb out. 'Hey, Billy, there's a kid over there hitching.' Billy pulled over and motioned the kid over."

18-year-old Steven Wells, who had a twin-sister and four other siblings, was a known homosexual who frequented gay bars in the Hollywood area. His father suspected Steven possibly used drugs and engaged in homosexual relations with friends while he lived with him in Riverside. He was six-feet-one-inches tall, 170 pounds with sandy blonde hair and blue eyes, just the kind of boy Bonin liked.

After working at the May Co. department store in Riverside, Wells moved to his mother's house in Norwalk, next to Downey, and started working at Porter & Griffin Printing Co. at 130 El Segundo Blvd., about 15-miles from Bonin's house. Steven had just gotten off work and was scheduled to meet with his father in Downey, an appointment Mr. Wells failed to keep with his son. The appointment was for them to be fitted with tuxedoes for the wedding of Steven's twin-sister, Susan, a family event he was excited about attending. During this time, he encountered Bonin and Munro.

"Billy leans across me from the driver's side and asks the kid, 'You wanna make some money?' The kid sez, 'Sure, what do I have to do?' Billy says, 'I was wondering about you and me and my friend, Jim here, goin' over to my house for a little sex party and then get a bite to eat. You up for it?' Bill was being real nice, he's older and kinda like a father, so it's easy to trust him.

"He asked him what he thought of gays, he told us was bisexual, but seemed kinda nervous, I didn't think he was gonna come with us, but

Billy's real smart, he reaches inta' his pocket and pulls a twenty and waves it at him. Man, that little asshole lights up like a rocket. The kid comes over and tries to grab the dough, 'Hold on,' Billy says. 'We got to go for a little ride and have some fun first.' He told me, 'I'm gonna get in the back for a little suckin' and blowin,' you drive.' Billy gets out of the van, pulls the back door open and tells the kid to get in, but the little shit pokes his head in but doesn't move. 'If you don't want to come with us it's okay, I'm sure some other young man would like the money,' Bonin tells him, then he got in the van.

"I heard Billy call the kid Steve, so I knew they was getting friendly. It was dark by the time we got to Billy's pad, his mother was out of town. 'You hungry Steve?' he asked the kid, not wantin' any trouble getting him in the house. I was sent out to get burgers and told to hurry back, the kid said he hadn't eaten all day and Billy wanted to keep him happy.

"I left and got pulled over by the police, I was scared cause I only had a Learner's Permit, the officer let me off and told me to drive straight home. I went straight back and made myself a sandwich. I could hear noises from the bedroom, I wanted to go in, but I was hungry, but I could hear 'em in Billy's mom's bedroom, I figured I'd get my turn.

"When Bonin finally came out of the bedroom, he motioned me to come back there. Then he tells the kid, 'I have a friend who likes to have some sex with a guy that's hogged tied and naked. This guy is willing to pay two hundred bucks for it. What do you think? Can you use some extra cash?' The boy tells him, 'Well it's getting late, I'm going to have to get home pretty soon. You said you would drive me back.' Bill told him, 'Well sure Steve, that's the plan. We will of course drop you off, well, you want the money?'

"Wells then says, 'Okay, but tell your friend to hurry, I got to get home.' Steve strips down and gets on the bed. Can you believe he lets himself get all tied up? Bonin tells me to grab the kid's shoulders and help him carry him out into the hall.

"I was bummed 'cuz, well, I could hear the sound of my favorite show comin' from the livin' room, and I still hadn't got any sex or anything, and now I had to help Billy carry this kid all over the fuckin' place. The kid started to yell and wiggle around, he was gettin' scared, so Bill grabbed the kid's shorts and stuffed 'em in his mouth, then he cinched up the rope from the ankles to the hands, so the kid was kinda bow shaped."

"Suddenly the kid let's out a big scream, Bill's laughing. He just done him a fast shot up the ass. See, he really gets off on that. 'Jimmy,' Billy sez, 'let's go in the kitchen, I need a drink of water.' We got to the kitchen and I sez, 'When's the guy comin' over to butt fuck him?' Billy sez, 'There's no guy, I just told me that to get him tied up without too much trouble.' I was kinda scared and said, 'So, well, when're we gonna let him go? We aint really gonna kill him, are we?' I asked Bonin, I couldn't believe he really wanted to kill him.

"Billy tells me, 'What else can we do? We don't have any choice, we gotta kill him now, he knows where I live, and I can't have any witnesses.' I couldn't believe it," Munro said with shame.

Munro realized Bonin fully intended to kill Steven Wells. He was seeing the side of Bonin he had never experienced, transformed from friend to calculating, vicious murderer with no compassion. And he had no choice; help or face the wrath as well.

"We go back into the hall and Bonin hits the kid in the chest with his fist, saying, 'You're gonna fucking do what I tell you to do.' He was sure scary when he got mad, but somehow the kid had gotten the shorts out of his mouth and now he's screaming, 'Please let me go, I'll give you anything you want if you just let me go, please, please don't kill me.' I look over at Billy, he's just smiling."

"Did you think about letting the boy go?" I asked.

"Shit no! Billy might have killed me. Then he goes back into the bedroom, gets the kid's wallet and takes all the cash. When he comes back, he sez to the kid, 'I'm just gonna' knock you out, put your clothes back on you, and leave you on a park bench somewhere.' Then he puts the kids T-shirt over his head, and around his neck, then tells me hold his feet.

"Shit, what could I do? I didn't want to make him mad. I didn't want to die, so I bend down and grab the feet. He starts tightening the shirt, twistin' and pullin' it and the kid's putting up a fight, making all these gaggin' and gruntin' noises. Almost made me barf, I tells him, 'He's jumping 'round too much, I can't hold him no more.' He yells, 'You got to, I can't stop now.' Billy just kept twisting and twisting and pulling, then I hear a snapping noise and the kid goes limp."

Young Steven Wells was lost to the world. A boy who fell into the net of Bill Bonin before finding his path in life; a boy just leaning on a tree when Bonin's Death Van happened to drive by on a mission of evil; a boy whose short adventure in life didn't deserve such a tortuous and painful ending.

"I was shocked, I sez to Billy, 'What happened? Is he dead or somethin?' Billy laughed, 'Yeah, stupid.' Then he pulled off the shirt and threw it down the hall. The kid's face is purple and puffy, it was awful. Bonin laughs and sez, 'You'd look that way too if you'd just been strangled. Haven't you ever seen a dead body before' I just shrugged like it was no big deal. He ordered me to get a cardboard box cause we're gonna take the dude for a ride."

Munro's attitude was repulsive to me, taking such a flippant attitude to brutalizing and helping to kill a kid not much younger that himself. I also knew Munro was putting up a front, even if he seemed to take pleasure in reliving the killing.

"I went outside where, it was dark by then, so I didn't think anybody was gonna see us. There's a little breeze, it felt good, I worked up a sweat tryin' to hold that dude down while Billy choked him. I wasn't in a hurry to get back in the house, it was really disgusting, and he stunk really bad. I didn't know what Billy was thinking, I decided first chance I get, I should hit the road.

"I guess I was takin' too long, 'cuz Billy comes to the side door and starts yellin' to get my ass back in there with the box from his brother's room. When I get back, draggin' the box, Billy tells me to help get him into the box, but first I had to untie him, I tried to untie the knots, but then I had to cut them with a knife. God, I didn't like touchin' him, but I had to get the ropes off.

"Billy tells me to pick up his feet so we can get him into the box. I reach down there, and geez that slug has pissed and shit all over himself and it stinks. I tried to grab his legs, but it was slippery and I dropped him. Bonin started laughing, but I didn't think it was so funny. Finally, we drop him in the box. I backed the van into the driveway.

"We slid the box across the kitchen floor, and we gotta muscle it into the back of the van. Then we went to Vernon Butts' house. They were good friends. He told me this Vernon got him inta killin' kids. When we get there, the house looks deserted, but I can hear rock music comin' outta the house. 'He's home, go knock on the back door,' Bonin tells me. By the time Vern opened the door, Billy was beside me and we went right in."

Bonin lied to Munro about the nature of their relationship regarding the killings. This was a common feature of Bonin; people being told the most convenient stories to suit his purposes. He was the master manipulator. Bonin learned this from years dealing with psychiatrists, psychologists and social workers in mental institutions and prisons.

"You shoulda' seen him, Munro looked at me smiling, this here guy is all dressed up like Darth Vader, out of Star Wars, with a black hood and cape and ever' thing! We follow him into the livin' room and he's got these bright strobe lights flashin' in time with the music. The furniture was shit, he had this coffin in the middle of the livin' room. Kind of a crazy place.

"Billy told Vern everything about what happened, they laughed about it and Bonin asks him, 'We got it out in the back of the van, it's a good one. Come on out and see it.' Vern gave us a couple of brews and then sez, 'Let's go see the stiff.' They crowd in around the back of the van, then Vern leans over and pokes at the kid. Then he sez, 'Great job, you really did good.'

"Vern patted me on the back and said, 'Welcome to the club.' We piled back in the van and headed down toward the beach. I had to open my window, it smelled bad in the van. We went past a cop on our way and Billy sez to him, quiet like, 'Hey mista pig man, you oughta see what we got here.'

"Then he laughed and laughed. We cruised down Pacific Coast Highway to Huntington Beach. On the way, we both got hungry, with his body still in the back we went to the drive-thru at McDonalds and picked up some burgers. You know, Bill used the money from the kid's wallet to pay for the food. We then just kept driving, eating along the way, till we found a closed gas station. After we were sure no one was around, we unloaded the kid and left. Bonin says, 'We had a good night, let's head home.' So, we went back to the house."

Munro was grinning, his legs crossed and his left leg kicking the front of the desk.

"What were you feeling?" I asked.

"Well, excited, nervous, really kinda scared cause I didn't know if Bonin might kill me," he said, not smiling anymore.

"Did you think about asking Bonin not to kill the boy?"

"Nah, why should I? I had to save myself," Munro said while shrugging his shoulders. I felt sick to my stomach; My God, they stopped for burgers with his body in the van!

In a bit of horrible timing the LAPD surveillance team arrived at 10:00 p.m., probably a couple of hours after they left the house. The LAPD report, from the start of the chapter, continues:

"At approximately 2315 hours (11:15 P.M.) Detective Harris, #11222, and Detective Krueger, #11638, observed the Ford green van arrive at the location. An unknown male, Caucasian (Jim Munro), was driving the vehicle and suspect Bonin was a passenger. Suspect Bonin was observed to open the side doors of the van and to remove what appeared to be clothing and roll it up into a bundle. These persons entered the residence."

Detective Krueger's testimony indicates how unaware Bonin and Munro were of the LAPD surveillance team parked nearby, "After wrapping what appeared to be a shirt and pants inside a dark, large, heavy item, which I believed at the time to be a jacket of some kind. I then observed Mr. Bonin go over to Mr. Munro. There was a conversation which I could not hear. There was a lot of laughter. This went on for three to four minutes at the side of the van prior to the two disappearing into the residence of that location."

Krueger recognized Bonin from his photograph but had no idea who Jim Munro was. Detectives were witnessing a post murder chit-chat without knowing of Steven Wells' fatal encounter. While the detectives sat outside, a macabre encounter between Munro and Bonin took place.

During Bonin's trial, in mid-November 1981, **LA Times** Staff Writer Gene Blake reported on what Munro said on the stand, "Munro testified that he and Bonin drove around dark side roads looking for a place to dump the body. He said the rolled down the windows when the van began 'smelling' from the body. Then they stopped at a McDonald's and ordered hamburgers, paying for them with $10 taken from the Wells youth, Munro testified.

"After dumping the body behind a gas station, Munro said, they returned to Bonin's home and began eating the hamburgers and watching television news to see there were reports of the body being found. At one point, Munro testified, Bonin took a bite of hamburger, looking heavenward and said, 'Thanks Steve,' then he looked downward and added, 'Thanks Steve, wherever you are.' 'He started laughing, and I started laughing too,' Munro told the jury."

His broken body was discovered just after midnight that evening. Jimmy Maguglin pulled into the Mobil Station, in Huntington Beach at the corner of Beach and Adams, because of a flat tire. He drove into the rear parking area of the station, to leave the tire, and found a dead body lying between two vehicles. Maguglin panicked.

He left the station, went to a local bowling alley, got a cup of coffee and called his girlfriend. She told him to call the police. Maguglin and his brother flagged down a police officer and returned to the crime scene. After inquiries were made, investigators were satisfied that neither Maguglin nor his brother was involved.

Here is the Huntington Beach Police Report:
"After the arrival of the SIB personnel, photographs of the victim were taken, and the area between the brown and white pickup and white delivery van was observed to have tire marks on the pavement. The tire marks were photographed as well as the surrounding area. Because of the similarity to other male nudes found abandoned the Orange County Sheriff's criminalist James White was called to the scene. He arrived at approximately 0230 hours and conducted a preliminary investigation. At approximately 0240 hours, the coroner was called and deputy coroner W. King at arrived at 0300 hours and reported taking charge of the case under Orange County Coroner's Office case #801943KG. After the victim had been examined briefly, the deputy coroner related that the body could be turned over, and upon being turned over, he observed what appeared to be possible teeth marks on the victim's left buttocks. We further observed lividity on the back shoulder area and buttocks of the victim, as well as an impression in the skin in the area above the right buttocks. Deputy coroner King stated that from his preliminary investigation, that it looked as though the victim had been dead for approximately ten hours, which would have placed the time of death at approximately 2000 hours, 6/2/80."

Immediately after Steven Wells was identified, the following agencies were officially notified; Orange County Sheriff's Department (Detectives Sidebotham and Esposito with four victims dumped in their jurisdiction); Westminster PD, where Larry Sharp was found); Stanton PD, next to

Long Beach; Long Beach PD, Homicide Division; Los Angeles County Sheriff's Department, Sgt. Kushner now with 10 victims dumped in his jurisdiction; Seal Beach PD, in Orange County; LAPD, Robbery-Homicide Division along with the Central, Rampart and Hollywood Divisions; Garden Grove PD, in Orange County.

43

Surveillance & Bonin's Final Arrest
June 3 to 11, 1980

Surveillance of Bonin continued after the Wells murder. Munro lived with Bonin and continued to ride to work with him at Dependable, even though he never got any driving assignments. They still went out partying around town as multiple two-man teams shadowed Bonin everywhere. Officers changed up close surveillance, switching cars in an effort to avoid alerting their target.

On night of June 3 Detective Banas followed Bonin and Munro to the Long Beach Naval Hospital, where Bonin visited his father, and then saw them go to Vernon Butt's house, where they stayed for about an hour. On the evening of June 5, at 9:30 p.m. while Detective Krueger and his partner sat in the car, Banas followed Bonin, Munro and another truck driver into the McDonalds at Telegraph and Washington, not far from Dependable.

While in line to order, behind Bonin, Banas engaged him in casual conversation about the weather and being lost in the industrial area. After getting a cup of coffee, Banas left and was crossing the street when he saw Bonin, alone, sprint out of the restaurant, get into the Chevette and speed down Telegraph Road.

Banas followed as Bonin clocked nearly 70-miles per hour before executing a U-turn and returning to McDonalds. As he pulled up, with Banas following in his plain clothes car, two uniformed Los Angeles County Sheriff vehicles arrived on scene. Turned out that, while officer Banas was departing the McDonalds, four men committed an armed robbery and that was what prompted Bonin's rapid exit and return. While Bonin was interviewed by uniformed officers, Banas, not revealing his true identity, walked up and informed officers he was in line and might be able to identity the suspect.

Bonin told officers he was chasing the suspect and if "they caught the person they'd have to do it very quickly since he was leaving town that night." Bonin was all set to fly back east on a truck run. Followed to Los

Angeles International Airport, Bonin and the other driver boarded a flight while Munro returned to Angell Street.

How ironic was this scene: A possible serial killer under surveillance for murdering an untold number of boys trying to capture a petty thief and ready to help the police identity him; comical if not so tragic.

When Bonin returned from New York, on June 9, he found out Munro sold his $130 radio and tools. Finding it hard to believe Munro's weak explanation for their disappearance, he decided to teach him a stern lesson.

"Take your clothes off, I'm gonna tie you up," Bonin ordered Munro.

"Why?" Munro asked in a frightened tone.

"This way I'll know you won't tell police," Bonin answered chillingly.

"Okay," he replied, unsure what was taking place.

Munro got undressed and Bonin tied him up in a macabre duplication of the murder scene with Wells, a week earlier. Munro lost his composure and began pleading for his life, the young man was scared to the core and feared Bonin was going to strangle him. Bonin motioned to put a white T-shirt around Munro's neck and stopped, letting the air hang with tension.

"You know I could kill you, and you couldn't do nothing about it," he said maliciously.

"Yeah, I know," Munro said, whimpering and sobbing, "just let me go." Having made his point, Bonin untied him. Enjoying the act of instilling fear in friends or co-murderers, Bonin built into them the terror of his being able to inflict pain, or worse, in those who went against him. He told many that he was connected with the mafia and knew people willing to do "favors" for him.

During those days Marion Perkins, the office manager at Dependable, noticed he was "worried to the point of distress." When questioned on the reason for his state of mind, Bonin dismissed it as worries about money and Perkins "didn't think anything of it." In contrast Munro seemed calm and not worried about much. He not only looked up to Bonin but was scared of him, going so far as to include his name in basic conversations with such statements as, "Bill said I could do this, or Bill said I could do that."

But Munro had other problems. Stan Hurd had been repeatedly calling him at Dependable to collect on an old debt. He threatened to break his legs and, when Bonin tried to calm him down, Hurd threatened him as well. Stan Hurd was a pimp who didn't like Munro because he interfered with his business.

On the morning of June 11 Bonin and Munro went to Dependable as usual. While Bonin was out on a truck run, Munro borrowed his Chevette and told the others to inform Bonin he would be back later in the day. Stan wanted to speak with him, so Munro went to straighten things out in North Long Beach. He ended up spending the night and partying with Tammie. When Munro failed to return by the end of the day, Bonin got a ride home from Ed Demler, the owner of Dependable.

When Bonin got into his van that evening, detectives were lying in wait ready to follow him, here is their report:

"On 6-11-80, 2220 hours, suspect Bonin, was observed leaving his house and entering the van. Suspect drove around the Downey area for a short time and then got on to the Santa Ana Freeway and drove to the Los Angeles-Hollywood area. Suspect got off the Hollywood Freeway at Santa Monica Blvd. and drove westbound to the area of Highland and Santa Monica. Suspect alighted from his vehicle and approached various lone males that were standing around the northeast corner.

"Suspect appeared to have conversation with theses persons. Suspect then left driving westbound on Santa Monica Blvd. Suspect would stop his vehicle and talk to lone males standing or walking on the street. Suspect made a U-turn back eastward bound on Santa Monica at Gardner and pulled to the southeast corner of Santa Monica and Martel, next to where Buddy Stark, M/C, was standing.

"Suspect and Stark appeared to have a conversation at which time Stark got into the passenger front seat of the van being driven by suspect (6-11-80 2320 hours). Stark appeared to by 16/17 years old, slim build, long dark blonde hair.

"Suspect drove to southeast corner of Santa Monica and Normandie where he backed the van against the building with the van facing west towards Normandie. Both persons left the driver's area of the van and went to the inside rear area of the van. Officers could observe the curtain inside the van to be approximately 1-2 feet apart. Detective Brooks approached the van and stood at the rear door of the van.

"Detective Brooks could hear voices and parts of the conversation between two people inside the van. During this time there was soft music coming from within the van. Parts of the conversation are as follow. 'You have a nice one.' 'Put it in more.' 'Do it faster.' 'I like making love to you.' 'I'm going to come.' During the above, the van was rocking from side to side. After approximately 10-15 minutes, Detective Brooks began to hear moans and groans coming from inside the van. At this time, headlights from a police vehicle were turned on and directed towards the inside and front of the van.

"Detectives Brooks, Harris and Krueger approached the front of the van and could observe both persons inside the van. Detectives could observe Stark on his hands and knees completely nude, facing the rear doors of the van. Suspect Bonin also appeared nude and had the front part of his body (private parts area) up against the buttock area of Stark and was moving back and forth. Suspect looked in the area of the detectives and the lights of the police vehicle, at that time detectives stated, 'police officers.'

"Suspect turned and pushed Stark forward and flat down on to the floor of the van. Suspect then pulled the curtains closed. Detectives could hear movement around inside the van and a few seconds later suspect appeared buttoning up his pants and then opened the driver's side front door and exited the van. A few seconds later, the double side doors of the van opened and Stark got out of the van buttoning his pants. As Stark got out of the van, he left the side doors open. While standing outside the van, detectives could observe in plain view numerous items of clothing, a fixed blade knife, rope, bumper jacket and tire iron on the floor of the van.

"Prior to beginning the surveillance of suspect Bonin, detectives of Detective Support Division, SIS, had information that the murder victims were probably hitch-hiking, bound with rope, and several hit with a hard object and strangled. A number of the murder victims had been sodomized. Due to the sounds (moans and groans) coming from inside the van, the activity of the persons in the van and the information detectives had about the murders, the detectives felt it was necessary to take immediate action for the safety of the possible intended murder victim Stark.

"Suspect Bonin was informed by Detective Harris that he was being detained for investigation of sodomy upon a juvenile and murder and was going to be transported to the police station. Bonin requested his van be taken to the police station and not left on the street. Upon seeing the items inside the van, detectives felt the van should be seized as evidence in the murder investigation. Suspect Bonin and Buddy Stark were transported to Robbery-Homicide Division where Stark was interviewed by Robbery-Homicide investigators.

"Detective J. St. John, Robbery-Homicide Division, advised booking William Bonin, 187 p.c. Bonin booked at Central Jail."

Bonin's recollections of that night also offer an encounter with Sgt. St. John, who was called in late, a detective who had been tailing him for days and his own conscience. Not knowing that Munro was in Long Beach, he began the night by searching for him to get his Chevette back.

"I told him that if Jim came in to call the police and have them take the keys away from him. I then went to where I worked, a short distance away. He wasn't there. I went to Hollywood and stopped at AJ's coffee shop and looked around, but I didn't see him or the car.

"Then I went driving down Santa Monica Blvd., westbound, and I spotted a youngster walking eastbound, so I turned around and approached him. I picked him up and had a conversation as we headed towards downtown. We stopped and got in the back of the van. He said he was 18. We were getting it on when I was approached by the cops. I looked out the front of the van and saw the headlights of a car facing in the van's direction. A man was outside the van. He put his badge to the window and said come on out.

"As I was getting out the cop said, 'What are you guys doing messing around in there?' The cop frisked me and then had the other guy get out. They frisked him. They told me the reason they were checking me out is that a bar nearby on Hollywood Blvd. was robbed and my van matched the description. They asked if they could search the van and I said okay.

"The cop said to me, 'You know there is a law against sodomizing.' I said, 'There wasn't between two consenting people over 18.' He said it didn't apply in a van in public. I saw the guy that was with me and said to him, 'You are 18, aren't you?' He said, 'Yes.'

"The cop said he was going to have to take us down the station as there were things that didn't look right. We were taken down to the station. This was around 11:00 p.m. The kid that was with me made a statement and signed it, using a false name and saying he was 18. They found out before he was released, many hours later, his true name and that he was 17. He had a Juvenile Warrant out on him.

"I was advised of my rights around 4:00 a.m. and St. John told me I had been arrested, indicating when I was brought down to the station. I told him they never told I was under arrest. So he read me my rights and told me I was under arrest for murder. I half knew it was coming and was playing it cool. When it came, I didn't know how I was supposed to react, so I just went silent and thought for a long time.

"St. John asked me if I wanted to call anyone, and I said I didn't know who to call. I then looked at him and said, 'You're not kidding, are you?' He said, 'No, I'm dead serious.' He asked again if I wanted to call anyone and I said, 'I don't know, let me think for a while.' It was all coming down at once. St. John had left the room for a while and then came in again and asked me again if I wanted to call anyone. I said, 'Yes, I wanted to call Todd Landgren, my attorney.'

"I asked him who I was accused of killing and no answer. Then I called Landgren's office in Tustin and they put me right through to him. Todd asked me 'What's up Willie.' Todd called me that, 'Willie.' I said I didn't know. Todd asked me if I was in custody and I said yes. He asked what for and all I could get out was 187 (Murder). He said, '187!' I said yes and broke down crying. Todd told me that he'd to see me that day and find out what it was all about. He told me not to talk to anyone until I saw him.

"He asked me if I was at the main jail and I asked St. John where I was, St. John told me I was at Parker Center, better known as the 'Glass House.' I relayed that to Todd. I was in tears through all of this. An officer asked me after I hung up, 'How was New York, Bill.' I was still crying and didn't answer, St. John told the cop to hold off.

"After I regained control, the cop asked me again, 'How was 'New York?' I said, 'What?' He said, 'You don't recognize me?' I said, 'No.' He said 'McDonalds!' Then I remembered he was there on the night I went to New York. That was the McDonalds on Washington. While I was there the place was robbed by four blacks. I flew to New York with my boss and one other guy to pick up three trucks and bring them back to California.

"The night of my arrest I found out that I had been followed since June 2, 1980, at around 11:30 p.m., when Jim and I returned home. Another thing, while I was trying to get a hold of Todd I was looking for his home phone number. I looked thru all my stuff, and as I looked at photos and cards, I reflected on all of it, knowing it would be a lifetime before I would ever see any of it again.

"I touched my ring. The only ring I had ever bought for myself. It was gold with a horse's head in the middle of it and one diamond chip at the bottom where the two ends of the horseshoe came together. I was reflecting on everything at once knowing that all was over. I was caught and it really hurt. That with talking to Todd and having to say 187 broke me."

Bonin's hurt feelings and crocodile tears could hardly stack up against the pain and suffering he inflicted on his victims, not to mention the families and friends who were left behind trying make sense of the madness.

Buddy Eugene Stark was released and must thank his lucky stars he was saved from a fate which had befallen so many others. As noted in the report, all of Bonin's favorite murder tools were in the van: rope, wire and a tire iron. Two knives were also found, one with the blade stuck in the dashboard next to the ashtray. Everyone involved believed Bonin had every intention of killing Stark that night.

In a twist of irony, Bonin later learned that Stark was the nephew of Sharon Tate, the beautiful actress brutally slain by the Manson family.

June 11, 1980 marks the official end of William George Bonin's reign of terror as The Freeway Killer, but the next chapter in his story will prove full of fascinating twists and turns.

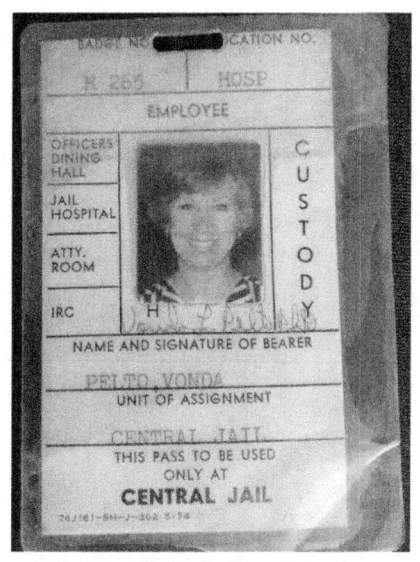

Dr. Vonda Pelto's LA Men's
Central Jail ID Badge.

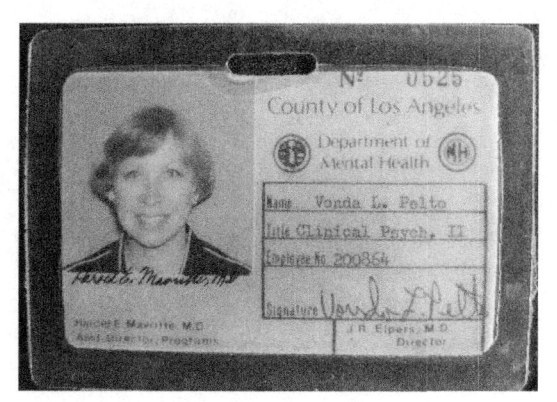

County of Los Angeles Department
of Mental Health ID.

Bill Bonin and Vernon Butts,
they killed six young boys together

12 of Bonin's victims.

WITHOUT REDEMPTION 261

Bonin's 'Death Van,' a term he coined.

Inside the van.

Bonin's mother house at 10282 Angell Street,
where Steven Wells was murdered

Vernon Butts house at 7310 Dinwiddie Street,
where Darin Kendrick was murdered.

Vonda Pelto sitting on Charles Manson's Bed
at LA Men's Central Jail.

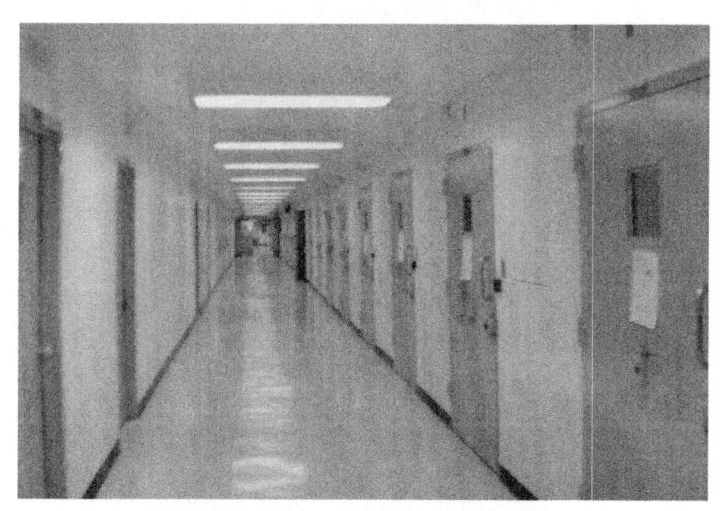

Cell Block where Vonda Pelto worked.

Halloween at LA Men's Central Jail.

Vonda's Jailhouse Office.

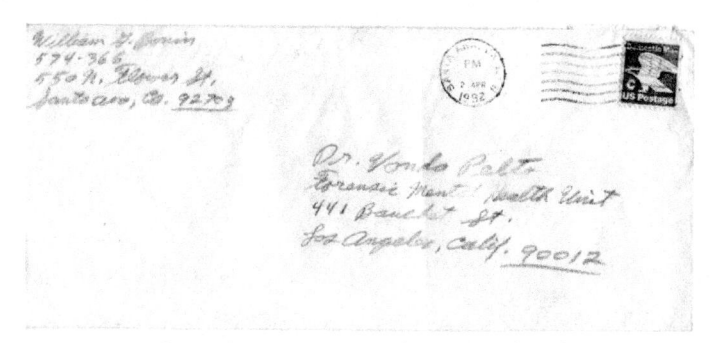

Letter from Bonin to Vonda Pelto, April 1982, sent from Orange County Jail after LA conviction.

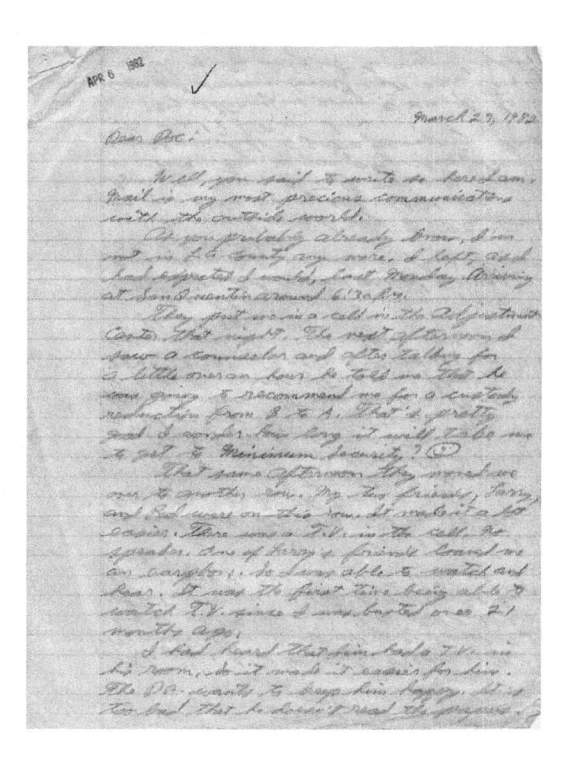

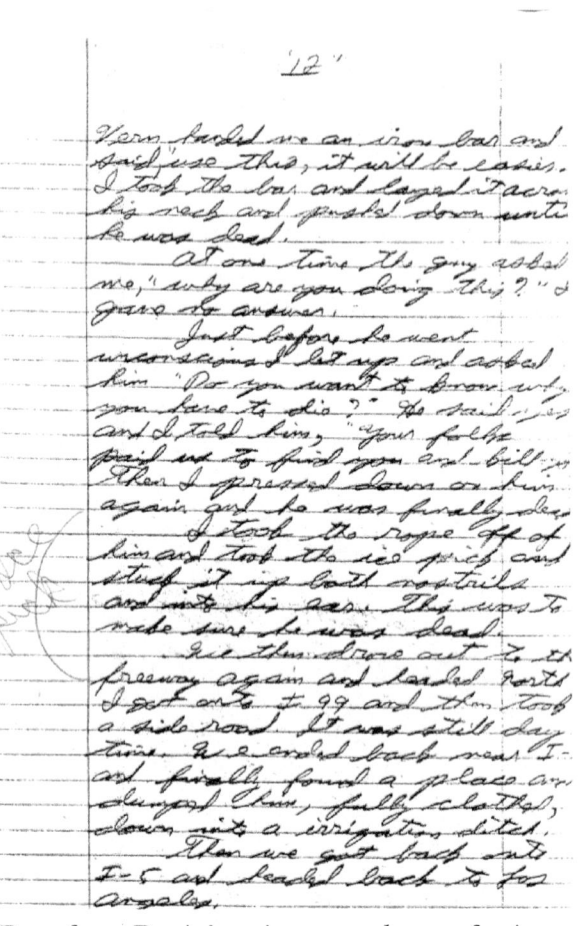

Page from Bonin's written murder confessions.

PART THREE
JUNE 12, 1980 TO AUGUST 1981

44

Bonin in Custody & Munro Skips Town
June 12 to June 29, 1980

A real lucky break led to progress in solving the Freeway Killer serial murder cases. This resulted in the arrest of Bill Bonin, however, evidence had to be found to prove he was the Freeway Killer and, if accomplices existed, arrest them as well. The public, afraid for their children, were panicked and right behind them were the press and politicians breathing down the necks of law enforcement agencies.

Since 1973, experienced homicide detectives, such as Sgt. "Jigsaw John" St. John of LAPD and Sgt. David Kushner of the LA County Sheriff's Dept., had been investigating a series of "homosexually oriented" serial killings. Slowly the situation deteriorated when Bonin started killing on August 4, 1979. For the next ten-months teenage victims showed up all over Southern California as Bonin murdered twenty-two teenagers; their bodies found like discarded like pieces of garbage along freeways, behind gas stations, in alleys, canyons and deserts.

With the victim count above 40, if counting from 1973, detectives were anxious to identify the victims Bonin might be responsible for and those to remain open cases. Detectives have many unanswered questions but strongly believe Bonin was their guy.

Although nearly twodozen departments devoted resources to solving the cases, Bonin left few clues to work with and distributed victims from San Diego to Bakersfield, from Palm Springs to Malibu and everywhere in between. Consistently disposing of clothing and ID papers, authorities often could only identify victims when family or friends reported a missing person or heard about the murder in the news.

In the end, William George Bonin killed six with Vernon Daniel Butts, two with Gregory Mathew Miley, two with Eric Marten Wijnaendts, one with William Ray Pugh and one with James Michael Munro. This leaves ten that Bonin killed alone, two in one day and the rest picked off one at a time. But only Bonin was in custody and detectives knew nothing about any accomplices.

He was initially charged with murder in connection with Charles Miranda, killed on February 3, 1980 with Greg Miley. While Bonin was in the waiting area for arraignment at LA Municipal Court, he was placed with an inmate who tried pumping him for info. Bonin later wrote, "Prior to that occasion Dennis was put in a room right next door to me up in 7000, which is the infirmary and also another place they keep protective custody people. He tried to get information out of me but I didn't give him anything. Either time."

Deputy O'Neal brought him down that day and months later, when he was Senior O'Neal and in charge of Bonin's row in 1700, informed Bonin it was indeed a set-up to gather info. Jailhouse snitches will play an interesting role in the months ahead.

Revealing the lack of evidence against Bonin, one-week later LA County District Attorney John Van de Kamp refused to file the single murder charge and he was instead charged with **Sodomy** and **Oral Copulation with a Minor**.

While law enforcement agencies and prosecutors made few statements, Deputy DA Sterling Norris was quoted in the June 17 edition of the *LA Times* as saying, "Investigators are examining the possibility that Bonin may have committed several murders in Orange County."

Northern California's *Napa Valley Register* reported that "authorities describe him as a 'continuing suspect' in the 41 homosexual slayings blamed on the Freeway Killer."

Norris asked the judge for a large bail in lieu of three facts: Bonin was a suspect in multiple murder cases, a convicted sex offender with multiple convictions and a strong flight risk; bail was set at $250,000 ($1.1 million in 2023). Bonin's attorney, John Barnett, said the prosecutors were buying time for "a case that isn't there."

First order of business for detectives was obtaining search warrants and questioning acquaintances, work associates, family and friends. Immediately after Bonin's arrest, affidavits for search warrants were filed in court by principal investigators seeking to search Bonin's cars, house and obtain access to relevant telephone records.

One search warrant wanted samples of Bonin's "blood, saliva, pubic hair, body hair, head hair, and teeth impressions." Several of Bonin's victims had bite marks on their body. The Ford Van was impounded as evidence and scoured by criminalists seeking forensic evidence.

One warrant from Sgt. Jack Fueglein of the LA Sheriff's Dept. sought items related directly to the Steven Wells case, listing those sought in the house and cars as follows:

1) All possible blood deposits or stains of any kind; 2) to luminol all areas to detect traces of blood; 3) all human hairs; 4) any clothesline types of rope or wire capable of being used as tight bindings; 5) any tent or green and yellow vinyl fabrics; 6) steak knives; 7) large cardboard appliance boxes big enough for a human body; 8) any identification papers in name of Steven Wells; 9) J.C. Penny brand NBA tennis shoes; 10) identification papers from Porter and Griffin at 120 El Segundo Blvd.; 11) nylon rust colored wallet.

The warrant also sought "all tools but not limited to jack handles, lug wrenches, tire irons."

Red blanket fibers were also sought from the Chevette. Another from his partner Sgt. Kushner listed items which may have been taken and saved by Bonin in the killings of Markus Grabs, Donald Hyden, James Macabe, Ronald Gatlin and Thomas Lundgren:

Items sought were: 1) Skate board with the words "Dog Town" writing with orange wheels (Thomas Lundgren); 2) Markus Grabs' passport and American Express Travelers Checks in Deutsche Marks, leather pouch 6x8 inches with neck strap, medallion and chain with Hebrew letter "Chai" (Markus Grabs); 3) Yellow T-Shirt, medium size (Donald Hyden); 4) A gold medallion and chain bearing the symbol of lightning bolt (James Macabe), White metal wristwatch, Seiko, 24-hour dial (Ronald Gatlin); 6) Samples of carpet fibers from the green Ford van license with license #948255, the blue Chevette #843ZXQ and from house at 10282 Angell Street in Downey, California; 7) Newspaper clippings of the Freeway Killings; 8) Any identification papers relating to the above named victims.

All the names above were cases assigned to Kushner and Fueglein of the LA County Sheriff's Dept. Sgt. St. John at LAPD filed the exact same Search Warrant Affidavit, and both were signed by renowned DA John Van de Kamp. During his years as District Attorney for LA County, 1975-82, Van de Kamp became prominent for successful reforms to the office; he hired large numbers of female district attorneys and established specialized units for gangs, career criminals, domestic violence, child abuse and more. Victims and witnesses got better treatment and a department was set up to monitor crime in the entertainment business. He was elected as California's Attorney General in 1982.

While detectives prepared Search Warrant Affidavits, on the morning of June 12 Jim Munro was waking up and driving back to the truck yard at Dependable in Montebello, unaware Bonin was in custody. After borrowing Bonin's Chevette the previous day, he ended up staying in Long Beach and partying with Tammie. Upon arrival, around mid-day, he found no Bonin. But Bonin was never late and always kept the office apprised of when he would arrive at work.

While sitting in the ready room, Munro heard on the radio that Bonin had been arrested and was suspected of being the Freeway Killer. He left and drove around the Lakewood area looking for friends, not entirely sure what to do next. He ended up back at Stan Hurd's, in late afternoon, and told him Bonin had been arrested. Stan told him to dump the Chevette. Munro dropped it at the Ric-Rac Tavern in Downey, an establishment frequented by Bonin's parents. Unaware they were under surveillance after dumping Steven Wells' body on June 2, and everyday afterwards, Munro couldn't have known the circumstances of Bonin's arrest, what detectives knew or if Bonin was spilling his guts.

Stan Hurd didn't believe Munro was involved in any murders but thought detectives might be interested in the time he spent with Bonin. Equally, Munro was curious about what they knew and if he was a suspect. Munro met with a detective friend of Hurd's the next day but didn't say anything and left. Staying around LA seemed like a bad idea, so he went to Las Vegas with a girl he had met, Margaret, and abruptly ditched her to hitchhike across country. Gallup, New Mexico and Nashville, Tennessee were two places he called Stan from during his travels. Back in Las Vegas, Margaret was found by police and instructed to report in daily even if Munro didn't contact her, but he never phoned or returned.

45

Scott Fraser Interview, Butts & Munro Arrested
June 30 to August 21, 1980

On June 30 Todd Landgren, an attorney who previously represented Bonin, was in court demanding Bonin's bail be reduced from $250,000 to $5,000, the normal amount for the ***Sodomy*** and ***Oral Copulation with a Minor*** charges.

While admitting it was "an egregious departure from conventional bail," Judge Lawrence Waddington refused the request based on "a field affidavit from Deputy DA Aaron Stovitz containing information of telephone calls allegedly made from Bonin's house." Landgren argued that prosecutors had nothing to justify murder charges and thus shouldn't be considered in the hearing, however, Bonin's previous record and being a suspect in numerous murders served to keep the bail high and deny Landgren info on current investigations.

With headlines and TV news coverage ever present, Vernon Butts must have been a nervous wreck, knowing at any moment police might come knocking. Among the other murder accomplices, Jim Munro skipped town right after Bonin's arrest and was on the road; Gregory Miley was living in Houston, Texas since the Miranda-Macabe murders four months earlier; William Pugh, who provided the key tip on Bonin, may have still been in juvenile custody but had probably been released; Eric Wijnaendts was at large, but he was raised in Garden Grove and thus was unlikely to have left town.

Vernon Butts was in deep, having been an encouragement to Bonin and a willing participant in six murders with knowledge of three others. Sgt. Kirk Mellecker of LAPD, and his partner Sgt. St. John, were convinced they had the right guy but lacked proof. Mellecker later said, "Bonin was no fool, he didn't leave much evidence."

Unsurprisingly, Bonin's arrest immediately set off a conflict between the two most prominent counties involved: Orange and Los Angeles. While a majority of Bonin's victims were from LA, the OC prosecutors were sizing him up for a number of murders cases. During those early days, according to LA Deputy DA Sterling Norris, his opposite number in OC, David Carter, "Directed deputies to snatch Bonin from the jail in Los Angeles for arraignment. Enraged prosecutors in Los Angeles hurriedly got a court order to return the suspect."

Scott Fraser, whose apartment was where Bonin met potential sexual partners and recruited accomplices, was known to LAPD from Billy Pugh. In the last two-weeks of June, St. John and Mellecker went to see Fraser. They wanted to know if Bonin ever told him anything about any killings. Fraser said no, and they left.

A few days later, Ray Pendleton contacted Fraser to buy drugs and was accommodated. Fraser later claimed he was introduced to Pendleton by Bonin a year earlier. Three weeks later, in mid-July, Fraser was arrested for selling narcotics and led to believe he would be charged and serve time. Previously convicted of a felony drug charge, he was told the arrest resulted from the sale to Pendleton.

Fraser was right in believing detectives investigating Bonin were targeting him, but the fact remains he was a drug dealer. Pendleton had met Bonin in prison and, according to Bonin's trial notes, he had been arrested for burglary and was working with police to alleviate his legal troubles. After hearing about Bonin's arrest, it appears Pendleton contacted detectives with information about Bonin and struck an agreement to run the sting operation on Fraser.

Bonin and Fraser were fairly close. He definitely knew about Bonin killing Markus Grabs but appeared unaware of anything else. Bonin later said, "We were fuck buddies and got together two or three times a week." Even after moving out of the Kingswood apartments, he was a frequent visitor to Fraser's party den.

On Monday, July 21 St. John and Mellecker came to speak with Fraser in jail, and he again stonewalled them. They informed Fraser that, if he cooperated, it might be possible to "get him home and out of jail."

Equally emphasized was the importance of getting solid information on Bonin. Fraser later claimed St. John and Mellecker never said anything about "cooperation for dropping the drug charges." Then Fraser's whole world changed when they showed him a hand drawn, detailed map regarding the April 10, 1980 murder of Steven Wood.

Interviewed in 1987 by George Zoroya, for an **OC *Register*** article, Fraser described it this way, "The map showed Bonin's house, where I lived, where the liquor store was, where Wood was walking. It just clicked, something just clicked. Bonin always liked young guys, he was going out at night." Mellecker recalled how Fraser's entire viewpoint changed in a flash, "The hair on his arm's actually stood up, you could just see the entire switch in his viewpoint once it dawned on him." Fraser took his gaze from the map, looked intently at Mellecker and St. John and said, "Ok, get out your pencils, you guys, get out your pads of paper."

When Bonin told Fraser his version of what happened in the August 5, 1979 murder of Markus Grabs, in a mistaken hope of creating an alibi, he lied and said Vernon Butts was involved. As a result, the start point for Fraser was Bonin and Butts both murdering Grabs, where the body was left, Bonin telling him it was self-defense and more.

Other subjects were the people Bonin met at Fraser's, such as Greg Miley, what he saw in the green van, Bonin's lifestyle and other pertinent info. Jim Munro might have been mentioned, but he was a recent friend of Bonin's and detectives were already searching for him. Miley was a new name and was added to their list for questioning.

Fraser, unaware it was Billy Pugh who tipped police on Bonin, probably didn't mention Bonin leaving with Pugh, from his apartment, the night Harry Turner was murdered on March 24, 1980. If Pugh was still in custody, it appears detectives didn't pursue the matter any further. Fraser may have failed to put the dates together; he was busy trying to remember events about a "friend" he just found out was a brutal serial killer.

At the same time detectives probably never asked about Pugh, which offers certain suppositions: 1) Detectives didn't bring up Pugh to protect a juvenile informant, 2) Detectives didn't bring up Pugh because Fraser may have then deduced Pugh snitched, which in turn might have become public knowledge or got back to Bonin, 3) Detectives didn't consider Billy Pugh a suspect and he may already have been released him from juvenile custody in the weeks after Bonin's arrest.

Eric Wijnaendts, who helped Bonin kill Larry Sharp and Sean King, was only at Fraser's a few times, however, he made a strong impression by being obnoxiously drunk on each occasion. His name was also left out by Fraser, for the time being, because he wasn't being sought for questioning either. Under pressure, trying to remember so much and not believing what Bonin had done, Fraser could easily have forgotten about Pugh and Eric.

With little to go on, detectives scrambled to match Bonin's activities to murder dates while collecting evidence. For example, detectives knew Bonin was in custody twice in the previous year for a total of 12-weeks, so any murders during those dates could be ruled out. Charges in the drug arrest were never filed against Fraser.

Blindsided and shocked must describe Fraser's state of mind during that "moment of realization." Knowing Bonin for nearly two-years meant he had no clue; in minutes Fraser's "friend" morphed from party buddy to predator. All his Bonin interactions swirling back to replay over and over: What was he doing and when? Who else might be involved and how had Bonin gotten them to kill? All those innocent boys tortured and murdered; all those families and friends put through hell; all those times he looked into the eyes of a serial killer and talked with him, laughed with him, had sex with him, partied with him, provided hospitality for him and introduced him to others who might have gotten involved!

At Bonin's trial he testified, "I thought I knew him very well and actually considered him a non-violent person."

Vernon Butts' house, on Dinwiddie Street in Downey, was immediately placed under surveillance. Having attempted suicide three times, he tried again on July 21, the same day Fraser was talking to detectives, using over-the-counter sleeping meds. Had he been successful, detectives would have been robbed of a major source of information. Despite what Fraser said about his involvement in the Markus Grabs murder, at the time he was only considered, according to testimony from Sgt. Fueglein, a "witness or informant." Third-party info proved nothing.

Three nights later, on Thursday, July 24, the surveillance team alerted detectives that Butts had returned home. St. John and Mellecker, from LAPD, and Fueglein and Kushner, of LA County Sheriff's Department, rolled up at midnight. He wasn't surprised; his suicide attempt days before, even if half-hearted, offers insight into his emotionally fractured state of mind. Already possessed with a nervous disposition, walking around with the secret of having helped murder six boys, and knowing about three others, was a difficult burden to carry.

One year earlier the strange chemistry between Bonin and Butts hatched a disaster which rippled out to engulf scores of innocent victims, directly and indirectly.

With little prompting, Butts readily admitted he was "present for six-murders and knew about another one." Knowing the game was up, he went to a small shed in the back and retrieved a "black address book" and various ID cards, belonging to Darin Kendrick, and gave them to Sgt. Kushner. Butts ignored Bonin's instructions to "lose the wallet" and investigators had a major piece of evidence. Butts also revealed the supply of Choral Hydrate used in drugging Kendrick.

After a short conversation, with questions about which victims came first and where they were dumped, he was taken to the Norwalk Sheriff's sub-station for questioning. Kushner and others stayed behind to search for more evidence. Discussions continued with Butts agreeing to accompany detectives to various locations where bodies were left and provide hair, blood and saliva samples. He was taken over to the Norwalk Community Hospital for those procedures.

Vernon Butts was booked on murder charges at the Norwalk sub-station, based on finding Kendrick's wallet and his information, and transferred to Los Angeles Men's Central Jail the next day. Before anything else, Bonin was charged and arraigned on Friday, July 25 for the murder of the West German tourist Markus Grabs. LA County District Attorney Van de Kamp, under tremendous pressure, decided to file the one murder charge in order to justify keeping Bonin in custody. Keeping his bail inordinately high for relatively minor offenses, when compared to murder, was becoming more difficult with each passing day.

An AP story in the Saturday, July 26 **Reno Gazette-Journal** reported that "an unidentified friend who allegedly witnessed the murder and helped him dump the body in Malibu Canyon is under surveillance said Deputy D.A. Aaron Stovitz." Disinformation was fed to the press as the alleged witness was not "under surveillance" but in custody. Stovitz also said police learned about the "unidentified friend," Butts, from a statement made "by a third man," Fraser. Both went unnamed and Butts' identity remained a secret.

Over the next four days the agenda for Butts was constant interviews and road trips; for example he took them into the Valencia area, 50-miles north of Downtown LA, in the mistaken belief that was where Mark Shelton, their first victim, was dumped (he was actually left in the Cajon Pass over 90-miles away); he also led detectives on a fruitless search to Crystal Lake, in the San Bernardino Mountains, where he thought Bonin said he left Sean King. Over 60-police officers went on that search, proving a huge waste of manpower and money.

One officer said Butts started "singing like a nightingale." He confessed to assisting Bonin with six of the murders by saying, "I was present, but Bonin committed them, I just went along with him. Bonin would talk to me like a drill sergeant, he had this dominate personality. But he also had a charismatic personality that hooked kids in and with me a very passionate lover." Butts felt drawn to Bonin, ten years his senior, while Bonin liked the excitement Butts brought into his life. Butts later admitted, "It's not smart to spill to the cops without an attorney present. I was there for a few of the killings, but you can't pin them all on me. Bonin actually did them. I just went along for the ride."

Playing the victim, Butts was lying because he was heavily involved in six murders and had info on three others: 1) Bonin told him about Markus Grabs and he saw blood splattered inside of the van; 2) He was with Bonin when he picked up Sean King, on May 19, and Bonin later told him, "You should have come along, it was a lot of fun." Butts had told Bonin he wished he had gone along; 3) He saw the body of Steven Wells in the van when Bonin and Munro came by the house afterwards. Later Cati Razook, Butts' fiancée, said she referred to him as "Timid Vern" and that friends called him "shy and easily led" by others. She wasn't surprised at how cooperative he was with the authorities.

When Butts became more sanguine, he said, "We shared a good little nightmare."

On Tuesday, July 29 a major announcement broke that Bonin and Butts were formally charged in Los Angeles with multiple murders and robberies in the "Freeway Killer cases." Carried in hundreds of newspapers nationally, the news must have made Miley, Munro, Pugh and Wijnaendts sit up and take notice. None were in custody, and all were involved in one or more Freeway Killer murders with Bonin.

Bonin was charged with 14 counts of murder, 11 counts of robbery, one count of sodomy and one count of mayhem, the final one in the Thomas Lundgren case because he was emasculated (He was not involved in Lundgren's death). Butts was charged with six counts of murder and three counts of robbery.

Todd Landgren, Bonin's attorney, and Joe Ingler, Butts' attorney, had the arraignments postponed until August 8 and 13 respectively. Bonin's sexual charges, from the June 11 arrest in Hollywood, were postponed and later dropped. A statement from the Los Angeles County Sheriff's Dept. shows how little was still known, "Bonin and Butts are believed responsible for the kidnapping, torture and murder of at least 21 young males between May 1979 and June 1980."

Immediately Sgt. St. John began eliminating Bonin from similar murders he had been investigating since 1973. He was quoted in the *LA Times* as saying, "Those 40 or so victims were not all victims of the same killer, that seems pretty much for certain, evidence gathered to date was unlikely to link Bonin or Butts to any murders stretching back that far." Once the interviews and road trips ended, leading to multiple charges, Butts shut down on advice from his attorney and fear of Bonin's reprisal. He was a "conflicted" soul in every sense of the word.

Back in Port Huron, Michigan the varied travels of Jim Munro were about to end. After ditching Margaret in Las Vegas, and hitchhiking around the country, he went back to LA for a week in mid-July. He stayed at a motel on Sunset Blvd. in Hollywood around July 13, the manager remembered him being with four other guys and "making lots of noise." At some point he spoke with Sgt. Mellecker on the phone, but after encouraging him to come in Munro got scared and hung up. He left town shortly afterwards and hitchhiked to Port Huron.

Beginning on July 25, aware Munro was involved in the Wells murder, officers were a constant presence at Stan Hurd's Huntington Beach office while prowling Downey, Long Beach and surrounding areas. They often visited Hurd's office and even offered money for Munro's bus fare. Word then arrived, through Margaret's mother, that Munro was somewhere around Detroit.

On Thursday, July 31 Munro was charged in LA Municipal Court with Judge Nancy Brown granting a motion, from Deputy DA Stovitz, that the complaint documents be sealed "to protect witnesses" in the case. That same day Munro arrived at this cousin's apartment on Nern Street in St. Clair, a suburb of Port Huron 50-miles north of Detroit.

In the late afternoon, Munro made a mistake and called Tammie in Long Beach. She told him to call back, and Stan alerted detectives Munro was about to ring back. Police in Michigan were notified he was in the area and may only be at the apartment for a short while. When he called back, Tammie kept him on the line for 30-minutes with talk of and sex and love.

Primed to hitchhike back to LA, Munro was quietly taken into custody at 5:00 p.m. EDT, 15-minutes after the call ended.

"He seemed surprised he had been found but not surprised he was being sought in connection with the series of killings," said Michigan State Trooper James Dowling. Detectives from LA were on the way to collect their prisoner.

In Michigan he was interviewed twice; once by Mellecker, who he had spoken with personally two-weeks earlier, and St. John from LAPD; the second time by Sgt. Bernie Esposito, from the OC Sherriff, William Tynes of OC District Attorney's office and Sgt. David Kushner, LA Sheriff. During the first interview with St. John and Mellecker, they asked what he had been doing for six-weeks? Munro said he was making money, hitchhiking at truck stops and that he decided to come back to California right when the police showed up and arrested him.

Before going into details about the activities of June 2, when Wells was murdered, a key part of the conversation reveals his state of mind.

Q: Why don't you tell us right now what's going on? What are you going to tell the court?

A: I'll just kept telling them exactly...because I'm tired of being, you know, sitting there being locked up in jail. This is the second time in my life I've ever been locked up.

Q: What are you going to tell the court what's going on?

A: I'll tell them the truth.

Q: Okay, do you want to start with me?

A: Sure. You know, me and you, you know, we're good friends, you know I'm tired of...oh, for one I was just going to tell them, 'Hey, I'm innocent, I didn't have nothing to do with that.'

Q: Nothing to do with what, Jim?

A: What's going on, I didn't have nothing to do with the...what they're trying to tell what they, have they, did they convict Bill for that or what?

Q: He's been filed on.

A: Well, that's what I'm saying. I know that now, now they're trying to think, trying to say I did it now. Is that what they got me arrested for?

Q: See, the court's going to want to know what you know about Bill Bonin before they're going to believe anything you say.

A: What I know about him? He's gay for one or bisexual, he's tried sexual acts with me...

Q: Why don't you start right now Jim. We've got a whole bunch of work. We've talked to a whole bunch of people. We know a lot of things and a lot of things about you. You start lying to us and we will know real quick, and I tell the court you're lying and can show you're lying, there not going to believe.

A: Yeah.

Q: So what do you know about Bill and his activities, particularly with kids?

A: The kids?

Q: The ones he's been picking up and killing. He charged with fourteen counts for Murder.

A: Jesus Christ, whew!!...

Mistakenly, Munro still thinks he might be let free if he talks, but he was rapidly disabused of that notion. Out of fear, he lies about the events of the June 2 Wells murder until St. John and Mellecker put the hammer down.

A: I just...Jesus I just want to go home.

Q: Listen, you've gone through your story. I've told you before there's been a lot of investigation in the last six weeks.

A: Yeah.

Q: Okay, and you're lying to us.

A: No, I'm not.

Q: Yeah, yeah. Okay, I know it and John knows it. And you know it. Okay? Now we came out here to talk to you. To get the truth about what happened.

A: Is this all I, you know, tell what happened, because I want to go home, you know.

Q: Yeah, okay. We want to find out what your activities were with Bill regarding the death of several young kids. Okay? Right now we hold a murder warrant for your arrest.

A: Why is that?

Q: Because we know you murdered somebody with Bill. We want to what your participation was. Was he the one that...it was his idea or was it your idea, did you both participate or did he make you do the driving, we want to find out what happened that night. We know you're involved, you know you're involved, John knows you're involved. And we want to find out the truth of the matter.

A: Well, Bill told me, you know, if I say anything, I'd get killed.

Q: Well, we understand that, but Bill is in custody now. He's not getting out.

A: Yeah, but he's got friends all over…yes, he killed someone.

Q: Okay, you want to tell us about it?

A: Can I have a cigarette, please? I need one. I'm tired of this, the hell with it. I'm telling everything, I don't give a shit. You know, my Daddy even told me.

Following this exchange, the details spilled out wholesale, although they differed from the actual truth. In the second interview Kushner pushed him hard, saying, "Listen to me when I tell you that you can't go back and change the past. There's nothing you can do about what happened, you have to just lay it out the way it actually happened. Don't change a damn thing." After a second interview with OC officials, on August 2, he was transported after waiving his right to fight extradition.

Reports of Munro's arrest coincided with more details about Bonin and Butts hitting the newspapers. On Wednesday, July 30 the **Fort Lauderdale News** reported that an LA based homosexual group, which put up a $50,000 reward leading to the conviction of a 'killer or killers,' was afraid police would stop "following up leads because they think they have their killers."

The next day, Thursday, July 31, the **Intelligencer Journal**, in Lancaster, Pennsylvania, reported the total number of Freeway Killings, 41, had been expanded to 44 with the addition of Sean King and two new "unidentified victims."

Number 44 was a young man who was found dead on Monday, July 28 alongside Santiago Canyon Road in Orange County. With six counties in Southern California possessing Freeway Killer cases, going back eight-years, the process of separation began with the cases of Bonin and his associates.

Doug Brown, in the **LA Times** on Friday, August 1, released the name of the "third man" informant as "Scotty," noting he had criminal charges pending when talking to detectives. He reported that OC Chief Deputy DA, Jim Enright, planned to seek grand jury indictments against Bonin and Butts. Furthermore, Bonin's attorney said he would fight for only one trial in LA and opposed the public defender's office taking Bonin's case. Todd Landgren, Bonin's attorney, believed all three informants were coerced and was prepared to challenge their veracity.

Based in Newport Beach, he previously represented Bonin on drug and sex charges and may have helped him avoid jail time during the ten-month murder spree. The article also noted Landgren's intention to become Bonin's court appointed attorney for the murder cases, sure to be a high-profile affair for any attorney involved.

On August 2 ***The Times Herald*** in Port Huron, Michigan published an article by Steve Spalding, ***LA Murder Suspect Asks to Return There***. It opened by saying that Munro, a former St. Clair resident, waived extradition rights and was "eager to return to California to stand trial." Claiming non-involvement in the Wells murder, he yelled at reporters outside jail, "I'm going back to LA to volunteer for court." Another article, in the same paper, had stories from people who grew up with Munro and a girl who saw him, the night before his arrest, at a local mini market. She was closing down when he ambled up for a soda and cigarettes; she knew him from childhood and didn't recognize him at first. As a final gesture he asked her out on a date. Jim Munro was characterized as someone who tried "too hard to become friends, asked too many questions and overstayed his welcome."

The last arrested, to date, was the first arraigned in LA Municipal Court. Fresh off the plane from Michigan, Munro appeared before Judge Barbara Jean Johnson on Tuesday, August 5. Before the pleadings, the halls had to be scoured for an attorney.

Marilyn Kopple was appointed but was unlikely to continue; she was nine-months pregnant. Reasons for the scramble were that the public defender's office was wary about representing Jim Munro because they might end up representing Bonin or completely avoid all the cases due to "legal conflicts." Munro, like Butts, blamed Bonin for everything and denied doing the actual killing of Steven Wells. He pled not guilty to one count of murder and his bail was set at $450,000 ($1.8 million in 2023).

Bonin was next on the docket before Judge Johnson on Friday, August 8 dressed in blue jeans with a paperback book stuffed in the back pocket and blue jail shirt, sporting shoulder length black hair and a thick mustache. He pled not guilty to all charges. Due to the chief public defender being on vacation, the preliminary hearing was delayed by Judge Johnson, who also approved Deputy Public Defender John Ryan as counsel along with extra phone calls and a haircut for Bonin.

Bill Farr and Kristina Lindgren's ***Los Angeles Times*** article, ***Freeway Killer Suspect Reported Talking Freely***, reported, "Investigators have been able to build their case against 'Freeway Killer' suspect William Bonin almost entirely on information give them by his young co-defendant, Vernon Butts, the ***Times*** learned Friday. Sources close to the case said Butts, a 22-year-old aspiring magician, 'began talking' almost immediately after his July 25 arrest, admitting he was present during six of the 21 murders linked to Bonin. Despite his cooperation, Butts has not formally turned state's evidence, and no deal has yet been made with him in return for his testimony. As a result of Butts' information, detectives have been able to develop other evidence they say corroborates his version about Bonin's alleged involvement in the series of slayings."

Not much had changed when, on Wednesday, August 13, Butts pled not guilty to charges amidst a swirl of rumors regarding possible cooperation. Waiving his right to a preliminary hearing within 10-days, Butts faced the death penalty with a "special circumstance" designation because of crimes involving multiple murders and robbery.

When asked about the rumors, by Tim Alger of the ***OC Register***, Butts' attorney Joe Ingler lashed out, "I wish somebody would let me know, everybody's talking about that, but I seem to be the last one to know. I have met with him several times but prosecutors have given me so little background material that our lawyer-client conversations have been superficial. We've got very little to talk about." Ingler was vexed about getting nothing about his arrest, house search, interviews and forensics. Unsure who delayed the reports—prosecutors, LAPD or sheriffs—Ingler said, "It doesn't help anybody if I don't have them."

Butts and Bonin were held without bail while detectives and prosecutors believe Bonin was the driving force behind the killings, either doing them alone or roping others to kill with him. Events quickly led to an internecine fight between counties wanting their pound of flesh. Along with OC planning indictments, San Bernardino, Riverside and San Diego counties were making noises as well.

Vernon Butts' interview transcripts were under wraps at the DA's office and Deputy DA Stovitz, chief prosecutor, refused to "comment on reports Butts' had admitted to his role in six slayings" and "evidence has been developed independent of Butts to connect Bonin to the murders."

Stovitz was serious about evidence being "developed" as criminalists from various divisions were comparing forensic evidence from Bonin, his van and his house. Richard R. Linhart, an expert in blood comparison with the LA Sheriff's Dept., matched a blood specimen from the van to that of Darin Kendrick; a semen finding lifted from a leg of Ronald Gatlin matched Bonin's blood type. Nylon rope from the van possessed detectable human blood stains; areas of van carpeting had blood stains someone tried to wash out; thirteen areas of blood detected in the van either proved not human or couldn't be proved to be human; four areas of blood were detected in Bonin's house on August 2, 1980. While absolute matches in blood comparisons wasn't possible with the technology available, statistical evaluation noting the percentage of population possessing certain blood types, combined with "genetic markers," provided "highly probable" matches.

Two hairs removed from the body of James Macabe, by Coroner's Asst. Mr. Frances Turney, were matched by Sheriff's Criminalist James Bailey to Bonin's pubic hair; a hair found on Ronald Gatlin's penis, supplied by Linhart, also matched Bonin. Hair found on upper right back area by Sgt. Kushner on Markus Grabs was similar to Bonin's; pubic hair found on James Macabe and Chapstick near the body matched Bonin.

Hair matching was not an absolute science as James Bailey explained in testimony:

"While he couldn't absolutely say two hairs are from the same person" it was possible to "absolutely eliminate some individuals when compared to a sample hair."

By examining the thin outer covering, thick middle portion and central core of a hair, each with different microscopic characteristics of length and curliness, he came to certain conclusions and the term "consistent with" was used by criminalists.

A fiber found near the mouth of Steven Wood matched carpeting in Bonin's van. OC County Criminalist Sandra Weirsema, with fibers found on Steven Wells, and LAPD Criminalist Linda Baxter, with fibers found on Charles Miranda, also matched them to the van carpeting. Fibers from the bodies of Steven Wells, Dennis Fox, Glen Barker, Russell Rugh and Larry Sharp matched as well. Monsanto, manufacturer of the carpet, confirmed the fibers came from the model of carpeting in Bonin's van.

46

Miley Arrested, Arraignments & Butts Interview
August 22 to November 13, 1980

Just two weeks after the murders of Charles Miranda and James Macabe, on February 3, 1980, Greg Miley moved to Houston, Texas with his family. He was arrested at 10:00 a.m. on Friday, August 22, 1980 while walking on the sidewalk near his stepfather's home. Scott Fraser had contacted him, as part of a trap, to talk about a girl who needed a place to stay. He asked Miley to meet her at the nearby Dairy Queen. A homicide officer was the bait and they wanted to lure him out of the house.

Bernie Esposito and David Kushner, of OC and LA Sheriffs, along with detectives from LAPD accompanied Houston PD on the sting operation. Miley walked about 200 yards from the house before multiple plain clothes vehicles closed in and Houston homicide detective, John Donovan, arrested him without incident. Uniformed officers transported him to the Detective Division where Esposito and Kushner interviewed Miley for two hours. Donovan informed Miley of his constitutional rights but didn't participate in the interview.

According to testimony, Miley immediately denied knowing Fraser, Bonin or knowing Bonin had a van or "anything like that." After hearing this nonsense detectives put the screws to him, and Miley began spilling out details regarding the Miranda and Macabe murders. The issue of what Miley said initially, and what he said later and why, was raised with detectives by defense attorneys at the preliminary hearings.

Miley was flown back and booked into OC Jail before transfer to LA County Jail for rebooking and arraignment. The multiple murder charges, done within hours of each other, carried the "special circumstance" designation signaling a possible death penalty conviction.

Preliminary hearings are supposed to take place within 60-days of charges being filed, however, in the opening months the Freeway Killer prelims were repeatedly postponed. Munro's attorney, Madelynn Kopple, had his prelims pushed from September 11 to November 6; while Miley's, set for October, took place in early December.

Two months after Bonin's arrest, four of the six co-murderers sat in custody. Billy Pugh and Eric Wijnaendts were not yet considered suspects.

Munro was a strong candidate for a deal while nothing was certain for Butts, who pled not guilty after getting a court-appointed attorney, James Goldstein. Miley, represented by Lawrence Steinberg, also pled not guilty and seemed ripe for a deal.

Criminalists identified two elements in the carpeting at Butts' home which tied him to Darin Kendrick's murder—Chloral Hydrate, used to drug him, and Kendrick's blood. Info from Butts prompted Kern County authorities to exhume the body of John Doe for possible identification. Picked up in Hollywood by Bonin and Butts, in November 1979, he was dumped in a farmland irrigation ditch near Bakersfield. AP reported on September 14, 1980 that Kern County Coroner Dick Gervais said he was 5-foot-10 inches tall, about 23 years old and 140 pounds. Having failed to ID the body, he was interred as a John Doe.

In the hours and days after arrest, Butts, Munro and Miley all gave up lots of information, a mistake for anyone! Detectives still had many holes to fill in the story and desperately wanted to confirm their main conclusion; Bonin bore primary responsibility for the murders and the others didn't operate without him on hand. Racked by nervous tension and fear, Butts' initial reaction seemed to be one of relief from the strain.

Upon further reflection he admitted, "Spilling my guts to police without a lawyer was probably a mistake." Munro, pressed by detectives just after arrest, cracked under the pressure and exclaimed, "I'll tell you everything, I don't give a shit." Greg Miley experienced the same scenario.

When the first of the three, Butts, was confronted by detectives they got a big surprise when he readily admitted to being "present for six of the killings." Days after his arrest, Butts again tried to kill himself, called a "joke suicide attempt" by deputies. He was then moved to a protected area of the jail. Within the tightly controlled High Power Unit, the hospital ward was where his four-by-eight-foot cell was located. It had a solid steel door with a porthole window, sink, toilet, small shelf and a towel rack three and one-half feet off the floor. Deputies made rounds every 30-minutes and "believed he wasn't seriously suicidal."

OC Register's Tim Alger secured an interview with Butts on Wednesday, October 15, 1980. Conducted through a thick glass barrier in a high-security room, the article, published two days later, provided a snapshot into what had transpired and his current state of mind. Butts told Alger the last year had been lived in fear for his life, and those around him. Early in the killing spree, from August to November 1979, Butts said Bonin's implied threats about keeping quiet were enough to shut him up and continue participating.

To the erstwhile reporter he appeared quiet, unassuming and a person "some might find it hard to believe would kill anyone." Claiming he liked drawing and was writing a book "somewhat like the Lord of the Rings Trilogy," Butts said he regretted "not telling police what he knew about the killings earlier, but at the same time he's convinced there's nothing else he could have done while Bonin was free."

Once the **OC *Register*** started publishing daily articles about the killings, starting on March 24, 1980, Bonin would come over to Butts' house with the newspaper to show him. On one occasion, when pictures of multiple victims were on display, Bonin pointed to a picture and read the name exclaiming, "I did this one…I did this one…I did this one…" Vernon Butts said that Bonin threatened both him and his fiancée, Cati Razook, who knew everything about Butts "aside from the homicides."

Terrifying fear followed him into jail, where he believed Bonin had "associates and friends" to do his dirty work. Both residing in the high security wing, they were accidentally placed in the same lawyer visitation room as Alger describes, "For one scary instant, he was face to face with the shorter, chunkier and much stronger man who he said had ordered him around like a dog for so long. Butts said he screamed at the guards and was removed—quickly."

At the same time, Bonin showed him a kindness in jail by paying for an engagement ring that James Meurer, the only other person besides Razook who visited Butts regularly, was sent to buy. While looking through the visiting area glass, Butts watched Meurer put the ring on her finger, and they became engaged.

Alger learned the DA, due to previous cooperation, offered Butts 25-years without the possibility of parole in exchange for guilty pleas, on all counts, and testifying against Bonin. Joe Ingler turned it down for a simple reason, as Butts explained, "I cooperated not because of making deals, the reason is I'm innocent. I don't need to make deals and now I'm being crucified by the state and everybody else." Stories about his occult activities playing a role in the killings bothered Butts, seemingly turning him into a kind of demonic monster. He told Alger, "I believe I am the victim, I am one of the few that remained alive—Miley, Munro and I and the other guy. People got the wrong idea. That I didn't expect."

Material from Alger's article was rewritten by the **Associated Press** (AP) and appeared in **The Courier** in Waterloo, Iowa under the headline, **Slaying Defendant Tells of Fear**, and **The Sheboygan Press** in Wisconsin with a banner reading, **Murder Defendant Says He Was Afraid**. Both reprints started, "One of the four men charged in the Freeway Killings case says he went along with co-defendant William Bonin on six murder trips because 'it was either go or become the next victim. When I'm petrified, I'm like a robot,' Vernon Butts said in an interview this week in the Los Angeles County Jail with The Register, an Orange County newspaper."

Vernon Butts was playing innocent victim, leaving out the fact he took an active part in six killings with Bonin. While certainly afraid of Bonin, it was their strange chemistry which helped kickoff the murder spree. Their fascination with death, combined with Bonin's aggressive sexual appetite for teenage boys, percolated under the surface in conversational fantasies and then burst forth when boredom and opportunity unleashed Bonin's monster within. For him, there was no turning back after he got the taste for killing.

No matter how much he wanted to deny his part, Butts couldn't escape his responsibility and guilt. Bonin would bring over new victims, and Butts went along for the ride. Months went by as he lived life knowing Bonin was out cruising for new victims, always on the prowl.

Four days after Alger's article was published, Miley and Butts were transported to OC to face murder charges stemming from grand jury indictments. Proceedings were delayed for a few days in order to determine who would represent Butts. Miley was charged with one-count of murder while both faced multiple charges in LA. Transported in separate Sheriff's Dept. vans, Butts rode with six other inmates, five men and one woman, for the 30-mile drive to the OC Men's Central Jail in Santa Ana. Bernie Esposito and James Sidebotham, the lead OC homicide detectives, decided to talk with the other riders in search of info.

Getting ready to board the van from a holding cell, the whispering about who Vernon Butts was and what he had done began to circulate. The inmates slated to board the bus tried to catch glimpses of the famous murderer from adjoining cells as jailhouse gossip swirled about. During the 45-minute drive the inmates began chatting with Butts, and he readily answered their inquiries. Three of the riders agreed to speak with detectives and were not promised anything or threatened.

Interview transcripts of Carl J. Hance, Juan Aviles, and Kenneth Wayne Hensen, conducted the same afternoon, provide an interesting snapshot of Vernon Butts at a crucial time. While all three freely offered info, it was Hance who spoke the most comprehensively. First to be interviewed, the proceedings with Hance began at 2:16 p.m. with J. Swenson of the OC Investigative Division providing transcription services.

The group conversation was easily heard by everyone in the back of the van, and all participated as Butts wove a series of whole-truths, half-truths and outright fictions.

Not holding back many details about Bonin, he was definitely editing his own involvement as he first told them about being "present or involved" in six murders and offering gruesome info about Bonin shoving a "stake into the victim's rectum till it came out his mouth" (never happened); that "Bill used a knife on the victim and that he (Butts) mostly just drove the van to help get rid of the bodies" (Bill did use a knife but Butts never drove, and he helped kill and not just get rid of bodies); about Bonin molesting 19-year old Darin Kendrick, drugging him and shoving an icepick in his ear (Butts participated in all aspects and actually drove the icepick in with a hammer blow, a move which shocked Bonin). He also told of dumping a body off a canyon and one in a Norwalk trashcan, the latter was Kendrick because all the other killings Butts participated in were dumped far away.

Was Butts trying to increase his prison credibility to enhance his survival chances? Butts alluded to knowing he would get 25-years and that he was already planning a book about what happened. While not revealing much beyond what detectives knew from the late July interviews, and road trips, there were bits and pieces that opened new windows for detectives to work with.

Hance told detectives that Butts related tales of his involvement in black magic, occult ceremonies and how Bonin would "just go out and get anybody, you know, every day, every time he went out he got somebody and killed 'em, you know, he told us how they carved stars and moons in their flesh and how Bonin strangled one with a crowbar in the back of the van." Bonin was never involved in black magic and no victims had stars or moons carved in their flesh, however, Bonin did indeed kill with a tire iron on the throat.

Continuing in this manner, to either disgust his audience or demonstrate criminal credentials, Butts told everyone they "hung up one by the balls and tortured him to death." This was utter fantasy and it caused a few of them to call him a "sick bastard with hopes he would get the gas chamber." Yet many of the group were fascinated by his stories and peppered Butts with questions of all kinds, which caused him to clam up at times. But Hance, with a more relaxed manner, got Butts to answer in ways which led him to conclude "he was fairly intelligent, I didn't see any insanity in him, but anybody who would go out and help participate in murders has to have something wrong with them, you know he laughed and smiled when he was telling us about bad stuff."

What struck Hance even more than the "laughing and smiling" was a distinct lack of remorse, "He told us he didn't feel any badness at all, and when I asked him if got out would he do something like this again, you know, he just said, 'I won't know till the time.' I asked if would testify against Bonin and he said 'no way' cause Bonin knew people who would kill him, he said if they convicted him of the six murders Bonin would know it was him." This lack of remorse and comical indifference was confirmed by the other two riders, Aviles and Hensen.

Hance proceeded to relate a story which appears to be a mixture of hope, fantasy and "his own" truth. Butts said he didn't want Bonin to think he was weakening from pressure to testify, so his girlfriend was having sexual affairs with various reporters in order to promulgate a story in the press favorable to a claim of innocence. He wanted the public to believe he was an unwilling pawn of Bonin's who went along out of "fear for his life," thus giving him a better chance of getting involuntary manslaughter rather than murder convictions.

Finding the notion farcical, Hance asked, "How can you expect involuntary manslaughter if you drove the van while Bonin killed, let him kill in your house and then brought a corpse over to your house with a friend to show you?" All Butts said was, "I just feared for my life."

Juan Aviles added these observations when asked if Butts seemed sorry for what he had done? "No, he didn't, he looked sick. I mean this guy was like, cool, like he was almost happy that he did it. He says he going to a write a book and be on TV to talk about it. A few of us told him he was sick; I remember I said that too. Because, he looked so, he looked insane by the way when he mentioned these things, he seemed casual, like it was nothing. And he laughed too, that was another one. A normal person wouldn't laugh at situations like that, you know!"

Kenneth Hensen was the last interviewed and one of his reactions proves insightful. Unaware Butts had actively participated in the murders, because Butts told them he just drove the van, Hensen saw through the veil: "After the first couple of killings he figured the police would come and bust 'em, and that would be all of it, but nobody came and nothin' happened, so he goes what the hell."

"But from what you're saying it sounds like he really didn't mind?" Esposito said, asking a key question.

"I know. That's what I think," Hensen said as he processed the notion. "He didn't to me, my opinion is that he was behind it all along cause if he could sit there and drive a van and the man can't get out, no way out of the van, why didn't he just drive to a police department with him in there, with bodies in there. He told us there was no way to get out, so he had to get out on every one of them and open the door every time to help get the body out."

Lastly is the amazing fact that Vernon Butts kept his mouth shut during the whole murder spree; never hinting or saying a word to anyone else about what had happened, what Bonin was still doing and what may happen again. Imagine the many months as Butts lived with the terrible secret, knowing he could save lives by calling the police. Finally, when the whole awful mess ended, Vernon Butts learns details, names and ages of all those so brutally and unnecessarily slain.

While in OC jail Butts was threatened by inmates, "You don't look so tough, you like to kill young boys, but you can't stand up to a man. We'll punk you pretty good."

This added to his nervous state of mind and increased his attorney's desire to seek increased protection for his high-profile client.

How long could Butts' false claims of coerced "non-involvement and feigned innocence" remain hidden from public knowledge? Bonin was the only other person who knew the truth, and he wasn't talking. Miley and Butts pled not guilty to all charges and were back at LA Men's Jail by the end of November 1980.

47

Hearings, Media, Snitches, Eric Arrested, Sgt. St. John's Letter & Secret Deals
November 14 to December 18, 1980

December ushered in the beginning of the Bonin Freeway Killer preliminary hearings, which had been postponed for months. On Thursday, November 13 Municipal Court Judge Randolph Moore, at the request of Deputy DA Stovitz, combined the Bonin and Butts LA trials and set the prelim hearings for December 11.

Stovitz argued that putting them together would "save the court's time" since charges against them were practically identical. A **United Press International** (UPI) article, published in the **Sacramento Bee**, reported he wouldn't seek to include Miley and Munro in "the same trial. The four men have been implicated so far with the killings of 21 of the 44 boys and young men found slain in five Southern California counties in the past eight years."

After three weeks at OC Jail, in mid-November, Butts and Miley pled not guilty as an AP story in **The Miami Herald** reported, "After the pleas were entered in Municipal Court, preliminary hearings were scheduled in January for Vernon Butts, 23, of Downey and Gregory Miley, 19, of Houston, Texas. Butts is accused of killing three teenage residents of Orange County in late 1979 and early 1980. Miley faces one murder charge in the death of a 12-year-old Orange County boy last February. Because of alleged special circumstances in the deaths, each faces a possible death penalty if convicted."

In early December Bonin began writing each murder story and giving them piecemeal to his trusted attorney, Todd Landgren. The final one was completed about two-months later. He also kept a diary which contained observations, thoughts, remembrances, personal stories, news stories, legal strategies, media strategies, jailhouse tales, interviews, case updates and more. Bonin believed the info within the pages, amounting to "written murder confessions," might be traded for a deal with prosecutors, resulting in Life Without Parole rather than the Death Penalty.

First up in LA were the Miley prelims on December 1 and 2, hearings which allowed prosecutors to present evidence while the defense generally sits idle. Should the judge deem a trial is warranted, a date for an arraignment is established which is then followed by a trial start date hearing. LA cases at the time transitioned from the Municipal Court, a lower court referred to by local lawyers as the "Muni Court," to the Superior Court (The LA Muni Court has since been disbanded).

Miley's attorney, Lawrence Steinberg, had the proceedings closed to the public so his client "wouldn't be tried in the public by one side of the story" for the February 3, 1980 slayings of Charles Miranda and James Macabe. Sgt. Kushner testified about Miley laying out the grisly story during his initial post-arrest interview, in Houston, where he agreed to speak to detectives without an attorney.

Steinberg argued Miley, with an IQ of 56, was unable to comprehend the situation and his Miranda Rights were violated, however, Kushner testified he was properly read and understood his rights before freely admitting he "decided to help Bonin kill someone." Miley's case was moving separately from the Bonin-Butts combined proceedings.

Satisfied with the evidence, the judge bound over Miley on all charges and scheduled a December 18 arraignment. Jim Munro's preliminary hearing was set for December 22.

Then out of nowhere the four Freeway Killer suspects became five when Eric Marten Wijnaendts was arrested, in early December, in connection with the Harry Todd Turner murder on March 24, 1980, a date which will play heavily in subsequent events.

Bonin met Eric in early March 1980, while both were serving short terms in Orange County jail. They formed a strong emotional connection and sexual relationship. Eric was in jail for intoxication and assaulting a police officer. Detectives asked Eric to come in for basic questioning on Thursday, December 4 and the session resulted in his arrest for helping to rob and kill Turner, which carried the "special circumstance" designation making him eligible for the death penalty. His arrest was kept totally secret until Monday, December 8 and the following day the story hit the newspapers.

Freeway Killer stories were news locally, nationally and internationally; a West German tourist was one of the victims. As hearings gained momentum UPI and AP, the two dominant print syndication services, had stories picked up by large and small newspapers throughout the U.S. and around the world. Articles from major newspapers, such as the *LA Times*, *New York Times* or *Washington Post*, were also syndicated to many regional and local newspapers.

TV news covered the story intensely and the public was anxious to learn details as they emerged. There was no Internet, no smart phones, no Twitter feeds; CNN began broadcasting on June 1, 1980, days before Bonin's arrest, and the notion of a 24-hour news cycle was still being tested. Media experts predicted CNN would rapidly fail. Most got their news through print media or local and national TV news, the latter generated by the three networks, CBS, ABC and NBC, and their local affiliates. There were also independent local TV stations in many places.

Many news articles continued to report that the Freeway Killer cases "may involve the deaths of as many as 44 young men and boys whose bodies were dumped near freeways in five Southland counties since 1972." However, authorities had informed the media that, due to his extended stays in mental hospitals and prisons, Bonin was not linked to any murders before 1979. Still the media used the 44 number in story after story and continued to do so for months. Detectives knew other serial killers were still out there.

On Tuesday, December 9 Bonin was in his cell when the inmate next door asked, "How many of you are there?" Bonin replied, "What do you mean?" He was told a fifth suspect had been arrested and Bonin immediately thought it was Billy Pugh, who helped him kill Turner. Bonin had deduced from court docs that it was Pugh who tipped off police, but he had kept his mouth shut about the murder. When he read the story in the *Herald Examiner*, he was shocked and dismayed to find out it was not Pugh but Eric! That same day Eric entered a plea of not guilty before Municipal Court Judge Giles B. Jackson.

Coincidences and an interesting chain of causality was about to transform the Bill Bonin story, revealing for the first time how and why, with Bonin's help, someone got away with double murder!

Following news of Eric's arrest, Bonin wrote in his diary about meeting him in OC jail, how much he liked the 20-year-old and looking out for him in jail. They exchanged contact info before Bonin's March 15 release and nine days later, on March 24, Eric was released and went to stay with his boyfriend on Leffingwell Road, near Valley View Ave. in South Whittier.

But he was locked out and at 11:00 a.m. he phoned Bonin, who lived six miles away. He picked up Eric and took him home to have sex. Bonin then rang up Scott Fraser and took Eric over to meet him. After a few hours, Bonin dropped him off back at Leffingwell.

That same night Fraser invited Bonin back to his place to meet Billy Pugh, knowing Bonin would be attracted to him sexually. They left together and murdered Harry Turner. Eric had indeed helped Bonin kill Larry Sharp and Sean King, but that was two-months after Turner, in mid-May. Six months after Bonin's arrest, on June 11, it seems most everyone was unaware of Eric's existence, except Scott Fraser, who may have temporarily forgotten about him.

Munro, Miley or Butts never met him, and Bonin never said a word about him. Logic dictates that, should Fraser have mentioned Eric during the July interview, he would have been questioned much earlier. Tracking all of Bonin's previous movements, detectives looked at Bonin's two six-week jail stints, at OC Jail, during the ten-month murder spree. In early March 1980, during the last two-weeks of the second stint from February 4 till March 15, Bonin and Eric established a bond which must have become visible to Sheriff's deputies.

Detectives put together three coincidences: 1) The Bonin-Eric jailhouse relationship in March; 2) Bonin and Eric's release dates and Turner's murder date; 3) Scott Fraser confirming Bonin had indeed brought Eric over on the afternoon of March 24.

Fraser remembered Eric for a simple reason; following his first encounter with Eric, Bonin brought him back twice and each time he caused a drunken ruckus. Fraser demanded that Bonin never bring him back.

When he gave St. John the Bonin tip, Pugh revealed that he met Bonin at Fraser's apartment, however, at the time of Eric's arrest detectives obviously didn't know that Pugh and Bonin met there on the night of March 24 and left together. Fraser hadn't been asked about it or volunteered the info; he could easily have forgotten the encounter.

Fraser couldn't know Pugh provided the Bonin tip, and detectives didn't mention Pugh to Fraser in order to protect a confidential informant, one who happened to be a juvenile.

Contemplating Eric's arrest and previous events, Bonin was confused and so struck by the coincidence of dates he had his lawyer request the

Turner file from the DA, saying he wasn't even sure Harry Turner was one of his victims.

His diary reflects that confusion, "I thought—wow, here Eric did this and I didn't even know it. I was with the guy and now I find out that he did the same thing I did. At this time I had not seen the file on Turner or the photos of where the body was dropped.

"I had seen Turner's photos in the newspaper and didn't recognize it. I found later it was an old photo. I started tossing it back and forth in my mind. I finally got the Turner file and read it. I glanced thru and felt it was still possible it was Eric. I finally read the file thoroughly and looked at the photos of the dumpsite.

"I had only a slight feeling that I was guilty and that Eric was innocent. I asked for more photos and received them. More photos of the area where the body was dumped. That's when I was positive that Eric was innocent. I knew who was with me, Billy! I knew I'd have to do something but I didn't know what."

When questioned, Eric had inadvertently led them to believe he was involved in the Turner murder. He failed a polygraph test and backtracked by saying he vaguely remembered "one night" with Bonin but was drunk to the point of repeatedly passing out, and that he "may have seen Bonin strangle someone."

Eric was driven to the alley in Downtown LA, where Turner's was found, and remarked, "That's a good place to dump a body." Eric also displayed strong emotional reactions to photos of Turner and other victims. All of it resulted in charges for murder and robbery in the Turner case.

Devising a remedy for Eric's quandary meant Bonin needed to inform detectives it was Billy Pugh, with no knowledge of what Eric had revealed while convincing them Eric wasn't involved in anything else. No forensic evidence connected Eric to Sean King, who was transported and raped in Bonin's Chevette, not the van, and murdered on a dirt patch in the San Bernardino Mountains before being discarded in the bushes.

Sean King's body hadn't been found. Larry Sharp was another question; it was certainly possible forensic evidence from Sharp's body might match Eric, they both raped him and were in the back of the van together with him for a while. Detectives must have been looking at all the evidence for a possible match.

Eric was arraigned on the same day Bonin learned of his arrest, Tuesday, December 9, and Bonin set events in motion the following morning. He wrote a letter to the ***Herald Examiner***, mailed by his attorney, and had the first in a series of interviews with a local TV news reporter, Dave Lopez of KNXT/CBS Channel 2 News.

Raised in South Gate, close to where the Bonin family lived, Lopez was an ambitious 32-year-old reporter who started with CBS locally in 1976. During journalism studies, at Cal State LA, he worked at a local radio station and then later transitioned from print journalism to TV news. By 1980 Lopez had won two Emmy Awards, for local coverage, and garnered other TV industry and journalism plaudits.

Meeting with Bonin, at the jail infirmary, Lopez later said that Bonin was emphatic when he told him, "I want you to say this because Eric is not guilty. He was not with me the night of the murder; he should not be jail." Lopez broadcast the story on the evening news and Bonin's efforts to help Eric were underway. Lopez's series of Bonin interviews, especially the one on January 9, 1981, created a firestorm amongst the media and attorneys for both sides.

By then Bonin had a new court appointed attorney, Earl. E. Hanson. The public defender's office totally bowed out of Freeway Killer cases and Todd Landgren's bid to become a court appointed attorney was rejected, although he continued to advise Bonin and represent him on other matters.

The Bonin-Butts prelim hearings commenced on Thursday, December 11 in Municipal Court with Judge Vincent H. Erickson. Bonin's attorney requested the hearings be closed to the public and, after granting the motion, Erickson refused to hear media objections before ejecting all reporters and spectators. Deputy DA Stovitz, who worked on the Charles Manson prosecution team in 1970, wanted them to remain open, "I would much rather have it open, I think the public should know how to protect their children and the children should know how to protect themselves." Bonin's attorney told Dave Lopez that, since current plans didn't include mounting a defense, he "had no choice but bar the press and public from hearing the evidence."

Stovitz anticipated they would take at least four days as the prosecution called over 50 witnesses, starting with a coroner's pathologist and including detectives, criminalists, witnesses, doctors, dentists, experts and jailhouse snitches. They lasted six-days. LA Sheriff's homicide detectives Kushner and Fueglein testified about their interviews with Butts. They laid out how he willingly revealed the sequence of murders he was "present" at, how victims were acquired, methods of torture, killing, body dumpsites, murders Bonin told him about, others involved and more. There were also discussions on legal technicalities between Butts' attorney and the prosecution.

Bonin's described the court proceedings, "During the preliminary hearing I watched Vernon Butts a lot. He's a weird person. He was so scared that the bailiff was reading his notes, he wrote them with symbols like little half and full squares with dots in them, like some code or something. When he was looking at the photos of the dead bodies and like when the necks were cut to show internal damage, he would laugh. He did a lot of laughing. I told him to knock it off and so did his attorney. His attorney said once, 'You're going to have to stop that.'

"To Vern it was and is a game. The D.A. wanted us to stipulate to the testimony of a dentist. All the guy was going to do was say he took some dental x-rays. The guy lived in Michigan. Everyone was for the stipulation except Vern. They flew the guy out for a 15-minute time span on the stand. I asked Vern why didn't stipulate and he said, 'It gives me one more day of information.' Incidentally, this same doctor had testified in Orange County a lot at the grand jury indictment of Vern and Greg Miley."

Bonin learned that two jailhouse snitches, Lloyd Carlo Douglas and one Dr. Fahey, were scheduled to testify on Wednesday, December 17. After pleading guilty to manslaughter and burglary charges, Douglas morphed into a "professional" jailhouse snitch; someone who talks up inmates for info, or invents stories, that might be employed to reduce prison time.

Douglas was doing the same in the Lawrence Bittaker and Joseph Zakaria murder cases. Earlier that month a sympathetic inmate, Benny, told Bonin about speaking with both of them at Chino Prison and their "conspiring and signed statements to the effect of the conversations revealed and what they were willing to testify about in court."

Through discovery, where prosecution documents are shared with the defense, Bonin obtained a copy of what Douglas told detectives and was planning to say in court. Having barely spoken to Douglas, Bonin was enraged as his statements were false assumptions and lies based on made up events, jailhouse gossip and news stories. Jailhouse snitches are despised by inmates. He wrote, "This Douglas is the worst kind of snitch there is. He is a living one." Coincidentally, Douglas was a relative of Larry Sharp, one of Bonin's last victims (Bonin didn't learn of this for months). So, the "professional snitch" had even more motives for wanting to see Bonin get the death penalty.

Bonin asked his attorney to contact the prosecutor's office to arrange a deal for him to tell them everything in exchange for concessions, such as possibly avoiding the death penalty. But Bonin also had other reasons for talking.

Six months on Sean King's body hadn't been found and detectives knew, from Vernon Butts, that Bonin killed him. He was with Bonin when he picked up King and, when it was done, Bonin said, "You should have come along, it was a lot of fun." Bonin came back to Vern's house immediately afterwards and told him everything.

Being the clever and successful homicide detective, Sgt. St. John of LAPD devised a scheme to possibly alleviate the problem. He wrote a fake letter to Bonin from Sean King's mother begging for him to reveal where her son was buried, so they could put him to rest and find peace. A key phrase read, "I forgive for what you did. I'm a born-again Christian, but I want my baby buried for Christmas."

It also contained a line Bonin found amusing, "She told me that they couldn't use the evidence against me. Obviously the attorney who told her this was lying. It really touched me."

Sgt. St. John's fake letter worked as designed. This was a serious breach of police ethics and posed a risk to St. John's career if not Bonin's case, but "Jigsaw John" took the risk as he was the legendary LAPD detective who had a TV show produced about his exploits. Whether other detectives knew of the letter's provenance is unclear, but St. John revealed his secret to Deputy DA Norris right before the trial started. Norris kept the secret from the public until he told the story as part of his eulogy at St. John's funeral, in May 1995.

In the speech, Norris told how the case was in trouble until Bonin received a "letter" from Sean King's mother and a "repentant" Bonin told them everything. "One day, as the trial approached, St. John sidled up to me and muttered in my ear, 'I've got to tell you something. It wasn't the mother who wrote the letter,'" Norris told the audience, which found it rather amusing.

It was written about by Eric Malnic in the May 9, 1995 edition of the *LA Times*. Bonin was still alive on Death Row at San Quentin, but nothing can be found about his reactions to this revelation. *LA Times* Staff Writer Ken Ellingwood retold the story in a Sunday, February 18, 1996 article about what happened to the judges, detectives, prosecutors and attorneys in the years after the Freeway Killer cases. Ellingwood's article was published five days before Bonin's execution.

Then there was the matter of Billy Pugh and Eric. Knowing Pugh pointed detectives in his direction as possibly being the Freeway Killer, and Eric was wrongfully charged in the Harry Turner case, Bonin wrote this and shows an interesting motive for finding a way to protect Eric—Love. Of course, there was also another common motive right behind—Revenge:

"I'm the only one besides Eric who knows what really happened. I've said it both ways. To some that he may by guilty and to some that he may not be guilty. The reason is simple. I haven't made up my mind what to do. I honestly love Eric more than anyone I have ever met. He's the closest thing to a perfect lover I've ever come to meet. It will be a very difficult decision. To put the person I've loved closest in prison to save my life, or to take my chances of getting a deal and possibly lose my life in the process. Yes, it is a big decision in my life."

Bonin is vague as his diary might be confiscated while the written murder stories were being completed piecemeal and locked away by Todd Landgren. Bonin believes that keeping Eric's secret about the King and Sharp killings may help him later in making a deal, which leads to Bonin's reasons for talking to detectives and prosecutors: 1) Discredit jailhouse snitches Fahey and Douglas, especially Douglas, 2) Avoid the death penalty by telling all and agreeing to reveal Sean King's burial site, 3) Get revenge on Billy Pugh and protect the one he "loved closest," Eric.

Again, it is worth reiterating that all these events and decisions are a result of what happened on March 24, 1980, the day when the paths of Bill Bonin, Scott Fraser, Eric Wijnaendts and Billy Pugh crossed.

Around 5:00 p.m., on Tuesday, December 16 in the middle of the prelim hearings and a day before the "jailhouse snitches" were set to testify, Bonin and his attorney sat down with Deputy DA Norris and seven detectives from three counties (Esposito, Sidebotham, Kushner, Mellecker, St. John, Kristis and Malmberg).

Facing Bonin were the detectives who had been chasing him for a nerve wracking ten-months; men who were fathers, husbands and brothers who dreaded hearing the phone ring while Bonin ripped innocent victims from family, friends and communities; men used to dealing with the worst of humanity forced to watch impotently as a murderous force of nature eluded their grasp; men now forced to swallow their rage as Bonin chronicled everything like an unrepentant tour guide describing his travels. One can only imagine the hatred running through their veins that day!

Ground rules were sorted and included tacit assurance his cooperation "might" lead to avoidance of the death penalty. All the arrangements were verbal and vague, except for a signed agreement stating that, if there was no deal, the interviews could not be used against him in court and would remain secret. Bonin believed he wouldn't be charged for King if he revealed the burial site. LA Deputy DA Norris told Bonin he had no influence over prosecutors in Orange or San Bernardino counties, the former having already filed against Butts and Miley while signaling a strong desire to charge Bonin on four murder counts.

Bonin's attorney, who encouraged Bonin to talk to detectives, departed and what followed was about 11-hours of taped interviews over three days. Right away Bonin angrily stated he didn't know Lloyd Douglas, saying, "I just want to let you know, right off the bat, you made a deal with someone who told you complete lies, including Dr. Fahey. I talked with Douglas for all of five minutes. I hope that after this deal here you won't have to use any of it, okay now we can start at the beginning."

Bonin's first two murders, Mark Shelton with Butts and Markus Grabs alone, were recounted in a forthright manner indicating a sharp memory for details. Detectives then had questions about the last murder, Steven Wells with Jim Munro, and the stop at Vernon Butts' house on the way to dump the body. This led to an interesting critique by Bonin of Butts, who claimed to have been "totally frightened" and "under the thumb" of the domineering Bonin, innocent of murder and a "victim" in all this. The commentary also touched on Bonin's ability to charm impressionable young men to kill with him.

"When we drove from my house we went to Vern's house, and I introduced Jim to Vern, and he welcomed Jim in and his words were basically like 'welcome to the brotherhood' or something—it was a real big thing with him, although me and Vern had a lot of conflicts. Vern wanted to be the dominant factor in the entire thing, and I wouldn't let him, for reasons that I felt if I let somebody else take control their gonna mess something up, and I wanted to make sure there was no evidence. So that's why I didn't let him take control, but Vern is not the very passive person he claims to be, and afraid of me, and he says in his statement that he jumps every time I talk.

"If you talk to some of the people that were at his apartment, when I got very insistent with him you'll find out he got very insistent back, he was not jumping. When he made all those statements, I guess the only thing he could do was make it sound like he was the very innocent person claiming to be tricked in a hypnotic way or something, it's not like that. I did come in contact with youngsters, or young people that were looking for something, and I suppose I fulfilled what they were looking for, and that's why they went along with what happened."

With that off his chest, Bonin proceeded to the most urgent matter, Pugh and Eric. Upset to the point of being unable to speak, Kushner instructed Bonin to "just relax. You want some water or something, would it help? You okay?"

"Yeah, anyway," Bonin replied, gathering his thoughts. "I read in an article you picked up a guy named Eric, it was very good article. I in turn wrote a letter to the **Herald Examiner**, which was mailed out by my Attorney. The youngster Eric is completely innocent of anything involved in this. Uh, you know, he's sitting in there and he's charged with all this, but he knows nothing about it, and I did meet him at Orange County. I did know you connected him being with me on that particular day.

"He was with me, I believe I took him over to Scott's apartment, and then I took him back home, and he was not with me after that. There was someone with me that day, and was involved in the Turner matter, and that's the guy that started this whole ball rolling, and his name is Billy Pugh. He's 17-years old. I met him at Scott's place, like his statement says. I told Scott I was gonna try to give him a ride home, and I did…"

Describing Pugh as a "real ruffian," Bonin then went through the whole evening when he met Pugh and what happened with Turner, chronicled earlier. Following a discussion about the route he took to the Sean King murder site, Bonin veered back to Eric:

BONIN: I'd like to ask a question at this time. Assuming that the D.A. does decide to make a deal, or even if he doesn't, I want to know what is gonna happen to Eric. He's supposed to go to preliminary next month.

KUSHNER: That's been continued, I think to the 23rd of January. If he's not involved he's not gonna be prosecuted.

BONIN: Okay

KUSHNER: Now there's been some statements from him though, you understand this, put him in the van with you all night. According to him he was, you know, he was so drunk and plastered that he didn't know what the hell was happening and all this that popping into his head is what we have to prove.

BONIN: He's got things mixed up. He drinks a lot, he was overstuffed, I believe that would be the day he was drinking over there. In fact one of Scott's statements was that he didn't want him back over there, he's that way. I can't remember any night he ever stayed with me all night. I did see him two or three times, brought him over to the house. We did get it on, uh, he was living with a person who was gay. I do not know if he ever got it on with the guy or not. When he was arrested, I couldn't believe it, I said this is a real coincidence, I even told my Attorney…"

A long explanation of events from Bonin ended with this statement, "I didn't know if Turner was mine or not, and I had to look at the pictures. I had to see the area where the body was dropped off, then I knew at a point a couple of days ago that Turner was mine, I knew that Billy was there and I knew Eric wasn't, that's clear to me."

Discussions ensued about why Eric would have talked about being in the back of the van and experiencing some rather traumatic events, mostly half-remembered. Bonin explained he had picked up Eric late one-night after he may have beat-up his roommate and called him for help; they had sex in the back of the van but didn't spend the whole night together.

Confronted with Eric's confused remembrances about seeing, through a drunken haze, two people wrestling or fighting in the back of the van, Bonin tries to close the topic, "The only thing I can say is Eric was never with me on any murders, I don't know how, I really don't know where he'd come up with that. I really don't. I'd have to hear something like from him, cause I just can't believe he would say something like that. I just don't believe that my memory is that bad, to where something could happen with somebody, and me not remember. Certain things I might forget such as whether I took the 60 or 10, or where, how to get to where I dropped off this icepick, but oh no he was not involved in nothing. I don't care what he says."

Noting that Bonin was doing the interviews to avoid the death penalty, Deputy DA Norris asked Bonin why he shouldn't receive such a verdict? Bonin had no real answer but acknowledged the DA had a difficult decision to make. Bonin told Norris that, for a deal, he was more than willing to testify against Vernon Butts. Before stopping the tape, the detectives wondered how Bonin would explain his extended absence to fellow inmates; he said an excuse about fighting with Butts and getting locked away should suffice.

Interviews for the night ended at 9:45 p.m. and soon afterwards Bonin set off with the nine detectives in four cars for the San Bernardino Mountains, 70-miles east of Downtown LA, to try and locate where Sean King was left. Bonin was handcuffed, with hands in front, the entire time as hours were spent retracing routes on various freeways while he looked for the key landmark—the Circle K market.

Finally, around 2:00 a.m., they found the place and the search began for the remains. When the King killing was discussed later in the interviews, Eric was left entirely out of the story. Bonin was hoping against hope that the wheels of justice might spin in Eric's favor; but if he extracted him from the Turner murder he could just as easily put him back in hot water with King and Sharp.

When the interviews resumed, on Wednesday, December 17, the issue of Scott Fraser was broached. Previously, Bonin had implicated Fraser in the Wood murder because he thought Fraser was reward hunting when he talked to detectives in July. Bonin was disabused of that notion and, after retracting the statement, he nonetheless talked about how Fraser had "lots of sex with underage boys and did a lot of drug dealing." With Eric ever present in his mind, Bonin continually brought up his "honesty" in the interviews so they might believe his claims that Eric "wasn't involved in anything."

Bonin later recounted an amusing aspect of the interviews, "Everyone had questions, of course, and at one point there was a particular detective that had a question and couldn't get in to give it. Others were talking all the time. I looked over at him and raised my hand slightly. The others noticed and let him ask his question. I had raised my hand in the way a pupil would when he wanted to ask a question. After that, for a while, they raised their hand and I called on them by looking at them and saying, 'Yes.' Another thing that happened was this conversation."

"What kind of knives did you use?"
"A steak knife."
"Really."
"Where did they come from?"
"Vern's apartment."
"Were they part of a set?"
"Yes."
"Vernon must have been running out of knives, was he mad."
"Probably."

Bonin was back in court on Thursday, December 18 for the last day of the prelim hearings. He relates what happened, "At the end of the Prelim on Thursday, December 18, 1980, Butts was held to answer on all counts except Count #8, the murder of Sean King. As we recessed for lunch Vern said to me, 'My attorney says they're going to drop all your charges.'

"I looked at him in disbelief. He really believed what he was saying. I said, 'You're out of your mind. They'll hold me to answer on all charges.' That's exactly what they did. During a recess, while the tape of Vern's 3-hour statement was being played, Vern told my attorney, 'Bill looks mad, I didn't say anything incriminating, did I?'

"My attorney relayed that to me. At the end of the playing of the tape when Vern and I was being brought back upstairs from the courtroom, Vern says to me, 'See, I didn't say anything too incriminating.' I just shook by head in disgust. Around the end of the day Sgt. Dave Kushner wrote on a napkin and gave it to my attorney, 'King found.' The District Attorney wasn't sure whether he could do anything. He didn't believe me and was saying I haven't given them anything. I only gave them everything including the body of Sean King and the real 5th person. They felt there were two others and that Eric was guilty and Billy was innocent.

"One reason they don't believe me to what I'm saying is that I said I was completely alone on the double murder of Russell Rugh and Glen Barker. They said Barker had a climax yet I didn't know about it. I felt he might have come thru me fucking him."

After the final day of prelims Bonin had his last interview with detectives, he describes leaving that night, "The last evening coming back I had no cuffs on with three detectives. I walked from the court building across the street thru a parking lot and rode in a four-door car. No extra locks on the doors. I had no thoughts of trying to escape as they had guns. Detective Dave Kushner told me they wanted to talk to me for a long time. It hurt.

"They wanted to know what happened. As he said it he jiggled a tape to his ear and got a smile on his face to emphasize the fact the he finally had the details even though he couldn't use it unless a deal was made. It was like he finally won the big prize. The story of what really happened in the van and what led up to certain things. Kushner once asked me if I got a kick out of giving the police a chase. I had to admit I thought they were fools to an extent and that I got some sort of kick out of hearing him say that he was baffled."

Bonin and Butts were held in connection for 14 of the 22 Freeway Killer slayings with an arraignment set for Friday, January 2. While the Bonin-Butts prelims wrapped up, down the hallway Miley was arraigned after his case moved up from the Municipal to Superior Court. Miley pled not guilty and the disturbing transcripts from his prelims, held in early December, went public with a trial set for Monday, February 23, 1981.

For the first time the public got a detailed, first-hand account of how the Freeway Killings occurred, allowing one to easily transpose the Miranda-Macabe murders to other killings. Steinberg was re-affirmed as Miley's court appointed attorney and pre-trial motions were set for Thursday, January 15.

A small paper in Northern California, the ***Auburn Journal***, reported that "Bonin sodomized the youth and he (Miley) attempted to, then held the boy while Bonin tied his hands, tied his feet, then tied his feet to his hands. Kushner, who testified at the preliminary hearing on Dec. 1, said Miley told him that Bonin then grabbed the boy's shirt, put it over his head and began to twisting it like a towel." The story also reported that Deputy DA Stovitz thought a Miley deal might be possible but had the impression his attorney might go the "insanity route."

In the ***OC Register*** Tim Alger wrote that Bonin's attorney, Earl Hanson, said his "client was 'shell shocked' by the testimony and couldn't believe how many people were 'lying and telling stories' about him."

On Monday, December 15 TV news reporter Dave Lopez had a second meeting with Bonin, and he expressed the same sentiment, "It is Bonin's contention that many people are lying about him to save their own neck. He expressed confidence that eventually the truth will come out and then he alluded to the fact that he could be found guilty of many things, but being the Freeway Killer, he said, is not one of them."

Truly fascinating; the day before he spills his guts to detectives about all the murders, he is proclaiming total innocence to Dave Lopez, who in turn broadcast his statement to the public. Bonin had to sit back and wait for events to unfold. Only one legal proceeding was scheduled before the New Year as the 1980 holiday season unfolded.

48

Holidays at LA Men's Central Jail
December 19 to 31, 1980

Three of the five Bonin Freeway Killer suspects then in custody have gone through their prelims as the Christmas season began. Munro will have his hearing on December 22. Bonin was going to spend yet another Christmas behind bars, but this time with no hope of ever gaining release. Three weeks of intense activity gave way to a short period of relative calm characterized by updates from concerned parties and enlightening snapshots of life in LA County Men's Central Jail.

On Friday, December 19 Bonin was filled with guilt and recriminations about "how I got mixed up in all this." He wrote that, once he started killing, it "became like a compulsion that I just couldn't stop. When I got up-tight I would go out and kill. Sometimes after I killed I looked for another on my way home. I got so I was always looking for a victim. I'd even use my money for gas before eating. The gas was necessary so I could search out more victims." He laid awake at night thinking it was the "end of a hellatious nightmare. I'm glad it's over."

Neglect, childhood abuse, war and institutional shortfalls all created the man which the world was learning about, however, as previously mentioned, a possible childhood frontal lobe brain injury may have also contributed to the disaster. Contemplating his mother seeing him get the Gas Chamber saddened him. Alice believed he was innocent and, like most everyone else, didn't know Bonin spilled the whole story to detectives in a bid to help Eric, and hopefully himself. Two months earlier, Bonin's father passed away from an extended illness due to a series of strokes.

During a visit with his mother, on Friday, December 19, he wrote about the struggle dealing with her, "The hardest thing to do was to sit and tell Mom that I was innocent. I knew I was guilty and I just had to keep saying that I was innocent. She read in the papers that Greg Miley confessed and wanted to know how he could say that? I told her he said that the day he was arrested. I pointed out that he still pled innocent at both the Municipal arraignment and the one in Superior Court. She told me that the truth had to come out. She didn't care what happened to her. The truth had to come out."

Bonin also told her to give Sgt. Kushner a photo album which contained pictures of Tony and Ralph, the latter having lived with Bonin for a month at Silverado in July 1979. Detectives wanted to question them both and Bonin knew they were innocent, at least of murder with him. Viewing it as a good faith gesture in his struggle to help Eric, Bonin needed to convince the detectives he was telling them everything, which of course was untrue. Bonin still held back certain info in order to retain at least some bargaining power.

Bonin describes his section at the jail and the daily routine, "The row I am on is in the High Power section. To get into the section you enter a door from the hallway, which is always locked. Once thru that door you find yourself in a small room like place. At the other end is a barred gate which is controlled from the booth by electronic means. Once thru that barred gate you're in High Power, which consists of A & B Row, 1700 Module, C, D, E & F Rows, 1750 Module plus other rooms, etc. To get to my cell you have to go thru another barred gate which swings open and then down to my cell, B-4, and in.

"The gates to the cells are all separated from inside the booth by electronic means and only one cell is open at any given time. The Row consists of 26 cells and the walkway that leads down the row in front of the cells is called the Freeway. That is why being let to walk up and down the row is called Freeway Time. Cell is 17 feet long 7 feet wide; the walking space 7x4 and the bunk 7x3. A small personal locker, combo metal sink-toilet unit and a small table is the rest of it.

"Everywhere I went outside the cell and row I was handcuffed hands behind my back until I got there. At the visiting room I was put in a single man cage of which they had six for High Power. At the attorney room I was handcuffed to the seat I sat in unless I used a booth. Then the officer had to stay in the attorney room if I used a booth. Most of the time I used a booth. When I was transported to the court and back I was shackled down a waist chain and handcuffed to it.

"Once they used leg shackles. Several times coming back to the jail they just used a single set of cuffs in front. Mostly every day I slept in the morning, noon and evening. A typical day would be: Wake up at 6:00 a.m., eat breakfast. Go back to bed, get up and eat lunch at around 11:00 a.m., go back to bed, get up eat dinner around 4:00 p.m., go back to bed. We had sick call and pill call around 8:00 a.m. in the morning. A nurse came around. We had pill call around 1:00 p.m., 5:00 p.m. and 8:00 p.m. also. There were days that I played solitaire to pass away some time or read a book.

"We had showers every other day in the mornings. Five minutes only. Sometimes we had on officer who would be good and let us slide with seven or eight minutes in the shower. They ran the showers one at a time. We had clothing exchange and bedding exchange usually once a week. There were times you had to force yourself to get up to change your bedding. You'd feel so tired of doing nothing but resting you wouldn't want to take five minutes to exchange your bedding. Some guys would just sleep thru it instead. There were guys who would skip their showers because they were tired. Myself I always took my shower. It helped to release the tension and I slept better afterwards.

"Lights went out at 10:00 p.m. but that didn't mean that people went to sleep. In fact it was anything but for several individuals. It was like when the lights went out their mouths went on. Talking louder than they needed most of the time. It would get real quiet say from 9:00 p.m. to 10:00 p.m. but then it got loud."

The blaring voice of a deputy, thru a loudspeaker adjacent to his cell, was ever present on the row. Located in a glassed-in control booth, the deputy moved lines of inmates down long hallways to and from the cafeteria. Bonin and other row inmates heard the instructions throughout the day, often prompting them to yell at the speaker in frustration. They went like this: "No talking, single file line, right shoulder against the wall, hands in your pockets gentlemen." With four rows in each module, like 2200 or 2400, they would hear "22 and 24, send your third line to chow" and each iteration of those instructions all day long.

Bonin continues, "Saturday, December 20, 1980: The trustee, an inmate with duties, came out to get the morning newspapers. He usually collected all the money in the early morning. As he was going out to get the papers Danny Young said he wanted a paper. Castro said, 'Forget it, if you couldn't take care of it when I made the collection, you could go without.' The thing is that when they call you to get the papers, you go out right away or you may end up not getting them. Anyways, when Castro came back in Young said something and Castro said, 'Hey, I wasn't even talking to you, punk.' That started off a verbal assault towards one another. That night Young and another inmate cluttered the Freeway, which is the walkway in front our cells, with milk, newspapers, shit, etc. That next morning Castro and Young had words that led to Young throwing bars of soap at him. It died down after about ten-minutes."

Danny Young was charged with the kidnapping and murder of his 10-year-old neighbor, Ronald Tolleson, Jr.

"Sunday, December 21, 1980: There was one heavy set trustee who worked in the kitchen part of 1700 and 1750 module. He was alright. He looked after us when we came back from court. He'd give us extra milk and food. Robert Cohen was his name. One time I came back from court at 9:30 p.m., after the second interview with detectives, and the Roast Beef was dry, so he gave me three milks and two oranges. When I first looked at him I thought he was in for embezzlement. I was later told by him he was in for embezzlement of securities. He always had a jolly look to him and had a smile on his face. One time a tall young trustee came to work down in the module. I told Bob to tell the guy I'd like him to come and cell up with me. Bob asked why and I replied, 'I'm horny.' Bob went away with a disgusted look on his face. He never did tell the guy what I said.

"A Sgt. came down the row carrying a piece of paper, a 115 for an inmate. A 115 is a disciplinary report. As the Sgt. was leaving the row I said, 'I'm innocent.' He looked at me and started to laugh and almost couldn't bring himself under control. Officer Vanecek told me over the speaker system to 'watch your gate, its coming open.' The gate to my cell was being opened so I could come out and take a shower. They usually say 'watch your gate' or something to that effect. When I got out of my cell I put my hands up to my eyes as if I was looking through binoculars and looked at the gate. When I got off the row and over to the shower I told Officer Vanecek, 'I watched the gate and it didn't go anywhere.'

"As he was letting me back in he said, 'Bonin, watch your gate, it is coming closed. Watch it closely it is going to move.' He did that a couple of times during the next couple days, it was just in a joking way. Officer Vanecek was the first officer I came in contact with at the central jail. He has always treated me fair and with a proper amount of courtesy. I have a high respect for him. Many times they would have tours come in and naturally they would point out the most notoriety prisoners such as Bittaker, Young, Buono and myself. The people would gawk. Bittaker made a sign once that he would put up when tours came by. It said, 'It's Okay to Feed the Animals! Throw Peanuts!'

"The person I talked with the most was Lawrence Sigmund Bittaker, I called him Larry and sometimes Sigmund. I found out he hated his middle name so I stopped. I even told him about everything eventually. I knew Larry from CMC East (state prison). Even though we only talked just a little there. When Larry ran out of money I loaned him some until he got himself together. I wasn't worried if he could or couldn't pay me back even. Though I knew he could. To me it was someone to help out. Yet Larry is like me. He'd rather give than receive. It was hard for him as it is for me. To receive without paying back. I didn't want to be in debt or owe anyone else.

"Bittaker and me would talk a lot about stocks. I even got him interested in the stock market. It was something to keep our minds off the reality of being in here. You have to keep your mind and mental thoughts on the outside even though your physical being is locked up. If you didn't it would get to you. A few months ago, Larry was going to commit suicide on his 40th birthday, September 17. Thru talking to him and showing him some hope and that there was still hope he changed his mind. Later he saw that there was some hope as things started looking a little more promising in his case. At least for passing up the death penalty."

Lawrence Bittaker, on trial for the torture, rape and murder of five teenage girls with Roy Norris, established an interesting friendship with Bonin. When examining their stories, one is struck by the eerie similarities in history, timelines, methods and personalities. Both were well liked amongst those closest to them and perceived as giving and kind; both were incarcerated at the California Men's Colony (CMC) at the same time in 1977-78. As seen above, they met briefly at that prison. Bittaker met Norris, his partner in crime, at CMC after rescuing him from prison gangs on several occasions.

Bittaker and Norris grew close during long conversations and hatched plans to murder teenage girls after gaining release, killing five teenage girls in four-months before getting caught. Bonin and Butts spoke for months about killing and murdered equally as many in the same amount of time before Butts backed off while Bonin continued. Bittaker and Bonin both decided they needed a van for their dirty work, and each assigned it a chilling moniker; for Bittaker it was "Murder Mac" and Bonin the "Death Van."

After warming up with a number of rape victims, Bittaker and Norris began killing on July 24, 1979; Bonin and Butts started ten-days later on August 4, 1979. Bittaker's streak ended in November 1979 after one of the rape victims, Robin Robeck, identified their photos; Bonin's streak ended in June 1980, after Billy Pugh told police he thought Bonin "just might be the Freeway Killer."

Bittaker and Norris killed five and raped 20; Bonin and Butts killed six and the final toll for Bonin, alone and with others, was 22. Fate then landed Bittaker and Bonin in adjacent cells on Row B in the High Power Unit at LA Men's Central Jail facing multiple murder charges and the death penalty. Lawrence Bittaker and William Bonin, like two-peas-in-a-pod, engaged in deep conversations about all aspects of life and looked out for each other. There was a distinct possibility their lives might end together on Death Row at San Quentin State Prison.

Bonin continues, "Monday, December 22, 1980: An 18-year-old came on the row. Jerry Naylor. He turned me on. He was talkative and said he was in for kidnapping, robbery, rape and murder. I couldn't help but feel sorry for him. I figured he had enough to worry about and decided to just be a friend to him. He never knew it but I gave him a nickname. I called him 'Freedom.' We talked and I gave him magazines and some books for him to read. I even called his father and mother a couple of times to ask them to come down. 'He wants to see you,' I told them.

"His mother gave me a message to give back to him. She said to tell him, 'Be good and that I love him very much.' One time on the row a guy tried to borrow a couple of dollars off Jerry and he said he didn't have enough. The guy tried to grab Jerry thru the bars. It really got me riled up as I like Jerry and he has enough problems without some gunsel who is still trying to prove himself doing something like that. What is more ironic about the matter is that the guy who tried to grab Jerry thru the bars was transferred to 'B' from 'C' Row because he was getting harassed. Then he turns around and does the same thing to someone else."

No major developments in the Freeway Killer cases took place during the holidays. Bonin, able to keep tabs on Eric through jailhouse contacts, was aware detectives don't buy his claims of Eric's innocence with Turner. The problem was that Billy Pugh was not available for questioning; at some point, following the May 29 key tip interview, he was released from custody and vanished. Detectives want him back to clear up questions raised by Bonin.

Sean King's remains were recovered, thanks to Bonin, but six-months after the killing will definitely yield no forensic evidence tying Eric to the murder. Authorities were working to confirm King's identity through dental records. At this point nothing has surfaced tying Eric to the Sharp killing. Another problem was detectives don't believe Bonin was alone when he killed Rugh and Barker on the same day. Certain aspects didn't match up and detectives were not buying his claim of having no help with those murders.

Able to arrange a conversation with Eric through an air vent, Bonin learned about his discussions with detectives and how he flunked the lie detector test and told them lies about being too drunk to remember anything specific. Eric was smart enough to not volunteer any information about Sean King and Larry Sharp, only answering questions regarding the murder of Turner in as vague a manner as possible.

On Tuesday, December 23 Eric's attorney George Elder came up to talk with Bonin, but he refused to see him even though Elder told him Earl Hanson approved of the meeting. Second thoughts about the detective interviews, done to help Eric, made Bonin reluctant to give out more info which might come back to haunt him in court. Diary entries flashed between anger at "getting bad advice from his attorney that sealed his fate" and helping Eric out of love.

An article in the **Herald Examiner**, about Munro's preliminary hearing, contained a line which Bonin highlighted in his diary, one he hoped Billy Pugh may have read: "Five men are charged in connection with 14 murders, and authorities are looking for at least one more suspect." Bonin noted, "That's Billy Pugh. Maybe they do believe me. Yet I may not get any deal as I've already told them everything I know. The only hope I have is that they need me to testify. I won't do it without a deal for me and hopefully the rest will follow suit. If they don't they risk the Green Room at San Quentin. I really hope they aren't stupid enough to try and beat this."

Phone calls to his old girlfriend, Mary, were a daily occurrence. A woman who lived with her, 18-year-old Ellen, started writing to Bonin and he sent return letters, some containing poems within the letters. Mary considered Bonin her "first love" and told her boyfriend, Pat, she would "love him through to the end." Bonin also had deep feelings for Mary as well as her children. He was extremely comfortable talking with Mary and even enjoyed it when she dominated the conversation with stories about family and work. Such social discourse took his mind off the grim aspect of the situation, at least for a short while.

On numerous occasions he wrote about "letting her go," but having someone like Mary to talk with remained an important distraction. As he became better acquainted with Ellen, their letters got more personal and, in December, she sent him a picture of her young daughter, Tamara, who lived in Utah with Ellen's mother, who had legal custody. Contact between them increased and developed into a fondness for each other, serving to create a strange series of twisted complications.

That evening proved amusing as Bonin explains, leading to entries on Christmas Eve and Day, "Tonight is one of those nights I'm listening to two people, Mike and Don, arguing about whether a boa constrictor snake will or will not crush an infant or bite a sleeping human being. Neither person will give in so they continue to argue. Finally someone yelled, 'Shut the fuck up.' The arguing continues. Now others join in telling them to shut up, finally after another hour goes by they shut up.

"Believe me you can hear all the authorities on all subjects in jail. And if you check on their stories, 75% of the time it's all bullshit, just things that were passed on from one person to the other. If a person hears a story that sounds good then it becomes fact to him and no one can make him change his mind, even if what he is saying is bullshit and has no merit to it. The reason mainly is the guys in jail hate to admit to another in jail that he is wrong.

"Christmas Eve, Wednesday, December 24, 1980: Thanksgiving dinner was pretty good. We should have a pretty good Christmas Day Dinner and New Year's Day Dinner also. X-Mas time is the time of the year the hardest to do time. You feel your being locked up more as it is more noticeable to you. It is a lonely time of year and the hurt just hurts more during the time span from Thanksgiving until after New Year's Day is passed. My brother Paul's girl had a baby girl, 7-pounds. They named her Autumn. I don't know what last name she got. She was born on Nov. 15, 1980. My brother Paul turned 31 on Nov. 23, 1980.

"It is X-Mas eve and the lights are out. The night shift left the radio on for us. All the music is Christmas music. It helps, yet it hurts. I love music, especially Church Hymns and Christmas music. This is the time on X-Mas eve when I reflect on my life. I don't like what I see. I can only try to control what happens in the present and future. The time for a change is long past and so I must make a change. The hate, the anger, the frustration and all the hurt must be left behind. Only good and love can go forward from this night forward. I shall try to live up to this promise I have just made to myself. Well it's 10:30 p.m. and they cut of the radio. So much for music on this X-mas eve.

"Christmas Day, Thursday, December 25, 1980: This morning breakfast was the usual SOS, Corn Flakes, milk and 2 donuts. I stayed up this morning as Freeway Time started on cell #1. Larry was 2nd out and then me. We talked most of the time. We talked about things that would have kept us out of trouble and alternative actions to things that have happened in the past. The results were quite interesting. It seems that the alternatives never occur to a person until it's too late.

"I feel people should get off by themselves once in a while and look at what is going on around them. I don't mean for an hour or two, I mean for a day or two or an entire weekend. Time to reflect on one's past and how to make the future better. See what they want in life and how to get it without interfering in other people's lives in an unlawful way.

"It was quiet almost all day today. They had X-Mas music on until 11:00 a.m. and then they switched to rock station. We had Christmas Dinner at 4:00 p.m. It consisted of 2 pieces of white meat, 1 of dark meat, turkey stuffing, mashed potatoes and gravy with a bun and butter and a carton of milk, French Apple pie with Neapolitan ice cream. They came around and gave us a 2nd thing of ice cream. I gave Larry a candy bar for a Christmas present. I had given him three candy bars yesterday. He gave me one. On Larry's birthday I gave him four candy bars as a present.

"My favorite religious songs are **How Great Thou Art** and then **The Old Rugged Cross**. There was no arguments tonight. Just some general talk and then everyone was silent. I like it when the row is quiet and I can relax and think. I enjoy it most when the lights are out as there isn't anyone that is walking around. If you want to relieve your sexual desires by manual means, you can do it in half-ass privacy."

"Friday, December 26, 1980: Got up for breakfast, scrambled eggs again. Then we had showers. They started at the front and I was the 3rd to take a shower. After my shower, I crawled back up in the rack and slept pretty good. The jail said there was a security problem, yet there was not too much of a security problem for Angelo Buono, one of the Hillside Stranglers. He has been going to the roof since before I got to the row. His son even goes with him now.

"They're going to the roof for an hour at 11:30 a.m. We had store today. So now I have over 10 candy bars. I make sure I have enough to last over the weekend. The store wouldn't sell me a newspaper as the guys on the other cells bought some. She needed them for the other rows. It seems like 'B' Row gets all the scraps most of the time. I guess it's because of all the people on the row that are charged with publicized crimes; Bittaker, Buono, Clark, Young and others to include myself.

"The person I have the most problem getting along with is Douglas Clark. We can start talking and be arguing in less than a minute. He constantly wants to talk about his case and comes off like he is an authority on everything. It's like no one knows more than him. And it is unnerving. The person who to me seemed to have knowledge and only gave it out as he believed, it was Angelo Buono. He used the most common sense and if he was wrong would admit and change his way of thinking. It was obvious to everyone he disliked his ex-wife and that she disliked him.

"Once his son Peter was making a phone call and Angelo said, 'Say hello for me.' Peter yelled, 'To my Mother.' Angelo replied, 'Heavens no, tell her I passed away.' Peter said, 'You really want me to say that?' And Angelo said, 'Yes, tell her I passed away.' When Peter came back Angelo asked him if he told her? Peter replied in the affirmative. Angela asked what she said and Peter said, 'She laughed.'

"I read an article in today's *L.A. **Times*** that made me weep. It talked about Sean King's body being found and his mother being told on Christmas Eve. They said an anonymous tip that led where the body was found. The real story is within these writings. I looked at the picture in the paper and read the words of his Mother as written in the paper; 'Sean's Christmas stocking is still in my bedroom. What am I going to do with an empty stocking.' And I say, 'Why? There isn't any answer in return.'

"Some people have the impression I thrive on news articles. That isn't the case. It hurts when I see news articles of all this. I think of how it is affecting my Mother and family and friends. I know how it is affecting me. There is a lot of questions and hurt going on inside of me."

Another quote he may have read, published nationally on December 26, also came from Sean King's mother, Laveda Gifford, "I had tried to keep that little spark alive, but time kept dragging on. Now I've been telling myself, 'Dear God, just let me get through Christmas.' But it didn't work out that way. I had a gut feeling it was him all along. Now I'm just trying to hold myself together."

When I arrived at LA Men's Central Jail, in September of 1981, I (Vonda Pelto) had dealings with Douglas Clark, the Sunset Strip Slayer, and Angelo Buono, one of the Hillside Stranglers. Peter Buono was Angelo's 23-year-old son from Mary Castillo, who bore Angelo four other children.

He was housed on the same row but not involved in any murders, which Angelo committed with Kenneth Bianchi. Peter was on trial for serious auto theft charges but was in the High Power Unit because his father was a high-profile serial killer, putting Peter's life in danger within general population. Mary Castillo was murdered with a gun by her grandson, Chris Buono, in 2007 before taking his own life.

Authorities took a week to identify Sean King's body, with dental records, and notify the family before releasing the news. Even though Bonin revealed practically everything, Eric's situation in the Turner murder case remained unchanged. Bonin's stories fit with those of Butts, Miley and Munro, but detectives believed he was protecting a co-conspirator, a common feature within criminal conspiracies. Billy Pugh hadn't been located and Eric's arraignment was less than a month away. Charges will not be dropped solely on Bonin's word and Eric's case moved forward.

Bonin reflected on the situation, "Sunday, December 28, 1980: Well today was more interesting. The guy in cell #18 was asking me some questions. One of the questions he asked me was, 'Why do you have so much loyalty to your family, friends and Eric?' I had no answer.

"My attorney told me that what the D.A. was going to do after he finished talking to me was offer a package deal to everyone. I told Earl I wasn't going to talk anymore until I had something in writing. Earl said he told the D.A. to come up with a deal before I was arraigned in Superior Court.

"I may end up with another attorney. Earl said he told the D.A. I may not want him on the case anymore, telling him, 'What have I done for him except get him bound over and get him to spill his guts to you.' He also told the D.A. he may himself not want to stay on the case. Thinking it all over I came to the conclusion that Earl really doesn't want to stay on the case anymore. I believe there is a lot behind the scenes I don't know about. I believe Earl gave me the worst advice in the world when he advised me to talk to the D.A. and Detectives before I had anything on paper. It may have made any chance of a deal not likely. My only chance is that they need me to get what they want.

"My impression of Sterling Norris the D.A. is that he is a cold-blooded person who is very deceptive. A person who will use any means to get what he wants. He'd make any promises necessary with no intention of using the promises so he can get what he wants. I received a letter from Ellen today. She told me that she is back in Utah with her family. She made a choice between Kevin and John. She chose Kevin and then he left and hasn't seen him for six days. It was rumored thru Mary that Kevin was still legally married.

"Tuesday, December 30, 1980: I talked to Senior Taylor, one of the top officers, this morning and asked him how Eric was doing? He responded, 'Okay, I see no signs of depression or suicidal tendencies.' I thanked him and told him I was just checking to make sure he was okay. I sent word thru his attorney that I wanted to talk to him. I figured I could at least find out from him how Eric was doing. I could also voice to Eric thru his attorney that I do care what happens to him. It may make a difference."

"Wednesday, December 31, 1980: "We had good coffee this morning as the coffee machine is now fixed. We also had French toast. It looks we are back to normal, as far as breakfast goes. I saw Todd today for two hours. We discussed what was going on. He gave me some confidence in what Earl has been doing and gave some hope again. It was really good to sit down for a long time and talk.

"He told me about his flight back from London. It seems that the scary thing that happened was that LAX was fogged in and they had to go to San Francisco and back to LAX later. Eric came over to use the exercise bike which is located in front of the 1750 module booth. As he is riding it he is facing right down my row. I got a message to Eric saying to have his attorney call me out and asked if he was okay. He stated he was okay and that he'd have his attorney call me out. I just want to give his attorney confidence in Eric."

49

Arraignment, Trial Dates, Pugh Arrested, Dave Lopez Interview & Butts Suicide
January 1 to 11, 1981

The New Year and a new decade started with jailhouse fireworks as Bonin described, "Last night the New Year was brought in by two guys throwing stuff onto the Freeway and making a mess. At breakfast a black guy in cell #1 threw stuff at the trustee and threats went back and forth. The black guy started it off by putting salt in the pitchers of coffee. Needless to say the entire row is after him. He was even going to snitch to the man after the trustee threw the pitcher of coffee, only the coffee, not the metal pitcher, at him. It should be quite interesting to see what happens between the trustee, who the whole row is behind, and the black dude in cell #1 who is an asshole."

An inmate on Bonin's row, Tom, told Bonin that Eric had been asking about messages from him on the way back from seeing visitors. He felt good knowing Eric had people on the outside "who loved very him very much, someone who believes in him and is standing by him." Bonin also learned, from Bittaker, that "jailhouse snitch" Douglas made an 8-page statement about Bittaker with the intention of testifying at his trial. His attorney was trying to discredit Douglas as a witness in his trial, which was about to start. Such a tactic, if successful, would in turn bar Douglas from testifying in any other trials.

On Friday, January 2 Bonin and Butts were arraigned in LA Superior Court, with a hearing set for a week later to establish trial start dates; they pled not guilty to all charges. Bonin was charged with 14 counts of murder and Vernon Butts five. Earl Hanson was re-assigned as Bonin's attorney and Joe Ingler remained Butts' counsel.

Entering the courtroom, Bonin recognized Dave Lopez from their December meetings and they nodded to each other; while the Sheriff's deputies, returning Bonin to jail, wondered if TV cameras captured their images so they might see themselves on the evening news. An inmate was transferred from Eric's row and Bonin heard Eric was doing well. This filled Bonin with ambivalence, writing how Eric was "involved in all this just because he knows me. He is innocent and pure of any of this. The thing that hurts the most is that I can't seem to find a way to prove he is innocent. They just won't believe me."

Bonin, playing a fiction of Eric's total non-involvement in his journal, showed his affection while knowing the writings might be confiscated at any moment. An AP article in the January 3 edition of the **Wausau Daily Herald**, in Wisconsin, reported that Deputy DA Stovitz said, "Bonin was more dangerous than mass murderer Charles Manson, who Stovitz helped prosecute in 1970."

Bonin's wrote about his somber mood, "Saturday, January 3, 1981: Talked to Terry today to let him know what has been happening. Then I called my Mom and she was telling me what Aaron Stovitz, the D.A. in my case, said about me. It was quite revealing. It made me cringe. I then talked to Dorothy, Mary's mother. Just said hello and talked a little.

"I then came back to my cell and the papers arrived. I didn't like what I read. It sounds like it will go to trial with no deals. That could make things very complicated for Eric. I am going to continue with the details of the case. I have to get them out of my head. If I don't, it will crush me. So I write them down and give them to Todd or Terry.

"Terry Giles didn't want me to write anything down as he wasn't sure who would read it. I simply told Terry that he could read it first and then decide what others could read, giving it to him in an Attorney-Client principal. He is representing me in matters of a personal nature. When the papers came out on the row I got harassed a little, mainly about being called the 'Master Mind' of it all. It didn't last long, but I got more later on. My attorney had told me that Stovitz was retiring in April. That might give me a chance to deal. The more I look at it though the more I can see that no deal will be made when the D.A. sees that he'll lose one or more of the others involved."

Terry Giles was a high-profile Los Angeles criminal defense attorney who represented one of the Hillside Stranglers. Giles and Landgren were advising Bonin on his case while handling Bonin's other matters, although Landgren seemed more involved than Giles. Bonin's fervent hopes of escaping the death penalty waned as he continued to worry about Eric.

On Monday, January 5 Lawrence Bittaker's trial began, causing Bonin to note that, since he would not see him much more, it "was like my best friend leaving on vacation and leaving me alone." He kept in touch by phone with Mary, worried about her kids, and continued to exchange letters with 18-year-old Ellen. Turned out that someone Mary knew was friends with Sean King's sister, a revelation Bonin found disturbing, "This hits really close to home."

A long conversation with Mary's Mom, Dorothy, brought him as much ambivalence as speaking to the jailhouse Catholic Priest and Protestant Chaplin the same day. Talking with both about the conflict of his Catholic upbringing, and his current Protestant leanings, did nothing to ease the struggle but led to a night of contemplation, "The night was quiet after lights out. I guess everyone was tired for a change. I cherish these peaceful nights because you can think."

On Wednesday, January 7 the start dates for two trials were set; Bonin's trial would be on May 4 followed by Butts on July 27. A deal with Butts to testify against Bonin would result in pleading the charges, with final sentencing after Bonin's trial finished. Miley's trial was set for late February, Munro had nothing set and Eric's preliminary hearing was two-weeks away. Legal wrangling, or unexpected developments, often altered arrangements. Both attorneys filed a motion to have the Bonin-Butts prelim transcripts sealed, at least till the trial started. Judge Keene denied the motion and, when released, they dropped like a bomb!

A Friday, January 9 **LA Times** article by Bill Farr, ***Youth's Story About Bonin Unsealed***, reported how an unnamed 17-year-old provided the tip detectives used to "focus on Bonin and place him under surveillance in June 1980." For the first time the public learns of the "big break" which helped roll up the Bonin Freeway Killers. Bonin was quoted by the "informant" saying "he liked to kill teenage boys on Friday and Saturday so he would have time to visit his girlfriend on Sundays." The girlfriend in question was Mary.

His article included nearly everything Pugh told detectives, chronicled earlier, which saved a number of young lives. A public hungry for details learned Bonin tried to recruit the boy to kill with him, but he said no and tried to escape but was prevented from leaving the van; then he was told by Bonin how he liked to "pick-up young hitchhikers and use their T-shirts to strangle them using a tire iron to increase his leverage for the twisting."

Even though the public doesn't know Billy Pugh by name, Bonin knew who the "informant" was and wanted him questioned in the Turner murder to help Eric. Detectives were also extremely interested in speaking with Pugh, but he was nowhere to be found.

Hearing transcripts include details of the Butts and Munro post-arrest interviews, Miley's were made public three-weeks earlier. Butts' interviews are by far the most damaging to Bonin because he was involved in six murders and knew about the killing of Grabs, King and Wells. While the public got a dose of Bill Bonin reality from the transcripts, detectives and prosecutors have been told all this by Bonin minus crucial facts: Eric helped him kill Larry Sharp and Sean King.

Bonin's writing reveals him losing hope of getting a deal. With more about the murder spree being made public, the political pressure intensifies for prosecutors to push for a Bonin death penalty. DA Van de Kamp and Deputy DA Stovitz know all too well that nothing less will satisfy Mayor Tom Bradley, the powerful City Council and an outraged public.

Pressure from LAPD and the LA Sheriff's Dept. was also intense, for it was their reputations Bonin damaged while killing like it was free. Knowing he spent 12-weeks locked up during the ten-month murder spree, it doesn't take a genius to realize Bonin claimed 22 victims in 28 weeks of freedom!

Offering both Miley and Munro deals, for testimony, is far less dangerous politically as they are known, and publicly perceived, as a small part of a bigger picture. Butts was a far different matter—since he was with Bonin during the first murder and a participant in five others, yet he is still a strong candidate for a deal. Despite many pronouncements from DA Stovitz that "enough evidence is being compiled independently" to convict Bonin, having the testimony of any of three, or all three, would boost their chances of obtaining a Bonin death penalty.

No-deal for Bonin meant the "confession interviews" will remain an unusable secret. Focus on the case is worldwide and the bill for his deeds was due and must be paid in full. Offering Bill Bonin a deal was all downside and no upside—politically, professionally and morally.

Vernon Butts was distraught with the release of the transcripts and an already nervous state of mind further deteriorated. Newspaper stories from around the country reported Butts claimed to be "present" for six murders but did no "actual killing," his job being to drive the van and help drop the bodies. Claiming to be in constant fear, he said, "I was taken by surprise by what occurred. After the first one, I couldn't do anything about it. Bonin would kill me if I didn't help."

Butts claimed he finally refused to "go along with Bonin one night when he picked up a hitchhiker near Butts' Norwalk home in the spring of last year," (Sean King, he told Bonin afterwards, "I was sorry I missed that one."); that he showed up at his house "splattered with blood and I helped him wash it off" (Markus Grabs); and that he used different knives, icepicks and Chloral Hydrate in the murders (Kendrick).

"Bonin really got off hearing the boys scream when he sodomized them," Butts recounted, "said it got him real excited, He would tie them up in the back of the van and sexually torment them to make them scream in pain, he loved to hear them scream. After Bill raped the kids; he got a big kick out of pushing their heads down into the toilet. Bonin jammed an ice pick into one kid's ear; he wanted to see how far it would go in before it hit a bone. When he got tired of torturing a kid, he would use a tire iron to tighten the kid's T-shirts around his neck and strangle him to death."

Embarrassed when the confession became public, Butts thought about his friends and family learning of his involvement. But the account, while basically true, was bogus regarding his role and what would those same people, and his fiancée, think when the truth came out?

His behavior at the preliminary hearings, as recounted from Bonin's diary earlier, indicated a loss of reality akin to a sort of mental breakdown. Bonin once accidentally saw Butts when he was getting moved around the jail and found it weird that "Vernon waved and smiled like he didn't have a care in the world."

Different circumstances could arise where Bonin will reveal everything and have nothing to lose, as he explains, "Thursday, January 8, 1981: Today I turned 34-years old. I'll probably spend many of them in here. About one-minute after I got up I got a wish from Larry when he said, 'Happy Birthday Bill.' The news came on after I was through eating breakfast and said the prelim transcripts was unsealed. It then gave a statement said by Billy Pugh in a statement written that I liked to 'kill young boys then take my girl roller skating on Sunday.' If only the media knew that he was the 5th person instead of Eric. I wonder what they would be thinking or saying. I can just imagine what Mary will be thinking when she hears about this. I truly hope that the truth will come out so that Eric will go free.

"The article made it sound like Greg confessed at the prelim. He made his statements when he was arrested. Greg was the only one, when he made his statements, who told the truth. All the rest lied. Munro saying 'that I forced him into it' or Butts saying 'that he had no choice yet never did any killings.' Bullshit! Every time they move me anywhere, Court Line, Attorney Room, or anywhere else, they always call around to make sure the others are locked down. They don't want any of us talking to each other. Or at least they don't me talking to any of them."

Events continued to move swiftly. On Friday, January 9, after a visit from his mother, Bonin had the third and most significant interview with CBS TV reporter Dave Lopez. Conducted for over two-hours in a private booth in an Attorney Room at the Central Jail, an unusual venue for such a meeting, Bonin was not handcuffed and there was no glass or screen between them.

Displaying a calm demeanor, Bonin shocked Lopez by telling him about all the murders in detail. As if in confession, Bonin unburdened himself with disturbing details about the murders of Kendrick, Wood, Wells and Macabe and many others. All those who killed with him are mentioned except, of course, Eric.

Lopez recalled Bonin telling him about Sean King, saying, "I got the kid in the van and killed him like I did the others. I always had a knife and knew how to tie up them up quickly." Bonin lied; Sean King was never in the van but always in the Chevette. He mentioned taking detectives to where King was buried in mid-December, something totally unknown to the public who believe the info came from "an anonymous tip."

Detectives and prosecutors misled the press in an effort to keep the Bonin interviews a secret. However, right after his chat Bonin learned, from his lawyer, that Lopez knew about the detective interviews and feigned surprise for Bonin, who noted, "Dave Lopez must be a good poker player." Bonin was also informed that the DA compelled Lopez to keep the confession interviews a secret.

Bonin told Lopez that Macabe, who was on his way to Disneyland, was the "easiest one" and that all the victims were strangled except the second one, Grabs, who was stabbed. Lopez produced a list of 21 victims and Bonin confirmed all but one, Thomas Lundgren, who was one of the 14 he was charged with in LA. His comment that Butts might have killed Lundgren was a nonsensical stich-up for Butts' statements against him.

Commenting about Butts "living in fear of him" Bonin said, "He was never afraid of me, and Vern told me a few weeks ago that the only way he will testify against me is if the D.A. offered to let him go."

When Lopez mentioned Scott Fraser, who provided early info and was slated to testify, he said, "I was mad at him at first but not now. I still consider Scott a good close friend. If I were in his shoes, I would have done the same." Setting the record straight about the icepick controversy, used by Butts to kill Kendrick, he said, "Vern got really weird that night and stuck icepicks in his head." Lopez was told he started killing in August 1979 and ended with his arrest in June 1980, eerily adding, "If I wasn't arrested that night, I would have killed the kid in the van." Buddy Eugene Stark was a lucky one, for few who entered the Death Van exited alive.

In a striking irony it was later learned he was the nephew of Sharon Tate, the most famous victim of the Manson Family ten years earlier. When Bonin learned this, from Sgt. Kushner, he wrote, "What a hell of a deal it would have been if I would have killed him. They would have called it something like a revenge for Manson and Watson being put in jail."

Bottom line: Bonin went through nearly every murder with Dave Lopez that day.

The express purpose of their first meeting, three weeks earlier, was to inform Lopez that Eric was innocent and Pugh guilty in the Turner killing. When the issue was raised, Lopez said Pugh had been picked up in Nevada on car theft charges and the DA expected him to break and confess. Bonin was one step closer to possibly seeing Eric set free. Pleased at the news of Billy Pugh's arrest, he in turn showed Lopez a love letter Eric sent to him recently.

Assured by Lopez he wouldn't use anything without permission, Bonin refused to go on camera but indicated he will "at some point." In turn, Lopez believed Bonin wouldn't speak to any other reporters. Exclusive interviews can boost the careers of journalists and news correspondents. When Bonin mentioned his plan to possibly pleading guilty, or doing a surprise court confession, Lopez told him to "be very careful."

This caused Bonin to speculate about Lopez and search his feelings, "I really can't decide, in my own mind, if he is really concerned. I'd like to feel he is, yet I don't understand how anyone else could have feelings for me when I appeared to have none for others when doing all these things. I thought at one time I didn't have a conscience, now it's catching up to me.

There's a lot of hurt and I still don't know how I'm coping with it. I guess it's my strong will to live. Even though at times it isn't a conscious effort on my part."

True to his word, Lopez kept the Bonin confessions secret and that night he broadcast four important points Bonin wanted the public to know:

1) He knew who the "unnamed informant" was and the person in question wasn't afraid of him, as he claimed, and is not as innocent as police believe, 2) Vernon Butts wasn't scared of him and would not testify, 3) He was not mad at Scott Fraser anymore, 4) Eric Wijnaendts was innocent of any murders.

Lopez also reported Bonin saying this about the upcoming trial, "I'm not looking forward to it, but I want it here in Los Angeles. I don't want a change of venue. I'm not looking forward to seeing the parents of some of the victims. I know there are people who want to kill me, but I can't worry about that now."

Lopez's January 9 broadcast on CBS Channel 2 News at 4:00 p.m. ended this way:

CONNIE: David, it is quite clear that when you met with him that he was clear of mind or did he seem very nervous, or what?

DAVID: No. He's extremely calm. He's very calm, he reads the stock market reports every day. He follows the market quite clearly. He was quite excited the way some of the stocks were going that he says he follows and he says he feels very comfortable, a little nervous, but he says he felt very comfortable today.

CONNIE: And you've spent a great deal of time with him and I understand there was a great deal of information that he gave you. You reported some of it, but did he keep any clamps on you from reporting information?

DAVID: Oh, there were lots of things discussed in the conversation, and he told me that he trusts me and that's all he put, that's all, he left it at that.

CONNIE: David, thank you very much.

Lopez later revealed Bonin's response to being asked this question, "What would you be doing if back on the street?" Bonin didn't hesitate, "I'd still be killing. I couldn't stop killing. It got easier each time."

Following the interview, Bonin phoned Sgt. Kushner at the LA Sheriff's Dept. and gave him facts on Pugh which could help in breaking him; these included "his ability to get out of the van, where he lived and that a police officer lived next door to him." Bonin also said he thought Ronald Gatlin, victim #14 on March 14, was "bisexual and that might account for the pubic hair that doesn't belong to anyone."

The dreaded secrets of Vernon Butts' true participation were still safe. Lopez, detectives, prosecutors and Bonin know, but the specious claims of him "being present and not participating" stands firm in the public mind.

Bonin then spoke with Eric's attorney, George Elder, and told him Pugh was in custody and would be charged for Turner, letting Eric off the hook. Wanting to see Eric, if possible, Elder said he would try to get it done while cautioning Bonin that "saying Eric was innocent and proving it were two different matters." When the attorney mentioned obtaining transcripts of his confession interviews, Bonin said Elder couldn't get access because of an "agreement with prosecutors."

A disheartened Bonin wrote, "I feel that Eric's attorney feels that Eric may be guilty. I got a birthday card from my Mom. Looking at the beautiful scene of a lake on the outside and a waterfall on the inside made me cry. I'll never see these types of things again. I'm thinking of all sorts of things to do. None of which is physical harm to myself. I'm talking about pleading guilty and letting the chips fall where they may.

"I may get on the stand at Eric's prelim two weeks from today. It all depends on what happens the next two weeks. I have a big weight on my shoulders and I want to get it off of me. I've done what I can for Eric at the moment and I've probably hung myself. I may have hit the green room (gas chamber) for what I've said already. I guess what I'm doing is my own way of making peace with myself before I meet my maker. I deserve Hell but I pray for different."

Bonin, commenting wryly about his portrayal as some "kind of guy with magical hypnotic powers," noted that a Bill Farr article in the **LA Times** got his age wrong, 31 instead of 34, and observed the tone of media coverage this way, "They want to make me into the worst thing that hit the Earth. It's like if they don't then they have nothing to show for all these killings. Maybe it's the only way they can live with it."

Bonin had an uneventful day on Saturday, January 10. He met with Todd Landgren, his personal attorney, and discussed media coverage, detective interviews and conversations with Dave Lopez.

Down the hallway, in the hospital ward, Vernon Butts was troubled by intensifying media scrutiny over his confessions. Safety concerns, from his repeated suicide attempts, was a primary reason Butts was in the hospital section. Skinny and lean, he was a timid guy with a less than intimidating physical presence. Sheriff's deputies had to keep the Bonin Freeway Killer inmates from personal interaction while trying to protect all 5,000 inmates in the massive facility, some serving time and others moving thru the court system and thence to prison.

Days earlier his attorney, Joe Ingler, raised safety issues in light of Butts' heinous crimes and being transformed overnight into a snitch, something viewed badly in jail and prison. During the arraignment process, in Orange County months earlier, inmates made threats, saying "You don't look so tough, you like to kill young boys, but you can't stand up to a man. We'll punk you pretty good."

Cells in the hospital ward are smaller, with the normal amenities and a solid door fitted with a round porthole window for deputies to look through during bi-hourly rounds. Since his arrest, in late July, Butts was visited steadily by his fiancée, Cati Razook, and occult mentor James Meurer. Both believe he is holding up well, however, like everyone else, they still believe he is a non-murdering, innocent victim of Bonin.

Ingler met with him twice during the week and found him "up even though he knew the confessions were about to be made public." Vernon's fiancée visited him for an hour that Saturday night and left at 8:30 p.m., seeing Vernon as "happy." He penned a letter to Cati, unveiling a depressed state of mind, a view into Vern's confused world he never finished.

At 12:10 a.m. the deputy made his rounds and Butts appeared okay, but he was well and truly lost in a stifling nightmare where every door opened to suffering, recrimination and pain. He saw nothing but darkness ahead when he looped one end of a towel around the towel rack, tied the other end around his neck, got down on his knees, and lunged forward to cut off the oxygen supply to his brain. Slowly the life drained out of him and with it all the fear, regrets and guilt; a life wrecked by fate, drugs, poor judgement and help from Bill Bonin.

While Vernon Butts' nightmare might be over, all the others left behind were emotionally scarred for life from the evil he unleased with Bonin, who had the aggressive tendency and needed only the right partner to push him over the edge. Once he got the taste of killing, Bonin found it easy to kill alone and recruit others. Vernon Butts couldn't have killed alone, and barely got into it with Bonin pushing him. After the first one, Bonin would show up at his house with a ready-made victim in the back of the van, and Butts jumped in for the ride.

At 12:50 a.m. the deputy discovered Vernon Butts slumped against the wall with the towel still tightly wound around his neck, dead by his own hand in nearly the same manner as the six boys he helped to murder. Bill Farr wrote in the **LA Times**, "Butts added his own name to the long, grisly toll of victims in the Freeway Killer case."

Deputies found the sad, unfinished letter to his fiancée "indicating he was upset" about the transcripts becoming public, but there was also a separate message written in a strange code, the same kind Bonin saw him scribbling in court. No signs of injury or a struggle were present and LA Chief Medical Examiner-Coroner, the famed Thomas T. Noguchi, reported Butts probably "lost consciousness in a matter of seconds after pressure cut off circulation through the carotid artery, but more than likely he did not die for another 10 to 15 minutes." At first Butts' attorney was skeptical about Noguchi's ruling, but he had previously tried it four times with a gun, plastic bag, natural gas and sleeping pills.

First thing Sunday morning Dave Lopez went to see Bonin, who knew nothing, on his way to an impromptu press conference. Bonin described the bizarre situation, "Sunday, January 11, 1981: Dave came to see me about 5-minutes ago. He told me that Vern had killed himself last night. He hanged himself. It was a total surprise to me. I don't know if it helps or hurts me and I don't really care. I told Dave that 'as I look back at the prelim I realize that Vern was flipping out.' The laughing he did when he was looking at the nude pictures, etc.

"I guess he must have found out about the news on Channel 2 and gave it some thought. He must have known that the truth was about to come out. That along with his girl finding out could have been too much. Then again maybe his girl heard the news and confronted him with it. She may have dropped him. Only time may reveal what really led him to kill himself. I came back from seeing Dave and asked the Senior if I could talk to Eric. I told him that I was very worried about him doing something stupid. I don't know if I could handle it if Eric ever committed suicide. It would be a very heavy feeling on me."

Bonin was wrong about Vernon's fiancée dumping him after the release of the transcripts. Razook told Dave Lopez that "he was very happy. It's the happiest I've seen him in a long time. And now, I just can't understand why he'd do it. Everything was going good. He told me that, we talked about the possibility that the D.A.'s office might offer him, you know, 15 years if he pled guilty second-degree murder, and asking me if I thought he should take it, if I'd wait that long. I told him I would."

Throughout the day Bonin received updates, news and jailhouse gossip. One of his fellow inmates, Castro, came back from a visit with his wife and reported what she heard on the news and some of it backed up what Razook told Lopez, "That the D.A. had offered Vern 15-years to life to testify against Bonin. That he tried suicide once before. That he had left a left a letter addressed to his girl who he was going to marry in March this year. That they didn't need Vern to get me. So time will tell just what will happen. I hope to see Earl tomorrow and find out what we do next."

Attempts by Bonin to reach Sgt. Kushner, who was called in at 2:00 a.m., proved futile. Major political fallout was descending on the Sheriff's Dept., which runs the LA Men's Central Jail, and the Mental Health Dept., responsible for psychological well-being of inmates.

County DA Van de Kamp was enraged, along with those from his office handling the cases, Stovitz and Norris. The prosecution team has lost the second most important suspect in the biggest mass murder case in Southern California history, and a possible witness against Bonin.

Already highly unlikely to be offered a deal, Butts' suicide put the notion on really thin ice as one of the only reasons for getting Bonin's testimony was gone. Giving up Eric was the last card Bonin had to play, and it was not nearly enough. Nonetheless, Bonin kept the Eric card in his back pocket. Frankly, prosecutors were in no mood to give Bonin anything and instilled with a burning desire to take everything.

The mental health team was not informed of Butts' growing depression and he fell through the cracks of the overburdened department. Were they made aware of Butts' previous suicide attempts, the Forensic Mental Health unit would have moved Butts to the inpatient hospital, prescribed depression medication and monitored him carefully.

Vernon Butts' suicide was how I, Vonda Pelto, Ph.D., arrived 8-months later to LA Men's Jail as a freshly minted Clinical Psychologist "to make sure this kind of thing doesn't happen again." Such a position at the jail had never existed previously and the experience would change my life!

50

Butts Suicide Fallout, Pugh Charged, Jailhouse Tales & Eric Released
January 12 to February 28, 1981

On Monday, January 12 news of Vernon Butts' untimely suicide, and what it meant for the Freeway Killer trials, exploded in the media internationally. Newspapers carried headlines like the one from *The Hanford Sentinel* in California, *Freeway Killing Suspect Hangs in Jail Cell*; or the *LA Times* with *Butts, Suspected in Freeway Killing, Hangs Self in Jail Cell*. Bonin read articles from the *Times* and the other local newspaper, the *Herald Examiner*, and recorded his reactions.

"Monday, January 12, 1981: I read both the *Herald* and *Times* account of Vern's death. Only the *Herald* stated at the end of the article that the D.A. thought Vern was not the passive one he was putting on to be. The investigators say they hope the three remaining co-defendants will turn states evidence against me. Munro and Miley may but Eric can't as he is innocent. That may help me. Along with the fact that investigators feel there is still one or two at large, I may still be able to make a deal."

Bonin wrote about the three others, Billy Gilespy, Johnny Malinca and Tony, who didn't kill with him but were suspected and in custody. He surmised that telling detectives of their innocence will only hurt Eric's chances as it will "appear I'm covering for up them as well as Eric." Showing a rational mode of thinking, Bonin analyzed the situation from different angles, "The investigators and the D.A.'s own greed may get me a deal. Their own narrow minds and desire for more to be involved and ego to not admit they are wrong may in the long run help me. At least I hope it does. A trial will get me the Death Penalty."

Bonin's attorney speculated that Vernon's death won't hurt their case and may even prompt a deal if prosecutors see trouble in obtaining a guilty verdict. Probably wishful thinking. Looking for scapegoats, a few detectives asked Dave Lopez if he felt responsible for Butts' suicide? According to Bonin, Lopez pointedly told them, "Go to Hell."

This exchange prompted Bonin to reassess the situation, "If anyone should feel responsible it's me. For many reasons. I got him into it and had Dave put the stuff on the air. I'm convinced at this time that Vern really wanted to die. He just couldn't handle the pressure of his loved ones and family finding out the truth about him. It came as such a shock that I couldn't even respond to it. It's still hard to believe yet easy to understand.

"In order to understand something you have to have been there. I'm there and I know what he was going thru. I'm going thru it right now. At times it really gets unbearable. I sometimes wonder how I'm getting thru it myself.

"I guess what it all boils down to is I can take more abuse than Vern and Vern's conscience got to him heavier than mine has at this point. It will all catch up to me as it is so far I can handle it. Yet I don't know how I do it. I guess it's just that I put it out of my mind when it gets too heavy. Maybe in a way I do have a split personality."

Deputies who ran the jail, pleased with the news, took every opportunity to ride Bonin with surly comments or insulting questions.

One had a hearty laugh and said, "Say, I see your partner died, what can I say." While playing solitaire, Deputy Campbell maliciously commented, "Well, well, well, one down and three to go." Bonin stayed silent and kept playing cards.

Another asked, "Do you feel sorry?' In reply Bonin said, "No comment." In contrast, Deputy Voyer showed compassion about his somber mood by saying, "Yeah, I can understand where you're coming from."

The Tuesday, January 13 edition of Munro's hometown newspaper, ***The Times Herald*** in Port Huron, Michigan, published an article, ***Testimony Tipped Victim to Suicide Method***, which reported that Butts picked up tips on a number of strangulation methods during the preliminary hearings. Deputy DA Stovitz commented that Vernon paid particular attention to a coroner explaining "how people can be strangled, choked or hanged—he was so attentive. I'm trying to say he learned how to do it. He had already spent six months in county jail; he had another six months until his trial. He had a life sentence to look forward to, if not the death penalty."

Stovitz uttered the best possible spin by saying, "Yes, a potential witness was lost, but he was just another defendant we were going to try in July."

They totally overlooked one cold fact: Butts possessed ample experience with strangulation—he killed six boys with Bonin using that method.

Headline in the **Sacramento Bee**, a major paper in the California capital, read **LA Coroner Rules Strangulation of Confessed 'Freeway Killer' a Suicide**. Coroner Thomas Noguchi announced, "Based on the available data, death was consistent with suicide." An **LA Times** article, **Butts Tried to Kill Himself Four Times: Coroner Calls Death of Freeway Killer Suicide**, explored many different aspects and noted further investigations would proceed for drug screening, psychological status and mental attitude through a careful examination of his brain.

Through Mary, he was informed that his new pen-pal, 18-year-old Ellen, had married her boyfriend Kevin during a road trip through Nevada on the way home to Utah.

Kevin, however, was married to another woman and Ellen was unaware when taking the vows. Bonin had a serious crush on Ellen and wrote she was "a very sweet looking young lady and anyone should be proud of being hooked up with her."

Bonin wrote about Lawrence Bittaker's trial and rationalized his situation, "Wednesday, January 14: Larry goes to court again. This is his eighth day at picking his jury. He has three more to go plus four alternates. He may still be at it till next week. I find myself quite relaxed this morning. I guess it comes with the passing of time. I've been in 7-months and 3-days now. I've resigned myself to being in a minimum of 30-years. In all actuality I may never get out. Yet I have to hold on to a spark of hope. So I say to myself that I stand a chance of getting out after 30-years. Even if I lived until I was 73 and then got out, at least I'd get out. That would be 40-years down the line. I know I don't deserve it. But I hope that people at that time have more compassion than I had before."

An article about Greg Miley sent Bonin into a tailspin about destroying Miley's life, and everything he had done. Unaware of his low IQ, Bonin now thought Miley didn't know what he was doing, and how he might be safe in Texas but for Bonin's interference. Bonin hoped Miley might get an insanity deal, thus avoiding heavy prison time.

He wrote, "I've ruined his life along with many other lives. Vern's life was ruined to the point of his taking his own life. Yet, I wonder if I myself knew what the consequences were. I feel I must be gravely mentally disordered to have not only committed these acts but to have taken with me so many others." Noting that he was too "chicken" to commit suicide, Bonin's mood saw him contemplating just pleading guilty and accepting the consequences. Through it all, Bonin searched for a "spark of hope" in the darkness that "keeps me going."

A meeting with his attorney, Earl Hanson, buoyed his spirits and brought him hope as they ran through possible deal scenarios in the wake of the confession interviews, Vern's passing and the arrest of Billy Pugh. Bonin was tasked with interviewing private detectives to work for him. Hanson had secured $5,000 ($20,000 in 2023) from the court to hire a private investigator in order to speak with the same people being questioned by detectives and prosecutors. Bonin found the prospect a welcome challenge, and distraction, from all the bad news filling his head and heart.

Dave Lopez was right; Billy Pugh quickly confessed to participating in the Turner murder. On Friday, January 16 the charges against Eric Wijnaendts were dropped by Judge Trammel, who ordered his immediate release after Deputy DA Norris informed the court that "charges will be filed next week against a new suspect in the slayings." Eric was released with an obligation to pay a small fine for a previous infraction. Pugh, now 18-years old, had his identity withheld from the public because he was a juvenile when the murder took place, however, a new law will allow prosecutors to file for permission to try him as an adult.

The next day Bonin was escorted into the Attorney Room for a meeting with Lopez. While waiting, the deputy asked him a couple of questions, which Bonin refused to answer. Undeterred, the deputy repeatedly told him the answers couldn't be used in court, that is until Bonin dressed him down with examples and then looked at him pointedly, in the eyes, for emphasis. The deputy ceased his inquiry.

Lopez told him about Eric's hearing and asked him what Billy Pugh was like? Bonin told him Pugh was a "real ruffian" and then Lopez told him Sgt. Esposito was out of state searching for a suspect. Bonin found this amusing, "I knew he was out of state and felt it was in connection with my case. Now I know for sure. He's spinning his wheels."

Lopez then pressed Bonin on whether he told anyone else about all the murders, the answer was no, and asked for permission to broadcast the whole story, repeatedly saying, "I'm sitting on the biggest story of the year." Bonin wrote, "I could see that he wanted to go on the air with it. His enthusiasm was so hyped up. He wants to tell it and yet he promised he wouldn't." Lopez kept his word, and the story remained a secret, this with Sgt. Esposito pressing him to reveal what Bonin said to him. Lopez could not be intimidated and refused to divulge anything else, much to Esposito's displeasure.

Bonin rang up Sgt. David Kushner and asked, "I assume Billy made some incriminating statements about himself?"

"Yeah, he broke," Kushner answered.

"He broke open and spilt about his part?"

"Yeah, he was easy, cracked right away."

"I want to thank you for whatever you did to get Billy to crack and get the charges against Eric dropped," Bonin said, pleased at being able to say the words.

"Well, thanks, I only hope he appreciates what you did for him."

"I think he does. It will be very interesting to see if he comes up after he is released."

"Well, take care Bill," Kushner said, ending the call.

Kushner and other detectives were correct about Eric being involved in killing with Bonin, but incorrect in their hunches about Gilespy, Malinca and Tony. Unlike those still in custody, Eric didn't "crack" when questioned and, with Bonin's help plus a bit of luck, he was released. He was smart enough to only answer the questions at hand and not volunteer anything. Among Bonin's friends or associates, only Fraser knew Eric, and then hardly at all. No forensic evidence connected him to either the Sharp or King killings, and for the time being he was safe.

In the weeks and months ahead Eric's foundation of innocence cracked and firmed up depending on circumstances. Bonin wrote this, "I've waited a long time to see these headlines. It makes me feel real good. I'll be able to rest a lot easier now. After reading the article I feel content. I'm glad Billy will be charged and I'm glad they will try and have him tried as an adult. They are prohibited from talking about what I said in my 3-days of talking to them. It's a real heavy feeling right now."

Eric was released on Sunday, January 18. Informed of this by deputies, when he attempted to speak with him, Bonin reflected on the situation, "So finally after a month he is back on the streets where he belongs. I may never hear from him again and wouldn't blame him. But I did what I felt I had to do and what I felt was right regardless of the consequences to myself. If Eric stays out of trouble and out of jail, that will be reward enough."

Bonin was baffled that someone like Eric, or anyone else, could still like or love him while he could barely live in his own skin, he then wrote that his "inner strength" would see him thru even if he lived the rest of his life behind bars.

An update on Ralph came through Sgt. Esposito, who had just returned from a trip to Dallas and Pennsylvania investigating more suspects. Ralph was a young hitchhiker Bonin picked up in July 1979. He stayed with him for a few weeks, in Silverado, just before the killings started. Bonin dropped Ralph at the I-10 to hitchhike back east, never to see or hear from him again. Later he was arrested for armed robbery, in Pittsburgh, and popped up as a possible suspect/witness.

Esposito learned Bonin had threatened Ralph, by putting a knife to his throat, and saying he would kill him and then leave his body in the hills. Ralph told Bonin he was 19-years old when he was actually 16. Bonin wrote in his dairy that the incident was true, but he done it just to scare the kid. Ralph was slated to testify at his trial.

Further discussions about Miley focused on Bonin telling Esposito why he should get an insanity plea. Esposito explained that, from his perspective, Miley may have been illiterate but not insane, which brought this explanation from Bonin: "He really didn't comprehend what he was getting himself into. I really believe that when I was talking to him about killing people that he thought I was kidding him." But referring back to Miley's post-arrest interview a different view is clear; he told detectives almost immediately, "I decided to go with Bonin and kill someone."

Rumors abounded as Jim Munro had his arraignment and the charges for Billy Pugh were prepared. Bonin spoke with Mary to reiterate his desire to marry Ellen, since her invalid marriage to Kevin cleared the way. She was probably returning to LA, and it appeared they had developed a strong bond through letters and phone calls. In the last week of January, Bonin phoned Scott Fraser and heard that detectives continued to ask more questions. Bonin told him to tell the truth, everyone was in custody and nobody else should get hurt.

He wrote, "I believe Scott knows that I am involved and that I'll do a lot of time. I miss his company and being able to talk with him. I guess that will never be again. That's something I'll have to live with or die with. My life on the streets is over."

Pugh was officially charged on Tuesday, January 28. The ***LA Times*** reported that he helped "Bonin kill Harry Todd Turner, a 15-year-old runaway. Turner's nude body was found in an alley near South Bonnie Brae Street in Downtown Los Angeles." Per a new juvenile crime law, his identity and charges would be revealed the next day, during arraignment, and he would be tried as an adult.

Bonin continued on the situation, "So finally Billy Pugh gets charged. I have no bad feelings for him getting charged as he is just as guilty of murder as I am. He knew what was going to happen before we ever left to go looking.

"He knew we were going to find someone, have sex with them and kill them. When he was in Juvenile Hall he would force youngsters to suck his dick and he'd fuck them. He told me that once a guy didn't want to do it. They were in the Day Room, no counselors were around. He swung at the guy and hit him and then told the kid to go to the head. They both went and Billy made the kid give him a head job. Billy told me how easy it was. After a guy did it once, no force was necessary.

"They could be talked into it quite easily. They knew what would happen if they didn't. I heard on the radio that Billy pled innocent today. I'm sure he's really feeling down in the dumps. So now he feels the way all the rest of us do. He started it all and now he's bringing up the rear. I only hope he gets what the rest of us gets. I hope that's life and not the death penalty."

The tape of Vernon Butts' confession in July was played again during Billy Pugh's arraignment and Dave Lopez, at a February 2 meeting, told Bonin that hearing it "made everyone in the courtroom sick." When played previously, during the Bonin-Butts prelims, it was during a closed session with no press or spectators in attendance.

For the press to hear the actual words, as opposed to reading transcripts, prompted a spate of new articles around the country with headlines like ***Tales of Homosexuality, Demonic Torture Unfold in California*** or ***Trail of 'Freeway Killers' is Lined in Horror*** or ***Grisly Murder Case in Court***. The first two paragraphs of a nationally printed AP article set the tone, "Southern Californians, inured to the horror of mass murder by the likes of Charles Manson, have been shocked anew by a grisly case now snaking its tangled way through the courts. It is called 'the Freeway Killer case,' and the gruesome details unfolding daily involve homosexuality, black magic and demonic tortures of perhaps 44 victims."

Irresponsible and understandable describe those paragraphs; the number of 44 victims for Bonin and company was, months earlier, cut to 21 and made public by investigators, plus Butts never said anything about using "black magic or demonic tortures" when he killed with Bonin. Just the same 44 "homosexually oriented murders," with demonic undertones, was juicy headlines for selling newspapers.

Now everyone knows who helped end Bonin's reign of terror, and that he is charged for helping with one murder. LAPD's Sgt. St. John took the stand at the arraignment and testified about his May 29 meeting with Pugh and how it broke the Bonin Freeway Killer cases. Bonin's ire about Pugh shows, "I'm glad his name is finally in print. I hope he ends up with life. He is potentially as dangerous as I was and if and when he gets out he'll probably kill again. I don't wish any harm to him, but I do hope he never gets out as he's just as guilty as I was of Harry Todd Turner's murder."

Kushner and Esposito's needling and ridiculing of Bonin, regarding Eric's sexual distaste for him, did the trick because on Thursday, February 5, Bonin phoned Esposito and dropped hints about his involvement. According to Bonin, the conversation went like this:

"Doesn't make sense to me for a guy to say he was at a murder scene if he wasn't," Esposito told Bonin.

"No, it doesn't, if Eric was involved in anything you'll have a hard time proving it, why don't you go to the Circle K store where Sean King was dumped off and see if they could ID me being there that night and with anyone else, and you might check and see if he has an alibi for that weekend. I'm not sticking my neck out if they couldn't prove it," Bonin informed him.

"What do you mean?"

"Check the Circle K out, if you come up with anything I'll talk."

"I'll do just that, by the way we think Billy Gilespy is a liar but wasn't involved in anything."

"Told you so," Bonin said with finality.

Bonin summed up his feelings, "I've been covering for Eric all this time as I love Eric very, very much. Even though it seems that it was one way I feel that I still love him. I don't usually look out for myself but maybe it's time. Esposito told me it would be sometime next week by the time they decided if they were going to file on me in Orange County. I told Esposito that I had everything written down and it was gone. That I wrote it down to protect myself."

Three points stand out: 1) Bonin hinting at Eric's "possible" involvement in Sean King, 2) Telling Esposito about hidden written murder story files, 3) Bonin waffling on Eric. This could be the first time Esposito heard about Eric in connection with King, but Bonin still left out being with him for Larry Sharp. Still on the hunt for more suspects, Esposito was probably pleased at rattling Bonin, seeing him crack a bit.

Detectives were probably unaware of Bonin's extremely deep feelings for Eric, feelings he was obviously rethinking constantly. Stuck with his love for Eric, the notion of giving him up only adds to Bonin's beleaguered sense of tragedy overwhelming his mind and soul. Diary entries repeatedly refer to "weeping during the night and asking God for help" before admitting all is "lost and not deserving salvation."

Two days of agonizing brought forth a third shift in his tenuous position; Bonin called up Sgt. Fueglein, LA Sheriff, and said he "gave Esposito a false impression" about Eric's involvement and didn't want them to think he "was trying to put Eric right back in the middle of it."

He described the emotional dilemma, "I thought about it the past couple of days. I just can't do it. It sounds stupid that a guy like me could have so much feeling for a kid like Eric that obviously has nothing in return, yet I care for Eric a lot. He's the lucky one. The one who got charged and held the only chance of going free, he is and was innocent.

"I just couldn't bring myself to do it. The homicide detectives are so convinced that there are other people involved that it left me desperate. So desperate that I was looking for anyone that I could put at the scene of any of the murders, even someone like Eric that I love. Even a neighbor that I love very much. I need to convince these people so they leave others alone and possibly give me a deal."

Who is the "neighbor" Bonin claims to love very much? Nowhere is there any mention of anyone who lived near Bonin involved on any level, especially murder! Is the "neighbor" Eric? Doesn't seem likely.

Three days later he phoned Esposito to make sure he knew the stuff about Eric was a lie, during which time he was informed Orange County was likely to file murder charges any day. Bonin called Landgren and told him to pick up the last of the written murder stories and the jailhouse diaries. If he got pulled down to OC for arraignment, all of it would be swept up and end up with the detectives. Those murder stories were part of Bonin's so-called "protection" for making a deal.

Life in jail could, at times, be rather colorful; stories from Bonin included inmates setting fires in front of their cells, two jailhouse deputies getting into a verbal argument and almost coming to blows, out of control inmates getting physically restrained and sent to the hospital ward. But most often it was boring as they passed the time reading, playing blackjack, walking and talking during Freeway Time or waiting for the next visit, hearing, attorney conference, shower or phone call.

One daily highlight was the mobile store which dispensed newspapers and candy bars each morning. Bonin's row was continually disappointed as the store reached their row last and was empty, eliciting bitter complaints to recalcitrant guards who said, "Sorry, nothing we can do about it."

Bonin wrote, "But there is something, they can start on our row once in a while." He believed it was revenge towards particular inmates on his row, particularly Douglas Clark, Angelo Buono and himself. The store also got emptied because Clark bought so much there was nothing left, which Bonin also complained about in the diary.

Ed Barrett, privately retained attorney for Billy Pugh, got a hold of Earl Hanson and requested a phone call from Bonin. All other attorneys were court appointed with fees and expenses paid by taxpayers. Days later Bonin learned Hanson had an upcoming lunch meeting with Barrett to discuss possible collaboration. Another aspect was that victims killed in a similar manner were recently discovered, leading to speculation on two fronts: 1) Copycat, 2) It was someone who was operating before Bonin killed anyone, and was at it again.

Seeking to work the system, Jim Munro was making up stories in the manner of Lloyd Douglas, the jailhouse snitch, about Bonin's friend Lawrence Bittaker. Housed in 7000, Munro was unaware that Bonin had grown close to Bittaker in the previous six-weeks, and it got back to Bonin, "Wednesday, February 18: Larry had a visit from his attorney and it seems that Munro told his own attorney that Larry had confessed to him. His attorney contacted Larry's attorney and they talked about it. Garber,

Larry's attorney, told Munro's attorney to keep him quiet. Munro then wrote a letter to the D.A. on Larry's case, Randolph, telling him that Larry confessed to him. The fact is that Munro and Larry have never met and have never had a chance to even talk face to face in all the time Munro has been in custody or before."

Munro was playing a dangerous game and would surely draw the ire of inmates for such behavior.

Hanson and Bonin found out what Pugh's attorney had in mind a few days before Bonin was scheduled to meet with him, on February 23. Barrett wanted all the attorneys to fight it out together on the grounds Bonin was crazy. Bonin was intrigued, "Of course if the D.A. offers me a deal, I'll take it. I think there may be a shot."

Barrett informed Bonin that Miley's trial was postponed for a month and then peppered him with a series of questions Bonin refused to answer, saying they were "irrelevant." Unhappy with the lack of cooperation, Barrett went on an insulting rant at Bonin's expense, one which he blithely ignored.

Not believing they could convict Pugh, with or without Bonin's testimony, Barrett ended the meeting by threatening him, "If you get on the stand against Billy, you're going to have one hell of a hard time." Bonin replied he expected "nothing less" and wrote, "What Ed Barrett doesn't know is that, if I get on the stand, he wouldn't be able to give me a hard time as I'd be telling the truth and he couldn't get to me anymore than the D.A. has already gotten to me."

More conversations with Sgt. Esposito followed and Bonin concluded, with help from his attorney, that the powerful OC detective "had been giving him the run around" on various deal scenarios. Bonin ruefully decided to return the favor and "see what he comes up with." Fearing the prospect of more charges from OC, Bonin's hope of facing one trial with better chances for a deal were fading, and Esposito confirmed it by saying, "No way you will get a deal off of anyone."

Another part of the conversation went like this:

"I'm glad you didn't use a Psychic in my case," Bonin said.

"What makes you think we didn't," Esposito replied with glee.

"I don't know that you didn't, did you?"

"I'll never tell," Esposito concluded, pleased at putting one over on Bonin.

The day next day Bonin learned his friend, Lawrence Bittaker, got a death penalty recommendation from the jury. One month later the judge would announce if he affirmed the jury recommendation. In the meantime, Bittaker received a new jail wrist band with a "Z" added to it, meaning death penalty.

After seeing a psychiatrist, where he was pronounced sane, Bonin had a meeting with Earl Hanson, who gave him a novel to read, **Blood and Money** by Thomas Thompson. This was the third book his attorney had given to him. The first one, **From Copernicus to Einstein**, was about the nature of the universe. Bonin read it carefully, wrote a detailed diary entry about the **Theory of Relativity** and ended it this way, "It's a very interesting subject and fascinates me greatly."

He discussed the topic rather cogently with Hanson, who was duly impressed and said, "Keep it up, I love it." Bonin's take on Hanson's comment was interesting, "He was referring to 'keep saying those things' as a psyche will think I'm crazy. I told him I meant what I said. I wasn't saying it for anyone's benefit to make them think I'm crazy. On the contrary, when it comes to the Universe and Space, I believe there is nothing that would be impossible to happen or be true. I believe it is possible to travel at faster than the speed of light. Yet you would probably become a ray or a very delicate atom. You would also travel in reverse time if and when surpassing the speed of light."

Near the end of the month, Bonin was able to straighten out some mixed communications with Ellen; she had received his letter in Utah but couldn't understand what he was asking. Mary set her straight; he was proposing marriage. After getting Ellen's phone number from Mary, he rang her up in Utah, charges reversed of course. With encouragement, she agreed to take his "suggestion seriously," while they both agreed on the disadvantages: Bonin was going on trial as a serial killer. Ellen will either move to Boston or back to Mary's, her marriage to Kevin was void and Ellen's daughter would remain in Utah, wherever she went.

A scuffle was brewing around Billy Pugh's case regarding the December confession interviews, when Bonin said Pugh helped him kill Turner. Ed Barrett was planning to file a request to see the transcripts of the 11-hours of interviews as part of discovery. In turn Hanson, since no deal was offered, would file to have it all destroyed. Bonin reasoned it this way, "It may go public at which time there would be no way that I could get a fair trial and the D.A. may have to give me a deal."

As February 1981 drew to an end a few things were apparent; 1) Bonin wasn't going to offer any more information without a deal in writing, 2) Sgt. Esposito had been and was a roadblock with deal negotiations, 3) The Pugh case may cause problems in the Bonin's case and trial, 4) All the pre-trial and trial hearings were getting postponed till spring and summer.

51

Hope for a Deal, Mind Games, Protecting Eric & Major Decisions
March 1981

March proved an event filled and fascinating month in the Bonin Freeway Killer cases. Each day brought new rumors, gossip, mutterings, news stories, and outrageous falsehoods. Eric continued to plague Bonin's mind while detectives diligently pursued various leads around the country. On Monday, March 2 Bonin's pre-trial hearing was moved to March 31. Other than the Billy Pugh hearings, everyone else was scheduled for April and May.

Other issues Bonin wrote about was his request for roof time and the judge deciding to let cameras in the courtroom, at least for part of the trial. Earl Hanson was told by the DA that he knew Sgt. Esposito, OC Sheriff, had been talking with Bonin but he said Bonin wasn't giving them anything. Bonin found this interesting, "Of course I'm not giving them anything. I've already given them everything at the beginning."

Bonin's phone call to Esposito later that day brought a confession he had indeed been "a stumbling block in the dealings earlier on. He said he would not deal with Butts." Bonin was hoping that Barrett's plan to force the DA to give up the interview transcripts might somehow lead to a deal. Kushner and Fueglein, of the LA Sheriff's Dept., came by on Tuesday, March 3 to chat with Bonin. After inquiring about one Eddie Owens and hinting about someone else in Ventura, but refusing to give a name, Kushner said he was convinced Eric and Gilespy "were involved in something." Following a bit of spirited banter, the conversation ended in a rather interesting manner:

"My partner says he'll give you 15 hamburgers or cheeseburgers if you give him Wijnaendts," Kushner told Bonin.

He laughed at the notion and said, "The only ones he could really possibly be involved in, if any, was Sharp and King. You should be convinced by now that Eric wasn't involved on Turner?"

"I don't know about that," Kushner blandly replied.

"Look," Bonin said sharply, "if he was there on Turner, Billy Pugh would have said something about it when he finally broke and told you his story?"

"Yes, I agree with that."

"Well, I had told you before Eric wasn't there, unless you think he was with Billy and me?" Bonin said in frustration.

"I don't know, was he?"

"Look, I know it sounds funny, me going out and killing 22 kids and now I'm holding back on one life that doesn't give a fuck if I live or die," he said a respectful yet mocking tone.

"Yeah, it sure does sound funny," Kushner admitted. "You're in a good mood today?"

"Yes, I am," Bonin said with satisfaction.

This seems to be the first time Bonin mentioned, to detectives, Eric's possible involvement with the killing of Larry Sharp. He had already dropped hints about Sean King, but now they have a second case to focus on with Eric, which probably sent them back to double-check the Sharp files. Eric's participation in both was clear from the murder stories chronicled earlier.

A new phone was installed on Bonin's row, making it easier to make calls. Previously an inmate needed a deputy escort to the shower area, which was often unavailable as showers ran all day. Allowed at least one call per day, Bonin had permission for additional "court ordered" privileges. Making calls during Freeway Time, out of cells, removed stress unless an inmate went over his allotted time.

Before meeting with Dave Lopez, another reporter contacted Bonin and he finally agreed to meet and speak with her. Barbara Riegle was an OC Correspondent for KFWB News Radio, a major news outlet in LA. She got back in touch, and he was ready to meet with her but then changed his mind,

"Saturday, March 7: I doubt I will see her on Monday as I just don't feel right about it. I was expecting her many months ago, not weeks. She never showed up. I'm not going to talk to these people when they get ready to talk. It's going to have to be when we both are ready. I was ready four of five months ago and they weren't ready. When I needed the media, only Dave Lopez came. I promised that I would talk to him and him alone as he helped me when I needed it. I also trust him, so far."

His loyalty to Dave Lopez held firm with each day offering new surprises. Bonin's attorney decided on a private investigator, Wayland Gilliam, for the task of looking into certain aspects of the case. Gilliam met with Bonin a day before having a "rare conversation with my older brother, Bob."

Two pieces of info came through Todd Landgren, his personal attorney: 1) The Orange County DA was reluctant about filing charges without Butts' testimony, 2) Sgt. Esposito wanted to compel Landgren to produce Bonin's written murder stories and maybe the diaries. He wrote, "I'll have to see if there is any way that Todd can be forced into giving up all the stuff."

On Wednesday, March 11 Bonin reflected on the situation, "I've been down 9-months today. I was called over to the Sgt.'s office and they asked a bunch of questions about other inmates and snitches like Douglas, asking if I knew he was snitching on me. I told them I found out the hard way, when he testified against me. They asked if I've been in the same cell all the time, I said yes. They were investigating another snitch and Douglas and I asked if they would prosecute Douglas if he was lying?

"They asked if I could prove it and the conversation ended there. Then I played chess with Peter Buono and it was a good series of games. He beat me for the first time because I made a stupid move and he is gloating continuously. I called Scott. I wonder how many people call witnesses against them. We talked and I asked him his opinion on things. I'm trying to decide if I should give Eric up or not? It's a very hard decision to make. I love him more than anyone I've ever met.

"I guess that he got released gave me the same feeling as I got when I did the 'En Passant' move on Buono in our chess game. Now it's looking like I have to decide whether I do something for myself, which means going against a loved one, not related though. Or passing and taking my chances of getting a deal another way. I also realize that if they get the evidence against Eric without me, that he'll go down and I'll get nothing out of it. The only consolation I would have then would be that I didn't help them get him. Maybe my love for Eric is only symbolic right now. Yet before, I felt it was true and very real."

According to Dave Lopez, who met with Bonin for 15-minutes the next day, Billy Pugh was set for a fitness hearing on Friday, March 13. Superior Court Judge Robert Altman would determine whether he should be tried as an adult and wouldn't offer a decision for a week. Bonin wondered if Pugh's attorney, Ed Barrett, would file to obtain the detective interview tapes as part of the discovery process. This issue was of particular interest to detectives, prosecutors and Bonin's attorney.

The atmosphere became tense as Lopez went through each murder to re-confirm which were done alone or with someone, causing Bonin to shut down until the subject changed. Lopez said he heard that OC didn't want to offer him a deal as Bonin explained, "They want to know who was involved in Rugh and Barker's death. They want it real bad. I mentioned that they'd probably give me a deal if I gave them that. He agreed with me. I told him I was thinking of giving them Eric. Lopez said, 'Now, that's interesting.' He mentioned that it was unusual that the others had 'diarrhea of the mouth and Eric was totally uncooperative, it just didn't jive.' All of this was off the record and it was just as if it never happened. He said he'd be back on Friday around 2 or 3 p.m. He said he was at every court appearance of everyone involved in the case."

Based on Lopez's reaction, this must be the first time Bonin spoke of Eric in connection with a murder other than Harry Turner. When Eric's arrest for the Turner murder was announced, on December 9, 1980, Lopez had his first meeting with Bonin, and he immediately broadcast Bonin's claim of Eric's innocence. Then Pugh gets picked up and it turns out Bonin was right, and Eric was soon released. Three months later, while going thru a crisis, he ends up telling Lopez he might give up Eric on a different murder.

Lopez must have been astonished, and what he did with the info proved interesting. Lopez had a valid point: Eric was a 20-year who faced a tough police interrogation and came away relatively clean. However, remember Eric told Bonin, after failing a polygraph, that he lied to detectives about being too drunk to remember anything. Maybe Eric Wijnaendts was just that smart, as well as being just that lucky!

That same Friday, Sgt. Kushner came to see Bonin and he had major slip of tongue, "I got up to leave and he asked me again who the other guy was. He had once asked if it was a girl and I said 'No.' I had Eric's name on my mind so as not to use it. Concentrating on not using it. He asked me again about if the attorney's put in to get the tapes?" The rest went like this.

"If Eric's attorney puts in…" Bonin said and stopped short, realizing the mistake.

"Wait a minute, Eric?" Kushner said with astonishment, "Don't tell me Wijnaendts is involved?"

"I have to go," Bonin said while rushing out in a panic.

Kushner must certainly have felt his suspicions were confirmed. Bonin quickly realized he should have calmly corrected himself by saying, "I mean Billy's attorney," rather than making a hasty retreat from the interview room. But confirmed suspicions did not mean Eric could be charged in different murder cases. Bonin had mentioned Sean King in connection with Eric but went back on the statement, then later he mentioned both Sharp and King in another conversation.

There was definitely no forensic evidence in the Sean King case, and obviously none for Sharp or Eric would already have been charged. All of Bonin's accomplices, except Fraser, knew nothing of Eric. Detectives were obviously re-exploring those King and Sharp cases, but it was clear they needed Bonin to talk.

On Saturday, March 14 fellow inmate Douglas Clark gave Bonin the April issue of **Hustler Magazine** and, much to his surprise, Bonin saw an ad for a new board game, the "Freeway Killer." Stunned, he phoned Landgren to see if they could get a restraining order against the manufacturer, the answer was no. On the issue of the KFWB reporter, Barbara Riegle, Bonin phoned her and agreed to meet on one condition: no discussion about the case during the initial interview. Lopez told him Riegle wanted to write a book, and a large monetary sum might be involved.

While Judge Altman was still deciding about Pugh's "Fitness" to be tried as a juvenile, the other parties scrambled for cover should Bonin's detective interviews become an issue. First of all, his attorney couldn't find the signed agreement stating the tapes couldn't be used in court, destined to remain a secret if no deal was offered.

But Hanson was not alone, Sgt. Kushner couldn't locate his copy either. He agreed to send his copy to Hanson when it was located, thus relieving Hanson of an embarrassing situation when, and if, he had to meet with the DA. In the meantime, they had to wait on events with the Pugh hearings.

Bonin explained it this way, "Wednesday, March 16: Earl had mentioned the possibility of, if the tapes were made public, we might have grounds for a federal lawsuit. Then the federal government could step in and order that I couldn't be brought to trial. That would mean I would get cut loose. That would be a hell of a way to end this case. I'd go so far underground that not even the oil drilling rigs would reach me."

Attorneys are always trying to buy time and find avenues to help their clients, no matter how far-fetched or tenuous the chances of success.

Kushner and Mellecker, LA Sheriff and LAPD respectively, showed up at 9:00 p.m. to talk with Bonin about a range of issues, but mostly Eric. Bonin cannily teased them with various word games and then the topic of the detective interview tapes came up:

"What would happen if it ever got out by Pugh's attorney trying to get it?" Kushner asked.

"I would be devastated. Can you get a change of venue out of state?" Bonin asked in a half-joking manner.

"Yes."

"Then that's what I'd have to do," Bonin exclaimed in surprise. "There'd be no way I'd be able to get a fair trial in this state."

"Want to know what Eric's nickname is with the detectives?" He asked with a probing eye.

"Sure, why not," Bonin replied, willing to take the bait.

"Well, you see, we call him 'Dirt,' and it fits because we know he's dirty for something and it involves you, somehow," Kushner said with malice while focusing on Bonin's reactions, "You know we could file on Gilespy and Tony and get past a prelim and then both would probably plead to manslaughter or 2nd degree murder, plus we could convict Eric of 1st degree murder right now. Beyond that we're not sure if anyone else is involved."

"You should really think of an escape," Mellecker said while winking at Kushner, hinting at Bonin killing himself.

"No, I had thought of it once but gave it up completely," Bonin replied without hesitation.

He wasn't about to take the Vernon Butts route; Bonin always seemed to look for hope in his hopeless situation. They were pouring it on to shake Bonin emotionally, but it was all smoke and mirrors. Saying they could "file" on two others and convict Eric Wijnaendts "right now" definitely comes across as a comical intimidation, and Bonin did not take the bait. He knew they would have already moved if possible.

The other powerful detective in the picture was Sgt. Bernie Esposito, OC Sheriff's Dept. Getting toyed with by a child murderer tried his patience beyond the limit; first, Bonin lays it all on the line to help get Eric out of the Turner situation, then hints at Eric being part of "something" before retracting the statement and then bringing it up again with Sharp and King.

Particularly keen about the Russell Rugh-Glen Barker murders, OC cases, Esposito was convinced Bonin had help and other detectives share his opinion. But Eric was in jail when Rugh-Barker took place, and they have nothing concrete to tie Eric to anyone else.

Afterwards, Bonin again struggled with the Eric issue, "I looked at the whole situation and see it this way. I can sit here and protect Eric from now until I enter the Gas Chamber and die protecting him. Or I can give him up and possibly save my life. I may, even though I gave him up, not get any deal because they can't corroborate it. Then I walk into the Green Room and then they find the corroboration and file on him. I really don't want to go against Eric, but I don't see that I have any alternative. Even if I don't, I feel they have enough to keep checking around until they finally find what they are looking for and file on him anyway. Then I'd get nothing as it didn't initiate from me.

"I thought for a long time and concluded that the homicide detectives working on the case are good enough, that even if it takes another year, they'll find what they need and get Eric. So I might as well leave my emotions behind and think for myself. I don't know what is or was or still is about Eric that is so binding. Maybe it's just my wishful thinking about what could have been, or me not wanting to ruin my memories. But it is a matter of something I have to do to save my life. If I die, memories aren't going to do me a damn bit of good."

Bonin got an earful of vitriol from his attorney after Dave Lopez called to say Bonin was holding out "on him" and had "one more name to give the police." Lopez didn't mention any name to Earl Hanson, but Bonin had mentioned Eric to Lopez in their last meeting.

Did Bonin believe Lopez stepped beyond the bounds of their agreement? Lopez had stuck to his promises by broadcasting what Bonin wanted and kept the secrets of their historic January 9 meeting; in turn, Bonin's "promise to go on camera" or allowing him to "run with the story" went unfulfilled.

What Lopez hoped to accomplish by calling Hanson was unclear?

Talking to Bonin's attorney about the ultra-sensitive subject of Eric, even though Lopez withheld his name, would not have sat well with Bonin. The next day, Tuesday, March 17, Bonin revealed his displeasure by siting down for his first interview with Tim Alger, a Staff Writer for the **OC Register**. Alger's work with J.J. Maloney broke the "Freeway Killer" story to the public a year earlier.

During Bonin's first conversation with Alger, the topic of the "alleged detective interview tapes" was raised, showing even if the public didn't know about them certain well-informed members of the press did. Another topic was the transcripts from Munro's first interview with police, which had been sealed by the court. Munro's attorney filed for them in discovery, had a closed-door meeting with Deputy DA Norris and came away empty handed.

Following the interview Bonin wrote, "I made a decision. I'm going to give them Eric and Mike if I get the deal. If not, they get nothing."

This is the first time a "Mike" has been mentioned in connection with any murders; was Mike the "neighbor" Bonin referred to earlier or someone else? A "Mike" was never mentioned in the written murder stories, detective interviews or in the diaries. Additionally, Bonin never says anything about police talking about "Mike" and the name hasn't been in the press. Six were charged; Butts committed suicide, Eric was released but was still under suspicion, four are in custody awaiting trial.

Issues with the press were heating up; that night Kushner told Bonin that "Dave Lopez and all his mates would be subpoenaed. Just the thing I needed to hear." The next day he met with the private investigator, Wayland Gilliam, and an amusing incident took place in the Attorney Room.

Deputy Campbell, who disliked Bonin, brought him over to the meeting room and made sure the handcuffs were on extra tight when affixed to a chair. After a few minutes of conversation with Wayland, Bonin blurted out his frustration to the friendlier Deputy Vanecek, "To hell with this, it's too tight. Do you mind if I get myself out of these?"

"No, just give me the key when you're done. Of course, if you slip from them, we'll bring you over in leg and waist chains next time," he replied with a laugh. Bonin used a paper clip to slip the cuffs in 10-seconds, threw it to over Vanecek and said, "That's the key." Vanecek laughed heartily at the absurdity of the scene.

Judge Altman's decision regarding Billy Pugh came down on Wednesday, March 18; he ruled that "William Ray Pugh was unfit to be tried as a juvenile, even though he was 17 at the time the victim, Harry Todd Turner, was strangled."

Bonin read about it the next day, "Well, Billy is finally where he should be. I would have never given him up if Eric wasn't arrested. My emotions and love was with Eric not Billy. I would have given Billy up only if I would have gotten a deal. Now it's the same way, except its Eric. I called Scott and talked to him for a short time. During our talk I made my decisions. I'm going to hand over the writings of what happened in the deaths of Sharp and King with Eric. During my talk with Scott, I insinuated that Mike C. was involved. This was to find out if he's talking to the cops. It's time to do it. Without a deal, I'm definitely dead. Especially with them going to call Dave Lopez to the stand."

Bonin is cracking a bit under the strain, and here again is "Mike" but now it is "Mike C." As it turns out, based on later writings, it was Mike Christenson. Even if Bonin was testing Fraser, this is the second time the name appears, and Fraser definitely knows Mike Christenson. Beyond that nothing was known, offering up two questions: Was Christenson also the "neighbor" Bonin refers to killing with? Bonin was cleverly keeping tabs on the info supply lines while probing what police knew, suspected, could prove and needed to learn. Then again, all of it could have been a ruse, just Bonin spreading disinformation.

Bonin's big trial was to begin in six-weeks, on May 4, and the pressure was building on everyone who was closely connected to all the cases. Stakes are high for the detectives, law enforcement agencies, prosecutors, defense lawyers, politicians, families and defendants. Neither Miley, Munro nor Pugh have agreed to testify against Bonin, and the wild cards in this deck were Bonin's many written murder stories, tapes from the detective interviews and Bonin dangling Eric in front of the detective's noses.

With no deal the confession interview tapes will be unusable in court and kept secret; no testimony from any of the co-murderers means prosecutors were relying on forensic evidence, expert testimony, witnesses like Fraser and detectives testifying about investigations and what Vernon Butts, Greg Miley, Jim Munro and Billy Pugh revealed during their first interviews.

Was that enough to convict Bonin and get a death penalty verdict?

On Friday, March 20 Bonin had his second meeting with Tim Alger, who was finding more favor with Bonin than Dave Lopez. Bonin chronicles the interview and circumstances, "According to the calendar, tonight is a Full Moon. About two weeks ago we had a welcome surprise. They served us steak. It was good and cut easily. Today Billy Pugh starts the long journey through the court system. I know that I will have to get on the stand unless I make a deal to plead guilty. I had a long talk, almost two-hours, with Tim from the O.C. Register. He said he'd come as often and as long as I wanted. I told him he could come up every day if he wanted. I enjoy the visits.

"I gave him some stuff he could write about. Mainly about Deputy D.A. Norris, I said things like, 'He was a publicity hound and that he was trying to use me as a steppingstone to a judgeship.' I also said, 'He was trying to be another Vincent Bugliosi, the man who handled the Manson case.' I called and talked to my brother Paul this evening. It was a revealing thing. He told about me about people driving by and yelling names all the time."

Bonin heard Billy Pugh was kept in restraints because he was "considered suicidal." Figuring Billy would get Life Without Parole if he pled guilty, he also knew Pugh's attorney didn't believe they could convict him even if Bonin testified. Another phone call with Scott allowed Bonin to tell him the "insinuations about Mike C." being guilty were bogus, saying it was a test to see if he was talking to the police. Scott told him Sgt. Esposito, convinced someone else took part in the Rugh-Barker murders, came by a week ago to quiz him about who was hanging out during March 1980 (They were both killed on March 21, 1980). Nothing more was discovered about "Mike C."

Two days later Kushner called to say he was bringing Eric's statement over and said it would "hurt to read it." Bonin pointedly told him the written murder stories "would remain locked away until I have a deal in writing. I purposely wrote them before having to read any Eric statements so I wouldn't get hot and exasperated."

When informed Bonin was talking with Tim Alger for newspaper articles, Kushner told Bonin to "be careful with him." Kushner said he knew, from reliable sources, Alger was having an affair with Vernon Butts' old girlfriend, and had been ever since Butts got arrested. With particular relish Kushner said she liked "anal intercourse and giving head jobs." This whopping yarn, designed to upset Bonin, was put to rest by Alger two days later. Alger said Razook had shown him a tattoo just above her breast, but the rest was total lies, Bonin wrote, "I believe him." Detectives were pulling out all the stops to get at Bonin emotionally.

A first in the life of William Bonin, now the world-famous serial killer, took place on Tuesday, March 24, 1981. In the evening, while escorting Bonin to the Sgt.'s office, Deputy Voyer told him it was his last week at the jail and asked for his autograph.

Bonin rapidly declined, but the next morning changed his mind, "Today I decided that he had given me fair treatment all the time I've been here. I gave him a short note and signed with the additional name 'Jonathan' that I adopted myself as a secondary Christian name, derived from the story of Jonathan and David. David was a taker, Jonathan a giver. I feel I'm more a giver than a taker, as ironic as it sounds." This tidbit reveals a multi-dimensional character who at least acknowledges his severe problems, ones he could never change.

In the evening, from 6:45 to 9:00 p.m., Bonin had another meeting with Tim Alger. Nothing of much substance was discussed, but after Alger had a disagreement with deputies, he promised to return Friday morning. Bonin believed he knew the reason, "I get the feeling he wants to put something in Saturday's papers. Maybe not though, as he told me I'd get to read it before it came out in the paper. I hope he does a good, honest and fair article." Dave Lopez had been supplanted by Tim Alger.

Things are coming to a head; Bonin called his younger brother, Paul, to tell him homicide detectives were supposed to be meeting with the DA on Friday, March 27, saying, "So one way or another I'd know, hopefully, if I'll be offered a deal or not?"

That Friday would prove, like March 24, 1980, another watershed day in Bill Bonin's story. In the morning, Bonin's cell went thru a shake-down that wasn't too disruptive. Deputy Robbins was "decent" in helping Bonin retain the stock of candy bars and apples he had squirreled away. Bonin's mother came to visit, and she became acquainted with Barbara Wood, there to see Lawrence Bittaker, while sitting in the waiting room. Wood was a divorcee with two young children, 10 and 12, who lived in Hollywood.

Bonin later struck up an extremely strange friendship with Barbara Wood after Bittaker was sent to San Quentin. It remains unclear how Wood knew Bittaker. Never one to miss a dig at inmates, Deputy Campbell asked Bonin and Bittaker, just before they entered the visiting area, "Have you counted up how many you have between you two?" Bittaker ruefully answered, "Huh, I don't know what you're talking about."

Tim Alger showed up are 3:20 p.m. and, as revenge, the deputies put him through the ringer taking ex-rays, searching his stuff and delaying his entry as payment for his poor attitude during the previous visit.

"There fucking with him?" Bonin asked when he learned what was happening.

"Yeah, that's right," the deputy replied.

Conventional wisdom in jail says don't mess with the deputies because they run the place; get on their bad side and bad things happen. A simple procedure was stretched to 40-minutes of hassle by the recalcitrant deputies. But his visit was short, and he promised to return in a few hours. While the detectives and DA were meeting down the street, Bonin learned a number of things from an inmate, Roy Norris, about Jim Munro and jailhouse snitch Lloyd Douglas. Norris was Bittaker's co-murderer and testified against him during the trial. He was housed with Munro for three months and said Munro was "talking with everyone who will listen." Munro had little money, no visitors and was "having a hard time." Bonin, experienced in prison life, adapted to the circumstances and looked for shards of light anywhere he could find them.

Bonin explained more, "I was also told that two different trustees told Munro that if he testifies against me someone will get to him and that the threat came from me. I never sent over any such threat. The only thing I can think of is the trustees didn't want him making any deal. They wanted him to go to trial and get the Gas Chamber also. Norris also told me that Douglas is trying to get out and intends to split the country and not testify against me at my trial.

"That may be bad for me, as then they would be able to use the prelim testimony. I hear that if he does go to the trial, he may state to the questions of he will tell the truth that he takes the 5th and then turn and be real dramatic and look at the detectives and say, 'Now threaten me.' It would be interesting to see just what he would do?"

Around 5:30 p.m. Bonin phoned Kushner at the LA Sheriff's office, and then Esposito at the OC Sheriff's. The conversations delivered conflicting messages: Esposito said Orange County, expected to file multiple murders charges, will not go for a deal unless he "pleads guilty and guilty with special circumstances in front of a judge."

Kushner said all the other counties will go along if LA decides to offer a deal. He wrote, "I suppose all I do now is wait until a decision is made in L.A., which will be sometime at the end of next week."

Tim Alger came back at 6:30 p.m. and they talked for two-hours. Bonin's attorney came in at 8:30 to pick up the private investigator reports, and they left shortly afterwards, however, his attorney returned five minutes later to talk with Bonin, and it wasn't good news. Earl Hanson didn't want Alger present for what he had to say.

Hanson picked up the transcripts from Munro's post-arrest interviews, Bonin had already read the Miley and Butts transcripts, and said, "I was just told today that both Miley and Munro took 2nd Degree Murder charges, which is 15 to Life, and will testify against you." Later that night Bonin wrote in despair, "That really blows any chance I have of getting any type of deal."

With solid testimony from Miley and Munro, who participated in three murders, prosecutors could proceed with confidence in obtaining a Bonin death penalty. There was no mention of Pugh testifying, but his case was in the early stages and his attorney, Barrett, appeared strident about taking their chances. OC was sure to file charges within days, and Bonin knew that as well.

Giving up Eric, or anyone else, became less relevant every day.

Shifting back to the detectives, for nearly a month they tried every device to get Bonin to give up Eric, and others. Relentless pressure, on a near daily basis with various strongarm tactics, was employed so Bonin might react through emotion rather than with logic. Reason dictates Kushner, Esposito, Mellecker and Fueglein, who were in Bonin's face throughout March, knew the Miley-Munro deals were close and Bonin would shut down afterwards, which is what happened. This was partially correct: Two-months later, in early June, Sgt. Kushner told Bonin he was unaware of the deals until they happened. Bonin wrote that "he was transferred over it because the Sheriff was pissed. Then he was reinstated. It seems LAPD was the one that was working with the D.A. on it."

Kushner's June statement, which rings true as he had no reason to lie, offers certain conclusions: 1) LA and OC Sheriffs were in the dark about the Miley-Munro deal negotiations, 2) Meaning Kushner's partner Fueglein and Sgt. Esposito, lead detective for OC Sheriff's Dept. and a respected officer, were out in the cold. OC had been fighting over Bonin since his arrest, desperately wanting to put him on trial first. OC had filed no charges and had been losing the "Battle for Bonin" since the beginning (They tried to kidnap Bonin from LA County Jail shortly after his arrest, and nearly succeeded).

This leaves only Sgt. Kirk Mellecker, of the politically powerful LAPD Robbery-Homicide Division, who knew the deals were close. He was the only detective from LAPD who visited Bonin during March, although it was not nearly as often as the other three. LAPD and the prosecutor's office worked closely together to protect their respective turfs and reputations—institutional, professional and personal.

Even if they weren't in the loop, Kushner, Fueglein and Esposito must have heard rumors of an impending deal. Going on the assumption they felt something was imminent, but not privy to details, might explain their unrelenting pressure during late February and nearly all of March. Kushner was ambushed by the revelations and transferred in the wake of his bosses' displeasure; however, his restoration two months later indicates Kushner was not held accountable.

All the same these four detectives played Bonin for weeks while knowing he wouldn't be offered a deal, ever! Even if only Mellecker possessed knowledge of how the various Munro-Miley deal negotiations were going, all involved saw nothing but trouble if Bonin was offered a deal. Death penalty was the goal, and indeed was the only one that would satisfy police, prosecutors, politicians and the public.

Bonin risked everything to save Eric months earlier, and he wasn't going to repeat the mistake of talking with nothing in writing. Hoping for a deal based on giving up one last person, or persons, was a fool's errand all along. Too much was at stake for LA County DA Van de Kamp to throw away the ultimate penalty on suspects who may or may not be involved. With or without testimony from any accomplices, Van de Kamp was going to charge ahead to obtain a Bonin death penalty verdict.

Bonin wrote that that if Miley or Munro was "offered a deal they should take it, I would," thus leading to the conclusion it wasn't much of a surprise. In the back of his mind, Bonin must have known Miley and Munro would take a deal rather than swing for the guy who led them to personal destruction.

Bottom line: The whole month of March was a big game to find out as much as possible before the betting window closed. Laying down in his cell that night, Bonin was determined to protect whoever else was involved.

Bonin read the entire transcript of Munro's police interview, in Michigan just after being arrested, and was amused with him lying to detectives, how they knew it and their methods of pressuring him to tell everything. Munro still lied about many aspects of the murder, which Bonin noticed and commented on while reading the transcripts.

One day before Bonin's pre-trial hearing, one of those classic scenes from jail took place as Bonin relates, "A Mexican guy was constantly yelling on the row and saying, 'I'm safe, there's bars between me and you.' Him and another guy, Rocky Glover, had visitors and the Mex was brought out first and got handcuffed. Then Rocky went out and ran over and punched the Mexican in the face. They put Rocky in the hole and when the Mexican came back he was yelling to be let out. He finally lit a fire and threw it on to the Freeway between the cells.

"Senior Deputy O'Neal and McWilliams came down and O'Neal screamed, 'Are you the one making all the noise?' while McWilliams put the fire out with an extinguisher. They prepared to take him off the row and O'Neal told him not to say anything as he was leaving. Voyer came on the row and I commented as the Mex was close to passing my cell. I said, 'Boy, it's sure hard times.' The Mex stopped and said, looking at me, 'That's a killer, a killer!' O'Neal told him, 'Shut up and move, I told you not to say anything you dumb fuck.' Later O'Neal said, 'I should have slapped him alongside his head the dumb shit.' I told him not to say anything. 'I've got to keep my cool,' he commented on the way out."

March 30, a Monday, was an interesting day as the tumultuous month ended: 1) It was his parent's wedding anniversary, and he wrote that "even though his father had passed away my mother will go out and celebrate," 2) Larry Bittaker left for Death Row at San Quentin, causing Bonin to note, "I'll miss him. I'll probably see him again," 3) Bonin had a pre-trial hearing and two murder counts were dropped, Wirostek and John Doe, both done with Vernon Butts early on, 4) Judge Keene granted a 90-day trial delay and set a new start date for early August, 5) U.S. President Ronald Reagan was shot, in front of the Washington Hilton, and nearly killed by John Hinkley, Jr., causing Bonin to write, "Looks like someone wanted to get famous."

On March 31 Earl Hanson came to talk to Bonin about hiring another investigator. Apparently the one he had mind, a man names Tides, wanted $75 an hour for a job he estimated would require 400 hours of work. The budget was unlikely to be authorized by Judge Keene, so it looked out of question. Rumors came from Joe Ingler, the attorney who represented Butts, about a TV show that contacted him about a series. Hanson told Ingler to have them contact Bonin, saying, "I'm his attorney not his agent." Bonin was indifferent and didn't expect anything to happen.

For a second time Bonin phoned Barbara Wood to chat, learning about her divorce 7-years earlier, birthday and more about the kids. He wrote, "I then wrote her my first letter. Hopefully I can develop a good pen pal relationship." They would get closer in the following weeks. Wood started visiting Bittaker a few weeks earlier, and she accidentally met Bonin when both were in the visiting area. Attracted by the celebrity status of these men, Wood took up with Bonin after Bittaker was shipped out to Death Row.

Bonin was to stand trial on 12 murder counts in LA with more charges anticipated in Orange and San Bernardino Counties. With so many moving parts still to be nailed down, the delay gave everyone four-months to answer unanswered questions, fill in story gaps and iron out sticky legal issues.

52

Why Bonin Helped Eric & March 24, 1980!

Bonin covered for Eric Wijnaendts, who committed two murders with him, for three basic reasons—Love, Revenge and Spite. Eric held a special place in Bonin's heart, and he helped him because of those feelings. The second reason was tied to the first and was a two-for-one-bonus: Eric was charged for a murder Billy Pugh helped him commit. By telling detectives it was Pugh they wanted in the Turner case, something he might not have done if Eric hadn't been arrested, he got revenge on Pugh for putting the finger on him as the Freeway Killer and helped the person he "loved most in the world." The last reason was pure spite: Detectives Esposito, Kushner, Mellecker and Fueglein, who all had extensive interviews and discussions with Bonin, all firmly believed Eric was involved but were unable to definitively prove anything. Bonin knew this and dangled the possibility of giving them Eric until it was clear doing so wouldn't help him avoid the death penalty. Letting Eric skate was a thumb in the eye of the detectives.

Don't forget that, in part, Bonin spilled his guts to detectives in December 1980 to help Eric get out from under the Turner murder charges, a move he never would have made if he wasn't in trouble. While the interviews were kept secret for many months, this decision changed everything.

And it all ties back to March 24, 1980—the day when the paths of Bonin, Fraser, Wijnaendts and Pugh all crossed, the day when, if one of those paths changed slightly, then events to follow would have been altered dramatically! It was also the day firebrand reporter J.J. Maloney, OC Register, broke the Freeway Killer story, the first of many front-page articles which shocked the public and put detectives under intense pressure.

53

Munro's Deal, Tim Alger's Articles, OC Files Charges & Lawyer Changes
April 1981

On April Fool's Day 1981, a Wednesday, many newspapers carried articles about two of the 14-murder charges against Bonin getting dropped, and the trial being postponed from May 4 till August 3.

Not a prank, it meant Bonin's reckoning would wait and be for two less killings. Thomas Lundgren, whom Bonin didn't kill, was still amongst the charges. Pressure eased with the trial taking place in four-months, rather than four-weeks, as a new phase in the Bonin story began with the Miley-Munro deals.

Delay also meant risk in the perilous environment of a highly publicized, high stakes serial killer murder trial. Regarding the testimony of Miley and Munro, the first step was a plea hearing where each answered a series of questions confirming they were of sound mind and understood the situation, then a plea was entered.

According to the ***Law Enforcement Institute*** plea bargains are viewed this way, "A defendant breaking a plea bargain is akin to a breach of contract, which will result in the prosecutor no longer being bound by his or her obligation in the plea deal. If a prosecutor reneges on plea bargains, defendants may seek relief from the judge. The judge might let the defendant withdraw the guilty pleas, may force the prosecutor to follow the plea bargain, or may apply some other remedy."

While federal and local courts are different, in most plea agreements, with promised testimony, a judge is unlikely to deviate from a prosecutor's sentence recommendations. This differs from a straight plea agreement where a judge can impose a different penalty, which is usually lighter, or the defense will rescind the plea. For a variety of reasons, such as extremis, change of heart or veracity, witnesses never deliver their court testimony, and this leads to one hard truth: Nothing is certain till a witness is answering questions in front of judge and jury.

On the road from cutting a deal to testifying in court, witnesses need to be protected and sometimes coddled, and that can be difficult in a place like LA Men's Central Jail. I, Vonda Pelto, was brought to Los Angeles Men's Central Jail in August 1981 for a purpose; helping to keep defendants and/or witnesses alive until their trials were over. Much had evolved in the Bonin Freeway Killer cases since his arrest, nine months earlier, and more will change in the days ahead.

Bonin was anxious to see Tim Alger, the **OC Register** reporter who interviewed him in March. Alger was writing an article series and Bonin was promised a look-see before going to press. He also wanted to see Todd Landgren, but his personal attorney was busy as Bonin noted, "Attorneys have to the busiest people in the world. They're always on the go or have a place they're already late at being there."

Irony ruled the day when Roy Norris, who testified against co-murderer Lawrence Bittaker, was moved to Bittaker's old cell on Bonin's row. During their many chess games, Norris told him he wanted to withdrawal his guilty plea in a belief his "civil rights had been violated." Norris got the deal, testified in court against Bittaker, now he wants withdrawal his plea on a flimsy pretense that won't hold water.

Bonin kept an active tally of how many chess games they played with wins, losses and ties dutifully reported in his writings. He learned from Norris, for the first time, that Lloyd Douglas, the jailhouse snitch, was Larry Sharp's uncle though a half-brother. Sharp was one of the last killed, with Eric, and Bonin found this news "interesting."

Bonin did not find a replacement friend for Bittaker in Roy Norris, as he relates, "I sure wish Larry was back. Roy is such a bullshitter. I hardly listen to him anymore. All I do is let him talk on and on and on. Every once in a while, I'll say 'yeah' or 'oh, ah ha.' While he's rambling on I'm writing or doing something else. I really don't know what he's saying as I'm not listening. I just make a grunt or something when he pauses, which is too often."

Norris and Bittaker were truly evil characters; their calculated torture, rape and murder of five teenage girls was heinous.

Fires continued to be lit up and down Bonin's row and deputies continued to put them out, but they were getting sick of the process.

Inmates down the row lit a mattress cover on fire and within minutes the area was choked with deadly smoke. Angry deputies rushed down with a fire extinguisher, put out the fire and sprayed the inmate in retribution.

Later deputies shook down the row, "When I got back to my cell I found my ***Playboy***, ***Oui*** and other magazines gone, along with some hard books I used as a pillow. They took my chess board but not my chess pieces. They took my playing cards also. All in all I came thru it with a very minor effect. I can replace everything in a matter of a day or so.

"The cards were getting old anyways. I had two $5 bills and change in my cell. It was still there when I came back. They took everyone's matches and even some cigarettes. I was left with two books of matches. They took a lot of extra bedding from the other end of the row. Since that is where the fire was."

He saw Tim Alger on Thursday, April 2. They spoke for about two-hours on a wide range of issues, he was especially curious about Bonin's views on Miley, Munro and their deals. When he departed, Bonin was left handcuffed and alone in the meeting room for over an hour because "the deputies are playing games with me as they don't like Tim Alger." He kept calling Barbara Wood and exchanging letters, learning she was a Born Again Christian and more with each encounter. She was amenable to being in contact, wanted to visit more and even encouraged Bonin to write letters directly to her young children.

Ellen was back in Los Angeles, staying at Mary's, and Bonin was on the phone with her on the evening of Monday, April 6. Her appearance meant discussions with Bonin about marriage were ongoing. Ellen mentioned she saw Munro on TV news about his deal, for second degree murder, with a sentence of 15-years to life. Bonin reacted this way, "I know he'll probably do 20 or more. It may be time to pull my safety valve on dear old James. It seems he is completely ignoring the fact. Possibly because I never said anything. Only time will tell, but it may end up old James gets bit in the ass by his past doings."

Was this a threat or just a comment about him probably spending the rest of his life in prison?

Details hit the papers and proved interesting reading. Munro's deal was constructed to protect the case as reported by AP in ***The Paducah Sun***, in Kentucky: "Deputy D.A. Norris told Superior Court Judge Everett Ricks that, after Munro pleads guilty to 2nd degree murder, prosecution will seek the maximum sentence, which means Munro would have to serve at least 10 years before he can be considered for parole."

Two additional counts of robbery and sodomy will be dropped at the sentencing hearing, which takes place after he testifies against Bonin. AP also reported that "Orange County will not file charges against Munro in the Wells murder if he testifies against Bonin" and that deal negotiations with Miley and Pugh were progressing.

After reading the newspapers, Bonin presciently wrote, "The first to fall. I wonder if he realizes that he'll do a minimum of 20 years before he has any chance of getting out. I do have to say though that he was smart enough to take the deal. I wish he would have held off though. Then they may have offered me a deal. I would have taken it and then he could have taken his deal. It is definitely not looking too good for me. It's always the darkest before the dawn."

Bonin was right; Munro is still in prison over 40-years later.

On Thursday, April 9, Jim Munro was moved downstairs from 7000 to Bonin's section in the High Power Unit. Located on the opposite side from Bonin on Row F, deputies were tasked with keeping Munro and Bonin apart. Norris went through the same type of move; prior to testifying against Bittaker he was upstairs to 7000 and roomed with Munro for three-months. Then he was moved down after Bittaker left; in contrast Munro was moved down right after making a deal and months prior to testifying at Bonin's trial. Highly agitated best describes Munro's state of mind after the move.

Through Norris he learned what Munro went through upstairs, "He told me tonight that the reason they had moved Munro into the same room with someone, namely him, was that they caught Munro fiddling with his sheets and corners, trying to put them around the grill to the vent in an attempt to commit suicide. The deputies had a 15-minute check on him 24-hours per-day for a long time and finally decided it was better to move in someone. That made it easier on the deputies and had someone around him all the time. Norris told me about two times he got so frustrated at Munro that he fired him up (punched out). Munro also beat Norris at a game of chess. He can't be as retarded as they say."

Bonin was up in 7000 and 8000 for a short time and hated it, "It was bad up there. They wouldn't give me and salt or sugar with my meals. They had me housed where all the diabetics were and wouldn't put any extra salt or sugar out for me. They said it was too much of a hassle. They also cut the radio speaker off that was piped to my room. That made it doubly worse. Guys came by gawking at me, making threats and one asked a deputy for five-minutes in the cell with me, I am pretty sure I could have taken him. No one to talk to and no music. They wouldn't let me have my radio in 8000 like they did in 7000. They ended up losing my radio when I got moved back to 1700 High Power. I put in a claim and no telling how long it will take before it is resolved."

Bonin caught a glimpse of Munro while moving about and noted "he looked squirrely as hell. It looks like he lost weight." Then he got a warning from Senior Taplin, who came over to the row gate for a chat.

"Bonin, stay away from Row F," the Senior Deputy told Bonin with stern authority.

"Taplin, you guys are full of surprises," Bonin replied in jest. "Does he know I'm down here?"

"Oh, he knew you were down here before he came down."

"He didn't want to come down, did he?" Bonin asked, knowing the answer.

"No, he didn't, and he isn't too happy about it."

Bonin concluded, "If Munro would have kept his mouth shut he'd still be up in 7000. Now that he's made a deal and is going to testify against me they'll mess over him some."

Bittaker wrote Bonin a letter from Death Row at San Quentin, which he received on Friday, April 10, "Got a letter from Larry tonight. He told me all about the trip up and things that happened after he got there. I enjoyed the letter until I go to the part where he said, 'Am thinking seriously about taking a trip to Carfus. Why not?' What he's referring to is suicide. It brought my eyes to a mist as I know what he is going thru. I'll have to get on his case about thinking that way. Although I wonder why. I sent a letter to Larry and tried to cheer him up. I hope I accomplish it." For the second time, Bonin was confronted with Bittaker's suicidal thoughts, and both times he sought to intervene.

That same day, following a visit with his mother and attorney, he met with Alger and was shown the first articles, Bonin was pleased, "I feel they were fair and gave me some good publicity for a change."

A phone call to Barbara Wood proved interesting as she wondered why Bonin had not asked her to visit. His explanation of a clogged waiting room made her more determined to visit soon, maybe even the next day. For her to possess such a keen desire to see him buoyed Bonin's flagging spirits.

Bonin reveals two mind sets, "Tuesday, April 14: There was a guy moved into cell #1 from 'A' Row today. He's no more than 19 or 20, blond hair and I believe blue eyes. Everyone on the row started telling everyone else that he was just 'what Bill likes.' Referring to me. I have to admit I wouldn't throw him out of bed. In my situation there's little that I would throw out of bed.

"I'm in no position to be choosey, not that I expect to ever get a chance to do anything with anyone. I received a letter from Ellen tonight. She says she has fallen in love with me. That makes me feel so good inside. She sent me three more photos of herself. She's some foxy looking young lady. I wrote and told her so. It would be a dream come true to have a good-looking girl like this to be my wife and Mother of my Child."

Days were filled with numerous calls to Mary, Ellen and his various attorneys, all producing a stream of mundane writing about kids, bikes, family gossip, occasional visits from Barbara and not much else. Deputies running the jail gave Bonin a new moniker and it became official when Bonin commented about it on Saturday, April 18, "When the deputies came around with a nurse he made the comment, 'Wild Bill, what's happening?' It seems that most of the officers are calling me that now. It's the first time I've had any type of nickname. Not that I like it fully, but it is better than being called by my last name."

Bonin got sanguine after speaking with his older brother, Bob, who criticized him over the phone for speaking with reporters too much. What Bob didn't know was that a major expose, done with Bonin's participation, was going to be published the next day.

Bonin reacted this way, "Sunday, April 19: If I would have had the time to talk I might have explained this. I talked to Tim Alger and Dave Lopez because I needed someone to talk to. I was hungry for someone to talk to. I can't seem to get it thru Earl's head that I want someone to talk to. He says that he doesn't want the D.A. to be able to say I'm getting any special privileges. It's hurting me a lot more not having someone to talk to. I'm just going to have to get someone here to see me and rap, in confidence, even if I have to end up paying them myself. That is, I'd have to promise them something when I have it. I'm all tense tonight. I'm trying to find a way out of the Gas Chamber. That ugly 'Green Room' that is only used for one purpose. To extinguish life."

Stuck in a void, fighting for a glimmer of hope in darkness, Bonin was in a state akin to the boys, who were led to believe all would be well, until he snuffed out their lives. Keeping hope alive, then seeing it disappear from their eyes, is elemental in a serial killer's stream of peccadillos. Exercising that power pushes people like Bonin towards the next rush; the process of hunting, capturing, raping and killing consumes them. With power over life and death resting with the government, Bonin was the one searching for a glimmer of hope, a shard of light in a darkening horizon.

Over a period of three weeks Tim Alger had spent about 20-hours talking with Bonin and the first of three articles, printed in succession, appeared in the **OC Register** on Monday, April 20. **Bonin: 'I Was on a Destruction Course'** was preceded by an Editor's Note indicating Bonin's "reluctance to talk to reporters" because, as he told Alger, "I now have nothing to gain by it."

Alger's articles were the first expose, with Bonin's complete cooperation, which appeared in the print press. Each article was skillfully crafted, carefully encapsulating many sides of Bonin's personality and giving the public a view of things from his perspective. Alger slid in at the perfect time, right when Bonin was miffed at Lopez and looking for another media outlet.

Chronicling Bonin's thoughts about each accomplice proved interesting: he couldn't understand why Billy Pugh believed nothing would come out after he fingered Bonin, also believing Pugh "was guessing" when he told detectives Bonin was the Freeway Killer (Fair assumption). Bonin claimed he never told Pugh about killing lots of kids by "strangling them with their t-shirts and using an iron bar for leverage" (Sounds like something Bonin might brag about, but he could be telling the truth). Lastly, Bonin said Pugh would probably never have talked if he hadn't been arrested (Also a fair assumption).

Bonin said Butts didn't expect to get caught as he "thought we weren't leaving any evidence behind." He said Butts was "very intelligent and a very good magician. Other than the murders, Butts was a good guy. But I think all magicians are pretty strange." Alger reported that Butts believed his house was haunted by ghosts, and that Bonin almost moved in with him until realizing he was a complete slob.

Going quickly through Bonin's history, the article ends with bullet points about his mother, Munro, and Miley. He said his mother believed he was "innocent but wants the truth to come out." Claiming he didn't know Munro was a gay "hustler" in Hollywood, Bonin thought he had just arrived in town and "was looking for something." He couldn't recall first meeting Miley at Fraser's but did recall "he would get drunk and obnoxious." He hadn't seen Miley since the murders, on February 3, 1980, unlike Munro whom he saw briefly at the jail.

Second in the series, **Bonin Directs His Hatred at Jailmate Snitch**, focused entirely on Lloyd Douglas, the "professional jailhouse snitch" who testified at Bonin's prelim, Bittaker's trial and was set to so in another murder trial. Not feeling betrayed by Miley, Munro, Butts or Fraser for talking, Bonin held a special enmity for Douglas. Expanding on regurgitated info from rumors and news stories, Douglas' veracity was severely damaged by claiming so many inmates "confessed" to him on the full extent of their crimes, and in detail.

Alger described an example, "Douglas claims that Bonin told him he buried bodies or tried to hide them first, but then began dumping them out in the open because the corpses were always found anyway. 'He told me how, to make it easier, on him, he'd just dump them off the freeway,' Douglas testified. 'He would, as he was pulling onto the freeway, he'd open the two sides (of his van) and just throw the body right out there and let it roll down a little in the bushes.' None of the boys Bonin has been charged with killing was dumped on a freeway or a freeway on-ramp. 'Now why would I tell him that?' Bonin asked, his voice raised. 'To give him a bogus story? Then why would I tell him the truth in anything else?'

"And Bonin says he's baffled by Douglas' statement that Douglas slapped Bonin when he 'would get into the graphic details,' but Bonin would come back, 'sniveling and crying,' to apologize. 'I've done over nine years in prison,' Bonin said. 'I've come across a lot of rough people. If I can handle guys putting pressure on me in the joint, why would I back down from a guy like this? It doesn't make sense to me.' Bonin appears to be a guy who wants to be trusted, but he's calculating in what he says—and what he doesn't say. Douglas, of course, has been to the 7000 block in the jail, a protective custody section that also was home for Munro until recently. Douglas has few friends back on 1700."

Alger reported that Douglas received a sentence reduction for his testimony.

Alger's final article, ***Bonin Sees Gas Chamber Waiting After Trial***, started with Alger going thru the other killers housed with Bonin, in section 1700, and noting he only "saw the sky" through grated van windows going to court. Alger pointed out that a conviction of the suspected 21 murders was "highly unlikely," but that the judge ruled there was enough evidence to schedule a trial. Bonin told Alger, "If the case goes to a jury, I think they would go all the way with me. Trial means almost certainly the gas chamber."

Accepting his fate realistically, Bonin said of course he wanted to get out but knew it was impossible, "I am willing to do anything I can to save my life as long as it's truthful. I would not put somebody involved that is not involved. I would rather take the death penalty."

Alger explored Bonin's dealings with detectives. Bonin's claim of telling detectives everything while admitting "he had lied" was incongruous as he also said, "If I could give them something, I'd use it in a hot second to get a deal." Alger reported that detectives still suspected others and were weary of Bonin offering truth and then telling lies, they were right.

He wrote about Bonin helping Eric Wijnaendts, after his December 1980 arrest, and giving detectives the right suspect, Billy Pugh. Breaking six-months of silence to help Eric, and revealing details on every suspected murder, Bonin didn't tell detectives "anything new and certainly nothing valuable enough for them to begin plea bargaining something in return for testimony."

As recounted earlier, Eric played it smart and said he was confused about one particular night, when he was extremely drunk and couldn't accurately recall events. Detectives utilized that confusion to help establish, mistakenly, his involvement with the Turner murder.

Alger described what happened, "Investigators drove Wijnaendts to the site where Turner's body was dumped in central Los Angeles. 'This would be a good place to dump a body,' he observed. And when detectives confronted him with their belief he helped Bonin kill Turner, Wijnaendts said, 'It all makes sense.'

"Bonin now says the investigators confused Wijnaendts, 'a kid who is absolutely innocent.' He shakes his head in disbelief. 'They were convincing this kid he committed a murder.' To get Wijnaendts off, Bonin insisted it was Pugh who helped, and Pugh subsequently confessed, police say."

Bonin said to Alger, "If I had kept my mouth shut, Eric Wijnaendts would have gone to the gas chamber and left Billy Pugh sitting outside, free. And Eric would have gone to the chamber thinking he might have actually done it." Alger described the dilemma; detectives convinced he will "never tell the whole story—if there are still others involved," and Bonin's disbelief they won't believe "what he tells them." Alger, of course, didn't know Eric was indeed involved in the deaths of Larry Sharp and Sean King, or that Bonin had dropped hints to detectives about Eric in both killings.

While the California Supreme Court stopped all gas chamber executions, during their discussions Bonin said he thought it would be used again, and probably soon. Alger's last article ended with Bonin arguing against capital punishment on religious grounds, a self-serving position when he said this about advocates for capital punishment, "You are killing and they are guilty for it." One detective said to Alger, "If Bonin doesn't deserve the death penalty, who does?"

Who learned what from the articles gives us a late April 1981 snapshot: 1) Detectives and prosecutors didn't pick-up anything new, but their faith in Douglas as a credible "jailhouse snitch" was embarrassing, 2) Media outlets received info hitherto unknown, especially about how events transpired with Eric and Pugh and Bonin's relationship with his accomplices, 3) Up till this time the public knew very little of how Bonin thought, spoke or viewed his current situation. Alger revealed many aspects of a more complicated and conflicted person than the public previously knew, 4) Dave Lopez, believing he had an exclusive arrangement with Bonin, felt betrayed and angry.

Lopez immediately visited the jail to personally express his feelings, as Bonin relates, "Wednesday, April 22: Dave Lopez came up and talked. He was hot about me talking to Alger. He said he felt I broke our agreement and that he was no longer obligated to that agreement. So he may run with the story on me saying I confessed to him. I told him that I couldn't stop him so I wait and see what he does and then handle it. He told me that Munro had an interview with the **Long Beach Press Telegram** and was stated as saying that I told him I killed 44, that Butts killed 16 and that Pugh killed 5 and that I sent a note to Munro saying, 'You're Dead.' I never stated these things to Munro and I never sent or wrote any such note. I was only out there talking to Lopez for less than 10-minutes. But I was exhausted once I was finished. I came back and had to lie down and rest.

"Earl showed up and brought me an 8-inch stack of reports of all sorts. He says he has more for me. He brought me several books. I chose three to read. So I'll have a lot to read now. I'll read as much as I can over the next two days before he comes back on Friday. At least he says he'll be back on Friday. He was upset with the call he got from Lopez. Lopez says he is going to run the story tonight saying I confessed to umpteen murders, etc. It looks like it will get darker then it will get lighter. The weight of it all is going to be heavy. I can visualize it all now."

That evening Bonin asked Senior O'Neal to watch Lopez reporting on Channel 2 News. He dutifully reported that Lopez talked about Billy Pugh being bound over for trial and a quote from Bonin about him. Lopez kept the confession secret and Bonin was relieved at not having to deal with the blowback, along with being grateful to Senior O'Neal for helping him out.

Lopez, furious at losing what he believed was an exclusive story, wanted to broadcast the story but two legal factors held him back. On December 18, 1981, a David Shaw feature article in the ***Los Angeles Times***, following Lopez's decision to reverse course and testify at Bonin's trial, reported that KCBS TV "would not let Lopez go on the air with the Bonin story then anyway, Lopez said, for fear of jeopardizing Bonin's right to a fair trial. They were also concerned that the story might result in Lopez being subpoenaed, he said."

While Bonin wrote that he told Lopez he "couldn't stop him," throwing up his hands in defeat, in Shaw's article Lopez's version of the encounter is a bit different: "Lopez conceded that Alger's stories, which contained some allegedly self-incriminating statements by Bonin, did not contain most of the details and the case-by-case confession that Bonin had given the television newsman.

"But Lopez said he still saw Bonin's disclosures to Alger as violating their agreement, thus freeing Lopez from his pledge of confidentiality. 'I went to Bonin in jail and said, 'You son of a bitch. You bastard. You broke our agreement. I'm going on the air,' Lopez said.

"Bonin denied having abrogated their agreement, Lopez said. He said, 'I told you I would confess, not that I wouldn't talk about the case at all.' Lopez said."

This issue would hang fire and flare up again in June.

Bonin became really depressed and ruminated about "getting the death penalty." He also saw it another way, "I really don't want to go to trial, but I'm forced to in order to have more and actually the utmost time on appeal." Finding light in the darkness was trademark Bonin.

Bonin used contact with Barbara as a way to keep communicating with someone, this despite a letter from Bittaker saying he told her "not to come and visit because Bonin can do without the visits." Barbara in turn told Bonin she enjoyed the visits and would continue the practice. Continued communication even saw her allowing Bonin to write letters directly to and speak with her two young children, over the phone. Interacting with them was a balm to his isolated and depressed state of mind.

Updates on Greg Miley and Jim Munro, through Roy Norris, introduced a new player into the story, criminal defense attorney William Charvet. Norris told Bonin he heard that charges against Miley, in Orange County, were dropped based on double jeopardy, where someone can't be charged for the same crime in different jurisdictions, or twice in the same jurisdiction. Munro wanted to switch attorneys, to possibly retract his deal, after realizing he could spend much more than the 10-years he was promised. It was ten-years before he was up for parole, so it was a promise with a proviso, and it got Munro nervous and agitated.

All these rumors came to Norris through his lawyer, Charvet, who secured him a deal in exchange for testifying against his friend and co-murderer. While a highly experienced criminal defense lawyer, his actions in a number of cases actions showed a nefarious streak. Conversations with Norris about Charvet created a situation which altered future events dramatically.

According to an appeal declaration, filed many times, Bonin revealed that "Roy Norris told me that, in an effort to obtain some money, he had entered into an agreement with an attorney named William T. Charvet to sell Charvet the book rights interest in his life story. Norris suggested that if I needed some money, I should contact Charvet and make a deal." This started the wheels turning between Bonin and Charvet, but it was a slow grind.

A stack of investigative reports delivered by Hanson, generated by their private eye, provided interesting reading and passed the time. Turned out Bonin's old girlfriend, Mary, was previously arrested for Child Cruelty. Not surprised, Bonin saw her children often and took them roller skating and on weekend outings. Reams of documents from Social Security, Bonin received benefits while in prison years earlier, and the VA rounded out reports about witnesses, victims, etc.

Bonin relates accidentally seeing Munro, "Wednesday, April 29: Jim was talking to the Senior, Stewart, this evening and looked over in my direction and we came eye to eye for two or three minutes. I just nodded and he nodded. I smiled and he smiled. I don't think he really expected to see me before he got to court and testified against me. I sure would like for him to take back his deal. It would give me a chance to get out of the Death Penalty."

The previous shows Bonin engaging in selective memory when reviewing the chain of events which led to the confession interviews, but he made some good points; his attorney only got tacit agreement that his cooperation might help, and a written agreement that his interviews could not be used in court without a deal. However, it looks like the interviews were somehow in play without a deal. Bonin had been adamant about speaking with detectives, for many reasons cited earlier, and so putting the blame back on his attorney was disingenuous.

Here is how he felt three months after, "I got very uptight when I think of how the D.A. conned me into telling him everything during those three days back in December 1980. Right after they started their game, changing their stories, saying I really didn't give them anything. I told about all 22 and how it all went down. I gave them Billy Pugh and got Eric cut loose. I showed them where Sean King's body remains were. But I didn't give them anything. They said it helped my case and hurt theirs when I gave them Billy Pugh. I changed him from being star witness to a co-defendant. They told me I knew all of the rest. They said there are more co-defendants still free. I had only given them King's body, nothing more! They now say there was no written agreement."

When it appeared Bonin was definitely going to be charged and arraigned in Orange County, an inmate sent Bonin a warning note, "Bill: What I am about to say is that I would appreciate it if you would allow me to explain to you how I came to learn this. There are a few from Psyche on

Third Row who need to be watched. I have never been to Orange County jail but I have learned there is no High Power there. Once you leave here to fight your case there, you will lose your life within four days you are there. All I can say is watch your step whatever you do. Don't put your trust in too many people's hands. I have said too much. Take care of yourself my friend."

Bonin wrote back, "There is a High Power there. I have done 9-years locked up. I have a natural born instinct and training and actual experience in Vietnam to use my instinct. I will rely on that instinct." That night Bonin had a strange dream. He was in Army boot camp walking behind a drill sergeant that looked from behind like fellow inmate Roy Taylor, who Bonin hated. His dream ended with Bonin using a machine to "shoot everyone in sight." With three-months till Bonin's murder trial in LA Superior Court, the only thing certain was that nothing was certain.

54

Witness Developments, Pugh Strategy, Jailhouse Tales & Bonin Gets Engaged
May 1981

Events continued to evolve as months of negotiations between prosecutors and attorneys settled a number of pressing issues. Bonin continued to talk with Barbara Wood, over the phone, on a near daily basis, and once spoke with her young daughter about a visit to Disneyland with her brother and father. Wood obviously didn't mind an accused serial killer speaking with her impressionable offspring, and in fact encouraged it. One wonders if Barbara's ex-husband knew about his children getting letters from and speaking with the notorious Bill Bonin?

Macabre jailhouse humor amid the tragic nature of human life was on display when Danny Young, accused of killing his ten-year old neighbor, saw an unlikely acquaintance, "Friday, May 1: Today has been quite interesting. The detective that questioned Young in Nevada came on a tour. They walked right past my cell and Young's along with every other cell on the row. They were on the other of the glass though. Young said to them that he was going to walk and made a walking motion with his hand and two fingers from his other hand. Then he made a written sign saying, 'You lose.' When they looked at him again before leaving, from the foyer, they saw the sign. The guy grabbed his own necktie and made like a hangman and laughed." Young's complex case proved troublesome and the fallout from it lasted for decades.

Following Tim Alger's three-article expose in the **OC Register**, Bonin's attorney forbade all further media contact. As a result, when Alger came by that afternoon, Bonin refused to see him but ended up speaking with Sgt. Esposito. Turned out the rumor about Miley's OC charges getting dismissed was only that, the hearing was just postponed. That morning, in LA, Miley pled guilty to 1st degree murder as part of a deal to testify against Bonin, set to yield him a sentence of 25-years to life. As with Munro, final sentencing would be delayed till after Miley testified and all the trials ended. Prosecutors were taking no chances on getting burned, causing Bonin to note, "He'll never get out, just like Munro."

Esposito said Pugh was going to trial and "wouldn't be offered a deal." Surely the detective was lying as everyone, except Bonin, were offered deals of some kind. All the District Attorney's efforts were focused on obtaining a Bonin death penalty verdict. Pugh's privately retained attorney, Ed Barrett, who leaned heavily on Bonin about testifying against Pugh, had a number of factors on his side which made going for a jury trial a viable option.

During the evening someone lit a bunch of newspapers on fire and threw them into the middle of the row, which went unnoticed by the deputies until they burned out completely and left a smoky corridor. Kitchen trustees were brought in to sweep up the mess.

Always thinking ahead, Bonin endeavored to find someone who might represent him during the appeals. Should he get the death penalty, the tactic was appeal as often as possible to delay the inevitable. He learned from Bob Acosta that Terry Giles, the latter advising Bonin on personal matters, had the best appeals attorney in the state, Bob App, working at his law firm. Bonin called Giles to arrange a meeting.

Two days later he reflected on Miley's situation, "Sunday, May 3: Greg made his guilty plea and will do the same in Orange County on May 15, 1981. I was expecting him to do so and he did. It still left an empty feeling in my stomach and head. I may just go ahead and do a plea myself to get all of this over. It will all depend on the answers I get next week. If I'm going to make a plea myself, I should make my decision before Greg does." The "answers" Bonin needed were the expected OC murder charges.

With Pugh's arraignment scheduled for Friday, May 8, Bonin wanted to speak with Ed Barrett, and it turned out the feeling was mutual. Both of them needed to know what the other intended or was thinking: Bonin if Barrett was going to advise Pugh to take a deal and testify against him; Barrett if Bonin would take the stand against his client.

On Tuesday, May 5 Barrett and a legal associate met with Bonin for two hours. The discussion started with Barrett's associate prattling on about his "feeling" that the kid Bonin and Pugh picked up was a different person (Sounds like speculation to muddy the waters). All agreed Pugh should only take a deal as a Youth Offender, this since he was a juvenile when the crime took place and because all other scenarios involved substantial prison time.

Bonin described the primary issues, "We talked about me getting on the stand. At least I don't have to worry about Billy testifying against me unless he's offered Youth Offender time and then I feel he should take it. Ed still isn't sure if he can trust me. I told him that if I say I'll do something I'll do it. Ed Barrett also told me that the homicide detectives suspect me of 44 murders. He said that they sincerely think this. Boy that's a bunch of crap."

Detectives long ago announced it was impossible for Bonin to have killed 44, something Barrett would know. A sharp operator with a keen strategic sense, Barrett was goading Bonin for his own purposes.

Knowing Bonin wasn't going testify against Pugh gave Barrett freedom to employ four solid arguments at trial: 1) Billy Pugh was a juvenile when the crime took place, 2) He was only involved in one murder, 3) Bonin was perceived as being able to lure vulnerable young men to help him kill, 4) Perhaps most important, Pugh freely volunteered the key tip which stopped Bonin's murder spree when authorities were totally in the dark.

Barrett banked on these factors leading to a much lighter sentence than the ones which Miley and Munro expected to receive. One fact was obvious: Without Pugh a few more, possibly many more, teenage boys would have been murdered because Bonin wasn't known to police when he sounded the alarm.

The next day deputies came through the row and removed all the glass mirrors from every cell. Aryan Brotherhood gang members were breaking off glass shards to fashion into "jailhouse shanks" for killing or injuring rival gang members or troublesome inmates. All of them would be replaced with plastic mirrors, which are safer but far less effective for grooming purposes. Devoid of a mirror for shaving, Bonin improvised by using his prescription sunglasses as a makeshift mirror.

Barbara Wood visited Bonin with a friend, "I saw Barbara on a visit. She brought her friend Nancy to see me also. I didn't talk with Nancy. It was an interesting visit. We were laughing throughout. Carl Hubbs wife went up and started asking Barbara questions in the visiting room. I got on Carl's case as he is an admitted snitch. I could just see having another informant against me. This evening they had some kind of press on C row. They had all kinds of Seniors and Sgts and a Lt. Three deputies had on helmets and flak jackets on. It ended with them taking a Mexican to A row."

On the morning of Saturday, May 9 Bonin saw an article in the **Herald Examiner** stating that Pugh would not testify against Bonin "without total immunity from all charges." Deputy DA Stovitz refused to comment on the matter.

Bonin wrote, "I'm glad to hear about this. It makes me feel halfway better. I just hope that he sticks by his guns. I doubt if they'll offer him complete clearance of the charges. He may get Youth Offender time though."

Later that day Bonin's mother visited and was forced to wait three hours. In the visiting area Bonin saw an old friend from Vacaville State Prison and received an affirmation regarding his notorious fame, "When I went into the visiting room I saw some fine looking homosexuals. Coming out I saw Bill Archibald. He had a white patch on his shoulder which denotes him as a homosexual. I asked the deputy if the guy was Bill Archibald. He said he didn't know.

"Then he walked over and told the guy, 'Let me see your wristband.' The guy showed the deputy his band and was wondering what was going on. Then the deputy turned toward me and said, 'Yes, he is.' Then Bill looked over at me and I nodded. He squinted his eyes and said, 'Is that Bonin?' I nodded again and smiled. As I passed him he told his visitors, 'There he is.' I'm sure he was telling them about me before I passed. His visitors must have asked him where he knew me as I heard him say Vacaville."

Following a phone conversation with Terry Giles, the notion of going to trial quickly if OC filed charges became a point of interest. Bonin decided that, if they filed, he would request a trial in 60-days, which was his right, in order to create as much confusion as possible between the two jurisdictions. There was little chance the defense team could "force" a trial in 60-days if the prosecution needed more time or extenuating circumstances existed, like another trial in Los Angeles.

A slice of jailhouse existence occurred that evening, "The guy in cell #1 was acting bitchy tonight. Talking tall shit to two Mexicans down the row who occupy cells #10 & 11. He calls the guy in cell #11 his daddy and tells the guy in cell #10 that he may get thrown off the second tier. That was after the guy in #10 said it to him. Cell #5, Young, and cell #6, Peter

Buono, really got cell #1 riled. They were talking about his wife and claiming to have had sex with her. He was crying by the time they finished with him. The man (deputy) had to tell him to shut up, he was yelling so loud. Anyway cell #1 finally asked the man if he could be moved. They told him it was up to the day shift. He told the man that Buono and Young were saying things about his wife."

Amidst squabbles with other inmates, phone calls to and visits from Barbara and his attorney, it turned out a celebrity of sorts was interested in meeting Bonin. Earl Hanson was representing Jacqueline Carlin in her divorce from comedic actor Chevy Chase. When she asked Hanson to write a brief, which he didn't want to do until learning more, he conjured up a fake client meeting at LA County Jail.

"You mean you'd leave my case and go and talk to a guy on some drunk driving case?" she acidly asked Hanson.

"As a matter of fact, the guy I'm going to see is more famous than you," Hanson replied bluntly.

"Ok, and who would that be?"

"Bill Bonin, the Freeway Killer, I'm sure you know about him," he replied while eyeing her reaction.

"Really… you know I'd really like to meet and talk with him," Carlin replied in all seriousness.

"You're kidding," Hanson exclaimed with surprise, "I'm sure after all the celebrities you've been around, with all their fancy parties and drugs, that you'd find him a very, very dull person to talk with. Bill is not into any of that stuff."

Hanson saw Bonin the next day and related the story, which he found intriguing, "I just do what I do. But no drugs or alcohol, etc. I hope she comes to visit. It would really be super."

Next was Miley's guilty plea in Orange County on Friday, May 15. Miley agreed to testify against Bonin and, since his final sentencing was not until November, it meant OC was sure to file against Bonin. With his LA trial set for Monday, August 3, Bonin reasoned they would have to "file now in order for my trial to go right after L.A. is through. What they don't know is that I intend on going for a trial in 60-days. I dread going to Orange County. Yet I know it is coming and I have to go through it. It's the only way I can stretch my appeal out to 10 or so years. If I could get Life

Without I'd plead guilty. I know I can't. So because of politics I have to go to trial and probably trials."

A damning article in the ***Los Angeles Times*** examined prosecutors' use of jailhouse snitches and their credibility, or lack thereof, as trial witnesses. Still mad about Lloyd Douglas testifying at his prelim hearing, and possibly at his trial, Bonin wrote, "If only people would realize how crooked the D.A. works. They, the D.A., will turn their back even if they know a guy is lying if it helps their case. Douglas, in my case, is a good example of how homicide detectives know that he is lying in areas and they are going to allow him to lie on the stand."

Ellen and Bonin continued to communicate and grew closer. Calls with her made Bonin happier and the strange idea of prison marriage was still a topic of discussion. Mary was a go-between but soured on the notion as it grew more serious. Jealous, as she considered Bonin her first love, Mary also felt responsible for young Ellen. Human behavior is mysterious; celebrities like Jacqueline Carlin who want to meet Bonin, women like Barbara Wood becoming his "friend" and young Ellen talking marriage to a serial killer she has never met facing the death penalty.

Less strange was Bonin's attorney informed by Deputy DA Norris that OC "wasn't going to file, period." Knowing the news would immediately get back to Bonin, this was a red herring designed to muddy the waters and keep Bonin and Hanson off balance. Bonin immediately called everyone with the news or, as he wrote, "the rumor of it."

With nightmares of another Vernon Butts suicide scenario ever present, one attorney rumor revealed that LA prosecutors, fearful of losing Miley or Munro as witnesses, desperately wanted the trial to start on August 3. Bonin wrote, "I'll have to weigh it all cautiously. I may decide to postpone again. It's my view that it may help me to get a life sentence. Earl brought me copies of the three articles by Tim Alger in the ***Orange County Register***. I'll add them into my file later on this evening."

The jail visiting room provided another fascinating coincidence in the life of Bonin, "Saturday, May 23: Yesterday when I went to my visit from my Mom, Saunders went on a visit also. He's involved in the Bob's Big Boy thing. It only took about four-seconds to realize who I was looking at. It's the first time I had seen him since the last time. The last time was the first time. He is the guy who was next to the door holding a pistol during the robbery of the McDonalds the night I was there before leaving for New York back in early June 1980.

"There couldn't be two people that look like that. That's when the rest fell into place. The guy sitting next to him was the guy standing next to the counter. The one Saunders said to, 'Stand in front of the counter as if you are a customer.' Freeman was one of the guys who went into the back to get money. I never did see the fourth person. I couldn't help but laugh and smile to myself."

Chronicled earlier, this incident occurred a few days before Bonin was arrested, on June 11, 1980. While under surveillance, he was in line at McDonalds, next to a plain clothes detective who was shadowing him. After the detective left, the armed robbery took place and Bonin followed them out, jumped his Chevette and chased the getaway car at 70 miles an hour before returning.

Bonin engaged in a brief conversation with uniformed officers and the undercover detective, not knowing who he was, before leaving. A year later, after all that had happened and only seeing them for a few seconds, Bonin was sitting next to two of the robbery suspects in a jail visiting area and recognized them immediately. Right up there with many other serial killers, Bonin possessed a keen intelligence and an eye for detail.

Two days later Deputy Duran came on the row to serve dinner and forgot he was wearing a baseball cap with a picture of an electric chair with the ominous words underneath, "Regular or Crispy." Realizing the mistake, Deputy Duran snapped the hat off his head, but he wasn't fast enough. The inmates started badgering him to see the hat up close, and the chastened deputy reluctantly showed it around.

Bonin told him, "It doesn't bother me, I can take a joke." Trying to make a point, Bonin called Duran over and looked him straight in the eyes and said, "What's your badge number?"

Flustered and at a loss for words, Duran angrily walked away and said, "Fuck you." After getting further away he yelled back, "You got my fuckin' name, that's enough."

"Duran," Bonin called him again.

"I'm not talking to you," he answered, hoping to end the conversation.

"Hey, wait a minute," Bonin said as the Duran came back close to him, "I just wanted to point out something to you. I don't really want your badge number. I just wanted to show you that I could take a jab, but you can't," Bonin said calmly.

"I don't really mean anything by the hat. I got it for $3.50 at a liquor store in Torrance," Duran replied, half-apologetically.

"Sure, I understand," he said with half-hearted sympathy.

Bonin wrote this about the incident, "I look at this way. If Deputy Duran didn't mean anything by the hat, then he would have never worn it in here in the first place. It was bad judgement on his part and one in very poor taste. I think he did mean something and sort of got caught with his hand in the cookie jar."

May of 1981 ended dramatically when word bean to spread that Ellen accepted Bonin's proposal of marriage. Barbara Wood was the first-person Bonin informed and everyone who heard was dumbfounded, except Mary who was extremely upset. Ellen pushed to finally meet Bonin in person and he arranged for his cousin's husband, Clyde, to pick her up for a visit.

This enraged Mary as she did not know Clyde, arguing against getting into a car with a stranger who was a relative of Bonin. After a heated exchange, Mary said she would tell Bonin not to phone anymore because of the costly charges, but Ellen found this order hollow since she paid rent and utilities. However, Bonin did phone Ellen on a reversed charge basis and that could get expensive since, at the time, calls down the block or cross country were charged individually. Phone service in the U.S. and Canada was an AT & T monopoly, broken up by federal government decree the following year.

Ellen's assurance that Bonin told her Clyde was okay made the situation worse. She screamed at her, "And you believed him?" After Ellen answered "yes" and argued he was part of Bonin's family, Mary upped the ante by saying, "How could you believe him, he's charged with 21 murders!"

Ellen weakly defended her position by saying, "I don't care if he's charged with 50 murders. He hasn't been convicted and remember he's innocent until proven otherwise."

Bonin's dealings with Ellen were not over, but it would be dicey as he tried to work every angle from confinement. However, the really fascinating aspect of this tale of star-crossed love was Bonin's immediate reaction to hearing what Mary said: "It really pissed me off that Mary brought up the part of me being charged with 21 murders, when it was only 12 at this time. And did it in front of her friends."

Quite frankly, that sounds like a famous comedic movie line.

55

Love Triangle, Reporters, OC Charges & Jurisdictional Fights
June thru August 1981

Two months until Bonin's LA trial and the tension was ratcheting up daily. OC hasn't filed any charges, but it was a near certainty despite rumors to the contrary. Miley and Munro cut deals, for testimony, and Pugh was going to a full trial and will not testify against Bonin, which may change if offered substantially reduced charges. Despite being a juvenile when he committed murder, he was a repeat offender for car theft and many other crimes. Problems abounded in the highly charged atmosphere of the biggest mass murder trial in Southern California history.

July fireworks started in June between Danny Young, accused of killing a ten-year old neighbor, and Bonin, "Monday, June 1: Danny Young and me got into it this afternoon. He's a rip-off artist and cons people into doing what he wants them to do. I told him that his ass is mine when I see him up north (San Quentin). I don't actually mean what I say, but it's a good way to release tension, especially towards him. He started saying, 'I'm going to fuck you and then kill you. Just like you did to those kids. I'm even going to use your own T-shirt and strangle you.' I told him, 'You should know, you have had some experience. You were so brave you had to tie the kid's hands behind him and then strangle him. I noticed you chose a 10-year-old white boy and not a black boy.' We went on like this for about a half-hour. I'll be pleased once he gets his time or whatever he gets and is gone. He'll never get away with that shit up north. Especially if he goes to Death Row."

Bonin continued to call and send letters to Ellen, hoping she might develop deep feelings for him, despite what Mary and others were saying. Efforts to get her to communicate with his cousin, Jeanette, as part of a plan to bring Ellen for a visit went nowhere, but he persisted.

Belying a sense of strange tragedy, Bonin wrote this as June ended, "It's very difficult for Ellen to say 'I love you.' At least that is what I assume is happening. She never says it verbally. She writes it though. I was the same way for a long time. All the way to when I was 28 years old it was hard for me to tell anyone I loved them. I told her twice on the phone that I loved her. Once I said, 'I send you all my love' then another time our conversation went like this. 'I want to tell you that I love you.' She said, 'Alright.' I replied, 'Are you sure?' She says, 'Yes.' I figure that if I show my love she will eventually be able to verbally tell me her emotions.

"She needs a lot of encouragement. Guys have lied to her and lied to her so often, she may feel I am doing the same. When she realizes that I mean what I say then it will make it easier for her. I honestly feel she has strong feelings and is searching, as I was, for love. She has it from me and I hope it works between us. Even though the future is uncertain in some respects and certain in others I feel that Ellen and I can make it work."

Two days later, wallowing in loneliness, contemplating a lack of visitors and unanswered letters to Ellen, Bonin swung from depression to elation when the unexpected happened, "Wednesday, June 3: I called Ellen today. It was a good day indeed. She was pissed at Mary. I tried to explain to her the side of Mary that was trying to help. Ellen said that Mary 'could try to talk her out of a relationship with me from now until doomsday and she could not change her mind.' I explained that it could involve a long time waiting. Ellen said, 'So, I can wait. I waited 18 years now, I can wait another 18.' I didn't know what to say. What really made the day was when Ellen said, 'I love you.' I said, 'I love you too.' It's the first time she said I love you, verbally, to me. So very encouraging. It made me feel very, very good. A positive factor in this week of disappointments."

On June 8, a Monday, award winning journalist J.J. Maloney, of the **Orange County Register**, broke another aspect of the unfolding Southern California serial killer stories. Maloney was instrumental in publicly breaking the original story, 14-months earlier, and coined the term Freeway Killer. His continuing research put together two plain facts; Bonin didn't kill before 1979 and similar killings continued after his arrest. He kept digging but the **Register** was recalcitrant about publishing his findings. Frustrated with his bosses, Maloney gave the story to TV reporter Dave Lopez, who broadcast it immediately and, as Maloney expected, it became a national story.

A detailed AP article in the **St. Joseph Gazette**, in Missouri, reported that Maloney went back to consult with forensic psychologist, Dr. Alfred

Rosenberg, after acquiring "a copy of police charts" produced by LAPD. Using the law enforcement charts, plus background info, Rosenberg created a "computer breakdown which indicated two separate patterns of killings—the group that occurred between August 1979 and June 1980 for which Bonin has been charged, and an earlier group of 16 killings between 1973 and June 1979. That earlier group of murders were dissimilar from those which Bonin has been charged in that the victims tended to be older, frequently were known homosexuals, most had alcohol or drugs in their blood, the bodies were mutilated and the bodies were dumped from a moving vehicle along a highway."

How Maloney obtained the document remains a mystery, but it certainly angered high-ranking officers and, again, put all Southern California law enforcement agencies on the defensive. LAPD responded that they always knew there was more than one killer, and investigations were active before and after Bonin's arrest. Reporters had been repeatedly informed that Bonin, due to extended incarcerations, hadn't killed prior to 1979, however, that failed to prevent the constant use of the "44-victims" number in Bonin articles. Since the public was now well aware Bonin was nabbed due to a lucky tip, and not police work per se, Maloney's revelation added unwelcome pressure for city and county officials.

J.J. Maloney had a dramatic impact on the "Bonin Freeway Killer" cases: his push at the **Register** in early 1980 to publicize the story created a media firestorm, forced law enforcement agencies to collaborate and led to Pugh seeing an article and revealing his suspicions.

Bonin was told about the story during multiple phone calls to Barbara Wood, his cousin Jeanette and Ellen, who all saw it on the evening news. The conversation with Ellen proved really interesting, "Ellen said that she was glad I called because she was depressed. She said that she was thinking about suicide but decided against it. I think it isn't anything to worry about. She quit her job today. She told me that it was one month since Kevin died. She said, 'It seems that everyone I fall in love with either gets killed or goes away.' I told her 'I wouldn't leave.' She said, 'Promise.' I said 'Yes.' She told she chose a date for our wedding, Oct. 16. She said it sounded like a good day. I told it was also Barbara's birthday."

Earl Hanson visited the next day and informed Bonin the story forced the DA to publicly admit Bonin's innocence in anything before 1979, while reiterating a belief he killed 22. Bonin wrote, "Of course they know that as

I told them that." In an effort to shed doubt on the prosecution's case, Hanson intended to file for documents on cases Bonin wasn't charged with and compare them. When told Bonin's fiancée wanted to get married on October 16, Hanson commented to Bonin "that everyone feels you are very photogenic."

Things got sticky with Ellen when Mary informed Bonin she was sleeping around and had given an STD to someone named Pat, who in turn gave it to Mary. Not caring about Ellen having to satisfy her sexual needs, he took Mary's accusations with a grain of salt. Ellen denied everything and the mess also involved another man, Phil, who apparently was the one who infected Ellen. Upping the ante, Mary told anyone who would listen about Ellen's problem. Here was a social nightmare not unlike those encountered in all of society.

Bonin reflected on the situation, "Tuesday, June 9: I feel I have a good thing going and intend on continuing with Ellen. I told Ellen that if she was in here and I was on the outside I couldn't go no prolonged time without sex and I didn't expect her too. Ellen also said, 'You have a sexy voice and that's what I fell in love with first.' Then my personality entered and she righteously fell in love with me. So I have an Oct. 16, 1981 wedding date. It's a Friday. We may have to change it because of it not being a Saturday or Sunday. I'll be in court on that day unless I get it postponed. I wrote Ellen a letter to reassure her of my love."

Two days later, Ellen tried to commit suicide with sleeping pills. She would be in the hospital for at least three days and Bonin felt guilty about confronting her on Mary's accusations, "I couldn't have known about her possibly overdosing. I guess all I can do is keep on writing to her. That way she'll have a lot of letters once she gets out." Not wanting to cause her unnecessary pain, Bonin kept the news about Ellen from everyone except Barbara Wood. They had a long conversation about Ellen on Thursday, June 11, and then Bonin wrote this, "I have to put my trust into her. I feel she needs it. If she is doing wrong, it may be the trust I put in her is enough to cause here to change. Until I hear thing as fact, I'll believe in Ellen. She's the one I want as my wife."

Accusations flew back and forth between Mary, Ellen and Bonin in the weird love triangle. Mary's desire to submarine the engagement got vicious as he relates after a phone update with Ellen, "The shrink after talking to Mary at the hospital in private walked into the room that Ellen was in and said, 'I want to ask you a question. I understand that you're planning to marry a guy name Bill, that you've never met. Is that true?' Ellen said, 'That's right, so what! Now I have a question to ask you. Who told you?'

"He told her Mary and then told Ellen she was 'nuts.' Ellen also said that Mary said she talked to Earl and that Earl said I don't have a 'snowball's chance in hell of not getting the death penalty.' I intend on talking to Earl about this and finding out if he did talk to Mary and if he did say that. If he did, I intend on letting him know that I don't want him commenting to anyone about the case in anyway. I intend on letting Earl know that I do not want him talking to Mary about me in any way, shape or form."

Peter Buono was sentenced to six-years in prison on Friday, June 12. Three days later, Bonin wrote that he would "be glad when he leaves." By the end of the week, a talk with Earl straightened out the Mary debacle and the rest of the month was largely centered on issues with these various women connected to the Ellen situation. Every time he called to reach Ellen, and Mary answered the phone, the charges were refused. Mary went to so far as to tell her mother not to speak with Bonin, a request she ignored and told Bonin to ignore it as well.

A cancelled visitation prompted a deputy to play with Bonin emotionally, "Thursday, June 18: Well, if everything goes O.K. I'll have a halfway decent day. Barbara should be here this morning along with Nancy. They may even bring Ronnie. That adds youth to the day. As I was writing this I got called out for a visit. Then they sent me back to my cell. They said that the visitors cancelled out. I don't know what happened but I guess I'll find out later when I call Barbara. When the deputy told me my visit was cancelled he said, 'Bonin, good news. You can go back to bed, your visit just cancelled. Not really, you're going home. No, they really cancelled just now.'

"When he said 'you're going home' a rush of adrenalin ran through me for a second. I thought, 'Could it be?' Then I felt sick that I wasn't going home. It all happened in a matter of a second. It reminded of that Friday, just after I was arrested in June, that they rolled me up for release and then told me I had a 187 hold on me. I knew I wasn't going anywhere. Yet I was hoping that someone had made a mistake and I was being released. When I found out that I wasn't going anywhere, I was drained of all emotion and strength. I knew then that it was going to be a long and difficult road back to freedom, if ever it happened. I might as well adjust to expecting nothing and being thankful for whatever I get."

Only a few things of interest took place in the last days of June. First, plain clothes detectives came by to talk with Bonin's brother, Paul. He ditched them out the back and the reasons for their visit were never discerned. Second, detectives also came by to speak with Mary and said they wanted all the letters, about a dozen, Bonin had written to Ellen. Third, it looked like all of the reporters who spoke with Bonin were going to be subpoenaed to testify in court. Bonin heard that Lopez was going to fight, citing his right to protect confidential sources, and hire his own lawyer if CBS refused to help.

If journalists folded up and revealed their confidential sources every time a subpoena showed up, no one would reveal anything to them. Shield law protections for journalists, under the purview of the First Amendment, vary around the U.S. and the Supreme Court's interpretation of those protections are solid yet vague. In July 2005 Judith Miller spent three months in prison protecting her source in the famous Valerie Plame CIA case, later agreeing to testify after her source signed a waiver.

On June 23, 1980 the shoe dropped in OC as Bonin explains, "Thursday, June 25: Well, it finally happened. I heard on the morning news that I was indicted on 33 felony accounts. So now what? I suppose I might be brought down to Orange County. Maybe I'll just stay up here until L.A. is finished. One thing I'm sure of, I'm also glad it happened in an indictment and finally one way or the other I know something. Now I'm wondering what the two plain clothes people were looking for my brother for? So much for O.C. not filing. Went to the booking front this morning at 8:30 a.m. I signed twice to show that I received notice of the Grand Jury indictments of Orange County. They sure like to slap charges (187-217-188-236-286-288A-297-209). 33 counts in all. Grand Jury Judge Murray, C-47500."

In Orange County Bonin was charged with seven counts each of murder, robbery and sodomy. A "special circumstance" designation was attached, making for a possible OC death penalty verdict.

Then two other big shoes also dropped: 1) Dave Lopez was finally able to broadcast about his January 9, 1981, confession interview with Bonin on KCBS TV, 2) The extensive and secret December 1980 Bonin confession interviews with detectives became public knowledge.

1) Dave Lopez, muzzled by the station in late April due to legal issues, blew his stack when he heard Bonin was negotiating for a movie deal based on his story. Having obtained station permission, on June 29 he revealed Bonin confidentially told him he "killed 21 young men and boys." Two factors restrained Lopez from going into specific murder details—lingering legal apprehensions from the KCBS executives and the amount of time allotted for broadcasting.

He was quoted saying, "I believe very strongly in protecting sources, but I also believe it's a two-way street. If he tells me something off the record and I find he's telling everyone, one detective even said to me, 'I don't see why you're being so secretive about his whole thing. He is telling everyone.' That did it for me."

2) How it happened remains a mystery, but the detective confession interviews with Bonin, during the preliminary hearings in December 1980, became public and created a firestorm. A Tuesday, June 30 article in the *LA Times* by Dave Lesher, ***Tape by Bonin Confession to Slayings Told***, said Bonin "reportedly confessed to 21 of the murders in a taped interview with Los Angeles police investigators, sources close the investigation said Monday. But for reasons that the prosecution has refused to disclose, the tape—comprising 11 hours of questioning—will not be used in Bonin's upcoming trial, the sources said."

The unnamed source said Bonin did the interviews to possibly avoid the death penalty and in response to a letter from Sean King's mother, which was actually a fake from LAPD's Sgt. St. John. Both reasons are true, but other factors came into play as chronicled earlier. Reporting that detectives never confirmed their existence till now, Bonin's attorney lied to the press by saying he "doubted" the existence of the tapes and that "under rules of discovery the prosecution would have been obligated to release the tape to Hanson to aid in the preparation of Bonin's defense."

Earl Hanson helped set up the interviews and was present when they commenced, on Tuesday, December 16, 1980, while Bonin was in the midst of preliminary hearings with Vernon Butts. Being kept secret for over six-months was an amazing feat since at least two members of the press, Alger and Lopez, knew about the interviews and the existence of the tapes. They were warned by detectives not to reveal anything. What, if anything, this meant for Bonin's trial remained to be seen.

Other developments included the OC Public Defender's Office bowing out because it previously represented Miley and Munro, both set to testify against Bonin. Hanson was appointed his OC attorney by Judge William Murray, who also postponed Bonin's arraignment till July 10. In the interim Hanson filed another motion for a delay, allowing for further preparation, which was opposed by prosecutors but allowed by the judge. The Bonin trial in LA was pushed back six-weeks to Monday, September 14. Bonin was moved to the OC Men's Central Jail and pled not guilty to all charges and Murray refused his request to be sent back to LA. Bonin hated the OC jail and told the judge he "feared for his life."

His preliminary hearing was set for Tuesday, August 18 and it produced a battle of wills between the powerful counties. Bonin had been sent back to LA and thence again to OC in early August, however, during the run up to the preliminary hearing Van de Kamp and Norris got nervous. In the Monday, August 17 edition of the ***Los Angeles Times*** it was reported that LA "shocked Orange County" by trying to get Bonin "removed from Orange County jurisdiction. Superior Court Judge William Murray denied a motion Monday by Los Angeles Deputy Dist. Attorney Sterling Norris to have Bonin immediately returned to Los Angeles."

This political turf war over Bonin had been going on since his arrest. At this key stage it involved three overlapping murder charges. The two most pressing involved eyewitness testimony and formed a foundation for death penalty convictions in both counties: James Macabe with Gregory Miley on February 3, 1980, and Steven Wells with Jim Munro on June 2, 1980.

The other double-charged murder in dispute was Darin Kendrick, with Vernon Butts on April 29, 1980, which didn't have eyewitness testimony but involved solid evidence of kidnapping, rape, drugging and murder with an icepick. Kendrick's wallet was recovered at Vernon Butts' house and the forensic evidence was more substantial than in any other Bonin murder. In addition, detectives could testify about Butts' post arrest interview where he freely revealed grisly details of the Kenrick killing.

Jerry Hicks of the ***LA Times*** went on to report, "Norris contended that Orange County could damage Los Angeles County's case against Bonin in the so-called Freeway Killings if it moves ahead with charges in any of the three slayings in which both counties have claimed jurisdiction. Bonin's trial is scheduled to begin on September 14." Norris was quoted as saying, "You can't split up those counts. A substantial part of our cases involves those three counts. If Mr. Carter were in my shoes, he would say the same thing."

Another worry for LA prosecutors was the offer made to let "Bonin stand trial without a jury." Norris said if he didn't "face a jury trial in any of those three overlapping counts it might hurt the chances of getting a death penalty verdict. The people of Los Angeles ought to be able to sit and hear the evidence against him. It is really an extraordinary thing to go to a non-jury trial." The article finished with OC Superior Court Judge Kenneth Lae saying he would "close the preliminary hearing to the public if Bonin's attorney requests it."

Bonin's preliminary hearing in Orange County commenced on Tuesday, August 18 and lasted three days. Behind the scenes negotiations got nowhere and the strange resolution became public as the final day of the hearings commenced.

Hicks' *Los Angeles Times* article, **Bonin to Get His Say on Who Tries Him**, reported that "the suspect himself will make the final decision today on which county will get to try him first." This unusual arrangement was commented on by Bonin's attorney, "This is just too important for me to advise him on it. Bill and I had a long talk about it at lunch. I told him he has got to decide."

At first Hanson didn't believe OC could complete a trial before Bonin's transfer date back to LA on Thursday, September 10, four days before the trial was to start. However, he became convinced otherwise by OC Deputy DA David Carter and most assuredly transmitted those feelings to Bonin. Conflicted on the matter, Bonin swayed between his dislike of OC jail and thinking it might be better to "get OC behind us" since he was already there.

Other issues were OC Judge Lae having to completely clear his calendar to accommodate the Bonin trial, on top of threats of ongoing appeals on Murray's ruling to keep Bonin in OC. Ultimately OC lost the battle of the three overlapping cases and would try Bonin for the murders of Dennis Fox, Russell Rugh, Glenn Barker and Larry Sharp.

Their strategy would adjust according to what took place in Los Angeles.

PART FOUR
AUGUST 1931 TO PRESENT DAY

Author's Notes from Vonda Pelto, Ph.D.

In the previous sections of this book, a fairly comprehensive picture of Bill Bonin has emerged. Quite a number of times Bonin was shown talking with me, Vonda Pelto, Ph.D., as the Clinical Psychologist at Los Angeles Men's Central Jail. Most prominent of these was his vivid and terrifying description of the Markus Grabs murder. Greg Miley and Jim Munro, in Part Two, also told me about several other murders.

In Part Four, as the Bonin trial is about to start and gets underway, my work at the jail gave me the opportunity to have a number of conversations with Bonin and many other notorious murderers. These encounters offer a small snapshot of William George Bonin as the last chapter of his life was being decided—whether it would be life in prison or the death penalty.

56

Vonda Pelto, Ph.D. Arrives at LA Men's County Jail
August 1981

My total fascination with people, and how they thought and behaved, was awakened when my sixth-grade schoolteacher gave me an introduction to a psychology textbook. Unable to completely grasp much of the language, and concepts, my curiosity pulled me towards becoming a psychologist when I grew up. After having two children, and becoming a single mother, I pursued that long buried goal while carving a new path in life.

The event which brought me to LA Men's Central Jail was the January 1981 suicide of Vernon Butts, chronicled earlier. Butts fell through the cracks of the overburdened forensic mental health unit, located in the jail, as they didn't know of his previous suicide attempts. Embarrassed and under intense political pressure, the LA County Sheriff's Dept., which runs the facility, and the Mental Health Dept., responsible for the mental well-being of inmates, had to prevent a reoccurrence with other high profile killers awaiting trial.

At the jail, aside from the four Freeway Killers Bonin, Miley, Munro and Pugh, there were many other vicious and notorious killers such as Hillside Stranglers Kenneth Bianchi and Angelo Buono, Sunset Strip Slayer Douglas Clark, Trash Bag Murderer Eli Komanchero and porn star John Holmes, being held in connection with the Wonderland Murders. The Mental Health Dept. decided they needed a psychologist to talk with high-profile inmates, which is how I came on to the scene.

After completing a Ph.D. in psychology, in June of 1981, I spent the summer looking for a job. With little experience, and no license, my options were limited. In August of 1981 I applied to the LA County Mental Health Dept. and was hired. With few positions available, I was assigned to work at the jail. The interviewer was skeptical I could handle working around 5,000 male inmates and mostly male deputies, but I was divorced with two teenage daughters and needed work.

My cell/office was located on the second floor, amongst the killers, and the assignment was simple yet complex: meet with high-profile murderers, and other sorted miscreants, on a weekly basis to detect any suicidal ideations. I was not tasked with conducting therapy. For those wanting to talk, I was there to engage in conversations which kept them on an even keel emotionally, acting as an always available emotional sounding board for all manner of chit-chat, which often got rather colorful.

Based on my findings, I could refer an inmate to a psychiatrist who might prescribe medication or transfer him to the hospital unit. A key aspect: there was no confidentiality since my office remained open and deputies periodically stopped by for a safety check.

So here I was, a small-town girl, raised in a strict Southern Baptist home in the desert community of Needles, California, thrown into the hall of mirrors world of serial killers. My daily digest of info came largely from reprobate killers, some who had engaged in unspeakable horrors. My dreams were haunted, and it nearly destroyed my waking life. Stress from all of it resulted in some self-destructive behavior and left me questioning many aspects of human life.

What caught me so off guard, as the months unfolded, was how intelligent and engaging these men were, leading me to think how easily people, myself included, could fall for their charm and disarming manner. It sounds crazy, but I was fascinating by the idea of seeing and conversing with serial killers. Their lack of moral bearing was a form of evil power all by itself, and I wanted to know how they thought, what led them to become uncaring and unfeeling monsters.

Bonin, arrested fifteen months before I was hired, had been asking for someone to talk about his proclivities and problems. Considering how many years he spent in psychiatric examination, it is not surprising he wanted to find a sympathetic voice, and ear, in the wilderness of incarceration. Bonin was betrayed by family, abused by people in positions of trust and battered by a system which failed to derail his drive towards violent behavior.

The following conversations will reveal much about the man whose story of personal evolution is contained in previous sections.

57

Pelto's First Session with Bill Bonin
August 31, 1981

"I hate Monday mornings," I mumbled to myself. Pushing open the door to my office, I took time to lock the bottom half of the Dutch-door, leaving the top half open. I inhaled the stale cigarette smoke still hanging in the air, giving the impression of a stale, smoky nightclub. Ashes flew airborne with the intake of air created from opening the door. The flakes settling down on the brown sealed envelope that was addressed to me, Dr. Vonda Pelto, at the Forensic Outpatient Unit, Los Angeles County Men's Jail.

Two half empty Styrofoam coffee cups, one with curdled cream floating on top, sat to the left side of my desk. Stains circled the bottoms of the cups leaving dried rings on the scared surface.

After I dropped down on the hard, wooden, swivel chair, wishing I would remember to bring in a soft cushion to sit on, I pulled open the crammed file drawer and pushed my purse into the tiny crevice created by jamming the files closer together.

"Good morning, Doc." I looked up to see James Munro, one of the Freeway Killers, leaning on the bottom half of the door.

"Good morning to you too."

"Can I talk with you later? I'm feeling kinda bad. By the way, it's those FBI jerks who sit around here shooting the bull at night, they make the mess while interrogating guys," Munro informed me.

"I'll have a deputy call you out." Munro was still leaning on the door when the ringing of the phone startled me.

"Hi Doc, this is Deputy Jerger down in 1750. Can you come down this morning to talk with Bonin? He saw you here the other day and asked who you were. Told him you're the shrink, I think he needs to see you."

"Sure, about ten works for you?"

"Works for me," he said.

Bonin's crimes and notoriety required the Sheriff's Department to house him in the High Power module (1700-1750), located on the first floor of the jail off the main corridor. Raping boys, a rung below raping girls, was on the lowest end of the prison hierarchy. This marked him as a prime target for someone in general population wanting to score points amongst other inmates.

Although it was more comfortable for me to meet with the high-profile inmates in my office on the second floor, they decided these inmates should not be removed from the High Power unit, 1700/1750 located on the first floor off the main hall. To be admitted into this module, which is the most secure area in the jail, trans versing through a sally-port.

On the other hand, module 7000 is located on the second floor and can be accessed only by an elevator located across from my office. This area also houses keep away inmates, those who have to be protected from the general population, designated as K-9, and K-10. K-9 and K-10 comprise serial killers, high profile inmates such as movie stars, judges, police officers, attorneys and their families, white color crime inmates and a few serial killers. The department tries to separate any partners in a crime by putting one in 1700/1750 and one in 7000, touched on in various sections of Part Three earlier.

The prospect of talking with Bonin, an accused serial killer, starting my heart racing. I locked the door, walked a few feet across the hall and pushed the elevator button with the number one imprinted in faded black, stepped in and watched the doors close. The urine smell was particularly offensive this morning, making me nauseated. Peeing in the elevator was the inmate's passive-aggressive behavior to get back at the staff.

I was extremely curious about Bonin and wanted to look for some type of psychopathology, some kind of mental disorder which allowed him to kill at least 22 teenage boys. According to reports sent to me, Bonin was the primary instigator of the horrific crimes, with all the accomplices influenced by his domineering personality. I wanted to find out if that was true. Bonin had a long history of kidnapping young boys, raping them and then releasing the traumatized children. Bonin used a gun and a knife in order to get the boys to cooperate with him, but usually didn't inflict further injury on any of them with the blade.

Then he started killing and couldn't stop. Bonin showed no concern for his victims, randomly dropping them all over Southern California with little effort in hiding them; and he didn't position the bodies like the Hillside Stranglers often did. The bodies were treated like unwanted trash.

Bonin strangled the boys because he liked the personal contact with and power over his victims. What changed him? What were the triggers that turned him into a cold-blooded murderer? How did he accelerate into playing God, choking the life out of his innocent victims with his bare hands?

The elevator doors pulled open, and I reluctantly walked toward the protected area where Bonin was housed. It was a relief to escape from the smelly elevator. A fishline of inmates were walking past me yelling obscenities like, "Yo, sweet little mamma, you wanna fuck?"

"Don't mad dog the lady." Deputy Salas, young, buff and looking sharp in his Sheriff's uniform, yelled at the offending inmate.

I knocked on the heavy metal door waiting to gain admittance. Another fishline of inmates were being herded like cattle down the long mustard-colored hallway toward me, their leg irons scraping along the concrete floor with each step they took. I shuddered inside, wanting to get into the module before they reached me.

Inside the massive jail complex, civilian staff members were issued keys on a daily basis to unlock their office doors. These keys never left the jail and were turned into the deputy's booth each evening when leaving. One of my first lessons was that failure to turn in keys would result in a deputy retrieving them from my house. A deputy was needed to gain admittance to any cell block.

After pounding on the steel door three more times, thankfully Deputy Jerger heard the noise and opened the outer door. Relief filled me stepping into the safety of the sally port, a room that resembled an air lock, that is dimly lit, and measures about three feet wide and five feet long. Each end of the enclosure is sealed with a locked metal door with a small window embedded in it. The second door does not open into the main cellblock until the exterior door is secured. This is the most protected area in the jail and houses the majority of the High Power inmates.

"Doc. You look a little rattled, you want a cup? The deputy asked as we walked into the module.

"You read my mind. I just let the inmates get to me."

"You're still a fish, you'll get used to these assholes." He followed his comment with a pat on my backside. I didn't know how to respond, laugh or slap his face. Then I reminded myself of what one of the female staff had said, don't ever alienate a deputy, they're your safety lifeline.

"Come on I'll get you a cup," he said. I smiled, but when he turned his back I gave him the finger. I followed him into the deputy booth and grabbed a seat at an empty desk.

"Want a cadillac?" Jerger asked.

"No, a john wayne, strong and straight, like my men," I said with sarcasm, trying to fit with the culture.

After a few sips and a bite of a donut, I walked over to the file cabinet and pulled Bonin's daily log out. I wanted to learn how Bonin was doing. It noted all the inmate's current behavior, such as problems with sleeping, poor appetite, lethargy and signs of depression. My job was to keep him alive throughout his trial.

Charged from my morning libation, I dropped my head down into my hands and thought about talking to this vicious killer. My job, I reminded myself, keep him alive! No more suicides like Vernon Butts.

"You ready for him Dr. Pelto?" I was deep in thought and the deputy's voice startled me. It took a moment to respond before I nodded yes.

The young deputy was not much older than the boys Bonin and his accomplices had murdered. The deputy didn't bother seeking out eye contact, reminding me that I was an impediment to his social life. I suspected he had a date with one of the nurses and was running late. The Deputy unlocked the door to the windowless interview room and flipped on a switch that allowed garish light to escape out into the hallway. The interior room reminded me of a crypt, with its gray cement floor and thick cement walls. A battered wooden desk sat opposite a standard leather barber chair for the inmate to sit in.

In short order the deputy appeared with Bonin. His slender five-foot-nine inches ambled into the office without making any audible sounds. The man who would ooze out the details of torturing and killing twenty-two boys didn't look like what I expected.

No, the man that cast a shadow into the office appeared rather ordinary looking, like someone that could have walked past me on a deserted street without sloughing off any imprint. No, I knew that he would never have been picked out of a crowd by anyone as a possible serial killer, no matter how trained or psychologically astute they were. No one could have suspected him of being the Freeway Killer.

Looking at his dead eyes started my heart pounding against my rib cage. The deputy pulled his cuffs and anchored one of Bonin's arms to the chair. I had thought that the inmates would be in chains. Would I be safe?

"Doc, let me know when you're through with him." The deputy called back over his shoulder as he left.

"Wait, aren't you…"

"I'll be around," he said while disappearing rapidly.

Even before Bonin slumped down onto the leather chair, his pervasive body odor permeated the space. His dead brown eyes stared ahead while the thick brown hair fell in dirty strands across his forehead; he didn't use any energy to push them away. A heavy mustache, in need of a trim, framed slackened facial muscles pulled down by gravity. Bonin's skin was paler than seen on the news broadcast, a look typical of jail inmates denied yard privileges.

His eyes, devoid of emotion, didn't blink but maintained a steady gaze. After Bonin spent some time exploring the dirty gray walls and dull overhead lights, he raised his head, sucked in some air, seeming to come alert. He settled back in the chair and addressed me.

"You the shrink?" Bonin said while eyeing me suspiciously with an edge to his voice I found disconcerting.

"Dr. Pelto."

"What's this all about?"

The truth; keep him from committing suicide like Butts. What do I say to someone who has admitted to killing 22 kids? I wasn't here to do therapy, thank goodness, what kind of therapy do you do with such a serial killer? My boss told me just to give him support. After reading some articles about him, I could hardly stand looking at him much less spending time with him.

"Look doc, I've had enough therapy to last me for a lifetime," Bonin said while yawning, not bothering to cover his mouth.

After collecting my thoughts, I explained my job entailed working with the high-profile inmates to give support and not therapy. I also warned him he would not have the protection of confidentiality. The deputies stopped by and listened outside my door. Heightened security was prevalent since Butts cheated the system by hanging himself.

"That talk therapy don't do nothin' anyway. When they sent me to Atascadero for treatment, I remember a social worker trying to do therapy on me, what a joke. Didn't take much to figure out what she wanted to hear and parrot the words back to her. She thought she was doing some great job changing me. They must have got her cheap cause she was still wet behind the ears."

I began to squirm around, remembering back to the day I met with my first patient. She must have thought the same about me. I didn't even know how stupid I sounded. Would Bonin see me the same way? This is no time to deal with my insecurities—I scolded myself, I've got to focus on my job and maintain the upper hand with this killer.

"Do you care if I call you Bill?" This man is a killer, why am I acting like we are having a tea party?

"You're new around here?"

"Hired in a little while ago," I said, quickly realizing staff don't usually ask an inmate if they can use their first name.

"I don't care what you call me, and it don't matter what I tell you, all the shit is all coming out in court anyway," Bonin's demeanor suddenly changed, catching me totally off guard, his body seeming to grow smaller as the voice softened and grew faint. "I keep thinking back to all the things people did to me. Did they make me like I am? Did those things make me...?"

Bonin seemed to be pleading for an answer. My stomach knotted; I didn't know what to say. Momentarily I felt drawn to him, wanting to tell him that everything would be alright. But I knew it wouldn't be, it was much too late for him.

Before I could answer, a deputy walked in and interrupted our little chat. "Excuse me, Doc. But Bonin's attorney is here." I looked up to see Deputy Burke leaning on the open door.

After releasing the cuffs, Bonin was led out of the office. I took a deep breath realizing I had been holding my breath. I was safe. I couldn't allow my waking self to realize how dangerous my job was. Ever present was the possibility that one of these killers might grab me for use as a hostage, but I couldn't fool my unconscious mind as it readily ferreted out the dangers.

Overriding the fears was the personal and professional curiosity which drew me to studying psychology, and here I was with a unique opportunity. I was able to freely interview serial killers, murderers and rapists, some of the worst genetics, fate and society have created were at my disposal for research. Additionally, I was on their turf, the interloper in their world, and that could be used towards my professional advantage. As for Bill Bonin, I wanted to know what made him kill.

58

Pelto's Second Session with Bonin
September 7, 1981

Only weeks into my new and crazy job, and I was already overwhelmed by the exhausting nature of dealing with the inmates and deputies on top of the sickening smells of urine, burnt toast and cigarettes. Being exposed to this highly toxic environment, on a daily basis, taxed every fiber of my being.

I reminded myself that I was hired to be an effective professional in a manner which inspires trust, this in a world where some think they are better off dead than confined for life.

Putting on a brave and false front for the hardened criminals, I also had to discharge my primary mission, preventing high-profile inmate suicide, by talking with men I viewed as evil and **Without Redemption**. Then, at the end of the day, I vainly tried to leave the horrors behind and transform into an attentive and loving mother for my two daughters. Since Bonin's primary accomplice killed himself in jail, my boss requested that I conduct regular meetings with him. As a result, the Senior deputy in 1700/1750 arranged a weekly session.

Monday morning and back to work. After getting settled in the office, I called 1700 to check on Bonin. Deputy Jerger answered and reported that Bonin had a really bad weekend, saying he didn't even leave his cell for the 30-minute Freeway Time to walk up and down the row. Although he was one of my primary assignments, I also had to deal with others in the same situation. My knowledge of Bonin was limited by what the media reported: Suspected of the torture, rape and strangulation of at least 21 boys and about to stand trial for multiple murders, plus additional charges, in two counties.

"Bring him up, I'll see him in my office," I told the deputy.

"Bout ten?"

"Great, thanks."

As soon as my coffee arrived, I turned my attention to plowing through the mail. In the stack the unit secretary dropped off, I found several large tan envelopes from the Probation Department, characterized by the distinctive stamp in the left-hand corner. My request for more info, in an effort to further understand Bonin, had been fulfilled. Before I had time to read anything, I heard a deputy calling for my attention.

"Doc, you ready for him?" I looked up to see the deputy leaning on the bottom half of the Dutch door. After nodding, the deputy pushed the bottom half of the door open and followed Bonin into my office. Then the uniform exited without asking me if I wanted the cuffs used. I smiled internally, cuffing this killer to the flimsy chair would be a joke.

"Would you like a cup of coffee?" I heard my voice, and barely recognized it. STRESS!

"Sure, never get it hot, usually a trustee spits in it. Cream and sugar, please?" A cadillac, I had learned to drink a john wayne, black, less hassle. Silence hung in the air as I arranged for our coffee. Bonin spent some time exploring the yellow walls of my office.

"Who did those pictures?" Bonin pointed to the two-penciled drawing taped to the wall.

"Ken Bianchi," I answered.

"He's the Hillside Strangler, yeh, I know his cousin Angelo from my row," he told me half-heartedly, "You talk to them too?"

"Yes, I do."

"Bianchi drew those pictures of Mickey and Minnie Mouse for you?"

"No, he asked a couple of guys down the hall to draw them, thought maybe they would cheer up my office," I said.

"This used to be a cell?"

"Only difference is the Dutch door, I leave the top-half open to let in fresh air."

"You're making a joke, there ain't no fresh air in this cement box," Bonin said while laughing.

"Funny you called it that. I called it a cement cracker box the first day I walked across the concrete walkway from the underground parking structure. When I saw the gray fortress looming up before me, cement cracker box came to my mind also," I replied, trying to make small talk with a vicious serial killer. I wanted to let out a nervous giggle but stifled the urge, knowing the need to develop a rapport was paramount.

I remembered being worried about what to wear my first day on the job, however, the real concern should have been what it was like working in a man's environment, or a men's jail with 5,000 inmates. I had never been inside any jail before, but there are jails and then there are jails; LA Men's Central Jail was and is the latter, with danger lurking everywhere. Grateful just to have a job, I also realized I never even thought to ask if there were any other women in the Forensic Outpatient Unit.

Thank goodness the trustee arrived with the coffee, giving me a chance to get my head straight.

"I will be checking in with you every week to see how you are getting along, I'm here to talk with and just shoot the bull, I don't report to the court or anyone else. If you need medication, I can refer you to the psychiatrist."

This offer of help was met with a blank stare and silence, I needed to change the subject.

"Bill, I heard on trial is getting delayed, is that true?"

"Yeh, lots of shit goin on, they want the death penalty for me. Doc, you know, no one listens or tries to understand that I couldn't help myself. I would try to stop killing but I couldn't stop, I just had to keep doing it," he said in a loud voice. I felt stunned, not knowing what to say.

I watched as a tear rolled down his cheek. He pulled a tissue and wiped his eyes. Was he crying for himself or maybe showing some regret for the boys he murdered? Was he a good actor? Grave doubts about my ability to handle this job jumped from one synapse to another, making my head hurt. I had no way to prepare for the Freeway Killer crying, and the ambivalent feelings Bonin evoked in me. His sadness seemed sincere, but was I being manipulated? I didn't know the answer. I felt fearful that I couldn't tell. Was I in over my head?

"When I think about all the things I did, it doesn't seem real. Feels like this all happened to someone else. See my life went on, then it all changed. All my feelings of anger came to the surface at the same time. I keep thinking I'm goin' wake up and find this is just a bad dream. Just know I couldn't have stopped myself," the accused serial killer said with a wry smile.

"Did you see Gregory Miley? I'm real worried about him," Bonin chirped up, now wanting to change the topic himself. "He's real scared and he's not bright. Guess you already know he did some of the murders with me and is testifying against me?"

"Yes, I know."

"I told Sgt. Esposito that Greg should go for an insanity plea. He asked me why? I told him that Greg was the only one who told the truth. He said he didn't think he was insane, saying he was dumb but not insane. I told him, well you had to be there to understand. Greg didn't know what he was getting himself into. Then it came right down to having Miranda in the van, I'm sure Greg thought I was going to let him go afterwards. It happened too quick for him to change his mind. I looked at him and said, 'You okay? You're sure you can handle this?' he said, 'Sure,' and then it was all over.

"But I don't hold nothin' against him. He's a kid really, I didn't know he was kind of, you know, not so smart, think I kind of ruined his life and I feel bad about that," Bonin said in a genuinely remorseful manner.

"I'll talk with him," I replied.

I looked up to see a disinterested and impatient deputy leaning on the half open Dutch door and wondered how long he had been eavesdropping.

"Doc, you through with Bonin? Its lunch time and I wouldn't want him to miss it." That translated into the deputy wanting to go to lunch with his buddies, and that was just fine with me. I needed time to work through my ambivalent feelings toward Bonin.

As I watched, Bonin's face flattened into a blank stare, looking out into a space known only to him, it felt like a curtain had closed. "I couldn't stop myself," he said barely above a whisper as he rose and walked out.

59

Bonin Lawyer Change & Trial Delay
September 14, 1981

Bonin's big trial in Los Angeles Superior Court, long delayed for a myriad of different reasons, was set to start in mid-September when the unexpected happened.

Months earlier Bonin became aware of criminal defense attorney William Charvet from inmate Roy Norris. Charvet represented Norris and got him a deal to avoid the death penalty by testifying against Bittaker, with whom he murdered five girls. In exchange for signing over the rights to his life story, Norris received legal representation with possible earnings from a book deal.

Norris said if Bonin needed some money, he might talk to Charvet about entering into a similar arrangement. Secret negotiations proceeded slowly thru late summer and fall. Charvet would be a privately retained lawyer, in contrast to Earl Hanson whose fees and expenses were paid by taxpayers as a court appointed attorney.

The amazing development was revealed by Bonin, during a court hearing on Thursday, September 3, when he "expressed his intention to move to substitute the law firm of Charvet & Stewart and its partners William T. Charvet and Tracy L. Stewart as retained counsel in the place of Hanson, and to request a continuance to allow new counsel time to prepare for trial."

Deputy DA Sterling Norris filed a motion in opposition based on three arguments:

1) The change would postpone and possibly damage the prosecution's case, 2) Previous contact between William Charvet and a vital prosecution witness, James Munro, posed a conflict of interest if his firm represented Bonin, 3) Bonin never expressed any displeasure with Hanson or wanting to change counsel previously.

On the day the trial was set to begin, Monday, September 14, Bonin threw a monkey wrench into the works and formally filed the substitution motion. Norris was against the motion for reasons cited above plus two others: "The motion was not timely made" and "that any retainer agreement by Mr. Charvet may involve book rights, creating an additional conflict." When questioned by the court, Earl Hanson admitted he "was never the attorney of choice of Mr. Bonin."

Bonin told the court he had a better "rapport" with Charvet and felt that "there is certain things that we cannot—that I don't feel I can discuss about the case" with Hanson. Despite Charvet's case law defense, Judge William Keene denied the motion and Bonin responded by threatening to represent himself.

The matter was appealed to the California Supreme Court and, a week later, Keene was forced to delay the trial till October 19. In the interim, Keene ordered that both attorneys prepare for trial and Hanson must "prepare Bonin to act as his own attorney."

Hanson dropped off eight boxes of the investigative information at the new defense attorney's office. When Charvet asked for additional time to prepare, Keene refused, stating, "This is a ploy on Bonin's part to buy more time." With this crush of time, Charvet needed additional staff and hired paralegal Melody Norris to assist in the preparations for the LA and OC trials. She later said, "You can't believe the mess they gave me to sort through and get into some organized form, it was a mess."

When Bonin was appealing his conviction, one of his arguments was that he had flawed legal representation. A May 1989 Appeal Declaration noted that "Charvet and I then negotiated an agreement wherein I conveyed a 50% interest in the literary rights to my life story. In exchange Charvet promised to ensure that at least one book was written and published, and that he would pay the writer out of his percentage of the rights.

"Because I was worried about my mother's financial situation, I required that my 50% would go to her instead of me. After Charvet and I agreed to this contract, my trial attorney, Earl Hanson, found out about it from Charvet. Hanson then came to see me and suggested that since Charvet had the book rights contract, he should also represent me as my trial attorney."

60

Pelto's Third Session with Bonin
September 21, 1981

My morning started out sitting at my plain, county issued desk looking at a stack of the interminable paperwork, one which I had put off for a week. A trustee delivered my first john wayne, black coffee, along with four warm cookies made by the inmates.

"Doc, you comin' down this morning to see your favorite asshole?" I recognized the deputy's voice, we both laughed. Based on the conversations I was now having with deputies, it felt like I had garnered a bit of acceptance over the last couple of months. In the beginning they thought, being a woman, I was being taken in by the inmates. Deputies saw me toughening up and must have appreciated the change. This is going to sound strange, but I would rather talk to this killer than do paperwork. I found it interesting trying to figure out how Bonin thought and reasoned.

"Ten, okay?" I asked, pleased to escape the paper stack.

"Yep."

"So's how's it going Doc?" Deputy Jerger asked as he admitted me into the module. "You got time for a cup?"

"I wish, got a pile of reports to get out today. Gotta check on Bonin first, don't want him offing himself."

I hadn't seen Bonin for two weeks, and a lot happened during that time. Bonin effectively delayed his trial for over a month by requesting an attorney change, in fact it seemed, according to rumors and the media, that he was forcing the judge to change his lawyer by threatening to represent himself. Barring other delays, the long-awaited Bonin Freeway Killer trial will start in a month. Once the proceedings began, his lack of presence around the jail might limit opportunities for sessions.

Since speaking with him last, I had carefully gone through the Probation Department reports and had developed a deeper and better understanding of his lifelong legal troubles, family history and the sexual/physical abuse he suffered as a child. Needless to say, at this point in time, I knew much less about his early life than what was chronicled earlier. But I still had plenty of info about Bonin's aggressive tendencies, arrests for raping young boys, war service, years spent at Atascadero, in State Prison and more.

What really caught my attention was how Bill's parents failed him. By four years old he had already been physically and emotionally abandoned by his mother, a woman damaged from years of abuse. This total lack of a safe and loving environment helped set him on a course towards extreme sociopathic behavior, of course that wasn't the only force creating the incapacity to love himself or others. Bill wanted and needed love, as well as protection, but instead he received abuse with no ability to protect himself. Not excusing Bonin's crimes, the family reports revealed how this might have contributed to the heinous behavior.

Another aspect, one referred to previously, was a possible frontal lobe brain injury Bonin may have suffered during childhood. Reports of beatings at the hands of various family members, or during stays the Boy's Home and Catholic Orphanage, are inconclusive but certainly indicate he could have suffered some kind of damage that altered his behavior.

Bonin knew the routine of stepping up into the leather chair and putting his left arm down to be cuffed, one ring around the chair arm and the other on the wrist. I knew it to. I had barely gotten seated behind the battered desk when I looked up and noticed Bonin smiling while watching the deputy tighten the cuff.

"Bill, you seem to be feeling a little better this morning?"

"Doc, just laughing cause these cuffs are a big joke."

"A joke?"

"Shit, I could get out of these in seconds."

"Really?"

"Loan me that paper clip."

"Okay, go for it." I watched as he unfolded the clip and with a couple of twist opened the restraint. "I did this for the deputies the other day. They couldn't believe it. Said that next time they might take me out in chains."

I started shaking. I wasn't safe at all. I looked over to the office door and could hear the deputy's voice. At least they were close by. With each meeting Bonin was becoming more open. I felt much less anxious about Bill Bonin killing himself.

"Last night some idiots at the other end of my row started a fire in front of their cells. The guards saw it. Some other jerks thought that was funny, so they started one. Deputies ignored it, shit, they hole up in their office shooting the bull, they don't care that smoke bugs the hell out of the rest of us."

"Does that happen often? It must be hard to get sleep?"

"That's not so bad cause the fires burn out pretty fast. The thing that gets me is the guys crying and yelling up down rows," then Bonin paused for second, getting more serious. "But, you know, I do often think back to all the stuff that happened in my life, no one could know what was going on inside of me, the hurt and anger, Wish I knew why I did a lot of the stuff I did, maybe someday I'll find out."

Suddenly I found myself wanting to reach out and comfort him. I thought of my own two daughters, and how I would react to them if they were in pain. I'd let my guard down, I had to be so careful, it was much too late for him. I noticed Bonin's tightly controlled exterior as he spoke generally about his horrible crimes, giving me a better understanding why no one suspected the depth of his rage or intense anger. Indeed, the face he showed to the world was far different from the hidden one buried deep inside, where the demons lurked.

"Doc, during all of this I had so many times when I showed the loving side of me to Mary's three kids." He shifted the conversation, then I realized he was talking about an ongoing relationship. My God, he was taking her children out for fun in between killing boys, I could barely look at him.

"I loved Mary's kids like they were my own, I would never have hurt them for anything."

"I understand that you did marry," I inquired softly, working hard at being civil.

"Short time, my mother pushed me into it. She couldn't stand me being a homo, wanted me to be normal, whatever the hell that is. Wanted me to be like her lady friend's kids are. I did want a son, someone to love me and look up to me. I just couldn't find the right combination. I didn't want a wife, I wanted a son. I don't know, maybe that would have changed me."

"How do you think that would have changed you?"

"Not what you think. Not for sexual reasons but to bring him up as a son. I needed someone to love me. Someone I could trust that I could love."

"You didn't feel loved by your parents?" I had read his history and knew the answer but wanted to know what he thought.

Bonin raised his eyebrows, looking straight at me. "What? I wasn't what they wanted. They didn't want any of us. Well, maybe they wanted my baby brother who died. They had us kids cause of the Catholic Church. If I would have had a son before this started it probably would have never happened. That's all I ever wanted, someone to love me, I went out looking for it, but I guess I didn't know how to ask for it. If I would have had a true lover, it would have never happened. One time I thought I did. He broke my heart."

"Do you want to talk about that?" I asked, but the topic changed again.

"I don't know what happened to me, how I got to this point? Just seemed like no one ever cared to take time to understand me or the struggles I was going through, guess I wasn't ever worth anybody's time," Bonin lamented, showing the fear of abandonment which colored his existence. "Thinking back, I just know I couldn't stop myself," he said, ceding all control of events to uncontrollable forces.

61

Session with Greg Miley
October 3, 1981

After arriving at work early, I headed down to the hospital kitchen to have some breakfast. Scheduled to meet with Greg Miley, at 10:00 a.m., I didn't want to speak with him on an empty stomach. I also checked in with the 1700 deputies to make sure Bonin was okay. They assured me he was, saying, "He didn't miss his 30-minute freeway time, walked down the row to get a little love from one of his buddies."

Walking along the corridor, looking into cells on either side, I saw Jim Munro, one of the four Freeway Killers who smiled at me; the Trash Bag Murderer, whose blank face was framed by the square window in the solid metal door; and Kenneth Bianchi, the Hillside Strangler who motioned for me to come over and talk with him. The sound of my heels on the floor had alerted them to my presence.

Aside from those who made a deal, all these killers faced a possible death penalty verdict. My own feelings on the death penalty were conflicted, becoming more so after each interaction with unrepentant murderers. Raised in a strict Baptist household, my religious teachings said it was wrong to take anyone's life. Wrestling with ambivalent feelings, I weighed ingrained ideas from my parents and clergy against a hardening belief that these men were animals. Despite my professional Hippocratic Oath, to "do no harm," I often found it difficult to stay detached and non-judgmental.

My boss reminded me the job was to keep them from killing themselves. They needed to be alive for trial and then the system will decide their fate, saying "That was the state's job. You are not here to do therapy, or analyze them, just give them support." In other words, give them coffee, cookies and chat about whatever they want. However, my boss never told me how to keep this job from damaging my mental and emotional health?

Feeling guilty about destroying Greg Miley's life, Bonin had voiced his concerns to me weeks earlier. He probably knew I was scheduled to meet with him based on a simple truth: inmates know everything because they are bored and eavesdrop on staff conversations, pepper deputies with questions, jailhouse gossip and info from waste baskets when trustees clean our offices.

Miley's story, chronicled in detail earlier, piqued my interest in regard to a psychological report revealing an I.Q. of 57, which indicates a defective level of intellectual functioning. There were no signs of cerebral pathology and/or overt psychosis. One psychologist's diagnostic impression was that he was "emotionally unstable personality disorder with a tendency to abuse drugs. Mild mental retardation."

Accompanied by a deputy, Miley arrived five minutes later at my office. He looked around the room, grinned at me, and without hesitation walked to the chair opposite and sat down. After getting comfortable, he looked at the deputy expecting to be cuffed down to the chair's arm. Without my nod of permission, much to Miley's surprise, the officer left without cuffing him.

Looking like a lost kid, Miley had long, flowing blond hair surrounding a face showing jailhouse pallor. The blue jumpsuit hung on his thin body, swallowing up his petite 100-pound, five-foot four-inch frame. I introduced myself, but Miley was uninterested in catching my name. After he checked the room out, he turned back towards me with a sudden look of recognition.

"Hey, I've seen you down in 1700 when you come to talk to Bonin."

"Bill asked me to talk with you, wanted me to make sure you are doing okay. He also wants you to know he isn't mad at you."

"What do you do here?" Greg asked while scratching his head.

"I'm a psychologist, for you to talk to. Just let a deputy know when you want to see me."

"Okay."

"I've read that you were involved with Bonin."

"Yeah, Mom didn't like him, thought he was weird, maybe a cop. Scared he might arrest me for drugs, but I tole her Bill weren't no cop. He was good to me, kinda like a father," Miley said half-defensively. "He bought me cloths, took me out to the movies, got me drugs. We were sex buddies, you know, he looked out for me."

"How did you get along with your parents?"

"Not too good. See, she got divorced and married again a bunch of times. She got pretty lonely. One time I came home from school, and she was sitting there on the couch in in her short, shorts. She patted the couch beside her and tole me to come and sit close to her. Okay? We talked a little and then she reached over and unzipped my pants and started rubbing my stuff."

"Had she ever done that before?"

"No, never."

"How did you feel about what she did?"

"Well, it was weird, but it felt good."

"How old were you?"

"Bout fifteen, maybe younger, holy shit I got a good boner. We made out for a while then she says we should go into the bedroom. I said sure. We go into there and really get it on. But see I had a girlfriend living with me. I got really nervous she might find out about mom and me and get jealous. Mom suggested we have dinner together, you know, to talk 'bout all of it."

"What happened?"

"We all started getting it on together. It was great," Miley giggled and slapped his hand on my desk, almost knocking my plant over. I jumped at this sudden bombastic behavior.

"When the cops picked you up in Houston, I read that you admitted to the police that you decided to kill someone with Bonin."

"Well, one night he comes over to my house and said he wanted to talk to me 'bout something. We go out and sit in his van and he says, 'You wanna go out and have sex with someone and then kill them? Well, I sez, why not," he said with a weird grin.

"I'd never done anything like that before, it sounded exciting. So, we go out and get this here kid to have sex and kill him."

"How did you feel afterward?"

"Well, I was high, feeling good. We got two that same time. One was only twelve and I told Bill he was too young, but he wanted another one, so we got him."

"How did you feel after killing the two boys?"

"Well, ya know, after the first kid I was tired and just kinda checked out. Just ready to go home and get some shut eye. I said that's enough, let's go home. But Bill said no, he said, 'I need another one.' Bill got what he wanted, fuck, I was too scared to say no to him, he might've killed me too."

"Did it bother you to kill the kids?"

"Well, a little, that one kid, the twelve-year-old goin' to Disneyland, I felt bad about that."

"Were you afraid of getting caught?"

"Nah, we was moving to Texas, I figured I'd be okay."

"Bill wants you to know he is not mad about you testifying against him. He cares about you," I told him not really believing Bonin did.

"Okay," Miley looked at the floor. "We through here?"

Miley was also a victim, consigned to a life behind bars for going along with Bill Bonin. I stepped out of my office and summoned a deputy to return Miley to his cell. Poor Greg Miley, own mother seduced him as a teenager, then he had a threesome with the girlfriend and his mother. Someone having a difficult time negotiating life, with little intellectual understanding, has to deal with this kind of twisted family psychopathology.

With parents like that, is it any wonder so many dysfunctional souls are running around.

Alone in my office, I had some quiet time to reflect on what Bonin told me during our last session. In between court dates, Bonin vacillated between boredom, anxiety and fear awaiting the trial. Life in jail rarely changed much. Bonin restlessly paced around his cell bumping into the walls after six steps by nine steps. He said, "My bed is anchored in the cement floor on one side of the cell, and the steel shitter is bolted to the floor, on the opposite wall, it's cold to sit on even in the summer."

Impossible to know if it was day or night outside, or if the world still existed outside the jail's stifling universe. He longed for the simple things he always took for granted. Being escorted along the walkway, from the bus into the courthouse, was his only time outside the jailhouse building. They weren't allowed roof time because of personnel shortages; keeping High Power inmates safe from the general population was paramount. If an inmate was lucky enough to take out a big killer, he would earn respect from the inmates.

Bonin's history revealed that he never liked doing anything alone, noted repeatedly throughout this narrative. His charismatic ability to recruit others, and lure victims into his grasp, are the hallmarks of a clever, shape shifting sociopath. Three of the five younger men he recruited to kill with him, Butts, Miley and Munro, were emotionally dependent people who were frightened of Bonin; they were not bright and easily led to destruction.

The same is not true of Billy Pugh and Eric Wijnaendts: Pugh first met and killed with Bonin on the same night, never to interact with him again except for brief encounter two days later. Eric knew him briefly in jail and they had a sexual fling in late May 1980, killed two kids, and then Bonin was arrested weeks later.

Butts, Miley and Munro were younger and exhibited moral depravity and weakmindedness by getting talked into killing with Bonin, but to compare them mentally to the others is a mistake. Pugh and Eric were smarter, in fact they were clever enough to get away much cleaner than the others for their involvement with Bonin.

62

Trial Starts, Lawyer Change, Jury Selection & Roadblocks
October 19 to November 3, 1981

On a grim Monday morning the long-anticipated Bonin Freeway Killer serial killer murder trial was about get underway, with all the heartbreaking and gruesome reality and recrimination that would entail. Knowing what Bonin did in general differs dramatically from parades of uncomfortable testimony, depressing photographs and forensic exhibits that will be available for the media to display and report about.

Journalists from around the world, interested spectators, victim's family members and many others were among those in attendance for Bill Bonin's long anticipated trial at the Criminal Courts Building at 210 W. Temple Street in Downtown Los Angeles. The biggest mass murder trial in Southern California history was being held on the 15th floor with Judge William B. Keene, a respected jurist who handled the Charles Manson trials in 1970, overseeing the proceedings.

First order of business was the official appointment of William Charvet as Bonin's attorney, a motion Keene denied a month earlier but was forced to accept after Bonin threatened to represent himself. The case went to the California Supreme Court for a ruling.

Before making it final, Keene heard from Charvet, "I've had only a little over one month to prepare, and I'm not as comfortable as I would be with two or three months, but Mr. Bonin says he still wants me as his attorney." Keene asked Bonin for confirmation and then installed Charvet.

Then, according to a UPI article, the "judge denied a defense motion to bar television cameras and tape recorders from the courtroom, but told broadcast journalists they would not be allowed to tape or photograph the jury selection process." Deputy DA Sterling Norris planned to call 100 witnesses of all types, at least 25 which would need "substantial cross examination."

Linda Deutsch's October 20 AP article, printed in the **San Bernardino County Sun,** described the scene, "The 34-year-old Bonin, clad in a blue jumpsuit, listened intently as Superior Court Judge William Keene began questioning prospective jurors on whether they could spend four months on the complicated case. Many said it would be a hardship. The trial's estimated length, coupled with heavy publicity about the case, was expected to make jury selection a longer task than usual."

Jury selection took an agonizing three weeks to complete.

Family members who were on hand, representing Bonin's victims, were easily spotted in the audience as many sobbed into a handkerchief or looked emotionally spent. Mark Shelton's mother, Ramona, informed reporters she would be there every single day, saying, "I feel it's just as bad being at home waiting. But now, I don't know. We want to get on with our lives, but we can't until this is over." She was seeing a psychiatrist to deal with the pain of losing her son. Barbara Biehn, mother of Steven Wood, said "How could somebody do what he's accused of doing? It's like a nightmare."

Sean King's sister, Randi Mancini, and mother, Lavada Gifford, were in attendance. The 24-year-old sibling told reporters that "there was simply no way to prepare emotionally for the trial. You just have to have your faith in the Lord and know that no matter what happens, when you leave here judgment will be passed. I pray for William Bonin. I pray for his soul. He's a sick man. He needs help."

King's mother, who was deeply impacted by Sean's death, said, "Faith has sustained us, for a long time, we just couldn't face getting up in the morning."

But before the prosecutors were able to make their opening statements, on Thursday, November 5 a defense motion to vacate all charges against Bonin had to be dealt with, and it all emanated from the December 1980 detective interviews. Kept secret for over six-months, their existence broke in the media and caused multiple legal issues to arise.

A feature article by **LA Times** Staff Writer Gene Blake, **Defense Loses Motion to Halt Bonin Trial**, described what happened:

"Accused Freeway Killer William G. Bonin furnished information to authorities implicating two accomplices who then pleaded guilty and agreed to testify against him, it was revealed Tuesday. But Los Angeles Superior Court Judge William B. Keene denied a defense motion seeking to have the case against Bonin thrown out on the grounds that the prosecution violated a tape-recorded agreement not to use the information supplied by Bonin against him. Keene said the trial will go forward with opening statements to a jury of seven men and five women, followed by testimony from the first of about 100 witnesses the prosecution plans to call."

Keene listened to the relevant portion of the tape, where Bonin talked about doing the interviews to avoid the death penalty and that, without a deal, they couldn't be used against him. Then he spoke with Miley and Munro, who were slated to testify but had just changed their pleas, with their attorneys present. Munro and Miley both pled guilty months earlier; Munro in LA and Miley in LA and Orange County

Blake sums up what happened:

"On the witness stand Tuesday, both Munro and Miley testified they changed their pleas to not guilty after learning that Bonin had made a statement to authorities implicating them in the murders. Munro, however, insisted that was only one of the reasons. Both Goldstein and Steinberg testified they advised their clients to change their pleas after hearing Bonin's taped statement.

"Because of their plea bargains with the prosecution, Munro and Miley will not face execution, but will receive sentences of up to life in prison after they testify against Bonin. Bonin's attorney, William Charvet, argued that the case should be suppressed because the prosecution will, in effect, use the information supplied by Bonin against him. But Deputy DA Sterling Norris said Bonin's statement will be introduced against him."

All the machinations amongst the attorneys for Bonin, Miley and Munro amounted to nothing. Bonin's trial will start on November 4, 1981 and the same issues will follow everyone down to Orange County for the next trial, and all through Bonin's endless appeals.

63

Opening Remarks & Family Testimony
November 1981

On Wednesday, November 4, 1981 the opening remarks in the William Bonin Freeway Killer trial took place. Nearly a year and a half in the making, the reputations of prosecutors, law enforcement and defense attorneys were on the line. Beyond that, politicians who governed counties and cities throughout Southern California were keenly interested in a proper outcome: A Bonin death penalty.

"Superior Court is now in session, the Honorable William B. Keene presiding." Without flurry the man in the black robe walked up the stairs to the bench and assumed his position in the black leather chair. In a bit of irony, later that day Charles Manson, whose trial Judge Keene presided over, would be denied parole for the fourth straight year. Billy Pugh's trial started a week earlier in the same building; he refused a deal to testify against Bonin and was taking his chances with a jury trial.

Deputy DA Norris had on display a massive chart with pictures of each victim and details of their murder—a billboard plain and clear enough for the jury of seven men and five women to see, read and digest.

"Mr. Norris do you wish to make an opening statement?" Keene asked.

"Yes, your honor.

"If it please the court, counsel, and ladies and gentlemen of the jury, let me indicate to you that the prosecution in this case is going to prove to you that the man seated over there, that has been sitting over there, William G. Bonin, is the mass killer of 12 young men and boys ranging in the age from 12 to 19. We will indeed prove in this courtroom that he is the Freeway Killer.

"We will prove to you that when William G. Bonin got into his van and started down the freeways of Southern California that he was driving a death van for many young men and boys. Mr. Bonin had decided they all would die, so there would be no one to go to the police. He had a premeditated plan to pick up young men and sodomize them before taking their lives, regardless of their sexual preferences.

"He would kick them while they were tied up, just kick them, having nothing to do with the killing portion of it, just kick them and thump them and beat them about the head as they lay there tied up like a hog, their arms behind their backs and their ankles tied, stuff some type of gag in their mouth, then take some kind of ligature, whether it be his T-Shirt, stick it around his neck and wind it around and choke and throttle that young boy to death.

"Some had skull fractures, one had an icepick driven through his ear, another's sexual organs were cut off. In one instance, immediately after killing one, Bonin said, 'Let's go get another one.' He had an insatiable appetite not only for sodomy but for killing. Part of his reason was to enjoy the killing of those humans, that he would stab them, stab them in the testicles, stab them in other areas."

During much of Norris' two-and-half-hour opening statement, Bonin sat calmly, only reacting to lean over and whisper something to his attorney, William Charvet. The jury sat stone faced as the litany of tortures and crimes were listed. He also related that two accomplices, Miley and Munro, would testify along with four informants who conversed with Bonin about various murders.

"Mr. Charvet, do you wish to make an opening statement?" Judge Keene asked the defense counsel.

"Yes honor, thank you," Charvet said in measured words. "The District Attorney told you things that are repulsive, repugnant to everybody in the world. No one here doesn't have sympathy for every parent or relative for every one of the children killed. The question is, can the district attorney prove beyond a reasonable doubt that Mr. Bonin is the one who killed these victims? There are a lot of inconsistencies in the statements that will be coming from witnesses. A man's life is hanging in the balance."

A UPI Article, ***Murder Trial Mothers Hear Cruel Words***, published by ***The Province*** newspaper in Vancouver, Canada described part of the opening day, "The mothers of four murdered teenagers sat quietly in court, occasionally glancing at each other as the prosecutor told jurors how the Freeway Killer had sexually abused, tortured and strangled a dozen young men and boys lured into his 'death van.'

"Two more mothers were among the opening prosecution witnesses Wednesday in the murder trial of William Bonin, a truck driver who allegedly masterminded the slayings. Mary Rodriguez choked back her emotions as she identified the bloodied face of her blonde and slender son, Donald Hyden, 15, in a photograph taken after his death. Violet Lerma, in an even voice, recalled she lost her slender, brown-haired son, David Murillo, 17, when 'he told me he was going to a movie theater.'"

Another grieving mother took the stand the next day. ***The Sacramento Bee*** published a UPI article, ***Moms Identify Grisly Photos of Sons in Freeway Killings***, which offered a view, "In a trembling voice, a mother identified a photograph of her son's body Thursday for jurors in the murder trial of accused Freeway Killer William Bonin, charged with 12 grisly homosexual slayings. Asked if the youth in the photograph was 19-year-old Darin Kendrick, Patricia Kendrick, fighting back tears over a quivering chin, 'Yes sir.'

"Kendrick said she last saw and heard from her son April 29, 1980, the day he disappeared while working as a box boy at a supermarket. Kendrick's nude, strangled body was found dumped near an industrial area in Carson. A Los Angeles sheriff's deputy testified that Kendrick had been stabbed in the ear with an icepick and a caustic solution had been poured down his chin."

The first week concluded, on Friday, with the jury being shown gruesome photographs of Thomas Lundgren, who was brutally beaten, stabbed and emasculated. Lundgren's father identified the pictures and Sgt. Kushner, LA Sheriff's Dept., described the gruesome scene in detail. Bonin didn't commit this murder and was ultimately cleared by the jury.

Many other relatives testified about actual Bonin victims as ***Los Angeles Times*** Staff Writer Gene Blake describes:

"Ann Jean Macabe of Garden Grove identified the pictures of her son, James Michael Macabe, 12. He was last seen on Feb. 3, 1980, in Huntington Beach after leaving the home of his older brother, William, to catch a bus for an outing at Disneyland. The Macabe boy's body was found three days later behind an industrial building in Walnut, near the Pomona Freeway.

"Sheriff's homicide detective Evan Dillon testified that there were ligature marks on the boy's neck, a bruise on his penis and an indentation in the back of his head. Found with the body were some Disneyland tickets given the boy by his mother. Folke Grabs of West Germany identified pictures of his brother, Markus, 17, and said he last saw him when he left Germany in February 1979, on a trip to Paris, London, New

York, Vancouver and Los Angeles. Earlier testimony showed that the Grabs youth was last seen alive on Aug. 5, 1979, near Newport Beach, headed for Mexico. His body, bearing about 70 stab wounds, was found the next morning on Las Virgenes Road in the Malibu Canyon."

The following week, after a number of coroners testified, James Munro took the witness stand as the first of two accomplices scheduled to appear as prosecutorial witnesses. Munro, who told the story as it happened except for a few details, was caught out by Charvet in a variety of inconsistencies designed to damage his credibility. But it was crystal clear Bonin ran the show; he decided to go out hunting and orchestrated the murder scenario, ending with Munro holding down Wells' legs while Bonin strangled him with a T-Shirt.

In the **LA Times**, on November 14, Gene Blake related a macabre story about what happened afterwards, one included earlier but one which needs repeating: "Munro testified that he and Bonin drove around dark side roads looking for a like place to dump the body. He said they rolled down the windows when the van began 'smelling' from the body. Then they stopped at a McDonald's and ordered hamburgers, paying for them with $10 taken from the Wells youth, Munro testified.

"After dumping the body behind a gas station, Munro said, they returned to Bonin's home and began eating the hamburgers and watching television news to see there were reports of the body being found. At one point, Munro testified, Bonin took a bite of hamburger, looking heavenward and said, 'Thanks Steve,' then he looked downward and added, 'Thanks Steve, wherever you are.' 'He started laughing, and I started laughing too,' Munro told the jury."

Steve Twomey, of Knight-Ridder Newspapers, had an article published on Wednesday, November 18, in the ***Detroit Free Press***, which reported on many different aspects of the trial, some not found in other articles. ***Killing—For Sheer Pleasure: Lurid Testimony in Calif. Freeway Murder Trial*** reported how Norris emphasized that Bonin "enjoyed the killing; part of his reason was to enjoy the killing of those human beings." Then Twomey offered a quote from Vernon Butts' "preliminary testimony" that was read aloud in the courtroom (Butts committed suicide 11 months earlier). Butts said, "He really loved those sounds of screams. He loved to hear 'em scream, he loved every minute of it. He would come over to my house and he would finally say, 'Hey, great, come on, let's get going. I wanna get another one.' He kinda scared me."

For all the public clamor and intense interest in seeing the Freeway Killer brought to justice, Twomey noticed something else, "Surprisingly, despite the lurid nature of the trial, the spacious, dark-paneled courtroom on the 15th floor of the Criminal Courts Building downtown has been empty save for the participants, several reporters and the families of the dead. Los Angeles, it seems, is bored with mass murders. There have been so many. Monday, in fact, in a courtroom just 30 yards away from where the trial of the alleged Freeway Killer is under way, the case of alleged Hillside Strangler was beginning. Angelo Buono, Jr., 49, a Glendale upholsterer, is accused of murdering 10 women in a pattern every bit as random as the Freeway Killer's."

To emphasize his point, Twomey listed a few of the other mass murder trials percolating through the LA court system.

Scott Frazer testified about the history of his relationship with Bonin. While largely true, Fraser lied about Bonin telling him he was the Freeway Killer while showing him ***OC Register*** newspaper stories. As shown earlier, Fraser had no clue Bonin was actually the Freeway Killer until over a month after Bonin was arrested.

That scene, in late July 1980, revealed how detectives showed Fraser a map, and other documents, which caused an immediate recognition of the truth; LAPD Detective Mellecker said, "The hair on his arm's actually stood up, you could just see the entire switch in his viewpoint once it dawned on him."

Fraser was also angling for a possible reward for cooperation.

Before Greg Miley delivered his testimony on the killings of Miranda and Macabe, Detective Krueger related how close the LAPD surveillance team came to stumbling on Bonin and Munro in the act of murdering Steven Wells. That rather tragic bit of mistiming is chronicled in Part Three.

On Friday, November 20 Greg Miley took the witness stand as described in a feature AP article printed in ***The Californian*** newspaper in Salinas, "A shocked hush fell in the courtroom Friday as Miley, seeming almost eager to give his testimony, told how he and Bonin strangled two youths—one of them a 12-year-old on his way to Disneyland. He said that before the two were dead, they were tortured with a crowbar, and said he and Bonin jumped on them until they heard their bones crack. In the midst of the testimony, one mother of another Freeway Killer victim rushed from the courtroom in tears. Others sat with their arms around each other as the testimony continued. The mothers of the two victims whose murders were described were not in court."

Charvet tried to discredit prosecution witnesses while postulating the root causes for his conduct: the physical, sexual and emotional abuse he endured during his early childhood and adolescence. Dr. David Foster, an expert on the developmental effects of violence and abuse on children, testified on his conclusions based on a psychological exam of Bonin. Foster stated that Bonin, from being abandoned multiple times, hadn't received the nurturing protection needed for proper development, thus creating an inability to understand the difference between violence and love.

In turn the prosecution called Dr. Park Dietz, a forensic psychiatrist and expert in impulse disorders and sexual sadism. Dietz testified Bonin's behavioral pattern didn't indicate to him an inability to control his impulses. Bonin's consistent actions reflected enough planning for Dietz to conclude he was a sexual sadist. Although he agreed Bonin also suffered from an intense antisocial personality disorder, he told the jury that neither of these conditions involved a lack of impulse control.

The following Monday, November 23, Miley was cross-examined with William Charvet using his only weapon of defense: discrediting witnesses and evidence. **Los Angeles Times** Staff Writer Gene Blake explained that Miley admitted that he "initially lied to police about his involvement in the strangulation murders of two adolescent boys," but then "told a Los Angeles Superior Court jury that he testified truthfully in linking Bonin to the slayings of Charles Miranda, 15, of Bell Gardens and James Michael Macabe, 12, of Garden Grove." Charvet pointedly asked Miley, "Would you lie to save your life?" After answering no Miley later said that "Bonin had not told him about committing any other murders."

Next came testimony from "jailhouse snitch" Lloyd Douglas, a witness Bonin's attorney tore apart on credibility issues. He brought up the fact that Douglas testified against a number of different serial killer defendants who all "supposedly confessed everything" to him in jail. To further damage his veracity, Charvet revealed how all of Douglas' cooperation got him an amazingly generous sentence reduction for murdering a drug dealer.

Lastly, the jury was told that Douglas was related to one of Bonin's last victims, Larry Sharp's father was his half-brother. Later on, Charvet brought in witnesses who further discredited Douglas.

Last on the stand for November was Phillip Gonzalez, who Bonin knew from Atascadero State Hospital, and Patricia Johnson, a Stanton police officer who arrested him in 1975. After strenuous objections from Charvet, both told the jury they heard Bonin utter a prophetic phrase at around the same time: "There will be no more witnesses."

Gonzales said he heard this twice, once at Atascadero and then again in Hollywood in 1975. Johnson heard him say it in the squad car during his arrest in 1975 and both instances were chronicled earlier.

December proved an action-packed month.

64

Lopez & Alger Testimony Rulings
December 1, 1981

December 1981 started with newspapers reporting that Judge Keene ruled against allowing Dave Lopez, TV reporter for KCBS, or Tim Alger, reporter for the *OC Register*, to testify about what Bonin revealed to them during numerous interviews.

LA Times Staff Writer Gene Blake's article, **Newsmen Barred From Testifying at Bonin Trial**, explained the ruling, "Both said they relied on newsman's privilege contained in state constitutional amendment adopted by voters in 1980. Among other things, the amendment protects reporters from contempt for withholding unpublished information.

"Defense attorney William Charvet argued his client's constitutional rights would be violated if he could not cross-examine the witnesses on details not contained in their news reports. Therefore, Charvet contended, all their testimony should be excluded. Deputy Dist. Atty. Sterling E. Norris countered that the reporters had waived their privilege as to the statements as they reported. He urged the judge to permit some cross-examination as to that material.

"However, Keene said the only way he could compel disclosure would be by the court's contempt power. 'As I read the Constitution, that power has been taken away,' the judge said. 'It is very clear.' Keene said evidence could not be offered unless it were to be volunteered by the two reporters. He then sustained Charvet's objection to all their testimony."

Both were under intense pressure to reveal everything Bonin told them in confidence. Lopez first helped Bonin get his message out about Eric's innocence, a year earlier, regarding the Turner murder and was rewarded with a confession interview a month later. But he was bound to secrecy by arrangements with Bonin, which Lopez felt Bonin violated with Alger for the article series. Lopez did finally go on the air, in June 1981, to reveal that Bonin confessed to him about killing 22 young men and boys, however, as noted above, he refused to divulge details from the interviews he hadn't broadcast. All of these dealings were chronicled in Part Three.

65

Bonin Gets Beat Up & Postponement
December 8, 1981

The second week of December started with Bonin's defense counsel calling to the stand another jailhouse snitch, who discredited Lloyd Douglas, and others who claimed they lied in court. But the real fireworks happened the following morning, Tuesday, December 8, when Bonin was attacked and badly beaten in a courthouse holding cell.

LA Times Staff Writers Jerry Belcher and Richard West's article, ***Bonin Injured; Says He Fell: Found in Cell with Broken Nose, Black Eyes***, reported what happened:

"Accused Freeway Killer William G. Bonin suffered a broken nose, two black eyes and a possible concussion Tuesday in what he told jailers was a fall, forcing postponements of final arguments in his trial. Bonin, 34, suffered the injuries while in a 14th-floor detention cell in the Criminal Courts Building with accused Hillside Strangler Angelo Buono and convicted murderer John W. Stinson, deputy sheriffs said. At 9:40 a.m., just 10 minutes before Bonin was to be taken up to the 15th-floor courtroom where he is being tried for the homosexual murders of 12 youths, a deputy outside the walled cell heard a banging on the wall, sheriff's Sgt. Tom Taylor said. The deputy opened the door and found Bonin standing, holding tissue paper to his bleeding nose, said Taylor, supervisor of prisoner security for Superior Courts in the building. 'What happened?' Taylor quoted the deputy as asking Bonin. 'Nothing, but I want to be changed to another holding cell,' Bonin reportedly replied."

They reported that Bonin had gotten along well with Buono, but Stinson was "a reputed member of the notoriously vicious Aryan Brotherhood, a prison-spawned outlaw gang, and faces a sentence of life in prison without possibility of parole." Bonin, experienced in prison etiquette, knew the best strategy was to take the beating and stay quiet.

Judge Keene, at 10:00 a.m., told the jury closing arguments were delayed because Bonin had "some kind of accident." He was taken to County-USC Medical Center for treatment, and all proceedings were delayed until at least Thursday. Charvet tried to use the incident for further delays, but Norris said he opposed further postponements. On Thursday, December 10, with Bonin in court wearing dark glasses and a nose cast, Keene pushed final arguments till the following Monday. No charges were filed against either Buono or Stinson, the latter having committed a number of violent attacks on inmates.

66

Pelto's Fourth Session with Bonin
December 11, 1981

While Bonin healed from his jailhouse injuries, I was able to see him on the Friday before his trial recommenced. Since late September, our contact was limited by his constant presence in court. I wondered how he was holding up emotionally. Rumors and jailhouse gossip about the incident, three days earlier, were swirling amongst deputies and inmates. Newspaper headlines reflected Bonin's statement of falling down, but the stories reported on the other inmates in the courtroom holding cell with him.

Didn't take much to figure out what happened, the deputies knew and were snickering about Bonin getting laid out by an inmate. Jails and prisons have a pecking order and serial killers like Bonin, with crimes involving the rape and torture of children, were the bottom feeders. Treatment meted out to child molesters are an infamous and gruesome aspect of prison lore.

"You sure you're up for Bonin today?" the deputy asked me with concern.

"He got worked over pretty good, busted nose, black eyes," he said while laughing. "Shit, he's a real mutha, for what he did to those kids, he deserves to get fucked up real good," he added with malice.

"Yeah, I know, sure, I'm ready," I said with resigned exhaustion, it had been rough week.

"He's been wanting to talk with you again. Pelto, you're popular with these perps."

"Thanks for noticing, right now I'm waiting for Jerger to break him out of his cell."

I turned quickly and saw Bonin closing in with a deputy trailing behind. Immediately my eyes went to his battered face, a white nose cast between black and blue eyes with a dark bruise on his cheek. He walked gingerly—I remembered reading that he had been checked for a concussion. An Aryan Brotherhood gangster caught him in the holding cell and did what so many inmates wanted to do; can you imagine if it was a group with time to operate? Bonin moved aside so the deputy could unlock the door.

Bonin never looked like I expected, he just didn't look like a serial killer, so many rarely do; but when speaking of the murders he sounded like one, which always made me queasy. Bonin was a beefy man, about five-feet-seven-inches, and today his appearance was rather scary. His stride was slow and deliberate, the round shoulders slumping forward. When he walked past, into the interview room, my nostrils filled with his body odor.

The deputy trailed us into the claustrophobic room while Bonin moved towards the barber chair. He stepped up and into the brown leather seat, obediently waiting for the deputy to cuff his wrist to the chair arm. The deputy efficiently clamped the handcuffs and exited. The stuffy room, with the overhead fluorescent lights buzzing away, seemed more so and a bit warmer than usual. Bonin turned to where I was seated, his bludgeoned face telling a story all by itself.

"Mr. Bonin, I understand you wanted to see me."

"Yeah."

"The deputy said you fell in the holding cell at court," I said, knowing reality was different and lying about the deputy.

"I didn't fall, that bastard beat me up," he answered brusquely while gently touching the injuries, "You probably read about it, that Aryan Brotherhood motherfucker, Stinson, grabbed me and shoved me into the wall, and then he started punching me in the gut, shit, he broke my nose. Blood poured out all over the place, I tried to defend myself, but I couldn't. He's real strong."

"Didn't the deputies hear what was happening? Didn't they help you?" I asked, knowing the answer.

"Nah! They don't give a fuck. While he was beatin' me, Buono was in there, he just sat and watched, smiling like I was gettin' what I deserved. That asshole didn't lift a finger to help me, shit, guess I didn't expect him to, I wouldn't have helped him," he said as I shifted uncomfortably in the wooden chair and listened. "In my life, I never had anyone to help me. My father beat the shit out of me, my mother never stopped it. They put me in one of those boy's homes, and I got raped by these older guys."

"Why did you say you fell? Stinson should be punished for what he did!"

"Look, Doc, that's not the way things go 'round here," Bonin said with ironic smile. "Stinson is a gang member, when the deputy opened the door, I was standing there with bloody toilet paper on my nose. He noticed Stinson's knuckles were bruised. He knew damn well what went down, he didn't do nothin, probably thinks I deserved the beating."

"Are you okay now?" I meekly asked, struggling to stay stone faced while recalling the murders, maybe he did deserve it.

"Yeah, they took me in for x-rays, thought I might've had a concussion, but I'm okay, I'll be alright. They said my nose will heal, nothing else broken. My whole body is real sore, shit, I ache all over. I guess all these assholes think they got some right to get a shot at me, ya know, getting punished for what I did, wantin me to say I'm sorry for killing those boys, but how can I say that when I couldn't stop myself—I had to do it. It wasn't my fault."

Stunned by his admission, I had no proper words to offer in response; did he want me to tell him he should be excused or forgiven for the murders? From my professional standpoint, I understood the concept of being driven by raging anger and poor impulse control to commit unbelievable acts; but as a thinking person with a sense of morality, I couldn't excuse such behavior. Finding it difficult to remain neutral, I fought my inclinations to perform my work effectively with Bonin, as well as the others.

I lamely suggested he ask for an individual cell the next time he went to court. Bonin covered his mouth, I thought he was going cough before realizing he was laughing at my naivete.

"Doc, you're too much," he quipped. "I did ask, but they're not going to listen to me. They don't give a shit."

His attorney wanted to postpone the trial till all the injuries healed, but the prosecution objected, and proceedings will commence on Monday. When meeting with him, a sense of sadness washed over me; at times difficult to believe he committed those crimes. When he talked about getting beat up by another inmate, I thought he might cry—not so much for the beating, but because no one came to help him—no one cared about him, no one comforted him, he was scared and alone.

I shared these same feelings. Being single and working to support two daughters, while in school, I often felt scared and alone when money got tight and there was no one to help. He exposed a vulnerable side, a human side we all have in common. Bonin was still the damaged child who hadn't gotten proper care. Many of us are that hurt child looking for love and approval, some more damaged than others, some better equipped to deal with the pain. I stepped to the doorway and called for a deputy to return Bonin to his cell, and to let me out of the module.

67

Dave Lopez Decides to Testify
December 14 & 15, 1981

Bonin's trial had been going almost two months, three if one counts jury selection. This was a grinding, pressure packed slog for attorneys, jury, judge, witnesses, families, reporters and the public. With the holiday season just around the corner, the prosecution was anxious to move thru the final arguments and get the jury working on the verdicts. The trial was delayed, due to Bonin's "accident" on December 8, right after the prosecution had rested its case. Charvet already indicated that no defense witnesses would be called.

During the weekend, while Bonin wrestled with his physical injuries, KCBS TV News reporter Dave Lopez was fighting with his conscience. As chronicled earlier, Lopez was the only journalist to whom Bonin confessed everything, well almost everything. Lopez flatly refused to divulge anything beyond what was already broadcast. On Monday, December 14 everything changed as **Washington Post** reporter Jay Mathews explains in his article, ***Reporter's Voluntary Testimony Fuels Journalistic Debate***, which was printed in ***The Charlotte Observer.***

"Prosecutors tried to subpoena Lopez's and Alger's notes and force them to testify. But superior court Judge William Keene ruled that the California shield law protected them. Up to that point, Lopez said he was fairly sure he did not want to testify. 'I kept thinking they've got enough,' he said. 'I am not a deeply religious person,' he continued, 'but I prayed a lot the whole time in January.' When the final arguments at the trial were suddenly postponed because Bonin was injured in what appeared to be a jailhouse fight, 'it made me realize that someone greater than me was trying to tell me something,' Lopez said, and at the last minute he told prosecutors he would testify."

Lopez told reporters he agonized over the weekend and, after making the decision, felt as "though a 100-pound weight has been taken off me." Deputy DA Norris was able to get permission, over Charvet's objections, to reopen the prosecution's case. Beyond Lopez revealing what Bonin said about the murders, what proved key was the jury hearing new info during a trial with over 100 witnesses. Before getting to specifics, it is worth knowing part of Lopez's ordeal transmitted to the jury during the defense's follow-up cross-examination.

Charvet, according to an AP story, had wanted to reveal "a conspiracy between the reporter and police to bring up the damaging testimony at a time when it would be difficult for the defense to counter it. Lopez said he had been urged to testify ever since he interviewed Bonin in jail last January. 'Several officers said that I would seal the case shut, but they've been saying that since back in January,' he said. 'I never knew I was so popular with the police.' Lopez said he was not pressured into testifying, that he followed his own conscience."

When Charvet suggested Lopez "offered or paid" a law enforcement officer $50,000 to acquire intel on Bonin, Lopez shot back disgustedly, "Are you kidding."

To the six points the jury heard, for the first time, from Lopez during his prosecution testimony. From an overall viewpoint, these were vital aspects of Bonin's story the jury needed to hear. Knowing his decision would elicit criticism and debate throughout journalistic circles, Lopez deserves credit for stepping up and taking the heat.

Gene Blake's **Los Angeles Times** article, ***TV Newsman Ends Silence on Interviews***, was the source for the quotes and info to follow:

1) Bonin revealed to Dave Lopez that he took police to the remains of Sean King in response to a heartfelt letter from King's mother, who was in the audience crying as Lopez told the story. Remember, that was a fake letter written to Bonin as a trick by LAPD homicide detective Sgt. St. John.

2) Bonin "related how he picked up King at a bus stop in Downey, Lopez testified. He quoted Bonin as saying, 'I got the kid in the van and I killed him the way I did the others.'" He was lying to cover for Eric Wijnaendts, as chronicled earlier. King was picked up in the Chevette and

killed in the San Bernardino Mountains with Eric. Of course, the jury and no one else knew that until the publication of this book.

3) Then there was the Kendrick murder: "Lopez said Bonin put the blame on Vernon Butts, initially a co-defendant with him in six of the murders, for thrusting an icepick into the right ear of the Kendrick boy. 'Vern got really weird that night and stuck ice picks in his head,' Lopez quoted Bonin as saying. Through Lopez, the jury heard for the first time that Butts, 22, had hanged himself in the County Jail last January. Charvet protested in vain to the judge, who had tried to keep any reference to the suicide out of the trial."

4) Bonin denied any involvement in the Lundgren murder.

5) Lopez was told the murders started in August 1979 and ended when he was "arrested with a youth in his van in Hollywood on June 11, 1980." Bonin said he would have "killed the kid in the van" if he wasn't arrested that night.

6) Lastly, Bonin chillingly said, "I'd still be killing. I couldn't stop killing. It got easier each time."

Reactions ran the gamut, with police and victim's families calling Lopez a hero to those in his profession offering praise and disapproval.

Jack Landau, **Director of the Reporters Committee for Freedom of the Press**, expressed both sides of equation: "Lopez demonstrated that in a sensational murder trial, the courts of California will uphold the reporter's right to confidentiality." Having prevailed in that fight, Landau believes he had every right as an individual with a conscience to testify.

A December 18, 1981 *LA Times* article, ***Newsmen Generally Criticize Lopez Decision to Testify***, by Times Staff Writer David Shaw broke down some of the arguments:

"***Los Angeles Times*** reporter William Farr was even more critical of Lopez. Farr spent 47 days in jail during an eight-year court fight over his refusal to disclose the source of a story he wrote during the Charles Manson murder trial in 1970, while Farr was a reporter for the ***Herald Examiner***. 'I sympathize with Lopez's dilemma, but I disagree with his choice,' Farr said. 'He says he's a citizen first and a reporter second, but Bonin talked to him because he was a reporter, not a plain citizen.'

"Lopez had no right to abrogate his promise of confidentiality to Bonin, Farr said, no matter what Bonin later told other reporters or anyone else.

'You can't break your promise just because Bonin did,' Farr said. 'If you do, if you're guided by situational ethics like that, I'm worried about the fallout. Will a source trust a reporter if he knows reporters don't always keep their promises of confidentiality?' Farr said he also worries that Lopez may have established 'a dangerous precedent' by testifying and that, if Bonin is convicted, prosecutors and judges in future cases may invoke Lopez's testimony as 'proof' that a reporter should testify to help convict a dangerous criminal.

"Several editors interviewed by **The Times** voiced this concern. Others, however, said Lopez's case was an aberration, in part because he testified voluntarily, not under court order. Even these editors were critical of his behavior, though. 'No reporter should take the confession of a murder off the record,' said Eugene Patterson, editor and president of the **St. Petersburg Times**. 'He (a reporter) should say don't talk to me in that situation. If you take that confession, you're duty about to step forward (and tell authorities). I don't think journalists can get themselves in the position of using the First Amendment to shield someone for murder. It seems to me he has damaged the California shield law. The purpose of the shield law is to help us expose things, not conceal evidence.'

"A few journalists, however, said they thought Lopez provided a valuable—and successful—test of the state's relatively new shield law."

Dave Lopez said that strangers stopped him on the street to express deep appreciation and a victim's family member sent him a card with "thank you written 100 times."

68

Final Arguments & Jury Gets Case
December 21 to 28, 1981

Eighteen months after his arrest, the final arguments in the Bonin Freeway Killer trial began on Friday, December 18, 1981.

Seven men and five women sat for over two-months hearing testimony of all kinds from detectives, victim's parents, accomplices, fellow inmates, coroners, doctors, forensic experts, informants, mental health experts, a TV news reporter who Bonin confessed to and just about everything in between. Deputy DA Norris, and the whole prosecution team, had run through a veritable gauntlet of obstacles to arrive at this point, when all the work was summarized and handed over to a jury of twelve citizens to decide Bonin's ultimate fate.

An AP article, *'Freeway Killer' Defense Team Hits Co-Conspirators' Stories*, printed in the **Times-Advocate** in Escondido, California contained interesting parts of the summation. "Bonin, a twice-paroled sex offender, faces the death penalty if convicted on 12-counts of murder. Since 1972, the bodies of more than 40 youths have been found nude along Southern California freeways. Police are unsure whether all the killings are linked. Bonin had pleaded innocent."

This is sloppy reporting as the "over 40 number" regarding Bonin had been put to rest by LAPD soon after he was arrested.

Next the article described an emotional part of Norris' arguments. He was quoted as saying, "If just one of these victims could take the stand and tell you about the humiliation, the degradation of ending his life this way, there would be no question what the result out to be." The article continued, "When he told jurors the 12 victims never would see their families again and 'will not see the coming Christmas,' the mother of victim Sean King hurried from the courtroom with tears in her eyes."

After noting certain commonalities with the murders—all young white men and boys strangled, sometimes with their own T-shirts, all discarded naked in desolate areas or by freeways—Norris said this, "Those dump sites are part of Mr. Bonin's habits—to use those freeways to put a body some distance from where it was killed. These ligatures are a trademark—it's like a signing Bonin on each and every murder."

In another example of unprofessional journalism, UPI got into the act with this paragraph from a syndicated article, *The Accused Freeway Killer Described as Animal on Prowl*, which was printed in *The Napa Valley Register* in Northern California:

"The Freeway Killer case was given its name by prosecutors who noticed the similarities in the slayings of 44 young men and boys, whose bodies, many of them sexually molested, were found near freeways in five Southern California counties from 1972-80."

1) As chronicled earlier, the Freeway Killer moniker was coined by J.J. Maloney, reporter for the *OC Register*, three months before Bonin was arrested.

2) Again, the use of the number 44 shows poor research. LAPD and LA Sherriff's told the media over a year earlier about multiple ongoing investigations before and after Bonin started killing and was apprehended.

Here are a few quotes from Norris' closing arguments that were reported in Gene Blake's *Los Angeles Times* article from Saturday, December 19, *Bonin Portrayed as Having 'Insatiable' Appetite for Killing*:

"He has an insatiable appetite for this type of killing, he fully enjoys the whole episode."

"He enjoys being the Freeway Killer in front of other individuals."

After laying out all the different scientific evidence—blood, semen stains, hair and carpet fibers—Norris said, "The only man that isn't eliminated is William Bonin."

Telling the jury about how Bonin found accomplices who were easily manipulated, pointing specifically at Munro and Miley, Norris declared that neither would have involved in murder "without that man right there—without Mr. Bonin."

Deputy DA Norris concluded his final arguments with this powerful statement:

"This evidence, this overwhelming evidence against this defendant has earned him convictions in these brutal deaths. Give him what he has earned. Give him what he deserves."

Judge Keene gave the jury final instructions after the Christmas holiday recess on Monday, December 28.

69

Jury Verdicts
January 9 to 20, 1982

On Wednesday, January 9, 1982, two days before his 35th birthday, the jury gave Bill Bonin an early present in the form of 10 murder convictions.

Judge Keene tasked the jury with making decisions on parallel tracks; 1) Decide guilty or not guilty on each murder charge; 2) Determine if "special circumstances," robbery and murder, could be applied in order to make him eligible for the death penalty.

The seven men and five women deliberated for six days before alerting the court they were finished.

An insightful **New York Times** article by Robert Lindsey, ***Los Angeles Jury Convicts Man Accused in 10 Killings***, described the proceedings:

"The reading of the verdicts lasted almost an hour. As the verdict was read in the dry tones of a court clerk, mothers and other relatives of some of the victims, most of whom were from blue-collar families in southern California suburbs, sat in the front row of the court of Judge William Keene. Several cried. Mr. Bonin, a muscular man twice convicted of sexual perversion and molesting children, stared ahead of him, showing no emotion."

The jury found him guilty with "special circumstance" on 10 of the 12 charges; he was acquitted in the Thomas Lundgren and Sean King cases.

Bonin was not involved in the Lundgren murder and his agreement with law enforcement, to reveal King's location in the San Bernardino Mountains, gummed up the works on that case.

"I think it's a very good verdict." Deputy DA Norris said. "A very just verdict that was fully earned by Mr. Bonin. We will ask for the death penalty."

Defense attorney Charvet, when asked by reporters if it was a "just" verdict, refused to answer but pointed out that TV newsman Dave Lopez's last-minute testimony had a "substantial, very substantial" effect.

This was a fair assumption: Lopez's last-minute decision to voluntarily testify, forcing the prosecution to reopen its case, made him, for all practical purposes, the final witness in a 10-week trial with over 100 witnesses. This meant the stories he related, some containing new info, were fresh in the minds of the jurors when they convened. Bonin's jailhouse confessions to Lopez must have made quite an impression on the jury. Two weeks later, on January 20, the jury recommended the death penalty, a decision Judge Keene would confirm or reject at a later date.

A syndicated UPI article by Mark Barabak reported the big story, "The jury that convicted William Bonin of 10 counts of murder in the brutal Freeway Killer torture-slayings decided Wednesday that he should be executed in the gas chamber for each of the homosexual killings. The mass murderer, dressed in blue jailhouse coveralls, sat silently with his chin resting in his hand as the court clerk announced 10 times, one for each of the convictions, 'the penalty shall be death.'

"Bonin's attorney said his client, who will become the 85th person on California's death row, 'expected nothing less' than the death sentence. When the court session ended, several relatives of the victims hugged and kissed each other, as well as police investigators who had put together the case against Bonin and prosecutors who had won the convictions and death penalty."

Barbara Biehn, the mother of a 16-year-old Steven Wood, put it bluntly, "I'll celebrate when they actually drop that pellet."

70

Death Penalty & Pelto's Last Session with Bonin
Monday, March 15, 1982

On the evening of Friday, March 12, 1982, two months after the jury found Bonin guilty, I was watching the NBC Nightly News when the anchorman made the announcement, "Today Judge William Keene sentenced William Bonin to die in the gas chamber for the murder of ten young men and boys. When Judge Keene pronounced the sentence, he described the murders as 'a gross, revolting affront to human dignity. Bonin had a total disregard for the sanctity of human life and the dignity of a civilized society. Sadistic, unbelievably cruel, senseless, and deliberately premeditated. Bonin is guilty beyond any possible or imaginary doubt.'

"Keene further ordered that if Bonin's death sentence were commuted to life, the sentences should run consecutively. He remanded Bonin to the warden of San Quentin State Prison, to await execution in the gas chamber. Bonin seemed unmoved by the verdict, having informed his attorney he expected the death penalty."

Knowing he would get shipped out right away, I decided to make it a point to see him Monday morning. I chuckled at the thought of how happy the LA Sheriff's Department would be to see the last of Bonin and his accomplices. At some point, in the near future, they would all come back to Orange County for a second trial, but that would have nothing to do with Los Angeles.

Quite sure Bonin was not the suicidal type, I was nonetheless duty bound to prevent such an occurrence and would cover all my bases. After my own dad's sudden death, from a heart attack, I realized how fragile life is and how much of my life's energy was getting chipped away dealing with serial killers. Little by little, slowly but surely, I was losing myself. Essentially, the person who first strolled into LA Men's Jail eight-months earlier was disappearing in small, possibly irretrievable, bits and pieces.

I was definitely more suspicious and less trusting—definitely more cynical and less lighthearted—and infinitely more able to believe the worst in people and less shocked at vile and atrocious human behavior. These were all the elements for an altered personality.

Another aspect was my increasingly shaky stand on the contentious death penalty issue; a strict religious upbringing, which taught that all life was sacred, was colliding with hard core reality, and reality was winning. How could I possibly defend all these malicious, unrepentant reprobates who so willfully snuffed out life, who seemed to have no cares or thoughts for the gaping holes they left in families, communities and society.

My perspective had shifted, and I concluded that Bonin, and many others, should be executed.

As if knowing my intentions, Deputy Jerger rang me up first thing to say Bonin was acting strange and I should see him. Not surprised Bonin was jarred by Judge Keene's decision, I gathered up my gear and went down to his module. Getting off the elevator, I walked the short distance down the hall and pounded on the metal door, using alternate fists while trying to get a deputy's attention. Finally, a deputy peered through the small window and recognized me.

"You here to see Bonin?" the deputy asked.

"Yeah." I said with a deadpan expression.

"Couldn't have happened to anyone more deserving," the deputy said while running a thumb across his throat in a cutting motion. "Occasionally, justice is served," he mumbled while I nodded in tacit agreement.

I checked Bonin's log and found the deputy's verbal report was correct. He was isolating himself, leaving the generally demanded Freeway Time outside his cell unrequested. Bonin's grooming was off as he refused to take a shower or change clothes—all possible signs of depression. After speaking with him, I would determine if moving him to the inpatient unit and suicide watch was appropriate.

Within a few minutes, the deputy appeared with Bonin, a defeated looking man whose stride was slow and deliberate as his shoulders slumped forward, his head hanging down. The deputy pulled out his keys, unlocked the door to the cold, windowless interview room, and flipped on the switch which ignited the overhead fluorescent lights. Without instruction, Bonin pushed the door open, walked to the raised chair and slumped into it as I took the desk chair.

During my time with Bonin, I constantly sought out and dug for some type of psychopathology or mental disorder, but like so many other doctors before me I found nothing. There were no hallucinations, voices or paranoid symptoms, however, he did exhibit the classic symptoms of narcissism and poor impulse control.

Thinking of his crimes, it was difficult to comprehend how he could be considered sane while being so vicious. Simple answer—human evil exists. Complex answer—his upbringing spat out a creature beyond help.

I scrutinized Bonin's face as he looked around the room. After inspecting the surroundings, he turned to face me. I waited for him to speak, tapping the underside of the desk, trying to relax.

"Well, Doc, I'm sure you've heard I've been sentenced to death, I'm going to the green room," Bonin said in a disbelieving yet resigned manner.

"I know." I said quietly, having nothing to add.

"Actually, I'm not surprised, they got what they wanted, but I couldn't help myself, the urge to kill was too strong. I was hoping for life, shit, I don't want to die!"

"But you were picking up boys for a long time, what changed, what made you start killing?" I inquired, knowing it might be last time I got ask him that question face to face.

"I met Vernon Butts, everybody liked him, we got along well. It was cool having him like me, well, he was into occult and weird stuff like that, games and rituals with death. Anyway, it all started at the drive-in movies, we got to talking about picking up a kid, having sex with him and killing him. After the first one, it didn't feel like no big deal.

"Besides, if I killed them then I didn't have to worry about some kid identifying me. Sometimes, I just felt horny and really restless, I'd get tense and think I was gonna go crazy if I didn't get a release, like my head would explode, so I'd go out hunting and killing. You know Doc, thinking about it got me so worked up, and doin' it helped me mellow out," Bonin explained in a confessional manner.

Listening to him didn't make me sick anymore, a development I found disconcerting at best.

"When you killed a boy, did you ever think about his family?" I asked, suspecting I knew the answer.

"Nah, I didn't feel anything for any of them, or their families, never," he said with a blank look. "Killing them was more important, going out and gettin one was what I wanted most of all," Bonin said, definitely feeling no guilt or remorse.

"If you hadn't been caught, would you have stopped killing?"

"Nah, there weren't no way I could have stopped myself."

"Do you think you wanted to get caught, like you deserved to be punished?" I asked, testing a common theory about serial killers. He looked at me, eyes wide open, as if I was the psychotic.

"You kiddin' me Doc, what a bunch of bullshit, sounds like some do-gooder social worker's theory. I'm only sorry I wasn't more careful, but I did get away with it for a pretty long time," he said with a wry smile and eyes which looked right through me, then he cryptically added, "I wouldn't have stopped unless I got arrested."

After that our conversation before more topical—other inmates, family, appeals to the death sentence, the next trial, etc. Bonin knew the ultimate sentence may not get carried out for years, maybe decades or never. Charles Manson got the death penalty and, on a matter unrelated to his case, had the verdict overturned by the California Supreme Court. Destined never to be carried out, Manson died of old age in 2017.

The death penalty in California was reinstated by the U.S. Supreme Court in 1976, but no one could predict how the political and legal winds might blow before Bonin was executed.

What I found striking, in so many different ways, was that Bonin had just gone through a trial where the complete and total dissection of his crimes caused mothers to break down and rush from courtroom, fleeing in tears to escape more reminders of the horror Bonin had forced them to live with. Yet there he sat, looking me in the eyes devoid of any facial expression, with no sympathy for the victims or the pain caused to friends and family.

Or how about the five men he roped into killing with him; without Bonin they probably would never become murderers.

What I gleaned is this: He was only sorry about not being able to hunt and kill anymore; not being able to taunt, torture and strangle anymore; not being able to see life drain away at his behest ever again!

71

Execution
Friday, February 23, 1996

Bonin was allowed to live 14 more years before his March 1982 Los Angeles County death penalty verdict was carried out.

One year later he was convicted of four more murders in Orange County and sent back to San Quentin State Prison, just outside of San Francisco, to live out his days on Death Row.

In October 1994, San Quentin's gas chamber method of execution, death by breathing cyanide, was deemed "cruel and unusual punishment" by U.S. District Judge Marilyn Patel. Installed in 1938, the gas method was used to execute 196 prisoners before it was outlawed.

One ironic story about the San Quentin gas chamber was told in a book, *Public Justice, Private Mercy*, by former and influential California Gov. Edmund G. "Pat" Brown:

A plumber, serving hard time in San Quentin for robbery, worked on the construction of the chamber and witnessed the gruesome deaths of the test pigs. He was soon paroled, committed murder and was later executed in the very chamber he helped construct. Brown's primary point was that even someone who witnessed the dreaded gas chamber in action was not deterred enough to end up there.

Ken Ellingwood's February 11, 1996, *LA Times* article, *'Freeway Killer' Bonin, 49, Nears Date with Execution This Month*, places Bonin's legacy in perspective, "If he is put to death, Bonin, now 49, would be the first in California to die by lethal injection and only the third state prisoner executed since the U.S. Supreme Court reinstated the death penalty in 1976.

"One of the most prolific mass killers in American history, Bonin helped define an extraordinary frightening period during the late 1970s when the nude bodies of dozens of young men were turning up behind gas stations or in the weeds along Southern California's roads. Bonin's deadly exploits also fed a fast-rising national frenzy over serial killers—a term that came to include such murderers as Ted Bundy, John Wayne Gacy and David Berkowitz.

"In the freeway case, investigators worked around the clock, crisscrossing the region in search of the monster responsible for such cruelty. In fact, there were two monsters out there. Only after Bonin was convicted of killing 14 people in Los Angeles and Orange County did police snare a second, unrelated predator, a computer engineer from Long Beach named Randy Kraft. To detectives, the methods were maddeningly similar. Both men picked up young male hitchhikers and then raped and killed them by strangulation or stabbing."

On a totally different note, Casey Goldberg's somber *New York Times* article, **Boys' Families Hope for Release as Freeway Killer's Execution Nears**, explained the tortured perspective of Sandra Miller, mother of Bonin victim Russell Rugh:

"If Sandra Miller's plans go right, the man who raped, tortured and strangled her 15-year-old son will receive a letter from her on Thursday that reads, in part: 'You taught me a few things: How to hate, that I feel I could kill you, little by little, one piece at a time. You'd best get down on your hands and knees and pray to God for forgiveness. I don't know if even He could forgive you. But I hope the Lord can forgive me for how I feel about you. P.S. May you burn in hell.' Then, a few hours later, Ms. Miller intends to watch William G. Bonin, better known as the Freeway Killer, who spread terror through Southern California by sadistically murdering at least 14-boys, get executed by lethal injection at San Quentin Prison."

Miller was quoted in the **Orange County Register** saying, "I had a very difficult time. I was so depressed until my grandchildren were born. That lightened my life. I was suicidal, I was in therapy. It was a tragedy you can't begin to imagine."

Bernie Esposito, who hunted Bill Bonin as an OC Sheriff's homicide detective, said, "I can't even put him in the category of an animal. An animal kills for food. I can't feel any empathy for the guy."

LA Times Staff Writer Dexter Filkins, in a Sunday, February 18 article **The Twisted Life That Led Bonin to Death Row**, explored his complete lack of remorse, "Bonin's many attorneys through the years offer claims of his humanity—his great love for his mother, his generosity to fellow inmates, his paintings and short stories.

"They do not speak of remorse. Except for a few isolated references in his psychological records, Bonin has evidently never expressed any shame for what he did, nor has he sought forgiveness. Lavada Gifford of Long Beach traded letters with Bonin for many months. Bonin confessed to murdering her son, 14-year-old Sean King, although he was never convicted of that crime.

"Not once, Gifford said, did Bonin mention the murder. She broke off the correspondence in the late 1980s. 'It was all about him and his favorite TV shows,' she said. 'He never acknowledged that he did anything wrong.' Just this month, Lavada Gifford decided to give Bonin one more chance and wrote him a final letter. If there is anything you want to say to me, the letter said, say it now. 'I was always hoping he would say he is sorry,' she said. So far, no reply."

The Day Before

Outside the stone walls of San Quentin rain drizzled down on a shivering crowd. In anticipation of raucous protests, which never materialized, 150 officers from 11 law enforcement agencies were on hand.

At the outside gates around 100 people marched back and forth carrying anti-death penalty placards like **Stop Executions**, **Death Penalty Isn't Humane**, and **Heal All Hate with Love**. Reporters also focused on the pro capital punishment marchers, some who carried a picture of a murdered child or signs such as **Burn! Bonin Burn!**

San Diego's **Union Tribune** reporter Anne Krueger wrote about a local protest:

"About 25 protestors showed up at the State Building on Front Street, carrying signs with such slogans as **Execution is not the Solution** and **Don't Kill for Me**. Michael Gilgun of Chula Vista, a school psychologist, and his wife, Lynda, a day-care worker, say the execution sends the wrong message to children. 'You can't teach someone that killing is wrong by killing them,' Lynda Gilgun said, 'If killing is wrong for the individual, then it's also wrong for the state to kill.' While reporters and TV crews were interviewing protestors, a man from a passing car screamed, 'Execute him!' Since his convictions, lawyers for Bonin vigorously filed legal appeals."

In the article it was also noted that an appeal to California Governor Pete Wilson, who could grant Bonin clemency, was met with a simple statement, "Bonin is a poster child for capital punishment." Peter Romanowsky, an ordained Protestant Minister in Sausalito, said, "If Mr. Bonin has not truly repented in his heart, he does not deserve to live."

Execution Day
Bonin hoped the 9th Circuit Court of Appeals would give him a reprieve, but they decided not to block the execution. Later that evening, at 10:47 p.m., the U.S. Supreme Court refused to hear any more appeals. With all judicial and political appeals exhausted, the execution would be carried out as planned.

One appeal was based on Bonin claiming his defense attorney, William Charvet, was compromised by financial arrangements outside the trial, a book deal, and abuse of prescription medication for a bad back, the latter especially during the second trial in Orange County. Charvet had left the legal profession, under the dark cloud of State Bar investigation, and was unreachable for comment.

On Wednesday Bonin had a radio interview on **KQED-FM** and gave this advice, "I would suggest that when a person has a thought of doing anything serious against the law, that before they did that they should go to a quiet place and think about it seriously."

He had these parting words for the family members, "They feel that my death will bring closure, but that's not the case. They're going to find out."

And this about the final act itself, "I think I've accepted the fact that this may come about, and I've made peace with it and if it happens, it happens. As far as how I'm going to feel at that very moment, I can't answer that question. I don't know. I don't think any of us would know until were there."

Late in the evening Bonin was visited by a Catholic Chaplain and the Warden of San Quentin, Arthur Calderon. At 11:30 p.m. he imparted a final statement to Calderon, "The death penalty is not an answer to the problems at hand. I feel it sends the wrong message to the young people."

When an execution takes place the prison goes into an all-day lockdown. At 6:00 p.m. Bonin was led to one of the two "death watch" cells, an ominous thirteen steps from the chamber and where he was continually watched by three guards.

Soon after arriving he was served the last meal. Able to order whatever he wanted, Bonin requested two pepperoni and sausage pizzas, three pints of coffee ice cream and a six pack of Coca-Cola. He watched the TV show *Jeopardy* while eating his final meal. At 11:45 p.m. he was issued a new pair of denim trousers and a blue work shirt. Allowed to keep one religious medal, Bonin was escorted into the execution chamber a few minutes before midnight and strapped onto the table.

The injection was administered from an anteroom, next to the chamber, which has two telephones, one an open line to the governor and other to the Supreme Court of California and the attorney general's office. IV needles were placed in both arms before the white curtains were drawn back between the chamber and the viewing area, according to procedure. The door was closed, and the warden issued the execution order to the volunteers who carry out the mission to fulfill state law.

Bonin was spared any discomfort when he departed this world, unlike the boys he raped, tortured and murdered. He was given more than adequate doses of valium to make him barely aware of the impending finality. Next was the 50 ccs of pancuronium bromide and potassium chloride, which paralyzes the diaphragm and heart while also preventing his face from distorting. Finally, the injection of potassium chloride stopped his heart instantly. Three minutes from start to finish, then the doctor made the official determination.

Gordon Dillow, from the **Orange County Register**, months later wrote about his experience as a "media witness" and the story of Troy Kendrick, the younger brother of one of Bonin's victim, Darin Kendrick.

"Six months ago, I stood near Kendrick in the death house at San Quentin State Prison. We were watching as 'freeway killer' William Bonin, who raped and murdered 21 young boys in Orange and Los Angeles counties, was executed by lethal injection.

"For me the execution was a straightforward affair. Watching Bonin die as potassium chloride was pumped into his veins, watching his face turn from jail-house white to blue to purple, was only slightly more dramatic than watching a guy go to sleep. Which in effect was what Bonin did. He went to sleep for all eternity, wearing a purple face. But for Kendrick, a soft-spoken 33-year-old Cypress resident, the execution was a bit more significant. Because 16 years earlier, Bonin had kidnapped, raped and murdered Kendrick's older brother, Darin.

"Kendrick wept for his brother as he watched Bonin die. Afterward I asked him if Bonin's death made him feel any better. 'I feel like I can get on with my life now,' he said. It was the sort of thing people often say about vengeance achieved—that everything is going to be different now.

"And things usually wind up pretty much the same as they were before. 'It's been wonderful,' he says six months after that night in the death house at San Quentin. 'I finally found peace. I've got my life straightened out now. And it (execution day) has brought my family back together again.'

"More precisely, the execution reunited Kendrick with his father, whom he hadn't seen since the day Darin was buried. Kendrick explained that his father had seemed unable to deal with Darin's death, and had drifted away from his family, hounded by his own personal demons. By the time of the execution, Bill Kendrick, Troy's father, didn't even know where Troy was living—and he was afraid to try and find out. 'After a certain time, you're afraid of what you're going to have to face,' Bill Kendrick, now a minister in Montclair, told me."

After Bill Kendrick heard Troy interviewed on a local TV news show, he decided it was time to "close another chapter" and he got back in touch with his long-lost son. After so many years of pain, estrangement and lost time, the Kendrick family was reconciled and "finally, at peace."

Here is an excruciating example of the damage wrought by Bonin and his accomplices, tearing a family to shreds and leaving behind a landscape of destruction and regret.

David McVicker, raped by Bonin as an innocent 14-year-old five years before began the killing spree, described the execution:

"We were guests at a dinner for the police dignitaries and family members then about 11:00 o'clock we were taken into the recreation room, used by the inmates on death row. It was a strange feeling walking around looking at the items the killers used, different games, books. A little before midnight we were lined up and told not to say a word when we entered the viewing room. I kept watching the clock tic by. Midnight came and passed. There was a rumor that the execution was delayed because they were having a hard time getting the needles into Bonin's vein.

"After three or four minutes they opened the door and we walked in. Two of Darin Kendrick's brothers were there but they only let one go in, I wanted to give him my place, but the guards wouldn't let me. They said my name had been cleared to go in. Then we went into a room with wooden risers, each one about a foot high, the room was dark. There were curtains covering the large windows looking into the execution chamber. It looked kinda like a bird cage, it is an octagonal room with steel plates welded together. There was a door on one side and a big window covered by draw drapes.

"There were 52 reporters, family members and dignitaries in the room, eighty in all. No cameras were allowed. After we all got settled, they opened the curtains and we saw Bonin lying on what looked like a gurney. His arms were outstretched and held in place by straps.

"I wanted to see his eyes, I wanted to see him looking around being afraid. Sandy Miller heard me say that and pushed me toward the glass. Bonin's eyes were closed, he looked like he was asleep. Then an unseen person upped the solutions, Bonin's chest rose, then his cheeks began to bulge, and his face turned purple, and he exhaled his breath. Then he was pronounced dead, and the curtain was pulled shut."

When word spread through the crowd, at 12:15 a.m., the anti-death penalty demonstrators lit candles and sang **Amazing Grace**. Long suffering families and friends of the victims drank champagne and prayed their nightmares might end. Sterling Norris, who led the prosecution team in Los Angeles, said, "Justice has been done."

Final Thoughts from Vonda Pelto, Ph.D.:
I recall what Bonin told me jail, "I keep thinking back to all the stuff that happened in my life, and I don't know all the reasons for what I did. I just know I couldn't have helped myself; no one could know what was going on inside of me."

I truly believe, in my heart and in my soul, that Bill Bonin was **Without Remorse** and **Without Redemption**.

72

Epilogues, Why Bonin Covered for Eric & the Importance of March 24, 1980!

Bonin's family refused to claim his earthly remains following his execution. Cremated in a private ceremony, with no family present, his ashes were scattered over the Pacific Ocean.

Gregory Miley received separate 25 years to life sentences as part of a deal to testify against Bonin in the Charles Miranda and James Macabe murders. Initially incarcerated at the California Substance Abuse Treatment Facility and State Prison in Corcoran, he was later transferred to Mule Creek State Prison. Throughout the years at Mule Creek, he was repeatedly reprimanded for violence and the sexual assault of inmates. On May 25, 2016, two days after he was brutally beaten on the prison exercise yard, Miley succumbed to his injuries.

Jim Munro was sentenced to a term of 15 years to life as part of his deal to testify against Bonin in the Steven Wells murder case. Despite numerous appeals, claiming he didn't know Bonin was the Freeway Killer till after the Wells' murder, and was tricked into accepting a plea deal, in January 2023 he was still incarcerated at Mule Creek. Munro has written to several California governors asking for execution rather than having to spend the remainder of his life behind bars for "a crime I didn't commit."

Billy Pugh rejected a plea deal to testify against Bonin and was charged in the Harry Todd Turner case with first-degree murder, robbery and sodomy. Convicted only of the far less severe voluntary manslaughter, it might be assumed the jury took the following into account in their deliberations: 1) Pugh's tip led directly to the capture of Bonin, 2) He was a juvenile when the crime took place despite being tried as an adult as per a new California law, 3) Bonin was shown to be a first-rate manipulator who convinced four others to kill with him. Billy Pugh served about four years in prison and was released in late 1985.

David McVicker, the 14-year-old who survived a 1975 rape and partial strangulation by Bonin, was initially traumatized and never discussed his ordeal with family or attended counseling. In the following years, plagued with nightmares, he dropped out of high school and began abusing drugs and alcohol. He described the experience of observing the execution as "the beginning of my life." After Bonin's execution, David McVicker actively campaigned to ensure Miley and Munro were denied parole.

Eric Wijnaendts was never charged with any other crimes in connection with Bill Bonin. Worth reiterating is the three reasons Bonin covered for Eric, who committed two murders with him—***Love***, ***Revenge*** and ***Spite***.

Eric held a special place in Bonin's heart, and he helped him because of those feelings. The second reason was tied to the first and was a two-for-one-bonus: Eric was charged for a murder Billy Pugh helped him commit. By telling detectives it was Pugh they wanted in the Turner case, something he might not have done if Eric hadn't been arrested, he got revenge on Pugh for putting the finger on him as the Freeway Killer and helped the person he "loved most in the world."

The last reason was pure spite: Detectives Esposito, Kushner, Mellecker and Fueglein, who all had extensive interviews and discussions with Bonin, all firmly believed Eric was involved but were unable to definitively prove anything. Bonin knew this and dangled the possibility of giving them Eric until it was clear doing so wouldn't help him avoid the death penalty. Letting Eric skate was a thumb in the eye of the detectives.

Don't forget that, in part, Bonin spilled his guts to detectives in December 1980 to help Eric get out from under the Turner murder charges, a move he never would have made if he wasn't in trouble. While the interviews were kept secret for many months, this decision changed everything.

And it all ties back to March 24, 1980—the day when the paths of Bonin, Fraser, Wijnaendts and Pugh all crossed, the day when, if one of those paths changed slightly, then events to follow would have been altered dramatically!

In addition, that was the day firebrand reporter J.J. Maloney, of the ***OC Register***, introduced the world to the Freeway Killer with his bombshell article, the first of many which shocked the public and put law enforcement under a microscope.

THE END

www.WithoutRedemption.com

Printed in Great Britain
by Amazon